Jewish
Spiritual
Direction

Books by Howard A. Addison

The Enneagram and Kabbalah: Reading Your Soul (Jewish Lights)

Cast in God's Image: Discover Your Personality Type Using the Enneagram and Kabbalah (Jewish Lights)

Show Me Your Way: The Complete Guide to Exploring Interfaith Spiritual Direction (SkyLight Paths)

Jewish Spiritual Direction

An Innovative Guide from Traditional and Contemporary Sources

Edited by
Rabbi Howard Avruhm Addison
&
Barbara Eve Breitman

JEWISH LIGHTS Publishing
Nashville, Tennessee

Jewish Spiritual Direction:
An Innovative Guide from Traditional and Contemporary Sources

Requests to the Publisher for permission should be addressed to Turner Publishing Company, 4507 Charlotte Avenue, Suite 100, Nashville, Tennessee, (615) 255-2665, fax (615) 255-5081, E-mail: submissions@turnerpublishing.com.

Library of Congress Cataloging-in-Publication Data
Jewish spiritual direction : an innovative guide from traditional and contemporary sources / edited by Howard Avruhm Addison and Barbara Eve Breitman.
p.   cm.
Includes bibliographical references and index.
ISBN-13: 978-1-58023-230-2
ISBN-10: 1-58023-230-2
1. Spiritual direction—Judaism. 2. Jewish way of life. I. Addison, Howard A., 1950- II. Breitman, Barbara Eve.
BM723.J486 2006
296.6'1—dc22
2006005276

10 9 8 7 6 5 4 3 2

Cover design: Tim Holtz

Manufactured in the United States of America

Published by Jewish Lights Publishing
A Division of LongHill Partners, Inc.
An Imprint of Turner Publishing Company
4507 Charlotte Avenue, Suite 100
Nashville, TN 37209
Tel: (615) 255-2665
www.jewishlights.com

To my beloved father, Henry,
and my beloved children, Mara, Jon, Leora, Arona, Aley,
and my most precious grandson, Amiel:
May God watch over you and always guide your steps.
—HAA

To my mother, Mary, for her abiding and sustaining love.
To my beloved daughters, Keyonnee and Kimberly:
May you always be blessed with love, friendship, good health, and
lives full of joy and meaning. Know that you are loved by an unending
love and by hands that uplift you even in the midst of a fall.
—BEB

Contents

Preface

More than ever before, contemporary Jews are seeking spiritual fulfillment. They recognize sparks of holiness in their lives and want to connect them with Jewish tradition, but don't necessarily know how. That's why the time is right for this book.

Spiritual direction has had a profound impact on the lives of those seekers and guides engaged in the process. It supports people as they examine their inner being and learn to recognize the sacred possibilities in everyday life. To demonstrate both the benefit and the promise that spiritual direction can offer to us as Jews, we thought that we might share with you the effect this sacred practice has had on each of our lives.

Rabbi Howard Avruhm Addison: When thinking about my spiritual journey, I often recall an insight attributed to Simchah Bunim of Pzhysha, a nineteenth-century Hasidic master, which I read in Martin Buber's *Tales of the Hasidim: Later Masters*. Reb Bunim observed that the difference between cognitive study and lived religious experience is akin to the difference between reading a playbill and personally experiencing the play.

Although my parents came from nonobservant Jewish homes, they wanted their sons to have strong religious foundations. Our Conservative synagogue on Chicago's Far South Side was the hub of a vibrant Jewish community, and throughout childhood and adolescence, my brother and I spent most of our after-school hours in Jewish study, worship, and youth activities. Upon graduating from college, I followed what seemed like my life's natural progression, entering the Jewish Theological Seminary. There I was privileged to study with world-class scholars, including Professors Moshe Zucker, Seymour Segal, and the revered Abraham Joshua Heschel. In rabbinical school our critical examination of classical Jewish texts was engaging and extensive. I was encouraged in my doctoral studies of philosophy, Kabbalah, and *Hasidut*. In retrospect, however, something was missing: Even our mystical texts courses offered faint instruction on how we might deepen our own connections to God. It was like reading about inwardness, *penimiyut,* from a playbill, with little opportunity to experience the play or learn how to join in the action ourselves.

I have spent most of the thirty years since ordination serving congregations according to the rabbi/scholar model I learned at JTS. As the demands of the pulpit, with its pastoral, scholarly, and communal responsibilities increased, my sense of calling grew ever more faint. Neither advanced study in the United States nor that in Israel helped me find an ongoing sense of spiritual connection. While sporadically welcomed, I was rebuffed more than once when seeking more traditional modes of study and guidance in the yeshiva world, due to my Conservative affiliation.

By the mid 1990s my life, while outwardly successful, was internally a wreck. Five of my nearest and dearest, including my mother, my brother, and a young niece, were dead; my home life was unraveling. At the suggestion of a Rabbinical Assembly colleague, I attended two seminars sponsored by the Alban Institute, an interfaith center dedicated to the ongoing support of clergy and congregations. Daily we deepened our contemplative practice; I was introduced to the Enneagram theory of personality and spiritual direction. My response was twofold. My mind, almost on its own, began to filter out the Christology and search for spiritual correlations and contrasts within our own tradition. More profoundly, my heart began to sing, as I sensed that here were hints of the experiential reality to which my previous study had but alluded.

Those Alban seminars over a decade ago impelled me to enter spiritual direction and to study further in both Jewish and Christian contexts. While I love the continuing intellectual challenge of mining Judaism's texts for their spiritual riches, it is the inner personal work that constantly proves transformative and amazing. During some very dark hours, it has literally been lifesaving. The insights gained and the changes I see in my own priorities, teaching, and behavior confirm that the Blessed Holy One is truly *Oseh Phele*, a God of Wondrous Surprise. More importantly, I have been privileged to witness among both fervently committed and marginal Jews, among those we've trained as *mashpi'im* and those I've been fortunate to companion, profound, life-giving spiritual changes as they—and I—try, like our Father Abraham, to "become wholehearted and walk continually before God" (Genesis 17:1).

Barbara Eve Breitman: I discovered spiritual direction during a time of loss and spiritual crisis. In the summer of 1995, a first cousin of mine was murdered; my then-husband and I took her orphaned children into our home. One year later my husband died suddenly. Life as I knew it and my understanding of God crumbled. As my beloved friends helped me put my life back together, I searched for Jewish wisdom about suffering, but could find little then that was helpful to me. It was in Buddhist writings, and later in spiritual direction, that I found more of what I needed to help me save my life, and, over time, to open myself up to a deeper, more embracing connection with the Holy.

I had difficulty finding the Jewish spiritual guidance I needed despite my involvement in the Jewish community and long-time commitment to Jewish learning. While attending Brandeis, I developed a profound interest in mysticism and Jewish studies. That led me, in 1972, to the University of Pennsylvania's doctoral program in Religious Thought, where I met the then-young professor Arthur Green. Though I didn't complete the degree, Art introduced me to both the academic study of Jewish mysticism and the *Chavurah* movement. For decades after leaving the Department of Religion, I was a student of depth psychology. I worked first at the Jewish Family Service, later taught social work at the graduate level, and have practiced as a psychotherapist for thirty years. My yearning to study Kabbalah and *Hasidut* persisted as a serious avocation, and I remained a committed member of the Mt. Airy/Philadelphia Jewish community.

But for decades there were only two Jewish contexts in which I could speak openly about my mystical experiences and relationship with God: circles of Jewish feminist women and gatherings organized by people in the Jewish Renewal movement. At B'not Esh, a Jewish feminist spirituality collective, we shared spiritual experiences and searched beyond exclusively male God-language for imagery that was truer to our experiences of the Holy. At B'nai Or (later P'nai Or, and finally ALEPH), I met Reb Zalman Schachter-Shalomi and an international circle of creative, unconventional people who took Judaism and spirituality seriously. Zalman taught us, loved us, inspired us, and gave us access to our people's mystical tradition, a tradition largely inaccessible in those days to women and liberal American Jews. I was fortunate to become part of an expanding *chevra* that created the Aleph Kallah and Elat Chayyim, two fragile but vibrant institutions that have been bringing together teachers and seekers of Jewish spirituality for years.

In 1995, the opportunity to join my passions for Jewish spirituality and depth psychology was offered to me when I was asked to teach a course in Pastoral Counseling at the Reconstructionist Rabbinical College. It was then and still continues to be a blessing to conceptualize this course, serve on a remarkable faculty, and contribute, in my small way, to this vibrant institution.

In 1996, though my husband had just died, I decided to begin chaplaincy training at a local hospital, as I had previously planned. As I shared my spiritual struggles and changes in the Clinical Pastoral Education group, a minister brought me a brochure from the Shalem Institute for Spiritual Formation. By 1998, I was ready to enter the institute's training process in spiritual direction as the only Jewish student in the program. At around that time, Rabbi Jacob Staub gave me the very precious opportunity to join a think tank to envision a program in spiritual direction for the Reconstructionist Rabbinical College and later to train a group of rabbis and therapists to serve as spiritual directors for the rabbinical students. I am deeply grateful to him for that opportunity and also to Rabbi Jeff Roth who, two years later, invited me to create a spiritual direction training program at Elat Chayyim. In 2001, Rabbi Zari Weiss, my coeditor Howard Avruhm Addison, and I began Lev Shomea, the first training program in Jewish spiritual direction not affiliated with a rabbinical college. In all these endeavors, I have felt "God's time" moving faster than my time. I've been deeply moved to witness as very gifted people have come forth to be "trained" as *mashpi'im* in response to their sense of calling and to the spiritual yearning among contemporary Jews. Our planet is in trouble, and it feels as if *Mekor HaChayyim*, the Source of Life, is breaking through every possible opening in human consciousness to remind us of who we are and of our deep interconnection with one another and the earth. All those involved in spiritual direction are in service to that calling.

Jewish spiritual direction is an emerging practice; this book a beginning step. We invite you to join intellectually and experientially in the task of uncovering God's guidance that is always available to us, if we are but open to it.

Acknowledgments

Pirke Avot, the Ethics of the Fathers, teaches that the acknowledgment of others helps bring redemption to our broken world. Therefore it is fitting, particularly in these turbulent times, that we acknowledge those whose wisdom, guidance, and effort have helped make this book possible.

First we are grateful to the contributors whose creative and often pioneering work is included in this volume. All of them are colleagues from whom we have learned, people whose friendship, vision, and creativity enrich our lives. We are honored that they were willing to collaborate with us in this venture and look forward to years of further collaboration.

We thank the Shalem Institute, especially Tilden Edwards, Rose Mary Dougherty, and Jerry May (may his memory be for a blessing), for their teaching and open-heartedness to our participation in the Spiritual Guidance and Contemplative Group Leaders Programs.

It is barely possible to acknowledge our indebtedness to Rabbis Jeff Roth and Joanna Katz, first of all for founding Elat Chayyim: The Jewish Retreat Center, a place that is truly *HaMakom:* a community that, under their leadership, has been a place where awareness of God is always central. Secondly, we are deeply grateful to Jeff for inviting and encouraging Barbara to develop a training program in spiritual direction at Elat Chayyim. Without his vision and encouragement, Lev Shomea: Institute for the Training of Spiritual Directors in the Jewish Tradition would never have been born. The opportunity of co-creating this program with Rabbi Zari Weiss has been among the most fulfilling and enriching professional experiences of our lives. We are grateful to all the students who entrusted their spiritual journeys to us, taught us so much, enabled us to share this practice with them, and opened up their hearts to each other, creating sacred community in which healing and miracles could and did happen.

Barbara Eve Breitman: I am extremely grateful to the Reconstructionist Rabbinical College and to Rabbi Jacob Staub in particular for his wisdom, openness, and faith in providing the leadership that brought the spiritual direction program at the College into being. He has been an extraordinary colleague in developing this program. I also want to acknowledge the amazing group of spiritual directors with whom I have worked for seven years and from whom I have learned so much. They have been dearest friends and fellow/sister travelers: Rabbis Mordecai Liebling, Yael Levy, Myriam Klotz, Elisa Goldberg, Shawn Zevitt, Marsha Pik-Nathan, and Simcha Raphael and Sandy Cohen.

To Reb Zalman Schachter-Shalomi, who saw into my soul, understood who I was, and whose love and teaching gave me roots and wings, I am deeply grateful. To my sisters in B'not Esh who "heard me into speech" in the early years, I am also deeply grateful. I particularly want to thank and acknowledge Sheila Weinberg, a *bat esh* and life-long spiritual friend, without whose constant love and companionship I do not know how I would have traversed the fierce landscapes of my life. We have been journeying toward God together for many, many years.

Finally, I want to acknowledge Bobbie Thalia, *z"l,* my first cousin and mother of the children we share in this lifetime. You somehow knew long ago our souls were intertwined. I can never repay you for the gifts of Keyonnee and Kimberly. They came into my life at such a terrible cost to you. That mystery has been and will continue to be an unfathomable meditation on the dark and light sides of God for the rest of my life.

Rabbi Howard Avruhm Addison: I was first introduced to the challenges and mysteries of Jewish thought during my college years by two rabbis, Edward Feld and Byron Sherwin. Each, in his own way, helped open for me the portals of our philosophic, kabbalistic, and contemplative traditions; for their teaching and personal examples I am ever grateful.

During a particularly difficult period I was privileged to attend two wonderful clergy seminars offered by Reverend Roy Oswalt of the Alban Institute. There I first learned of the Enneagram theory of personality and the practice of spiritual direction. I am thankful for these precious gifts, which remain sustaining pillars of my life.

Over the last eleven years I have been blessed to have three wonderful spiritual guides: first, Sister Elizabeth Hillman in Florida; for many years Sister Barbara Whittemore in New Jersey; and now, Sister Bernadette Kinniry in Philadelphia. Their open hearts and sensitive insight into the movement of the Spirit embodies the finest in what spiritual direction can offer to seekers of all denominations and faiths.

I thank my colleagues in the Intellectual Heritage Program at Temple University whose sharing from diverse perspectives and disciplines brings texture and clarity to every academic exchange. My congregation, Melrose B'nai Israel Emanu-el, is truly a "Little Shul with a Big Heart" that proves weekly how warm, unpretentious, and welcoming synagogue life can truly be.

To my children Mara and Jon, Leora, Arona and Aley, and my grandson Amiel: The spirit of God and our people moves differently but vibrantly in each of you and it is my privilege to receive light from the glow that is uniquely yours. And to my father Henry, who we pray will be with us for many long years: your loving smile and big heart remain the best spiritual teachers of all.

Before concluding let us thank everyone at Jewish Lights, especially Stuart M. Matlins, publisher; Emily Wichland; and Lauren Seidman for helping see this project through to fruition. Finally we thank the Holy One of Blessing for bringing us together that we might teach, write, and companion one another as we explore both the tangible and spiritual pathways of life.

Introduction

To Revitalize the Spirit of God: Toward a Contemporary Practice of Jewish Spiritual Direction

Acquire a companion for yourself … to reveal all your secrets, both in matters of Torah and in matters of the world

AVOT deREBBE NATAN 8

From its inception Jewish tradition has recognized that seekers need spiritual companionship along life's journey. In antiquity the role of spiritual guide was, in part, fulfilled by both priests and prophets (I Samuel 1, 3; II Kings 4). *Pirke Avot,* Ethics of the Fathers (1:6), seems to stress the importance of acquiring a spiritual companion even above securing a teacher. In most instances such spiritual friendship was exchanged freely between students and colleagues. However, in his commentary on this passage, the fifteenth-century Italian sage Ovadiah of Bartenura literally interpreted the verb used to connote acquiring, *uk'neh,* to indicate that, if necessary, one may even pay for such companionship.

For the last two centuries formal guidance has been offered in Orthodox yeshivot by spiritual supervisors known as *masgichim* (sing. *mashgiach*). The *mashgiach* is responsible for the personal and religious development of the yeshiva students, interacting with them in the hall of study *(Beit HaMidrash)* and offering public talks *(schmoozim)* on the inner, spiritual aspects of Jewish observance and the Holy Days. During the nineteenth century it was often the *mashgiach* who introduced the insights of *Mussar,* the Moralist movement founded by Rabbi Israel Lipkin Salanter (d. 1883), into the Lithuanian yeshivot.

In Hasidism the primary spiritual guide is, of course, the rebbe who meets with his Hasidim in private encounters known as *yechidut* or *pegisha.* Listening to the Hasid's problems, the rebbe offers a combination of spiritual counsel, practical advice, blessings *(brachot)* and intercessory prayer, all in an effort to help the Hasid align himself with God's will for him. However, in larger Hasidic communities *mashpi'im* (sing. *mashpia*), spiritual prompters, offer guidance and instruction both in support of the rebbe and when the rebbe is absent. In the *Tomchei-Temimim* yeshiva network of the Lubavitch Hasidim, a *mashpia* is assigned to each grade—both to monitor and facilitate the spiritual growth of the students and to formally teach Hasidic practice and texts.[1]

In liberal Judaism, ongoing spiritual guidance to help further personal religious growth and deepen one's connection to God has, by and large, not been available. In part, this is attributable to the founders of the liberal movements, whose revolt against Orthodoxy rejected any form of counsel that seemed to dictate how one should think or feel. It also reflects liberal Judaism's modern/scientific bias, which favors Western therapeutic modes over traditional forms of counsel that have been deemed restrictive, supernatural, and untrustworthy. Increasingly, however, liberal Jews seem to desire a form of companionship on the spiritual path that is personal, intimate, contemplative, and structured as a regular practice. Contributors to this volume are among those who have been developing such a contemporary model of spiritual companionship.

What Is Spiritual Direction?

For many, spiritual direction might best be described as a contemplative practice through which people companion one another over time as they reflect on their spiritual journeys and expand their awareness of the sacred dimensions that underlie the ordinary and extraordinary events of life. Through reflection, spiritual practice, study, and response, seekers are encouraged to cultivate *penimiyut,* their inner lives. The guide's function is to help seekers discern the *kivun,* the spiritual direction of their lives, to recognize how the Source of Life might be calling them to greater meaning and growth. A guide might be ordained or may have completed a training program in spiritual direction. However, the guide's main qualification is to be receptive and "see to his own interior life [through] prayer and meditation, since you [can't] give others that which you don't have."[2] Ultimately, the guide's main role is to help nurture intimacy between the seeker and God. The guide serves as a listening, reflective presence, creating an atmosphere of trust and openness that supports an individual's growing awareness of God's presence and the obstacles to an awareness of that presence in everyday life and prayer.[3]

Unlike psychotherapy, which helps people gain a stronger sense of self by facing unresolved childhood or family issues, or pastoral counseling, which invokes the insights, archetypes, and practices of religious traditions to help individuals navigate both the joyous and challenging transitions of life and death, spiritual direction focuses on our unfolding relationship with God. Spiritual guidance points the seeker beyond the "normal," to see the Divine that underlies and transcends the everyday. To quote longtime spiritual guide Carolynne Gratton:

> Spiritual guidance ... though it may get its impetus from the changes required by a particular life situation, does not usually aim at dealing with the situation itself. Spiritual guides are more interested in how people connect their living of certain situations (perhaps difficult ones) with their inner desire to live a loving relationship with the divine Other whose call the situation represents.[4]

Because normative Judaism emphasizes Torah study and observing mitzvot as the legitimate pathways to God, many Jews may feel uncomfortable with the idea that we can have an unmediated, personal relationship with the Divine. However, classical Jewish texts offer a variety of metaphors to describe how we might derive guidance from just such a relationship. Psalm 40 speaks of coming before God with a scroll of our experiences inscribed upon us and God's Torah written within our viscera, the seat of our deepest desires. Speaking theistically, the Talmud (*Moed Katan* 14b) depicts a heavenly voice offering daily guidance on issues ranging from the financial to the intimate and personal, while medieval Jewish philosophers wrote extensively about *hashgachah pratit*, individual providence. Employing mystical imagery, the kabbalists imagined each of our souls as rooted in one of the ten manifestations *(sefirot)* of God's personality located on the Tree of Life *(Etz Chayyim)*. The contributors to this volume plumb the riches of the tradition and their own experience for additional language, imagery, and texts to enrich and elucidate contemporary Jewish discourse about God.

As postmodern, post-Holocaust theologian David R. Blumenthal writes: "[I]n developing a way to talk about God, it is the vocabulary of the realm of religious language and experience that must be primary; it is also necessary to state that ... language about God begins in the ineffable but includes other universes of discourse: the moral, the rational, and the aesthetic."[5] No effort has been made in this volume to articulate any singular or comprehensive theology. This is not only because it is an anthology, but also because the purpose of spiritual direction is to enable each of us to develop greater awareness of and bring expression to our unique experiences of the Holy. The reader will hear different voices in this anthology: not only the voices of the authors but also brief echoes of conversations between spiritual directors, seekers, and God. We encourage you to listen for moments of both harmony and dissonance.

Beyond Inwardness

In many ways spiritual direction is an intimate practice that helps seekers expand their recognition of the Holy and develop their own inner lives. However, the work of inner cultivation is not in and of itself the goal. Rather, spiritual direction seeks to engender what Jacob Agus calls "Inter-subjective potency,"[6] an ever-deepening understanding and responsiveness to our fellows and our world that can grow from probing the inner depths of our being. When illuminated by the light of Spirit, that inner probing can prove transformative, offering possibilities of divine healing for the individual, our community, and, hopefully, our world.

Early in the twentieth century, Rabbi Abraham Isaac Kook, chief rabbi of pre-Israel Palestine, surveyed the dynamics shaping the nascent Jewish community in *Eretz Yisrael*. On one side, he saw an "Old Force," exclusive and insular in its traditionalism and religious certainty. On the other, he saw a thoroughgoing secularism that discarded the Holy. Dedicated to land and nation, it nevertheless subverted the foundations of religion and alienated its adherents from the light of God. In contradistinction to those extremes, Rav Kook spoke of a "Second Force," of which he himself was a leader, just beginning to gain recognition in the Holy Land.

This is the force that proclaims it is our duty to revitalize the spirit of God in our people and gain respect for Torah and mitzvot through the acquisition of all cultural resources active in the world.... We must take whatever is good from any source where we find it to adorn our spirit and our institutions.... We shall infuse the living creative spirit that knows our generation and is capable of influencing it, toward the love of all things holy and beloved of God.[7]

Given Rav Kook's mystical consciousness, which transcends the particularities of time and place, and his redemptive concern for Jewry and all humankind, it is little wonder that his words still resonate today. The insular and the assimilationist trends that he observed among the Yishuv Jewish community are still present in contemporary Jewish life, in both Israel and the United States. Sadly, the forces of secular materialism and religious fundamentalism, which he but glimpsed a century ago, have grown virulent and threaten our very world today.

Many of the contributors to this volume, though already learned and knowledgeable Jews, encountered, received training in, and practice a contemplative form of spiritual direction they learned under the auspices of programs grounded in contemplative Christianity. Many have had both Jewish and Christian spiritual directors. Some have been profoundly influenced by Eastern traditions. Others have developed models solely through Jewish sources. As contemporary American Jews and as members of the wider human community, all these writers believe we need to help foster a contemporary "Second Force": a creative living spirit "to adorn our souls and institutions through knowledge of and respect for Torah, deepened through active encounter with what is good among the world's spiritual resources, leading [hopefully] toward the love of all things holy and beloved of God."[8] We believe that the evolving practice of Jewish spiritual direction can play a small but helpful role in nurturing this potentially healing "Second Force" within both the Jewish community and the wider context of our world.

Assimilation, Survival, and Contemplative Judaism

Among the many forces impacting American Jewry today, there seems to be a dichotomy growing among those of Jewish ancestry. On one side, there is a trend among many toward weakening, if not dissolving, their ties to Judaism, as evidenced by high intermarriage rates, dropping affiliation numbers, and the graying of the core Jewish community. Conversely, we see a significant if relatively small number of Jews becoming *ba'alei teshuvah* by making countercultural choices to adopt the dress and observant life patterns of Eastern European Orthodoxy. Even in the non-Orthodox world, we find organizations whose stance toward American life was highly integrationist during their early phases, including the Federations and JCCs, developing ever more insular, inward-looking Jewish agendas. Some now fund new "Jewish continuity" initiatives by curtailing interfaith and communal relations activities that in the past strengthened responsible Jewish participation in the community at large.

In the midst of this assimilationist/survivalist split, we have witnessed the emergence of a new dynamic—the resurgent interest in Jewish spirituality. As indicated by contemporary theologian Arthur Green, this resurgence is occurring within the context of a wider American turn toward the inner life as an "answer [to] the moral failures and impending disasters brought about by excessive faith in the technological revolution and the belief in science."[9] Mystical teaching, meditation, music, dance, and healing all have helped mark the shift among Jews and the wider American community to include the aesthetic and devotional in what had previously been their predominantly rational religious lives.

Some may consider the contemplative to be a form of religious privatism that undermines Judaism's core message of communal responsibility and social activism. As indicated by several chapters in this book, however, we are witnessing a growing synthesis of contemplation and activism, as more Jews invite the Holy into their lives not only for self-transformation, but for greater clarity and inspiration as they discern how best to help "perfect this world as the dominion of God."[10] More profoundly, contemplative spirituality offers an alternative worldview that can experientially reinforce the call to justice and compassion voiced by Israel's ancient prophets. By summoning our attention to the sacred in others, in our planet, and in ourselves, it can help us detach from a corporate capitalist ethos that increasingly views every natural resource as a commodity, every community as a market, and every human being as a consumer. By providing islands of reflective calm amid our consumerist frenzy, the contemplative can challenge the drive for acquisition and consumption, with all its attendant inequalities, that is sadly sweeping our world today.

It is within this context of renewed spirituality that the practice of contemplative Judaism in general and Jewish spiritual direction in particular has arisen. Research done by Linda Thal for the Circle of Support of Contemplative Judaism[11] and our own experience reveal that this phenomenon has deepened the religious and social commitment of many practicing Jews while opening personal gateways back to Judaism for any number of those who have been alienated from our community and our faith.

The Emergence of Jewish Spiritual Direction

Pioneers

How did the longing arise for a form of spiritual guidance that at once went deeper than and transcended the traditional-survivalist and secular-integrationist impulses prevalent among Jews? The experiences of two Jewish spiritual direction pioneers can offer us some insight. Dr. Carol Ochs of the Hebrew Union College–Jewish Institute of Religion in New York began her encounter with spiritual direction in the 1970s. As recorded in her book, *Jewish Spiritual Guidance* (with Kerry Olitzky; San Francisco: Jossey-Bass, 1997), she found upon graduating from college in the early 1960s that the traditional paths to rabbinical school were blocked to her because of her gender. She opted instead for a career as a university professor where she could teach philosophy to those who wished to grapple with spiritual issues. While at Simmons College, she found students approaching her with questions they felt unwilling to ask the psychologically trained staff at the counseling center. This led her to find her own spiritual guide, Sebastian Moore (later Abbot of Downside Abbey in England), so she could better help her students and facilitate her own spiritual growth. After joining the HUC-JIR faculty in 1994, first one then several students sought her out for spiritual guidance. Her experiences with guides, seekers, and colleagues, both Jewish and non-Jewish, have led her to the realization that "There can be no community more genuine than one that grows up around a shared love of God."[12]

Burt Jacobson is the founding rabbi of Kehillah in Berkeley,

California, one of the first Jewish Renewal congregations in America. Ordained by the Jewish Theological Seminary, he found himself leaving the bounds of traditional halachic (Jewish legal) practice and belief early in the 1970s. However, he desired a source of religious guidance that would go beyond what he could read in books and the dictates of human conscience, which he feels are too conditioned by prevailing social norms. As he told us, "The human element and conscience are not enough. We need to go to a transpersonal place, to get in touch with the inner voice that moved Abraham and Moses." In 1982 he received a card inviting him to attend a class in "Pilgrim Companionship" at the Desert, an urban retreat center in Berkeley. For the first time, he glimpsed in spiritual direction a form of guidance that could be helpful beyond the dictates of tradition and the practice of psychotherapy. Ten years later he enrolled in the spiritual direction training program at the Mercy Center in Burlingame, California, graduated in 1995, and has since brought the practice to Kehillah and the wider community.

While Ochs's and Jacobson's experiences differ, they both represent what Professor Jonathan Sarna has called, "a discontinuity that [has] worked to promote Jewish continuity."[13] Neither found fulfillment within the confines of tradition or within accepted communal pathways and insular activities. Their search for sources of guidance outside of Judaism testifies to their comfort with the culture at large, but shows no impulse to integrate wholesale into that culture. In spiritual direction they each found a form of counsel whose insights go deeper than any Western scientific models of psychotherapy can do alone.

Mutual Irradiation

While some might be uncomfortable that Jews have sought out people from other traditions for spiritual guidance and learning, our own tradition cites Melchizedek of Shalem and Jethro of Midian serving as spiritual guides to Abraham and Moses, respectively.[14] History is replete with examples of intercultural sharing among mystics and contemplatives from different traditions, including Buddhist monks and Taoist roshis from as early as the first century of the Common Era;[15] Jewish, Christian, and Hellenistic Gnostics in the first centuries of the Common Era, followed by their Muslim, Jewish, and Christian counterparts in thirteenth-century Spain;[16] and Sufi sheikhs and Hindu gurus in Mughal-ruled India from the mid-sixteenth to mid-seventeenth century.[17]

In our current age of rapid travel and instant communication, unprecedented opportunity has been afforded for personal exchange among those from both Western and Eastern traditions. These encounters point toward the realization succinctly voiced by Sister Rose Mary Dougherty of the Shalem Institute, that "God is bigger than any one church." In this post-9/11 era, these exchanges take on added importance when tribal and religious fundamentalism threaten to divide our world into warring factions, each utterly convinced that God is exclusively on their side and that their enemies are demonic and worthy of destruction.

Significantly, such encounters between contemplatives deeply grounded in their own traditions has not led to religious syncretism or to the commodification of spirituality evident in much of the New Age phenomenon. Instead, these connections engendered among contemplatives might best be characterized by the term *mutual irradiation,* first articulated by the Quaker scholar Douglas Steere as:

> a relationship ... [i]n which each is willing to expose itself with greater openness to the inward message of the other, as well as to share its own experience and to trust that whatever is the truth in each experience will irradiate and deepen the experience of the other.... It is not likely to leave any of the participants as they were when they started.[18]

As indicated above, the development of Jewish spiritual direction in its current form was, in part, catalyzed by the learning that many of the contributors to this volume did in training programs under Christian auspices. Our exposure to the Christian practice of spiritual direction irradiated deeper truths within our tradition and within our souls. This, in turn, has inspired us to mine the treasures of our classical sources to recover, translate, and contextualize their wisdom on spiritual counsel for contemporary seekers and guides.

The evolving practice of Jewish spiritual direction continues to provide opportunities for mutual irradiation and, in its own small way, contributes to the healing of rifts along interfaith boundaries. Today Christian directors also attend workshops on classical Jewish approaches to spiritual counsel. Spiritual Directors International, once exclusively Christian, is now an interfaith organization serving as a worldwide umbrella for guides of all traditions. As the essays in the final section of this book indicate, the process continues as some Jewish spiritual guides irradiate their own work with the insights and techniques of Eastern traditions as well as the visual, literary, and performing arts. As Douglas Steere observed, none of us have been left where we started.

Where We Are Today

Much has transpired in recent years. Many of the authors in this volume have been offering spiritual guidance in various forms and formats over the years. Recently, however, more structured programs have emerged to make ongoing, personal, and intimate spiritual guidance more readily available to contemporary Jews in the United States, Europe, Oceania, and Israel. In 1998 the Reconstructionist Rabbinical College began preliminary discussions to explore the establishment of a spiritual direction program to serve its students. That program, instituted in 2000, now enables rabbinical students to engage in ongoing individual or group spiritual direction throughout their seminary careers.

It was the first of what is now a variety of spiritual guidance offerings made available to students by each of the Conservative, Reform, and transdenominational rabbinic training programs in the United States. Elat Chayyim, the Jewish Retreat Center, offered an initial weeklong workshop in spiritual direction during the summer of 1997; under its sponsorship Lev Shomea (A "Hearing Heart"), the first institute for training spiritual directors in the Jewish tradition, welcomed its first class in 2001. A second training program, Morei Derekh ("Guides along the Way"), initiated by the Los Angeles Metivta Institute and now under the aegis of the Yedidya Institute for Jewish Spiritual Direction, started in 2003. Lev Shomea and Morei Derekh have attracted rabbis, cantors, Jewish educators, therapists, healers, artists, and others who feel called to the work of spiritual companionship. Those who have completed these programs are now bringing group and individual spiritual guidance into synagogues, Hebrew and public schools, hospitals, prisons, hospices, and various communal agencies in the United States, Canada, Australia, New Zealand, the Netherlands, and Israel, in addition to offering spiritual direction privately as professionals and as volunteers. The Jewish Spiritual Directors Association listserv reaches scores of directors worldwide. While this summary is by no means exhaustive, it does offer a glimpse of how the practice continues to grow.

What's Ahead?

While no text can fully convey any lived experience, the chapters in this volume attempt to highlight different aspects of spiritual direction. The first section, "An Evolving Practice," explores some issues of theology, Jewish authenticity, and the cultural challenges inherent in this emerging field, as well as how classical Hebrew texts and terminology can be recovered and transposed to help shape a contemporary practice of Jewish spiritual guidance. The essays in "Practicing Spiritual Guidance" offer an extensive and insightful exposition of the varied elements that underlie and comprise the art of offering spiritual companionship. As its title indicates, the chapters in "The Jewish Path" richly show how the experiences of seekers can be both validated and informed by the prayers, sacred calendar cycles, life passage rites, master stories, and moral wisdom of our heritage. The fourth section, "New Dimensions in Spiritual Guidance," offers a glimpse of the exciting possibilities inherent in body and energy work, poetry, movement and dance, and the visual arts. These creative outlets can offer keys to unlocking the soul and openings to deepened awareness of the Divine. Finally, we will provide some practical advice for those who wish to enter spiritual direction and those who wish to learn the practice.

We pray that this anthology will increase your understanding of the practice of Jewish spiritual direction and its potential as one of the forces helping to revitalize the spirit of God in our community and our world.

Notes

1. On the Hasidic rebbe as spiritual guide, see Zalman Schachter-Shalomi, *Spiritual Intimacy: A Study of Counseling in Hasidism* (Northvale, NJ: Jason Aronson, 1991).

    For further information on *Mussar,* see Alan Morinis's essay in this book, "Soul-Traits in Classical *Mussar* and Contemporary Jewish Spiritual Direction" (pp. 239–253).

    Special thanks to Rabbi Ebn Leader of Hebrew College in Boston for his research on the traditional roles of the yeshiva *mashgiach* and the Hasidic *mashpia.*

2. Thomas Merton in Tilden H. Edwards, *Spiritual Friend* (New York: Paulist Press, 1980), 129.

3. From a handout prepared by Rabbi Nancy Flam of the Institute for Jewish Spirituality, 330 Seventh Ave., Ste. 1401, New York, NY 10001; 212-774-3608; www.ijs-online.org.

4. Carolyn Gratton, *The Art of Spiritual Guidance: A Contemporary Approach to Growing in the Spirit* (New York: Crossroad, 1998), 54.

5. David R. Blumenthal, *Facing the Abusing God: A Theology of Protest* (Louisville: Westminster/John Knox Press, 1993), 39–40.

6. Jacob Agus, "Preface I," in *Abraham Isaac Kook: The Lights of Penitence, the Moral Principles, Lights of Holiness, Essays, Letters, and Poems,* trans. Ben Zion Bokser (New York: Paulist Press, 1978), xiii.

7. *The Letters of Rabbi Abraham Isaac Kook,* vol. II, #427, quoted in Bokser, *Abraham Isaac Kook,* 15–16.

8. Ibid.

9. Linda Thal, "Rekindling of the Jewish Soul: Contemplative Judaism Takes on the Challenge" (New York: Circle of Support of Contemplative Judaism, 2005), 7.

10. From *"Aleynu," Siddur Sim Shalom* (New York: Rabbinical Assembly, 2002), 81.

11. For further information on the Circle of Support of Contemplative Judaism and *Rekindling of the Jewish Soul,* visit www.jfunders.org/knowledgecenter.

12. From Carol Ochs and Kerry Olitzky, *Jewish Spiritual Guidance: Finding Our Way to God* (San Francisco: Jossey-Bass Publishers, 1997), x.

13. Thal, *Rekindling of the Jewish Soul,* 8.

14. On Melchizedek, see Genesis 14:18–20 and *Bereshit Rabbah* 43:6–7.
    On Jethro, see Exodus 18 and *Mechilta Yitro* 2, 59b–60a.

15. Wm. Theodore De Bary, Wing-tsit Chan, and Burton Watson, *Sources of Chinese Tradition,* (New York: Columbia University Press, 1960), vol. 1, chap. 12.

16. James Webb, *The Harmonious Circle: The Lives and Work of G. I. Gurdjieff, P. D. Ouspensky, and Their Followers* (Boston: Shambala, 1980), 513–19.

17. Wm. Theodore De Bary and others, *Sources of Indian Tradition* (New York: Columbia University Press, 1958), vol. 1, chap. 16.

18. Douglas V. Steere, *Mutual Irradiation: A Quaker View of Ecumenism* (Wallingford, PA: Pendle Hill, 1971), 8.

SECTION I

An Evolving Practice

Jewish Theologies and Jewish Spiritual Direction

Rabbi Jacob J. Staub

Is the practice of spiritual direction authentically Jewish? The question arises because the field of Jewish spiritual direction has developed over the last fifteen years by North American Jews who have borrowed the practice from Christians and who have sought to integrate it into their Jewish lives.

The answer to this question depends on one's understanding of what makes something "authentically Jewish." There are some who assert that, by definition, anything that is borrowed from another religious tradition (especially from Christianity) is not authentically Jewish. There are others who believe that any authentic practice must have precedents in the history of Jewish practice, and there certainly are many documented instances throughout Jewish history in which Jews have sought regular spiritual counseling and mentoring from rabbis and sages.[1]

My premise in writing this piece, coming as I do from a Reconstructionist perspective, is that the evolution of Jewish beliefs and practices throughout Jewish history *always* involves cultural borrowing—borrowing *and* adaptation into a Jewish idiom that makes a practice Jewish. Jews have always lived in dynamic historical contexts, and we have developed our ways of life in response to the cultural trends that have surrounded us. I assume that most innovations made by Jews through the ages have not survived because they have not been adopted by significant numbers of Jews; we do not even have records of most of them. Those innovations that do survive, however, are then accepted as authentically Jewish and are generally assumed to have been Jewish from the time of Sinai.

Thus, I believe that the "Jewishness" of Jewish spiritual direction will depend on whether significant numbers of people who lead serious Jewish lives continue to find this practice to be a meaningful, enriching, deepening aspect of their Jewish lives. Toward that end, I will offer here a definition of spiritual direction, Jewish theological tropes that express some of the teachings of spiritual direction in Jewish terms, and reflections on some of the challenges that may be encountered in spiritual direction by Jews who may not believe in a God who literally intervenes supernaturally in our lives, literally hears and responds to our prayers, or literally "calls" us, individually and personally, into service. My goal is not to demonstrate that spiritual direction, in anything resembling its current form, has precedents in the Jewish past, but rather to explore how it might have a place in the lives of Jews, now and in the future.[2]

Defining the Practice

The practice of spiritual direction (SD) occurs when two people sit prayerfully and reverentially in the presence of the Holy. Since a central principle of SD is that the terms of their conversation are defined by the directee or the seeker, it may be in the presence of God—however the seeker images God—or in the presence of the Holy, or of the Mystery, or of the Infinite, or of the Ultimate, or of the Process.[3]

The director tries to get himself "out of the way"—to listen openly and nonjudgmentally to the seeker, noticing if and when his own beliefs, biases, emotions, and the like obstruct open listening.[4] The director is there in the presence of the Holy and in the service of the seeker's relationship to the Holy. He is not there to solve the seeker's problems; when necessary, the director will refer the seeker to appropriate helping professionals. Rather, the director is there to witness the way in which the Mystery unfolds in the life of the seeker and to help the seeker to discern the Presence in her life.

Toward that end, the director accompanies the seeker on the journey and notices where the supernal light shines through in the seeker's narrative, helping the seeker to discern it. The director may offer texts for the seeker to contemplate or suggest spiritual practices that the seeker may find helpful. The director also may share what she observes about the seeker's unspoken yearnings or about obstructions the seeker may be placing in the way of perceiving various aspects of the Presence in his life. The seeker comes to the director with an initial, often unarticulated yearning to open or deepen a connection with the Blessed

Holy One. The director provides a welcoming, safe place in which the seeker can journey, in the ways and at the pace in which the Mystery works in and through the seeker.

Ultimately, the goal of this practice is for the seeker to develop the habit of discernment in all aspects of his life, noticing the sacred traces[5] of the Holy in even the most mundane activities, looking and listening for opportunities to do the will of God, developing a level of comfort in asking for assistance and guidance.

Translating into "Jewish"

My initial introduction to SD occurred in 1998 when, as academic vice president of the Reconstructionist Rabbinical College, I found myself directing a program, funded by the Nathan Cummings Foundation, to offer Jewish spiritual direction to rabbinical students.[6] Initially, I convened and chaired a study group to examine relevant Jewish sources and to read and discuss the literature of SD, written by contemporary Christians.[7] Most of us in the group found it very difficult to understand, on the most basic level, the vocabulary and images in the literature, until we ourselves began to meet with spiritual directors. Experiencing the practice, we were able to formulate it in our own terms. In the next section of this essay, I offer brief formulations of basic SD vocabulary, in the hope that some may find it helpful.

Discernment

As Jews, we may not be accustomed to looking for God in all areas of our experience. We sanctify our lives and the world by performing mitzvot, thereby invoking God's presence by following the commandments. It is more indirect than finding God *in* things. We wear kippot on our heads to foster an awareness of God *above*. We look at tzitzit, the fringes on our prayer shawls, to remind us of the commandments, and, *indirectly,* about God. But we may find it odd to ask, "Where is God in this conversation? In this experience? In this feeling?" We are the descendents of Jacob, who woke up at Bethel and said, "The Lord was present in this place, and I did not know it!"[8]

The idiom may seem alien, but the concept is not. *"Bechol deracheha da'ehu,"* we read in the Book of Proverbs, "Know/acknowledge God in all your ways, and God will direct your paths."[9] There is perhaps no more fundamental principle of Jewish living. Our relationship with the Blessed Holy One is based on an awareness that we ideally maintain at every waking moment. In the *Amidah* (the silent, standing prayer) of every Jewish prayer service, we say, "*Modim anachnu ... al kol nifla'otecha vetovotecha she-bechol et erev va-boker ve-tzaharayim*—We acknowledge and are thankful for all of your wonders and good works, [which occur] at every moment, morning, noon, and night." The Jewish practice of reciting at least 100 *brachot* (blessings) each day is one traditional way that Jews have sought to maintain this awareness. By acknowledging every bite of food we eat, every sunrise or clap of thunder, every bodily function, we seek to avoid a functional atheism in which we forget where everything comes from and lapses into self-reliance, whether out of pride or despair.

The mitzvah of continuous awareness of God applies whether we have a belief in a more transcendent or a more immanent God. If you pray to a God who creates and sustains us perpetually from afar, you recite the *motzi* blessing over bread by way of appreciating the (transcendent) Creator's uninterrupted sustenance of creation. If you lean more toward a paradoxical identification of the (immanent) Creator with creation, the *motzi* is an opportunity to see the Blessed Holy One *in* the bread—indeed, in everything. In the words of the early Hasidic masters, "The fullness *(melo)* of the entire universe *(kol ha'aretz)* is God's glory *(kevodo)*.[10] Most Jews, however, fall somewhere between those two poles. My maternal grandmother, *z"l*, who was raised in czarist Russia, serves as my "text" here. My *bubbe* spent her days in the Bronx engaged in perpetual conversation with the *Ribbono shel Olam* (Master of the Universe), thanking Him, appealing to Him, squabbling with Him, reproaching Him. He was a constant companion, present everywhere, who *also* was the majestic Creator.

My main point here is that the discernment practice of SD is completely consonant with the Jewish view of God's omnipresence. Living in Western secular society, we tend to forget that Jews have never before divided sacred and secular time and space. Their awareness of God was not limited to time spent in the synagogue or engaging in rituals. The practice of SD is thus one important tool for reclaiming the "cosmic" or "unitive" consciousness of our ancestors, welcoming an awareness of the Divine back into our lives between our visits to the synagogue.

Grace

"God in goodness provides the whole world with food in grace *(hen)*, love *(chesed),* and compassion *(rachamim)."* So begins the *Birkat HaMazon,* traditionally recited after every meal. "Our Father, our Sovereign, respond to us *(aneinu)* with grace *(honeinu),* for we have no [meritorious, deserving] deeds," we sing in the *Avinu Malkeinu* on the High Holy Days. The word *hen* (grace; unearned blessing) occurs frequently in our prayers, but for so many of us, it is unintelligible. The very notion that we may be the recipient of blessings that we have not earned can be disturbing.

There are many factors that have contributed to this state of affairs. Following political emancipation in Western societies in the nineteenth century, Jews were faced with the challenge of distinguishing Judaism from Christianity in order to justify our existence, and we embraced Paul's, the Christian apostle, (inaccurate) characterization of Judaism as based on works (deeds) rather than faith.[11] Jews, we have proclaimed proudly, do not believe, as Christians do, that we are inherently sinful and thus depend on God's grace. Rather, we believe in the possibility of *teshuvah* (return or repentance), in our own capacity to make amends and thus be *deserving* of God's love.[12]

Similarly, following the elevation of autonomy (self-reliance, independence) over heteronomy (obedience, subservience) by the philosopher Immanuel Kant, liberal Jews sought to emphasize the human half of the Rabbis' Divine-human partnership. Indeed, Judaism's suitability as a religion for modern, free people has often depended on a redefinition of the mitzvot (commandments) as opportunities for humans to act justly and piously in order to *merit* our good fortune.[13]

The underlying issue here is control. After millennia of powerlessness, subject to the whims of hostile rulers and brutal natural forces, praying for divine intervention to bring the Messiah, Jews in the modern world have embraced autonomy and self-reliance. On a political plane, Zionism emerged out of our need to take our destiny into our own hands.[14] On a personal level, modernity has led to an assertion of self-reliance: if I work hard, I will succeed in my career; if I eat right and stay fit, I can expect to remain healthy.

We run into difficulties, however, when the formula fails us and we lose control—or realize that we never had control in the first place. If we claim that we merit our blessings, we must also merit our misfortunes. In fact, Jewish teachings have always emphasized our dependence on a gracious God whose blessings overflow perpetually and sustain the universe, whether we deserve them or not. "Surely goodness and love shall pursue me all the days of my life."[15] Commenting on this verse, the Hasidic rebbe Moshe Hayyim Efrayim of Sudilkow affirms that we are each indeed pursued by blessings at every turn—blessings from which we flee because we think we are undeserving or that we simply do not discern.[16]

If we were able to recall some of the fortuitous coincidences that have led us to our current life situations—if we had been able to discern and appreciate them when they occurred—then we might begin to approach a sense of what we mean when we pray in the Shabbat morning service, "*Nishmat kol chai tevarech et shimcha*—Every breath we take testifies to the divine blessedness of our lives." The practice of discernment in SD inevitably involves noticing and appreciating how much of what we take for granted is unearned blessing—*hen*.

Forgiveness

A teaching attributed to the Kotzker Rebbe cites a midrash that understands Adam in the Garden of Eden[17] to be telling God that, not only did he eat the fruit, but that he would be likely to continue to eat the fruit in the future—that he was powerless to overcome his *yetzer hara* (evil inclination). Rather than viewing Adam as hopelessly sinful, the Kotzker praises Adam for possessing the great spiritual attribute of self-awareness.[18] The message is that human nature is flawed and that we should not seek to be pure, but rather to be mindful of our sinful propensities.

But doesn't Jewish teaching insist that we do *teshuvah* and make amends before we ask for forgiveness? It's Christians who believe in "original sin" and that they are forgiven through their faith, isn't it? Yes and no. Yes, we are obligated to engage perpetually in *teshuvah;* even the most righteous *tzaddikim* (whom we might have presumed had little about which to do *teshuvah*) are said to be so engaged.[19] But a look at the High Holy Day liturgy, for example, shows that sin is presumed to be a constant of human life. We appeal to God to save us *despite* the fact that none of us is meritorious. In our appeals, over and over again, we pray that we should *not* get what we deserve. And the promise is that, year after year, God moves from the Throne of Judgment to the Throne of Mercy, always giving us another, unmerited chance.

It's not God who has difficulty moving from judgment to mercy. It is we who have difficulty forgiving ourselves (and, consequently, others). Five months into my work with my spiritual director, I noticed that I was only discussing sparkling, luminous experiences, even though those moments constituted only a small fraction of my days. When my director suggested that I close my eyes, sit in God's presence, and recall darker moments, I was startled to discover that I couldn't. I could recall my struggles, and I could sit in God's presence, but I could not do both simultaneously. Just as I had been raised to dress up to enter the synagogue, so I needed to be the "good" Jacob, putting on my best face, in order to sit in God's presence. It was a profound realization—that I could only let God into the parts of me for which I needed God least.

And so there followed months of serious daily practice, in which I brought *all* of me—the parts of which I was proud and the parts of which I was ashamed—into my prayer. It was a contemplative practice in which I began to imagine God as more than a stern Judge before Whom I was absolutely accountable. I reached deeply into my personal storehouse of memories, imagining gentle, forgiving mentors, intimate friends and lovers, my mother holding and hugging me—all as images of God, as embodiments of aspects of God that I had never noticed and allowed to embrace me because of my shame and guilt.[20] And gradually, I was able to sit prayerfully in God's comforting arms, as it were, caressed and fully known by a gentle God of compassion and forgiveness.

Prior to this process, I had related to the words of Psalm 139 with the greatest discomfort:

> O Lord, You have examined me and know me.
> When I sit down or stand up, You know it;
> You discern my thoughts from afar.
> You observe my walking and my reclining,
> and are familiar with all my ways.
> There is not a word on my tongue
> but that You, O Lord, know it well.
> You hedge me before and behind;
> You lay Your hand upon me.[21]

I had read this psalm as a banner example of the traditional, *Mussar* theology in which I had been raised and educated and from which I had fled—God portrayed as an all-knowing supervisor, perpetually looking over my shoulder, aware of my every wayward thought, judging me, determining my reward and punishment. But then one day, during a walking meditation that alternated between *hitbodedut* (the Hasidic practice of talking to God out loud) and singing a *niggun* (wordless melody), I realized that God's stern judgment was *my* addition to the Psalm's words. It struck me that it could be understood instead as an affirmation that God knows *all* of me, every thought and feeling I have, knows me better than I know myself, and that, nevertheless, God hedges all around me.

I detail my own story at such length not because I think it is unique but because it is a story I encounter regularly in my work in SD with Jewish people. Much of the spiritual work in which they engage is about overcoming their sense of God's distance. Frequently, that sense of distance arises out of their feeling that they are unworthy, that they are either not sufficiently observant ritually, or feel guilty or wounded about the way they've treated family or friends, or in some way harbor a sense of not being sufficiently righteous. They are synagogue-attending Jews who have somehow missed the Yom Kippur message that God says, "*Salachti kidvarecha*—I have forgiven you as you have asked."[22]

The practice of discernment inevitably entails, I believe, work on forgiveness. "*Elohai, neshamah shenatatah bi tehorah hi,*" we recite each morning. "God, the soul that you have given me is pure." Unless the seeker can come to believe that her soul is pure and unstained by the thoughts, feelings, and deeds that she regrets—unless, that is, the seeker can experience self-forgiveness—it is difficult to accept divine forgiveness and to discern the Presence in us and all around us.

Love

God's love *(chesed)* may be another, related, problematic concept. God loves me? Isn't that Christian and not really Jewish? This is another example of Jews accepting proudly the Christian contrast between the two traditions, a contrast in which Judaism is not presented in an accurate, positive light. In this case, however, the difference may be substantial.

"*Ahavah rabbah ahavtanu,*" we recite before the morning *Shema,* "You have loved us with an abundant love." In the evenings, we refer to God's *ahavat olam,* eternal or unending love. *"Baruch atah ... ohev amo yisrael*—Blessed are You ... Who loves Your people Israel." It's not that Jews don't refer to God's love, but that we tend to think of God's love as directed to the Jewish people as a whole, and particularly, in the past, in the formative narratives of our people. Or that God's abundant love is manifested in God's revelation of the Torah, so that the manifestation of God's love is (exclusively?) in the gift of the commandments, and does not apply to our unique, individual experiences.

"God loves *me,"* by contrast, may be a phrase that sticks in the throats of many of us, perhaps because it sounds too much like, "Jesus loves me." We may be more comfortable with *"gomel chasadim tovim,"* as we say in the first blessing of the *Amidah,* "God causes loving and good effects." God lovingly sustains the universe. Or, returning to Psalm 23, verses 1 and 6, "The Lord is my shepherd ... [and, as the result of God's shepherding,] surely goodness and love will pursue me all the days of my life." As long as it's not personal.

There are traditional images of love between the individual and God, but they tend to be about an individual's love for God, rather than God's love for the individual: the psalmist's "My soul thirsts for You," or the rabbinic interpretations of "I am faint with love" in the Song of Songs as describing our love for God.[23] God certainly is said to act lovingly toward us as individuals—God is proud of us, God asks us for favors, God weeps for us, God protects and rescues us, God knows us and forgives us—but the actual L word is difficult to come by. The traditional Jewish distance between Divinity and humanity shows up even in kabbalistic writings, where the *sefirot,* aspects of the divine, play an intermediary role. The Jewish seeker in SD may thus need to venture beyond inherited words to describe the divine love that he discerns. All I can say is that when a serious Jew, who prays Jewish prayers, studies Jewish texts, and lives in Jewish time, discerns the presence of a caring, loving God, the Jewish authenticity of the experience is apparent.

One issue here can be Jewish seekers' resistance to an image of God that is so very personal. I will address this issue in the next section. As a director, I focus rather on whether the seeker feels worthy of being loved. When the obstruction of unworthiness surfaces and is discerned, and the seeker is able to discern the blessings of grace and forgiveness, it matters little whether he believes that God "loves" him. I believe that this is a place where Jewish SD differs from its Christian counterpart.

Asking for Help

"Asking for help" is not exactly a theological term. The corresponding term would be Divine Providence *(hashgachah pratit)*. The "translation" issue here is not whether God governs and watches over creation; traditional Jews believe that as much as traditional Christians. The issue here is the seeker's comfort in asking for assistance and opening up to the unknown.

My spiritual director is a minister in the United Methodist Church who is a model of the director who witnesses and accompanies the seeker's journey, using the seeker's terminology, without introducing her own beliefs or vocabulary. In over seven years, there has been only one occasion when she spoke to me in a foreign language. It was a moment in which I was in great distress, facing terrifying personal challenges with no easy solutions. She said, "Jacob, just give it to God." I let the comment pass—understanding each word in the sentence and therefore not registering that I didn't understand her meaning—until she repeated it a few more times. When I told her I didn't understand, she apologized and explained that she meant, "Offer it up and ask for God's help."

This may have been the most challenging moment I've experienced in SD. My difficulty arose in part because the God in whom I believe does not watch over and is not aware of the moment-by-moment details of my life, so that asking for help in a specific situation did not make sense to me. But I know from subsequent experiences with seekers with whom I work that this is not simply a question of naturalism versus supernaturalism. No matter what their personal theologies, many Jewish seekers have no experience asking God for help. Some know how to ask God for something specific; the Jewish liturgy is replete with petitionary prayers *(bakashot)*. But when you ask for something specific, you already have some clarity about what it is you seek. Turning to God in confusion is another matter. "Taking it into prayer" is another way that contemplative Christians talk about this.

Engaging in this practice requires a lot of trust *(emunah)*. You are acknowledging that you need help, that you don't know how to proceed, and that you can't do it alone. That's an admission of great vulnerability. Further, you are positing that if you let go—if you release your grip on ways of thinking and feeling to which you are attached and which are keeping you stuck in your current predicament—you may receive insight, comfort, and guidance to which you do not currently have access. That can be comforting, but, at least initially, it is also frightening. Admitting your helplessness, you are also opening yourself up to the unknown. You don't know what will arise. There may be truths that you are reluctant to face.

The effects of doing so are powerful. Reality changes when you say, "I can't do this alone." Your isolation diminishes. You are reminded that, while you may habitually operate on the premise that everything depends on your efforts alone, that is never the case. A prayer for help is immediately answered—not by solutions that fix your problems quickly, but by support. "*Somech Adonai lechol hanoflim*—God supports all those who fall," we read in Psalm 145:14. Sometimes, we have to let go and fall in order to get divine support.

Cultivating the practice of asking for support is especially helpful in discerning where God is in those aspects of ourselves of which we are not proud—our anger, our jealousy, our pride. Often, as discussed above, we are ashamed and feel as if we need to be worthy in order to turn to God. But when we discern that God is always there, we can also discern in our flaws an opportunity or an invitation to turn to God for support—not despite our flaws, but because of them.

Relating Personally to a Nonpersonal God

For some of us (and I include myself here), the greatest stumbling block in SD may be that we don't believe in a personal God who literally watches over each of us and is aware of the details of our journeys. How then can one experience a relationship with a God who forgives, acts graciously, comforts, supports, and loves? In this section, I will try to explain how SD has nevertheless served as a powerful, transformative practice for me. I do not seek here to influence either those who believe in a personal God or those who understand the Ultimate as nonpersonal and have no need to develop a personal relationship with God. I offer this as my own path, in the hope that it may speak to others who identify with it.

Maimonides

I begin with the philosophy of R. Moses ben Maimon, the Rambam, Maimonides, as he articulates it in *The Guide of the Perplexed (Moreh Nevuchim)*.[24] A twelfth-century Aristotelian philosopher, he is known as a rationalist, but I read him as a postrationalist, as close as a traditional Jewish philosopher comes to postmodernism. The Rambam argues forcefully that *anything* positive that we say about God is, by definition, idolatrous, because we must use language in our descriptions that refers to creation. Thus, for example, if I say that "God is good," the term *good* is a concept that refers to an aspect of creatures, who are multifaceted, while God is one; creatures are ever changing, while God is immutable; creatures are finite, while God is infinite, and so on. I may think that I am praising God by attributing goodness to God, but the Rambam argues that if I intend the attribute literally, I am associating God with what is not God (the goodness of creatures)—the very definition of idolatry.

How, then, can we speak of God? The Rambam offers two alternatives. The first is that we speak of God in terms of attributes of action that do not describe God at all but rather describe the effects of God's causation. I can say "God is good" if what I *mean* is that the effects of God's causation are such that were a human being to act and cause such effects, I would call that person good. The second is for us to speak of God in terms of negation of privation. I can say "God is good" if what I *mean* is that God is not evil. Neither of these leads me, however inadvertently, to think of God Godself as literally resembling a finite creature. The critical point for our purposes here is that God is, by definition, beyond human conception. Everything we think and say derives from our experience of this created world.[25]

According to the Rambam, how then does Divine-human communication occur? God continuously and immutably sustains the universe through an overflow of forms that are embodied in matter. As humans develop their knowledge of the universe and thus of the divine overflow, we come to know God more and more. The overflow remains constant and unchanging. Our individual reception of it, however, varies according to the receiver; the message we grasp varies with the individuality of the person. Those with the most highly developed understanding of the divine overflow are prophets, who also possess perfect imaginations and can apply the generalities of divine laws to specific situations.[26]

To summarize: According to the greatest Jewish philosopher of the medieval period and, arguably, in Jewish history, (1) we cannot know anything about God, who, by definition, is beyond our conception; (2) what we can know about God comes indirectly, through our understanding of the effects of God's causation; and (3) all experiences and accounts of Divine-human communication—including the revelation of the Torah to Moses!—are filtered through the specific intellect and imagination of the human reporter, and reflect more about the human reporter than about the unchanging divine overflow.

Maimonides and Spiritual Direction

Following the Rambam, I believe that God underlies, permeates, and sustains all aspects of existence but that we cannot know God in Godself. To say with certainty that God is a person or that God is impersonal is to claim to know more than a human being can know. We can only know what we discern of God, and our discernment takes place through our own individual lenses. God's overflow is filtered through me and colored by me. Whatever I say about God is idolatrous if I mean it as the literal truth.

I believe, therefore, that discernment is a never-ending process by which I open up to noticing where God is and to becoming more receptive to taking it in. God's aspects are infinite and are reflected, in part, in the array of human characteristics. The universe, created and sustained by God, is harsh and gentle, for example, just and merciful, judgmental and forgiving, loving and antagonistic, supportive and distant. It is all of these things simultaneously and constantly. What I discern varies with what I am able to receive.

To return to my personal story above, at the point at which I could not bring my problems to God, I was limited to discerning God's judgmental aspect but not God's comforting and supportive aspects. My reception of God's blessings was filtered through an image of God as an impersonal, removed, immutable Force. For months, I worked at a practice that expanded that image. I imagined God as *Ruach HaOlam*—the Spirit of the Universe, but also the Wind of the Universe. I sat imagining God as the air that envelops me like a womb, as the inhalation and exhalation of my breath, as the breeze that caresses my cheeks. I sat with a black and white photograph of my mother, in her skunk coat and feather hat, holding me at age six months, pressing her cheek gleefully against mine, while I grimaced, and I imagined God in a skunk coat and feather hat, holding me, over-flowing with loving pride and annoying me by squeezing my cheek.

Do I believe that God is the air or that God looks like my mother did in 1951? No more and no less than I believe that God is a king or a rock or fiery volcano. Every one of our images is potentially heart-opening *and* potentially idolatrous if we think it is literally true and defining. In Maimonides' terms, every image can be held idolatrously as an essential attribute or nonidolatrously as an attribute of action.

One of the insights that I internalized in those months of practice is that thinking of God as an immutable, impersonal force—like grav-ity or electricity—is no more or less naturalistic, scientific, or sophisti-cated than thinking of God as a mother who whimsically hugs her child too hard. Both gravity and maternal love are natural.

Another lesson that I learned is that it is a culturally conditioned notion, not a timeless principle, that being helpful or loving, for exam-ple, is more virtuous and godly than accepting help or taking love. I discovered that part of what blocked me from asking for help or ac-cepting comfort was an inherited value system that severely limits the masculine virtues. I discovered this by lowering my guard and taking my vulnerability into prayer. Asking for comfort and forgiveness, I dis-covered that comfort and forgiveness had always been there for the asking. And so I found myself building a personal relationship with a nonpersonal God whose presence can be experienced in personal ways.

The Faith Required

But do I believe that God actually *does* anything? When I felt caressed or comforted, was I being caressed and comforted by God? I do not believe literally that God was aware of me, heard my prayers, and de-cided to caress and comfort me. I do believe that at all times, God's presence can be felt as caressing and comforting, and that I experience it at particular moments because I become open to receiving it at those moments.

In what sense is such a belief in a nonpersonal God worthy of the term *faith*? It is faith because, unlike Sigmund Freud or Ludwig

Feuerbach, I do not believe that I am projecting my yearnings and needs up onto an illusory God.[27] By contrast, I believe that it was God whom Moses encountered at Sinai and whom each of us discerns and encounters in peak experiences and in quiet moments of intuition. The rabbinic image of the Voice that calls to us *every day* from Sinai, saying, "Return, return, you wandering children," gets it right. At every moment, we are beckoned, invited to see and hear what we have not discerned before. What we discern, however, is the encounter filtered through our own eyes and soul.

After one presentation on SD at a synagogue several years ago, I was confronted by a serious but disturbed congregant, who is an accomplished scientist. "But how do you *know*?" he asked. "How do you know if what you think you discern is really divine?"

First, I explained the practice of SD as a way of admitting possibilities that go unnoticed because we do not admit that they are possible. Then, I spoke about the intersubjective aspects of SD and how one shares what one discerns. I went through four or five different ways of addressing his question, only to have him raise it again: "How do you *know*?" Finally, I said, "Bill, you *don't* know. That's why it's called *faith*!"

The practice of discernment takes place in the realm of mystery and paradox. We do not want for other kinds of explanations that function in the realm of what we *can* know—explanations in the field of biology, endocrinology, neurology, psychology, sociology, anthropology. One who seeks to discern that which cannot be known with certainty, however, seeks intuitions that are not subject to verification, messages that can't be recorded or preserved. Discernment is definitely subject to the pitfalls of self-delusion. To insist, as I do, that all human reports of divine intuitions and encounters reveal more about the reporter than about God is to acknowledge the pitfalls.

On the other hand, the denial of any experience that cannot be verified scientifically—the denial of the possibility that God exists and can be discerned—is no less a position of faith than the affirmation of those possibilities. When you invest the time and effort to develop a relationship with God, just as time and effort are required for the development of any relationship, you are engaged in the same type of activity—psychological and cultural conditioning—in which you engage when you view the world "scientifically." In the end, self-delusion is avoided not by a faith-based adherence to verification, but rather by a Maimonidean discipline of humility, in which you remind yourself that all images and experiences of God are colored by our own human, limited souls.

Surprises

And yet, one certainty emerges for me, over and over again, in my own journey and in the journeys of others that I witness: the certainty that we are not in control, that no matter how much we think we have the territory mapped, there are always surprises. We are buffeted. There are forces at work within us and around us that move us in unpredictable ways, and once we open our hearts and let them in, things happen that we did not think possible, things of which we did not think ourselves capable. Moments of grace and surprise, moments of uncontrolled exuberance, moments of unimagined compassion, moments in which wounds are healed and minds open up. Moments that Jews have traditionally understood as caused by a God who is aware of each of us and governs our lives providentially, but that are also experienced powerfully and lucidly by those of us who believe instead in God as a nonpersonal Mystery, the Ground of Being. The blessings are there for all—there to be discerned by all who open their eyes.

Notes

1. Howard Avruhm Addison's essay, "Reciprocal Grace: The Vocabulary of Jewish Spiritual Direction" (pp. 53–60) has documented some of these instances. Also see Zalman Schachter-Shalomi, *Spiritual Intimacy: A Study of Counseling in Hasidism* (Northvale, NJ: Jason Aronson, 1996).
2. For a similar attempt, see Amy Eilberg, "Jewish Theologies of Spiritual Direction," *Presence: An International Journal of Spiritual Direction* 11, no. 3 (September 2005): 26–32.
3. I am restricting this definition to one-on-one direction with a spiritual director. The practice takes other forms—namely, group spiritual direction and spiritual *chevruta*, in which the interactions are reciprocal. The principles, however, remain largely the same.
4. Indeed, often enough, the director may perceive her own reactions to the seeker as divine promptings, calling the director to his own work. The director's focus, however, remains at the service of the seeker.
5. For one instance of the use of this term, see Bahya ibn Pakuda, "*Sha'ar Habehinah*," in *Hovot Halevavot (Duties of the Heart)*, trans. Menahem Mansoor (London: Routledge & Kegan Paul, 1973), 150–175.

6. For a full account of the development of that program, see my article, "'I Keep God before Me Perpetually': The Development of a Jewish Spiritual Direction Program," *Presence: An International Journal of Spiritual Direction* 11, no. 4 (December 2005): 10–16.

7. At that time, *Jewish Spiritual Guidance* by Carol Ochs and Kerry Olitzky (Jossey-Bass, 1997) had just been published. The only other Jewish writing on the topic of which we were aware was Zari Weiss's article, "Contexts and Cultures in Jewish Spiritual Direction," *Presence: An International Journal of Spiritual Direction* 5, no. 2 (May 1995), and Schachter-Shalomi's account of Hasidic practice (see above, n. 1).

8. Genesis 28:16.

9. Proverbs 3:6.

10. *Likutim Yekarim* #161 (Jerusalem: Kolel Mevakesh Emunah, 1974), p. 63b. The text, traditionally ascribed to the Maggid of Mezerich, is believed to be a compilation of unattributed teachings by the first generations of Hasidic rebbes.

11. See *Romans*, especially chaps. 1–5.

12. For just one articulation of this dichotomy, see Leo Baeck, *Judaism and Christianity: Essays* (Philadelphia: Jewish Publication Society, 1958).

13. One clear example of this revised view of human nature can be found in the rich writings of psychologist Erich Fromm, who goes as far as to define religions that promote autonomy as "healthy," in contrast to "unhealthy" religions that infantilize adherents by demanding obedience and surrender to a Higher Power. See, for example, *Escape from Freedom* (New York: Farrar and Rinehart, 1941) or *Psychoanalysis and Religion* (New Haven: Yale University Press, 1950).

14. Leo Pinsker's seminal essay that launched the movement in 1881 was titled "Auto-Emancipation!"

15. Psalm 23:6.

16. Degel Mahaneh Efrayim (Jerusalem: Mir, 1995), 233.

17. Genesis 3:12.

18. A. Y. Greenberg, ed., *Itturei Torah* 1:37 (Tel Aviv: Yavneh, 1972).

19. The Rambam, Rabbi Moses Maimonides, affirms the rabbinic teaching that one who acknowledges and overcomes temptation is greater than one who does not acknowledge such yearnings. See *Shemoneh Perakim* (Eight Chapters), in *A Maimonides Reader*, Isadore Twersky, ed. (New York: Behrman House, 1972), pp. 376–379.

20. See my accounts of this process in "God as Comforter," in *Reconstructionism Today* 7, no. 1 (Fall 1999): 1, 4–6, 15; and in "Bless Us, Our Father: Parenting and Our Images of God," *The Reconstructionist* (Spring 2000): 4–11.

21. Psalm 139:1–5, translation taken from the Jewish Publication Society *Tanakh* (Philadelphia, 1985).

22. The phrase, from Numbers 14:20, that follows *Kol Nidre* and that precedes each of the *Selichot* (confessional) services of Yom Kippur.

23. Psalms 42:3, 63:2; Song of Songs 2:5, 5:8; see also Shir HaShirim Rabbah.

24. See Shlomo Pines, trans., *The Guide of the Perplexed* (Chicago: University of Chicago Press, 1974), or Isadore Twersky, ed., *A Maimonides Reader* (New York: Behrman House, 1972).

25. *Guide,* 1:51–60.

26. *Guide,* 2:32–45.

27. See Freud's *The Future of an Illusion* (New York: Norton, 1975) and Feuerbach's *The Essence of Religion* (Amherst, NY: Prometheus, 2004).

Suggested Readings

Alpert, Rebecca T., and Jacob J. Staub. *Exploring Judaism: A Reconstructionist Approach.* Wyncote, PA: Reconstructionist Press, 1985. Revised and expanded edition, 2000.

Fischer, Norman. *Opening to You: Zen-Inspired Translations of the Psalms.* New York: Penguin Compass, 2002.

Kaplan, Mordecai M. *The Meaning of God in Modern Jewish Religion.* Wyncote, PA: Reconstructionist Press, 1962.

Muffs, Yochanan. *The Personhood of God: Biblical Theology, Human Faith and the Divine Image.* Woodstock, VT: Jewish Lights, 2005.

Rabbi Jacob J. Staub, PhD, serves as professor of Jewish philosophy and spirituality at the Reconstructionist Rabbinical College, where he established and now directs the program in Jewish spiritual direction. He is the author of *The Creation of the World according to Gersonides* and the coauthor of *Exploring Judaism: A Reconstructionist Approach.*

Creating Jewish Spiritual Direction: More Than an Act of Translation

Linda Rabinowitch Thal

Y ou know," said Sister Mary Ann Scofield (one of the founders of both the spiritual direction program at Mercy Center in Burlingame, California, and Spiritual Directors International), as I was conducting the research on which this chapter is based, "I am both touched and somewhat puzzled by the interest we are getting from Jewish people in spiritual direction. After all, we got it from you!"

Indeed, exposure to Christian contemplative practice and the theology of spiritual direction has challenged us to examine Jewish texts and traditions with new eyes, discovering elements that are part of our legitimate heritage but that have been lost to most contemporary Jews. It is possible to understand the process that those of us building this field are engaged in as one of reclamation.

Reclaiming the contemplative and experiential dimensions of Judaism has required a process of "translation." One of the rabbis who trained in spiritual direction at a Christian center that welcomes trainees from all faith traditions explained that it took three years for him to complete the first year of the training program. "Two years in a row, I never went back after the fourth session, which was on prayer. It just felt too Christocentric." Another, a rabbi who trained at a different center, speaks about "those 'What the hell are they talking about?' moments" that she frequently experienced at the beginning of her training.

Many of the chapters in this book deal with very specific issues of translation. The research on which this chapter is based approaches the problem of translation from a somewhat different perspective, by broadening the comparative possibilities from which Jewish spiritual direction might develop. In addition to describing the model(s) of Jewish spiritual direction that are emerging in the practice of directors who have been trained in Christian institutions, it also examined alternative possibilities.

The contrasting models, which, for the sake of convenience, I refer to as *spiritual counseling* rather than *spiritual direction,* illuminate some of the issues that may need to be considered as we develop and refine the emerging model(s) of Jewish spiritual direction.

The Research

The core of the research consisted of interviews with thirty Jewish spiritual guides, fourteen of whom had been trained in Christian spiritual direction programs (called *Jewish spiritual directors* in this study) and sixteen of whom provided spiritual guidance without reference to the Christian model of direction (called *spiritual counselors* in this study).[1] The second group of interviewees roughly fell into groupings that I have elsewhere characterized as following a "rebbe-teacher" modality of spiritual guidance, a "healer-therapist," mode and the mode of traditional *"mashpia."* These groupings, which emerged from the data, are not comprehensive models, but they are suggestive of alternative modes of spiritual guidance. The interviewees in both the Christian-trained and the non-Christian-trained categories included rabbis and laypeople, men and women. Their denominational affiliations included Reform, Conservative, Reconstructionist, Renewal, Modern Orthodox, and Chabad.[2] The interviews were conducted between January and July of 2001. Thus they provide a snapshot of spiritual guidance at a particular point in time. The field has developed rapidly since that time, but I believe that the issues illuminated by contrasting the practice of spiritual directors and spiritual counselors remain salient to the thoughtful unfolding of Jewish spiritual direction.

The accompanying chart (see pages 24–25) and key findings summarize the most significant differences in viewpoint and practice between Jewish spiritual directors and Jewish spiritual counselors. The remainder of this chapter summarizes the issues, based on these findings, that seem most important to place on the agenda of those who are developing and teaching this new practice.

Key Findings

The following key findings emerged from an analysis of the interview data collected from fourteen Jewish spiritual directors and sixteen Jewish spiritual counselors:

1. Jewish spiritual directors' primary and explicit focus is on the seeker's relationship with God. To this end they pay particular attention to the directee's subjective experience, listening for indications of God's presence in the seeker's experience and awareness and orienting the seeker toward the (implicit or explicit) question of "Where is God in this?"

2. Jewish spiritual counselors focus more on the seeker him- or herself—on "soul work"—than they do directly on God or on the counselee's relationship to God. They foster individuation, identification with a unique soul-self and its spiritual journey, and the removal of obstacles that block the seeker's transcendence of self.

3. In spite of their focus on God, using explicit "God language" is problematic for a significant number of spiritual directors. They often use alternative words, or sometimes strings of descriptors, to refer to God, such as the Mystery, the Source, the Flow (or Web) of Life. Others speak about God without any seeming discomfort.

4. Spiritual counselors engage in less explicit "God talk" than do spiritual directors. Several acknowledge their disinclination to speak about God directly, allowing God to remain implicit in their work with counselees. Others use the very concrete tropes of biblical and rabbinic Judaism without distinguishing literal from figurative use.

5. Spiritual directors believe that the challenges they have encountered in adopting Christian models of spiritual direction are issues of translation rather than essence. They have sought language from Jewish tradition for the concepts encountered in their spiritual direction training. However, they generally have found there to be few concepts that are essentially incompatible with traditional Jewish perspectives.

6. *Discernment* is the issue around which Jewish spiritual directors feel most challenged. Although they recognize discernment to be at the heart of spiritual direction, they struggle to find Jewish language and precedents within the tradition. Spiritual counselors, on the other hand, expressed a wide range of views about the role and efficacy of discernment, including profound skepticism and concern about self-deception. Few individuals in either group

Differences in the Views of Jewish Spiritual Directors and Counselors

With Respect to	Jewish Spiritual Directors	Jewish Spiritual Counselors
Focus and Goals	Relationship with God. The focus is on experience. "Where is God in this?"	The seeker's soul journey. The focus is on soul work and refinement of the soul.
God Talk	Abundant use of direct, explicit reference to God.	God is often implicit.
Discomfort with God Language	Use of alternative referents, e.g., Source of Life, Mystery, the Web of Life.	Use of biblical/rabbinic tropes and/or avoidance of explicit references to God.
Spiritual Guidance as a Contemplative Practice	Spiritual direction is perceived to be a contemplative practice: holy listening. God is the real director.	Spiritual counselors play more varied and active roles. The counseling session itself is not necessarily perceived as prayerful.
Discernment	Although often unable to name an equivalent Jewish concept, JSDs accept discernment as central to spiritual direction.	JSCs do not use this concept. When asked about the role and possibility of discernment, their responses range from comfort to profound skepticism and concern about self-deception.
Spiritual Development	The goal of growth or development is perceived to be judgmental and prescriptive.	JSCs are comfortable with the idea of spiritual growth/development. Most have only a vague religious anthropology/spiritual psychology.

With Respect to	Jewish Spiritual Directors	Jewish Spiritual Counselors
Prayer	Prayer is of central interest. Primarily interested in spontaneous, personal prayer. Prayer may occur during a direction session. May use meditation or chanting of a liturgical phrase, but communal, liturgical prayer is rarely addressed.	Recommend meditations and chanting of liturgical phrases and *hitbodedut*. Some attention paid to communal, liturgical prayer. Prayer is less central than other traditional Jewish practices.
The Role of Spiritual Practice(s)	Study, communal participation, and the observance of mitzvot receive little attention.	Study, communal participation, and mitzvot are perceived to be important to the spiritual journey. May be perceived as pathways to self-transcendence.
Jewish Text and Tropes	The use of Jewish textual references and tropes is largely determined by the directee's familiarity with them and proclivity to use them.	Jewish texts and tropes are used more frequently and deliberately. JSCs introduce counselees to the Jewish spiritual vocabulary.
Teaching and Directiveness	Wary of taking on a teaching role, JSDs introduce texts, tropes, and practices only with caution and self-restraint. Direction comes from the directee and God.	JSCs do not perceive teaching to be antithetical to their role as counselors. Some may do their counseling over a Jewish text.
Variation	With the exception of one director who favors a "masculine model" (and, to a lesser extent, one director who introduces more explicit Jewish content), JSDs' descriptions of their practice are quite similar one to another. Their practice is based on and congruent with the contemporary contemplative Christian model of SD.	JSCs' descriptions of their practice manifest much greater variability. Three tentative models-in-action of Jewish spiritual counseling can be discerned in the data: the rebbe-teacher model, the healer-therapist model, and the *mashpia* model.

were able to articulate a coherent view of discernment in terms of Jewish texts and tropes.

7. Jewish spiritual directors have adopted the contemplative model of spiritual direction in which "God is the real director" and in which the human director's role is receptive, facilitative, and nondirective. Spiritual counselors do not conceptualize spiritual guidance as a contemplative practice, one in which God is actively present. Although generally not prescriptive, their counseling role is more active than that played by spiritual directors and they incorporate more teaching into their guidance.

8. Jewish spiritual directors are reluctant to use the concept of spiritual growth or development because it carries (for them) connotations of judgment, hierarchy, and a preset agenda. Spiritual counselors do not share this reluctance. Counselors are more likely to have at least a fledgling religious anthropology that guides their understanding of spiritual growth and their practice of counseling.

9. Jewish spiritual counselors express significantly more concern about the role of the traditional Jewish practices of study, mitzvot, and community in the spiritual lives of their counselees than do spiritual directors. Jewish spiritual counselors sometimes articulate a connection between these practices and spiritual growth, particularly self-transcendence.

10. Jewish spiritual directors express significantly more concern about the role of prayer in the spiritual lives of their directees than do spiritual counselors. Spiritual directors encourage spontaneous, personal prayer; they may suggest using a liturgical phrase as a chant or meditation, but the role of communal, liturgical prayer is rarely addressed in their practice. Spiritual counselors are more likely to encourage participation in liturgical and communal prayer and less likely to place emphasis on personal prayer.

11. Jewish spiritual counselors use Jewish texts and tropes more explicitly than do spiritual directors. They do not eschew the role of teaching within their role as spiritual guides. Directors engage in teaching and the deliberate introduction of Jewish texts and tropes into the direction process only with great caution and self-conscious restraint.

12. Guides' theological beliefs often do not easily support the development of a "relationship with God." The espoused and operative theologies of Jewish spiritual directors are often at variance with one another. The key theological themes and issues raised as problematic by Jewish spiritual guides were the following: naming God without idolatry; God as Mystery; Flow and radical Oneness; the dark side of God; divine love; and personal providence. The monistic theology embraced by most of the spiritual guides interviewed does not easily lend itself to the idea of "relationship," nor do most guides' more specific beliefs about God.

13. Meaning-making is not an explicit part of the current conceptualization of Jewish spiritual direction. Although Jewish spiritual directors engage in theological reflection and personal narrative theology when discussing their own spiritual journeys, they do not consider these important elements of spiritual direction. Contrariwise, Jewish spiritual counselors—because of their comfort with the idea of spiritual development and their conceptual frameworks with respect to soul work—are more likely than directors to incorporate elements of theological reflection and personal narrative in their practice.

An Agenda for the Emergence of Jewish Spiritual Direction

Two very general conclusions may be drawn from these findings:

> Jewish spiritual directors' stated practice closely parallels the current contemplative model of direction that is described in the contemporary literature and taught in Christian and interfaith training centers.

> Jewish spiritual counselors' practice is more varied, privileges different aspects of spiritual experience, and provides a rich set of additional possibilities—in both viewpoint and practice—for Jewish spiritual directors to consider.

In the four years between the completion of the research interviews and the present, the number of Jewish spiritual directors has grown exponentially, several programs for the training of Jewish spiritual directors have emerged, Jews have presented workshops at Spiritual Directors International, an annual national Jewish Spiritual Directors Kallah has been developed, and a week long program of advanced training has been offered. Consequently, we can assume that if the same directors were interviewed today, their thinking on some matters, particularly issues involving translation and those related to theology, would be more highly developed than it was in 2001. In spite of the changes that may have taken place in the intervening years, I believe that the key findings still provide an accurate reflection of the state of the field. And, I would argue, they should prompt us to ask whether a specifically Jewish form of spiritual direction ought to differ in some significant ways from the model in which the pioneers in this discipline were trained. In essence, I am suggesting that we at least ask ourselves whether the development of Jewish spiritual direction requires more than mere translation.

As a preliminary step toward responding to this question, I would place the following issues for consideration, research, and discussion on our agenda for the ongoing development of Jewish spiritual direction.

The Central Focus of Jewish Spiritual Direction: Relationship with God/Refinement of the Soul

Spiritual directors and spiritual counselors use very different language to talk about the primary focus and goal of spiritual guidance. Directors speak of fostering or deepening one's "relationship with God." Spiritual counselors almost never use that expression. Many of them exhibit varying degrees of discomfort with God language altogether, finding it "too noisy" and preferring to leave God's presence implicit, or adding "whatever that means" to the word *God*. The shared content of counselors' very different approaches seems best characterized as "soul talk."

Although articulated in various metaphors, there is an underlying sense that the seeker's soul is on a journey of development or unfolding. For those who dislike the journey metaphor, the soul may be seen as overcoming or freeing itself of the obstructions, impediments, or obstacles that prevent it from manifesting its true self or fulfilling its particular destiny. Just as counselors engage in relatively little God talk, directors speak only infrequently of the soul.

In spite of the apparent differences, it may be most appropriate neither to equate these two perspectives nor to assume that they can be completely separated from one another. Although spiritual counselors were rarely explicit about the connection between soul work and relationship with God, they seemed to assume their interrelatedness. Soul work, according to various counselors, has the potential to make one "more transparent to the Divine Light"; it leads to a "transcendence, a spirituality ... beyond the concerns of the soul." One counselor suggested that working at the soul level of *Ruach,* or what he called the "heart space," invites a higher kind of work that is connected to a more "universal world" and is experienced as a moment of grace. Another spoke of reaching a state in which he could no longer "distinguish the perceptual mechanism of 'I' from the Mystery of the Universe." As individuals who are unlikely to use the phrase "relationship with God," their words indicate that they do believe that soul work leads to the development and deepening of the Divine-human relationship, to *devekut.*

Similarly, spiritual directors affirm that the growth of a directee's relationship with God is attested to by the directee's greater display of character or soul qualities, such as compassion, equanimity, honesty, trustfulness, clarity, joy, presence, openheartedness, and prayerfulness. These are among the qualities explicitly cultivated in traditional Jewish soul work—*Mussar* texts such as *Duties of the Heart (Hovot Halevavot), The Path of the Upright (Messilat Yesharim), The Book of the Choicest Virtues (Sefer Maalot Hamiddot),* and the like. Nevertheless, perhaps because of their commitment to keeping a directee focused on God and on his relationship with God, Jewish spiritual directors spoke very little about the need to reflect, let alone work directly, on the soul-self.

What seems to be lacking in the responses of virtually all interviewees—counselors and directors alike—is an explicit, conceptual connection between soul work and relationship with God. Spiritual counselors were more likely to express an implicit understanding of these two sides of the spirituality coin, but the emphasis they place on soul work over relationship with God is only slightly less disproportionate than the nearly exclusive attention that directors pay to the directee's relationship with God. Without some conceptual as well as experiential understanding of the dynamic interconnection between soul work and relationship to God, spiritual guides are likely to have a smaller repertoire of ways to both understand and guide seekers.

Jewish spiritual direction will most likely be differentiated from other forms of Jewish spiritual guidance by its abiding focus on experience of and relationship with God. When interviewees spoke about their initial attraction to spiritual direction, they indicated that they had been responding to the absence or inadequacy of God talk and discourse about personal spiritual experience within their Jewish communities—both in seminaries and in synagogues. Nevertheless, it seems important that Jewish spiritual directors ask themselves whether, while maintaining their explicit focus on the directee's relationship with God, the director doesn't also need to understand that relationship against a background that includes both theology and religious anthropology/spiritual psychology.

There are a variety of Jewish tropes that provide conceptual frameworks for bringing soul work and relationship with God together: exile and return, *teshuvah,* soul levels that extend from the individual's animal soul to the divine soul, and others. Jewish spiritual directors may discover that there are particular individuals and/or particular times in an individual's spiritual life when it is beneficial, if not necessary, to be able to focus directly on the seeker, whether this is manifest as work on *middot* (qualities of character) or on understanding where one is in the journey of one's soul (personal narrative theology). In a similar way, spiritual counselors might ask whether they need to pay more attention to the relationship-with-God side of the spirituality coin.

Thus, the first issue that I would place on the agenda for additional work is *developing a Jewish conceptual framework that clarifies the overlap between "relationship with God" and "soul work," theology and Jewish religious anthropology.*

Theological Foundations for Jewish Spiritual Direction

At the heart of the Christian model of spiritual direction in which most Jewish spiritual directors have been trained lies a set of theological presuppositions that God initiates, invites, communicates with, and directs individuals in ways in which one who is contemplatively attentive can discern. This theology refers frequently to the Holy Spirit "speaking" to individuals. The spiritually attuned individual becomes increasingly adept at perceiving and interpreting the "inner stirrings" of the Holy Spirit, as well as reading the "signs of the times" (the messages of Divinity contained in the events of the external world).

Jewish spiritual directors may claim that "God is the real director," but Jewish tradition lacks an explicit descriptive term for God that is fully congruent with the Christian theology of the Holy Spirit. For some Jewish spiritual directors, neither theology nor Jewish language is particularly important; their own experience assures them that "There is guidance in the world." Others have developed phrases of their own, like "the deep place of knowing," to express a religious truth for which they have no name. Still others have adopted metaphors and searched for traditional tropes and images that provide Jewish language for the issue of discernment: *kol d'mamma dakka* (the still, small voice), *lev shomea* (a listening heart), *annanei hakavod* (the cloud of Glory that guided the Israelites in the wilderness), *merechefet* (the fluttering of God's creating Spirit). While these and other Jewish tropes may function suggestively, they are not elaborated into a system of discernment that can help the individual distinguish between the *kol d'mamma dakka* or the guidance of the cloud of Glory and the voice of ego.

Judaism does have a traditional trope with which the possibility of humans receiving divine messages can be acknowledged. But the term *Ruach HaKodesh* is in itself problematic, even apart from the potential for confusion with the hypostatized Holy Spirit, which forms part of the Godhead in Christianity. There is considerable ambivalence within the tradition about *Ruach HaKodesh,* and central to the ambiguous nature of this trope is disagreement about whether or not *Ruach HaKodesh* "ceased in Israel" after the death of the prophets Haggai, Zechariah, and Malachi. Nevertheless, whether reserved for formal prophecy or applicable to individuals whose learning and devotion have brought them unusual merit,[3] the claim of *Ruach HaKodesh* generally carries with it the connotation of great personal holiness. This makes it an uncomfortable if not dubious trope—let alone theology—for those engaged in spiritual direction. Moreover, *Ruach HaKodesh,* as it has traditionally been used, is too powerful and extraordinary a phenomenon for what we might want to call "ordinary" or "everyday discernment": the cultivation of receptivity, the willingness to wait in patient openness for greater truth to unfold over time, the conscious effort to find one's "most honest, *teshuvah* place," the attempt to live with a sense of interconnectedness and to see "with a God's-eye perspective."

One trope that emerged in interviews with several guides, both directors and counselors, is that of *teshuvah*. Unlike *Ruach HaKodesh*, which is problematic because it is generally reserved for extraordinary human-Divine contact, *teshuvah*'s disadvantage may be that it is a bit *too* ordinary. Liberal Jews are accustomed to speaking of *teshuvah* primarily as repentance for particular misdeeds or, perhaps, for more enduring failures of character. Having lost touch with the intentional recitation of the daily liturgy, many Jews are unaccustomed to thinking of *teshuvah* as the need to continually realign oneself with God, or, as Adin Steinsaltz suggests, "return to one's own paradigm."[4]

Rabbi Abraham Isaac Kook, first chief rabbi of prestate Israel, is among those who have elaborated upon *teshuvah* in a way that bridges theology and religious anthropology. According to Kook, this return to one's authentic Self is "the soul's surge for perfection, a reach for reunion with God, an effort to rise above the limitations of finite existence." It is the "effort to return to one's original status, to the Source of Light and Higher Being." Kook writes that "the finitude of the human self blunts"[5] the soul's capacity to receive divine light, but continuous refinement of the soul's receptivity is possible, and it is that process of returning and refinement that Kook means by *teshuvah*. While repentance for a specific sin or for sinfulness is one level of *teshuvah*, ongoing *teshuvah* includes:

> attentiveness to one's inner sensibilities through meditation and the withdrawal from worldly distractions, serious study of spiritual and moralistic writings, and exposure to great spirits, the true *zaddikim* [*tzaddikim*: righteous ones] by whose light others can also see light.[6]

This constant process of reorientation toward God, based on "attentiveness to inner sensibilities," is somewhat akin to the various processes that Christians call discernment. Those inner sensibilities are not the message itself but rather a felt sense that requires interpretation within a framework that provides a language and a set of values associated with *teshuvah*—and, of course, Kook would assume, commitment to *halachah*. Thus, *teshuvah* expresses a process that is expansive enough to include a range of religious orientations from repentance for specific sins to *devekut* (cleaving to God).

Teshuvah is only one of many possible tropes that might be developed as Jewish spiritual directors attempt to elaborate a theology of spiritual direction and particularly of individual discernment.[7]

Indeed, it was possible to delineate at least five theological issues in addition to that of discernment that emerged as problematic in the interviews: naming God without idolatry; God as Mystery, Flow, and radical Oneness; the dark side of God; divine love; and *hashgachah pratit* (personal providence). The monistic theology held by most of the spiritual guides interviewed does not easily lend itself to the idea of "relationship," nor do most guides' more specific beliefs about God. These issues are not only central to spiritual guides' theological discourse, they are also the issues around which the conflict between guides' espoused and operative theologies are most apparent.

Thus, the second issue that I would propose for an agenda of future work is the *development of theological underpinnings, as well as suggestive traditional tropes, for Jewish spiritual direction and for individual discernment.*

Spiritual Development and Spiritual Dynamics

Interviews with spiritual directors revealed a disparity that exists between the spiritual direction literature, which generally asserts that "the only valid objective in spiritual direction is the *growth* of the directee,"[8] and the discomfort expressed by Jewish spiritual directors around the issue of spiritual development. Typical responses to my questions about spiritual growth included, "Am I making a judgment by saying directees two and three have spiritual maturity and directee one doesn't?"; "None of the literature on spiritual development rings true.... I find it boring. I can barely read it"; or "I think spiritual maturity is a function of developmental maturity. What is spiritual maturity? I don't know; I'll let you know when I get there."

There are legitimate arguments for caution in adopting particular developmental schemes,[9] but spiritual directors' reluctance to entertain the subject of growth was rarely expressed in terms of these issues, but rather out of a concern that setting spiritual growth as a goal would introduce human judgmentalism and prescriptiveness into a practice that should be contemplative and guided by God.

This leaves Jewish spiritual directors with no conceptual framework for understanding or fostering the dynamics of spiritual growth. Even Gerald May, who argues that a purely developmental model cannot account for instances of children or young adults who manifest more mature perceptions of God or far greater compassion than their sophisticated elders, has developed his own developmental scheme, based on "progressions of love." And, like one of the spiritual counselors interviewed, who, in spite of believing that "Some people *are* at higher levels than others," finds the idea of spiritual levels more useful when applied intrapsychically than comparatively, May argues against a purely progressive or comparative use of developmental schema and suggests that

> It is wise to hold all concepts of stages in spiritual growth very loosely, using them only at the most gross levels of understanding and remembering constantly that the manifestations of grace in a person's life can never stop surprising us."[10]

But holding stages loosely does not mean spurning all focus on spiritual growth or the development of conceptual frameworks for observing, understanding, and fostering growth. Spiritual guides need conceptual frameworks and language that will help them remain aware of the complex dynamics of spiritual development: the identification with soul, the disidentification with the ego-self, the growing identification (or *devekut*) with God. These processes of identification and disidentification, like May's progressions of love, have a developmental valence, even if they do not follow a neatly sequential process.

Given their concentration on soul work, spiritual counselors are aware of the need to foster individuation as part of the spiritual process. They referred to this in various ways, including, "identification with one's pure soul" and "following the journey of one's soul." Both transpersonal psychologists who work from a model of Eastern spirituality (e.g., Ken Wilber) and those who follow a Western paradigm (e.g., Michael Washburn), build their models for self-transcendence on the prior consolidation of an established ego-self.[11] But just because individuation is a step on the path of spiritual—as well as psychological—development, it is hardly its pinnacle.

The inability to differentiate among the levels of ego, authentic self, and soul contributes to the charge of spiritual narcissism, which is often leveled against the New American Spirituality.[12] Those who see Jewish spirituality as the problem rather than the solution, or as little more than "warm fuzzies," are reacting to this confusion.[13] The very ease with which the legitimate recognition of the individual's holy uniqueness can be co-opted by the secular culture of narcissism makes it particularly important that spiritual directors have sources of guidance and wisdom that are spiritual rather than psychological against which to read the unfolding lives of their directees.

Another dimension of spiritual development, one that I would call *spiritual dynamics* was found in a small number of the interviews with spiritual counselors. This term highlights the processes rather than the content or quasiprogressive levels of spiritual growth—for example, *yeridah l'tzorech aliyah* (descent for the sake of ascent) and the alternations of *mochin de gadlut* and *mochin de katnut* (expanded and constricted consciousness). This dimension was surprisingly absent from most of the interviews, although it is noted in Schacher and Hoffman's study of Hasidic counseling.

> Reflecting this all-encompassing love, the rebbe saw the hasid as one growing and evolving—not as a stationary entity.... Hasidic leaders emphasized that this internal ascent is not always a smooth one. Rebbes knew that "between one level and the next, before one can reach the higher one, he must 'fall' from the previous rung." In these moments, the hasid indeed felt stricken with despair and hopelessness; he feared that his difficulty might endure forever—and desperately sought the rebbe's solace.[14]

These dynamics may occur over an extended period of time or they may appear as almost daily vacillations. Christian literature refers to extended periods of *katnut* or *yeridah* as dark nights of the senses or of the spirit. Thomas Keating describes the more episodic periods of "psychic nausea" that occur at certain stages of Centering Prayer in much the same way that the Hasidim describe the *machshavot zarot* ("strange thoughts"—illicit sexual, idolatrous, prideful, or even murderous desires) that seemed to arise during intense prayer, when, in the fervor of unselfconscious devotion, the ego's mechanisms of repression are relaxed. In longer and more intense periods of *yeridah* or *katnut,* the shadow elements of the personality may emerge as strong waking urges. They may be acted on as either ethical or ritual violations of *halachah*, or they may emerge as depressive states experienced as *galut* (exile) or abandonment by God (*hister panim*, the hiding of God's face). Transpersonal psychologist Michael Washburn refers to these processes as "the regression of the ego in the service of transcendence." He argues that this spiraling downward to reconnect with the energies of the Ground of Being in their primitive and personal forms may be necessary before the next phase of growth, openness to transpersonal spiritual energy, can begin.[15]

While Hasidic literature provides a conceptual vocabulary for spiritual dynamics, it may be helpful for spiritual guides to read it in conjunction with the literatures of Christian spirituality and transpersonal psychology, which are more systematic in their presentation. The Christian literatures tend to be more explanatory than the Hasidic literature, which is largely descriptive and prescriptive. Given the Hasidic preoccupation with the power of sexual thoughts and the fact that Hasidic remedies sometimes involve an elaborate use of the complex sefirotic system of the Kabbalah, this literature sometimes appears to be arcane and hopelessly dense. However, juxtaposing Hasidic literature with that of Christian (or Buddhist) spirituality and with transpersonal psychology suggests that spiritual guides can deepen their understanding of spiritual development by using diverse but mutually revealing lenses.[16]

Consequently, the third area of work to be placed on the agenda is *the location, juxtaposition, and analysis of wisdom about spiritual development and dynamics gleaned from Jewish textual sources, from the spiritual literature of other traditions, from transpersonal psychology, and from the practical experience of guides themselves.*

Traditional Jewish Spiritual Practices as Paths of Self-Transcendence

The research revealed that Jewish spiritual counselors express significantly more concern about the role of the traditional Jewish practices of study, mitzvot, and participation in community in the spiritual lives of their counselees than do spiritual directors. Spiritual counselors frequently articulated their understanding of the connection between these practices and spiritual growth, particularly self-transcendence.

On the other hand, directors generally approached discussion of specifically Jewish practices with reticence and with concern that they not violate the nonprescriptive nature of spiritual direction. Below is a brief consideration of a few of the ways in which mitzvot, study, and communal participation can function as paths of spiritual growth toward self-transcendence.

Study and Self-Transcendence

Since the rabbinic era, *Talmud Torah,* the study of traditional texts, has been understood to be a primary path to God. Indeed, rabbinic tradition generally gives study precedence over prayer. Here the contrast between directors and counselors was stark. Counselors who work in the rebbe-teacher or *mashpia* mode may actually conduct a counseling session around the study of a text, letting the student discover and explore her own issues in conversation with the text as well as with the counselor. Others, including those who work in the healer-therapist mode, often make reference to Jewish texts and teachings in their work with counselees.

Only two spiritual directors, both of whom acknowledge that their work is something of a departure from the modes of direction they were taught, feel fully comfortable picking up on opportunities that arise for the teaching of Jewish material during a session. One explained that he had increased the "intellectual content" and the reading material that he gives directees as "homework." "They're Jews, after all!" he noted. He does this "not to bring in Jewish authority but to help people locate themselves Jewishly." Most spiritual directors, however, were much more cautious, often curbing their natural proclivities as Jewish teachers. As one spiritual director commented,

> So that is a question for me: to what extent is it appropriate for me
> to teach or prescribe or even associate with issues of Torah study
> as opposed to just being open to the possibility of that arising in
> the same way that I would be open to any other manifestation of
> Divine Presence that a person might bring into direction? I'd want
> to be very cautious about this.

Recent spiritual autobiographical writing by Jews who have found their way back to Judaism through the gateway of study attests to some of the ways in which *Talmud Torah* may lead to self-transcendence.[17]

Self-forgetful absorption in the text, the appropriation of a set of values that transcends self-concern, and identification with a transhistorical, transgeographic community that has grown up around the text are among the various ways that study can serve as a mode of self-transcendence. In his book on Jewish spirituality, Lawrence Hoffman even argues for the spirituality of immersion in oft-disdained *pilpul*—argument over details that have no real-life applicability.[18]

Given the potentially transformative power of *Talmud Torah* and its centrality in Jewish spirituality, to what extent might either study itself or the exploration of the directee's experience with Jewish study (including his nonexperience) take place in Jewish spiritual direction?

Community and Self-Transcendence

Jewish spiritual directors also were reluctant, in ways that many spiritual counselors were not, to prescribe community affiliation or participation.

> Now as a rabbi, I am very attuned to the possibility that a seeker may find God primarily through community, but as a spiritual director, it's my primary duty to say, "Let's listen together to how God is working in your life." And, from that perspective, how do I come off saying, "You ought to belong to a shul!" There's something discordant about that.

By contrast, a number of counselors, believing that community is an essential element of Jewish spirituality as well as a path to self-transcendence for the individual, may even try to facilitate a counselee's entrée into some form of communal affiliation or participation.

> The community is the essence in Jewish spirituality. Judaism holds the individual in great regard, but not apart from the extended *mishpacha* of the community. Jewish spirituality is about relating to, and from, and in that community.... I don't want to demean meditation, but if you only did that, we wouldn't label you a *Jewishly* spiritual person.

To the extent that we understand spirituality as the search for the connection between the Transcendent and that which is deepest within the individual,[19] or as the letting go of one's narcissism in order to surrender into Mystery,[20] a communal spirituality might appear to be an oxymoron. Mark Verman, in his book on the history of Jewish mystical practice, acknowledges the long-standing nature of the "dialectical tension that exists between an individual who wishes to achieve spiritual elevation in isolation and the centripetal force of Judaism which requires Jews to function as members of a national community."[21] The negotiation of this tension is also acknowledged as part of spiritual work in paradoxical statements by Hasidic masters: "it is good to practice separation *(prishut)* in the company of others" or "it is good to practice *hitbodedut* (aloneness) by acquiring a partner."[22]

Although participation in communal spirituality may take very conventional forms, it may also provide a developmental challenge for those moving into postconventional ways of relating to the world. Engagement in community may be a form of self-transcendence, placing communal welfare before personal welfare, but also requiring one to actually perceive oneself as a differentiated part of a larger organic whole. Even when Jews begin their spiritual journey as a private search, they almost inevitably are drawn into community, which offers the possibility of identification with something larger than the self and the humility of discovering that one's unique, individual story is neither unique nor individual, but rather part of a larger sweep of spiritual history.

Without becoming prescriptive about how a directee links herself to the Jewish community, should a Jewish spiritual director nevertheless seek to explore directees' experience (and non-experience) in Jewish community, help them reflect on how it affects their relationship with God, and encourage them to find and contribute to communities that support their spiritual growth—even if the "support" that is provided is the challenge of not falling prey to that community's particular weaknesses? It may be especially important for Jewish spiritual directors to pay attention to this issue of connection to some part of the larger Jewish community—to explore the ways in which community is or is not successfully mediating a directee's experience of God—because the very privatized, dyadic nature of spiritual direction can easily provide a countervailing message.

Mitzvot and Self-Transcendence

Whereas Jewish spiritual directors are extremely cautious about being prescriptive with respect to mitzvot, even hesitating to follow up on practices that a directee might have expressed a desire to try at the previous session, spiritual counselors frequently prescribe various forms of traditional spiritual practice. "You need some kind of structure that isn't self-created," explained one counselor. "[Practice] moves one from the purely personal ... into a place that knows complexity, knows the other, and can make discernments in the world." One counselor unabashedly described her prescriptive approach to point up the difference between her directee's and her own religious priorities (*hachnasat orchim* [hospitality] as opposed to full Yom Kippur observance):

> One of the women I work with does a lot of entertaining. She has a wonderful home and she entertains beautifully. So it was before Yom Kippur and she mentioned that she was going to go home on Yom Kippur around 3:00 so she could cook for her guests. I said, "What? Cook? Prepare it early!" And I was very firm that she stay at synagogue throughout Yom Kippur. This led us to a whole discussion of how you decide to serve God. Do you do what you think is your service for God or do you do what the Torah says that God wants? She stayed in synagogue. It was very hard for her, but it was a tremendous opening for her. Once we clarified the issue, she was able to do a little *misseras nefesh* [self-sacrifice], going beyond herself. And that was a tremendous source of growth for her.

Arthur Green, writing about his own religious struggle with willfulness and surrender, explains, in classic covenantal terms, the way he understands the relationship between mitzvot and self-transcendence.

> In my own religious life, I have come to recognize the need for submission to God as a part of religious devotion. I fought long and hard against this aspect of religious life, but I now, perhaps with long delayed maturity, have come to accept it. I believe there is no room for God—however defined—in our lives until we can overcome our own willfulness. To thus submit, to "negate your will before God's will," is essential to accepting the covenant as I have described it, the readiness to serve as a channel for divine presence in the world.
>
> In Judaism, this submission, usually described as *kabbalat ol malhut shamayim* ("accepting the yoke of divine rule"), is joined to *kabbalat ol mitzvoth* ("accepting the yoke of the commandments"). For myself, I recognize the necessity of this link, the sense

that religious awareness only becomes constant in life through the regularity of religious discipline.[23]

Consideration of mitzvot raises issues of both practice and theology. Traditionally, the Jewish relationship with God is rooted in an act of communal surrender or submission—at Sinai. So for a Jew living according to *halachah,* the act of surrender has already happened. To what extent, and based on what kinds of theological understandings, should Jewish spiritual directors, then, at least be prepared to help Jewish directees explore the system of traditional Jewish spiritual practices as a path to self-transcendence?

A fourth area for Jewish spiritual directors to explore is that of traditional Jewish spiritual practices. *Spiritual directors need to reflect on and understand more fully the ways in which traditional Jewish spiritual practices—mitzvot, study, communal engagement, and liturgical as well as personal prayer—can mediate God's presence for individuals.*

Text, Trope, and Teaching

After exploring and rejecting a series of essentialist options for capturing the unique nature of Jewish spirituality, Arthur Green has concluded that it is "the text itself" that serves as the "binding substance for the variety of Jewish spiritual expressions." The text, according to Green, impacts Jewish life in two primary ways: practice (mitzvot) and language—particularly Jewish tropes.[24] Jewish discourse is constructed around text-based tropes that evoke sets of associations. These associations, in turn, spark the engagement, insight, and creativity that are part and parcel of Jewish spirituality. Within Jewish thought, language itself is divine. Creation takes place through language; letters and words are perceived to be the building blocks of the universe.

> Words, especially proper names and common names, do not arbitrarily refer or apply to individual things or categories; they refer to them by virtue of expressing their natures or essences. The essences of things, wedded to their names, are the meanings of the names; the names as it were, abbreviate descriptions of the essences or their bearers. Hence, the speaker ... who knows the meaning of ... the names ... *ipso facto* knows the natures or essences.[25]

Consequently, when the halachic system of mitzvot cannot be assumed, the use of Jewish tropes becomes that much more important as a hallmark of Jewish spirituality. The importance of familiarity if not facility with the Jewish conceptual vocabulary raises the issue of teaching, something that Jewish spiritual directors are wary of doing.

Directors, using basic counseling skills, by and large join in the directees' own mode of religious expression. Consequently, directees who themselves use Jewish tropes, references, and concepts will be met by directors happy to engage them in that language. Directees who lack the Jewish conceptual vocabulary, however, may not necessarily be introduced to it in the spiritual direction context. We note the extreme caution with which one director said she would offer even an image or association that had arisen for her as she listened to her directee.

> When I have listened very carefully, and in one of those moments when I am sure that I am not interrupting, when I am sure that I am not robbing the person of his own time to really, quietly, deeply listen to what God is saying to him, then, if an association with the *parasha* or to a holiday that is coming up or to a passage in the Siddur arises for me—something sort of small, that is very much a response to what he is wrestling with—and I think it would be helpful to his struggle, then, I will certainly say it.

We might then wonder what happens when this level of reticence encounters a directee with little fluency in Jewish text and trope. Would the amount of teaching necessary to make the association meaningful preclude its being offered? And, if that is the case, given the role that language plays in Jewish spirituality, is there some very basic way in which the "Jewishness" of this direction experience is being undermined?

This cannot be answered in the abstract. For a directee who feels alienated from Judaism, the introduction of a specifically Jewish trope or concept will have a different resonance than it does for a directee who is eager to return, explore, or learn. One director concluded that the very fact that "Jews often know so little and are adrift and in need of guidance" means that he must temper the very receptive model in which he was trained. Struggling to discern when to "hold back" and when to "give some direction," he remarked, "with Jews … direction is partly what they are coming for. They are not coming just to reflect.

They want a little bit of the 'lowdown.'" This director was suggesting that for directees who lack basic Jewish literacy, work that would ordinarily be considered spiritual formation may need to be included within the context of direction.

As Jewish spiritual directors begin to consider the question of whether Jewish spiritual direction is particularly Jewish, we should remember that the issue of language has both practical and symbolic import. If Jewish spirituality is intimately tied to the particularity of Jewish tropes, directees who are unfamiliar with these tropes not only lack access to the Jewish conceptual vocabulary but, on a metalevel, they may not be able to perceive their spiritual journeys as "Jewish." As one director reported, offering an alienated Jewish woman the trope of *neshamah t'horah* (a pure soul), can have a pivotal impact on her ability to nurture the spiritual side of herself and to locate herself within, as opposed to feeling excluded from, the Jewish spiritual universe.

Given the communal nature of Jewish spirituality, being able to reflect on personal spiritual experience in the shared religious language may be the linchpin of a specifically Jewish spiritual direction. Perhaps rather than limiting Jewish spiritual direction to "holy listening" and "mirroring," the director may sometimes refract the directee's speech and experience through a specifically Jewish prism, breaking the speech of generic spirituality into the more nuanced speech of a specific tradition—in this case, Judaism.

Thus, the fifth issue to be placed on the future agenda we are creating is that of teaching. *Jewish spiritual directors need to reflect on the extent to which and the conditions around which teaching— Jewish tropes and basic concepts as well as specifically Jewish practices—should enter into their conduct of spiritual direction. They will need to consider when their primary commitment to following the directee's lead, to listening for God experience wherever it manifests, and to letting God be the director give way to a slightly more active introduction of—and possible advocacy for—specifically Jewish spiritual pathways and participation in specifically Jewish discourse.*

Meaning-Making

Only three of the spiritual directors interviewed made any reference to meaning-making as a goal of spiritual direction, and those references were only made in passing. Maintaining their explicit focus on the immediacy of experience—taking notice of and "dwelling in" those moments in which God's presence seems to have been manifest—most directors eschew additional levels of meaning-making. By contrast, several directors did engage in theological reflection and personal narrative theology when they were speaking about their *own* lives or *reflecting on* the experiences of their directees. For example, after describing the work she had done to help a directee find Divine Presence in his visit to an elderly grandparent suffering from Alzheimer's, a director added,

> I think one of the hardest questions we have to deal with is that we grow up from utter dependency to relative independence and strength back to increasing dependency. And that's the normal human trajectory. Moses is the exception. And what do we think about that trajectory? Is it just an accident or is there something meaningful going on there that we are supposed to be learning? Because we lose each of the things we thought identified us: First of all, we lose our physical appearance, and then we lose our physical strength; and then we lose our sense of status; and we lose our sense of being able to do things. So now we're being rather than doing. So you see all these things being stripped away. And you say, maybe this is stripping that we should have been doing, and because we didn't do it, it happens to us.

This is a rather profound piece of theological anthropology, but there was no indication that it had been part of the director-directee conversation. In fact, in the spiritual direction model, as described to me by most of the Jewish spiritual directors I interviewed, the director's introduction of her own theology in this way would have been considered "too directive" and not sufficiently focused on the directee's felt experience. Tilden Edwards's admonition that spiritual direction is about "apprehension not comprehension"[26]—and William Barry and William Connolly's warning that the search for meaning can be a distraction from contemplation with its focus on experience[27]—have been taken to heart by Jewish spiritual directors.

Because so many of the examples discussed by directors in interviews lend themselves to being interpreted as incipient forms of theological reflection or narrative theology, I remain unconvinced that Jewish spiritual directors do not in fact legitimize and even encourage these forms of meaning-making. What does seem clear, however, is that this is not part of Jewish spiritual directors' conscious model of direction.

Elsewhere, I have argued that Jewish spiritual direction would be enriched by directors' reflective awareness of how theological reflection and narrative can deepen a directee's experience of God.[28] Brother Don Bisson has argued that some directees actually need to begin with cognitive understanding before they can come to awareness of their affective experience.[29] Indeed, William James, looking at pinnacle moments of religious experience, found that a noetic element is an essential part of mysticism.[30] From the perspective of inquiring about how Jewish spiritual direction may be particularly Jewish, theological reflection and personal narrative create opportunities for expressing spiritual experience in the text-and-trope language of Jewish spirituality. And, of course, the very introduction of Jewish texts and tropes into the conversation is an act of theological interpretation and meaning making.

The sixth item that I would place on the Jewish spiritual direction agenda, therefore, is *the need to explicitly explore the dynamics and the potential power of theological reflection and personal narrative theology for the interpretation and integration of experience.*

Relationship with God, Contemplation, Discernment, and Ongoing Revelation

I have delineated six issues that constitute future work for those who wish to contribute to the development of Jewish spiritual direction. Each of these items extends the boundaries of the phenomenon studied: Jewish spiritual direction as articulated by its current practitioners. The composite agenda implies that elements found in the practice of those who are providing Jewish spiritual guidance based on other models might be incorporated into the heart of a specifically Jewish practice of spiritual direction. Nevertheless, this agenda is proposed alongside the recognition that all that we have learned from the contemporary Christian model must also be protected.

Jews have become interested in spiritual direction because they were not finding outlets in which they could comfortably talk about

God directly or reflect on their relationship with God openly within the Jewish community.[31] They have been attracted to the contemplative mode as a complement to the more communally validated intellectual mode of encountering God, and they have been inspired by becoming witnesses to the ongoing nature of divine revelation rather than teachers of revelation that has already occurred.

Therefore, my seventh recommendation is that *the agenda outlined in this chapter include a commitment to maintaining the centrality of spiritual experience and personal relationship with the Divine, that the* ruchaniyut *(spirituality) of Jewish spiritual direction continue to be grounded in* penimiyut *(interiority), and that the commitment to a contemplative modality be maintained.*

A Future Agenda for the Development of Jewish Spiritual Direction

Based on a review of the central issues raised by this the research, I would propose the following agenda as fruitful future work for Jewish spiritual directors:

1. Developing a conceptual framework that acknowledges and clarifies the relationship between "relationship with God" and "soul work."
2. Articulating the theological foundations and related Jewish tropes for Jewish spiritual direction and for individual discernment.
3. Studying and synthesizing the wisdom on spiritual development and dynamics that can be gleaned from Jewish textual sources, the spiritual literature of other traditions, transpersonal psychology, and the practical experience of Jewish spiritual guides.
4. Reflecting on the role traditional Jewish spiritual practices can play in mediating God's presence and in providing paths of self-transcendence.
5. Rethinking the role of teaching in Jewish spiritual practice and developing sensitivity to conditions under which the introduction of specifically Jewish practices and traditional tropes will enrich or hinder the deepening of a directee's relationship with God.
6. Exploring the dynamics and the potential power of theological reflection and personal narrative theology as ways in which directees interpret and integrate their spiritual experience.

7. Maintaining a commitment to the centrality of religious experience and personal relationship with the Divine within the practice of Jewish spiritual direction.

Conclusion: Toward a More Comprehensive Model

The contemporary contemplative Christian model that is being taught at interfaith training centers is only one of many forms that spiritual direction has taken through the centuries. In developing a model of Jewish spiritual direction, it is not necessary to assume that the contemporary model is complete or comprehensive. The model graphically illustrated in the accompanying chart represents a schematic for combining and integrating elements that emerged in interviews with spiritual counselors with those that were described in interviews with spiritual directors.

The model recognizes both foci found in the research: a more meaningful relationship with God and a strengthening of soul work, each characterized by the three components that were identified

Toward a Model of Jewish Spiritual Guidance
Holy Listening/Holy Teaching/Holy Healing

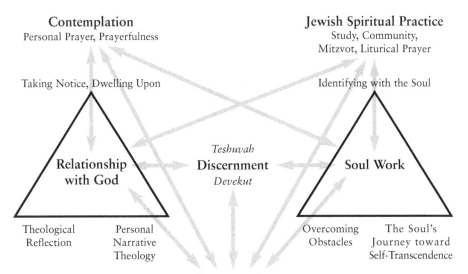

Contemplation
Personal Prayer, Prayerfulness

Jewish Spiritual Practice
Study, Community,
Mitzvot, Liturical Prayer

Taking Notice, Dwelling Upon

Identifying with the Soul

Teshuvah
Relationship with God — **Discernment** — **Soul Work**
Devekut

Theological Reflection — Personal Narrative Theology

Overcoming Obstacles — The Soul's Journey toward Self-Transcendence

Jewish Text and Trope

through analysis of directors' and counselors' descriptions of their practice. I have suggested, however, that rather than imagining the deepening of relationship with God and the refinement of soul as separate goals or foci, they be seen as two sides of a single coin, as two aspects of a single integrated process that can be talked about from one perspective as *teshuvah* and from another as *devekut*. These central Jewish spiritual concepts point toward the dynamic interaction that exists between relationship with God and soul refinement.

Prayer and contemplation are very directly linked to the establishment and deepening of relationship with God, but they also play important roles in soul work. The number of Jewish spiritual counselors who prescribe contemplative meditations and *hitbodedut* (prayerful crying aloud to God) attest to their understanding of this connection. Traditional Jewish spiritual practices provide direct opportunities and structures for identifying with the higher self and for moving toward self-transcendence, while contemplation and spontaneous personal prayer foster the *kavannah*, which makes these practices truly spiritual rather than merely religio-cultural practices.

These practices themselves—study, participation in acts of communal ritual and responsibility, the performance of mitzvot, and liturgical prayer—immerse the Jewish seeker in the text and tropes of traditional Jewish life, but if we are to take Green's understanding of Jewish spirituality seriously, the Jewish conceptual lexicon needs to be applied to all aspects of the model. So, for example, Jewish spiritual directors might encourage spontaneous personal prayer as a form of *hitbodedut* and might consciously provide directees engaged in theological reflection and personal narrative work with the Jewish textual references and tropes that would help them express their experience.

Such a model is not to be taken as a program for directees but rather as the conceptual framework within which Jewish spiritual directors can view their work. It is the beginning of a map that might help directors locate their directees at any particular point in their journey, a tool for asking themselves whether there are directions in which the directee might be ready to grow or whether there are gaps in a directee's spiritual life that might be addressed if the director were sensitive to a timely opening.

Notes

1. For the purpose of this study, I reserved the term *Jewish spiritual direction* to designate the one-on-one spiritual guidance provided by Jews who are consciously adopting and adapting the Christian model of direction as they understand it. I use the designation of *Jewish spiritual counseling* to describe the counseling done by a wide range of counselors whose work has *not* been influenced by experience with Christian models. I use *spiritual guidance* as a generic term to embrace the work of both of these groups. There is no common agreement on these terms, nor am I suggesting that the way they are used here be widely adopted. Individuals trained in spiritual direction may actually prefer to call themselves *guides;* those whom I am designating as counselors may understand themselves to be *Jewish* spiritual directors. The differences among spiritual guides may increase in the coming years, and clear, alternative models may emerge; alternatively, the differences may fade, as directors, counselors, and others converse and exchange their practical wisdom. Meanwhile, it is my hope that the work of those whose practice is based on the direction model will be enriched and deepened by seeing their words placed within the context of these other sources.

2. The research population and the three groupings within the category of spiritual counselors are further characterized in "Where Is God in This? Issues in the Emergence of Jewish Spiritual Direction" (Linda Thal dissertation, Columbia University Teachers College, 2003), chap. 2, app. 1.

3. Maimonides, *Guide to the Perplexed*, 2:45. Moses Hayyim Luzatto, *Messillat Yesharim: The Path of the Upright,* trans. Mordecai M. Kaplan (Philadelphia: Jewish Publication Society, 1966), pp. 452, 456. Rabbi Hayyim Halberstam of Sanz: "I do not know why you doubt that *ruah ha-kodesh* exists even now for the one who deserves it, even though prophecy was abolished … for prophecy is one thing and a holy spirit of wisdom *(ruah ha-kodesh de-hokhmah)* is something else. This (holy spirit of wisdom) was never abolished, and only a heretic will deny this." Quoted in Norman Lamm, *The Religious Thought of Hasidism: Text and Commentary* (New York: The Michael Scharf Publication Trust of Yeshiva University Press, 1999), 319.

4. Adin Steinsaltz, *The Thirteen-Petalled Rose* (New York: Basic Books, 1980), 127.

5. Abraham Isaac Kook, *Lights of Penitence* (New York: Paulist Press, 1978), 39, 87.

6. Ibid., 189–190.

7. Rabbi Zalman Schacter-Shalomi uses *kavannah* as his central trope for redirecting the soul toward God.

8. Sandra Marie Schneiders, "The Contemporary Ministry of Spiritual Direction," *Chicago Studies,* Spring 1976: 126–30. Also in Kevin G. Culligan, ed., *Spiritual Direction: Contemporary Readings* (Locust Valley, NY: Living Flame Press, 1983), 48, 50, and 52. Also see Janet Ruffing, *Uncovering Stories of Faith: Spiritual Direction and Narrative* (New York: Paulist Press, 1989) 18.

9. In literature, among the most frequently mentioned reasons given for caution when using developmental schemes are the following:

   • Developmental schema are often affected by religio-cultural values that are assumed but may go unrecognized and unacknowledged. See, for example, Brant Cortright, *Psychotherapy and Spirit: Theory and Practice in Transpersonal Psychotherapy* (Albany: State University of New York Press, 1977).

   • Many developmental schemes conflate psychological and spiritual development, although there is a great deal of evidence that these kinds of development do not necessarily occur in tandem. See Gerald May, *Care of Mind: Care of Spirit* (HarperSanFrancisco, 1992), 22.

   • Developmental approaches cannot account for many transformative or conversionary experiences. Gerald May, *Will and Spirit: A Contemplative Psychology* (San Francisco: Harper and Row, 1983), 167–171, and *Care of Mind: Care of Spirit*, pp. 21–31.

   • Developmental approaches deal with differences in worldview or ways of knowing but have little to do with the way religious traditions self-define. See Craig Dykstra, "What Is Faith: An Experiment in the Hypothetical Mode," in *Faith Development and Fowler,* eds. Craig Dykstra and Sharon Parks (Birmingham, AL: Religious Education Press, 1986), 45–64.

10. May, *Care of Mind: Care of Spirit*, 22.
11. Ken Wilber, *No Boundary: Eastern and Western Approaches to Personal Growth* (Boulder: Shambhala, 1981) and *A Brief History of Everything* (Boston: Shambhala, 1996). Michael Washburn, *The Ego and the Dynamic Ground: A Transpersonal Theory of Human Development,* 2nd ed. (Albany: State University of New York Press, 1995) and *Transpersonal Psychology in Psychoanalytic Perspective* (Albany: State University of New York Press, 1994).
12. Elizabeth Lesser, *The New American Spirituality: A Seeker's Guide* (New York: Random House, 1999).
13. Michael Chernick, "Ki Hashem Elokekha Esh Oklah: Spirituality and Danger," in *Paths of Faithfulness: Personal Essays on Jewish Spirituality* (Hoboken, NJ: KTAV, 1977), 17–20, and Charles Liebman, "Post-War American Jewry: From Ethnic to Privatized Judaism," in *Secularity, Spirituality, and the Future of American Jewry* (Washington, DC: Ethics and Public Policy Center, 1999), 11.
14. Zalman M. Schachter-Shalomi and Edward Hoffman, *Sparks of Light: Counseling in the Hasidic Tradition* (Boulder: Shambhala, 1983), 112.
15. Washburn, *The Ego and the Dynamic Ground* and *Transpersonal Psychology in Psychoanalytic Perspective*.
16. See Louis Jacobs, *Hasidic Prayer* (New York: Schocken, 1972), chap. 9; Thomas Keating, *Open Mind: Open Heart* (New York: Continuum, 2000), 73; Washburn, *The Ego and the Dynamic Ground* and *Transpersonal Psychology in Psychoanalytic Perspective*.

17. For a look at the ecstatic transcendence of falling in love with Torah, see Lee Meyerhoff Hendler, *The Year Mom Got Religion: One Woman's Midlife Journey into Judaism* (Woodstock, VT: Jewish Lights, 1999). On the transcendence of rigidly held assumptions, see Lisa Schiffman, *Generation J* (HarperSanFrancisco, 1999). On the transcendence of psychic wounds, see Emily Benedek, *Through the Unknown, Remembered Gate: A Spiritual Journey* (New York: Schocken, 2001). For insights into the transcendence of death, see Leon Wieseltier, *Kaddish* (New York: Alfred Knopf, 1998).

18. Lawrence Hoffman, *The Journey Home: Discovering the Deep Spiritual Wisdom of the Jewish Tradition* (Boston: Beacon, 2002), 72ff.

19. Ewert Cousins, "Introduction," *Jewish Spirituality: From the Bible through the Middle Ages*, ed. Arthur Green (New York: Crossroads, 1986).

20. Daniel Evans offers the following definition of spirituality: "Spirituality consists primarily of a basic transformative process in which we uncover and let go of our narcissism so as to surrender into the Mystery out of which everything continually arises [p. 4]. [Mystics tend to agree that any authentic spiritual transformation] involves shedding of narcissism, self-centeredness, self-separation, self-preoccupation, and so on" (p. 158). Daniel Evans, *Spirituality and Human Nature*, cited in Jorge Ferrer, "Transpersonal Knowledge," in *Transpersonal Knowing: Exploring the Horizon of Consciousness*, eds. Tobin Hart, Peter L. Nelson, and Kaisa Puhakka (Albany: State University of New York Press, 2000), 220.

21. Mark Verman, *The History and Varieties of Jewish Meditation* (Northvale, NJ: Jason Aronson, 1996), 21.

22. Moshe Leib of Sassov, *Tzevvaot Ve-Hanhagot*, 101, and R. Eliahu de Vides, *Reishit Hochma HaShalem, Shaar ha-Kedusah*, 6:19.

23. Arthur Green, *Seek My Face: Speak My Name: A Contemporary Jewish Theology* (Northvale, NJ: Jason Aronson, 1992), pp. 132–133.

24. Arthur Green, "Introduction," in *Jewish Spirituality: From the Bible Through the Middle Ages,* xiii.

25. Joseph Stern, "Language," in *Contemporary Jewish Religious Thought: Original Essays on Critical Concepts, Movements, and Beliefs,* eds. Arthur A. Cohen and Paul Mendes-Flohr (New York: Scribner, 1987), 544.

26. Tilden Edwards, *Spiritual Friend: Reclaiming the Gift of Spiritual Direction* (New York: Paulist Press, 1980), p. 4.

27. William Barry and William Connolly, *The Practice of Spiritual Direction* (New York: Seabury, 1982), p. 18.

28. "Where Is God in This?" Thal dissertation, chap. 8.

29. Don Bisson, "Melting the Iceberg: Spiritual Direction for Men." *Presence: An International Journal of Spiritual Direction* 6, no. 2 (2000): 31. In personal communication, Bisson has also stressed the importance of meaning-making in spiritual direction.

30. William James, *Varieties of Religious Experience: A Study in Human Nature* (London: Longmans, Green & Co., 1911).

31. See Thal dissertation, Appendix C.

Linda Rabinowitch Thal, EdD, is codirector of the Yedidya Center for Jewish Spiritual Direction and its spiritual direction training program, Morei Derekh. A pioneer in the early work of synagogue transformation, she serves as a consultant to the Rabbinic Spirituality Committee of the Central Conference of American Rabbis. Receiving her doctorate in a joint program at Union Theological Seminary and Columbia Teachers College, her dissertation stands as a major scholarly work in the field of Jewish spiritual direction. She trained in spiritual direction at Fordham University and in spiritual direction supervision at the Mercy Center in Burlingame, California.

Reciprocal Grace: The Vocabulary of Jewish Spiritual Direction

Rabbi Howard Avruhm Addison

Introduction

Language plays a vital role in the Jewish understanding of reality. According to Genesis, God created the world through speech. Medieval Jewish philosophers referred to the human species as *midaber,* creatures who speak. Jewish mystics view the name of each object and being as constituting its reality and essence.[1] Therefore, if we are to look for authentically Jewish models of spiritual direction, a good place to start is with the Hebrew words traditionally associated with this enterprise.

As found in all faith traditions, spiritual counsel dates back to the earliest stages of Judaism. Scripture reports instances affirming spiritual guidance as essential to the work of prophet, *navi,* and priest, *kohayn.*[2] Classical rabbinic sources allude to guides, known as a *Morei Derekh,* and the prime importance placed on acquiring a spiritual friend, called a *chaver.*[3]

Two additional terms for spiritual guides have appeared during the last 250 years. The title *mashgiach,* or spiritual supervisor, arose within the context of the Lithuanian yeshiva, based on the model established in the nineteenth century by Rabbi Hayim of Volozhin. Charged with the students' religious development, the *mashgiach* often was the one who introduced the teachings of *Mussar,* the Moralist movement founded by Rabbi Israel Lipkin Salanter, into the yeshiva. *Mashpia* is the name given to the spiritual prompter within Hasidic communities, who teaches and provides ongoing counsel both in support of the rebbe and when the rebbe is absent.

Traditionally, the *mashgiach* and *mashpia* have offered more authoritative, ritually prescriptive forms of counsel than we usually associate with modern spiritual direction. However, an examination of the Hebrew words that form the roots of their respective titles can give us insight into classical Jewish theology and its attendant conception of spiritual guidance.

The *Mashgiach*

As mentioned above, the word *mashgiach* is commonly translated as "supervisor." However, if we look at the term and its associated enterprise, *hashgachah*, we find that both are derived from the verb that means "to pay attention." Thus a true *mashgiach* is not one who merely uncovers flaws and prescribes correctives, but one who is attentive and mindful. How so? We can cite two instances where the word *mashgiach* first appears in the Babylonian Talmud:

> Are the utensils of one ignorant of the Law [*am ha-aretz*] pure or impure? He [Rabbi Joshua] replied, "Impure ... but if you tell him so, will he pay attention [*mashgiach*] to you? He'll reply, 'Mine are pure; yours are impure'" (*Hagigah* 22b).

> Rabbi Nathan said, "It [the verse "He has despised God's word"] applies to those who pay no attention [*mashgiach*] to the Mishna...." (*Sanhedrin* 99a).

The first quotation focuses on how to guide those unacquainted with the intricacies of Jewish law. Rather than putting them on the defensive, those who offer guidance need to be attentive and speak sensitively, lest their counsel provoke only resentment. The second source speaks of the need for guides to be mindful of current needs and the resulting evolution of tradition. Rabbi Nathan declared that anyone who would derive Jewish practice solely from Scripture without paying attention to Rabbi Judah the Prince's guide to Jewish law and observance, the Mishna (codified circa 200 CE), was not to be considered as faithful, but as one who disdains God's ongoing revelation.

Medieval Jewish philosophy began to speak of God as the ultimate *mashgiach*. Debates raged over whether God's *hashgachah*, Divine Providence, provides only general direction to the universe as a whole or supervises every aspect of each human life. The following two passages however, imply that God might not be the immediate

cause of everything that befalls us. Instead, the Source of Life is portrayed as ever-mindful of us, the One whose omnipresence never leaves
us totally abandoned or bereft:

> A person must examine those opinions that strengthen the heart's
> complete trust in God. The first concept is to know clearly that
> God shows mercy to humanity beyond that shown by any other
> comforter. God pays attention [*mashgiach*] to humanity in both
> hidden and revealed ways (*Orchot Tzadikim*, Gate 9).

> How does one acquire Reverence? By contemplating two truths:
> The first is that the blessed *Shechinah* [Divine Presence] is found
> everywhere in the world and pays attention [*mashgiach*] to all
> things small and great. Nothing is hidden from God's eyes. (Rabbi
> Moshe Chayim Luzzato, *The Path of the Upright [Messilat
> Yesharim]*, 25: Italy, eighteenth century).

These sources indicate that as the divine *Mashgiach,* God's loving, attentive presence is everywhere. Therefore, to be a human *mashgiach,*
the guide must also be attentive and present. Through prayer or chant
or meditation or through lighting a candle, a "sacred container," a
contemplative space free of physical and emotional distractions must
be created. Then through attentive, "holy" listening might the guide
help the seeker recognize the Loving Presence as it unfolds in the great
and small details, in the revealed and hidden patterns of the seeker's
life.

The Mashpia

The word *mashpia* is derived from the word *shepha,* which means, "to
overflow" or "to pour abundantly." Literally, a *mashpia* is a channel
or a conduit, a tube or pipe through which liquid flows. In kabbalistic
terminology, *shefa* refers to the divine radiant energy of the unknowable, limitless Divine *(Ayn Sof)* that overflows and enlivens the configuration of God's personality, the Tree of Life *(Etz Chayyim)* and then
brings vitality and blessing as it pours down on our world.

Judah Loew of Prague (d. 1609), philosopher, talmudist, and legendary creator of the humanoid *golem,* conceived of God as the ultimate
Mashpia, Who conveys goodness to the world. It then becomes the

godly task of the righteous to place themselves consciously within the stream of blessing and to channel divine goodness and guidance to others, according to their needs. Both the human *mashpia* and the one receiving the guidance will find themselves transformed by the experience.

> It is the way of the Blessed One to convey [*lihashpia*] wholeness.... And permission is given to those who receive it to do as they please. What do the righteous do? They channel [*mashpia*] that goodness (Judah Loew of Prague, *The Eternity of Israel [Netzach Yisrael]*, 25).

> Concerning the receiving of Torah ... it was given to Moses because he was prepared for it. Therefore the Torah was given exclusively to Moses who, because of his generous spirit, was a channel [*mashpia*] to others. Thereby Moses conveyed [*lihashpia*] Torah's guidance to Israel exactly as its psyche needed (Judah Loew of Prague, *The Splendor of Israel [Tiferet Yisrael]*, 49).

> The essence of Torah guidance is derived when one acts as its channel [*mashpia*] to others.... [T]hose who receive the greatest wholeness do so through acting as a channel [*mashpia*] for others and thereby actualize their Torah. This act of serving as another's Torah channel completely actualizes them and brings them supernal wholeness.... When one channels Torah to another, it represents something new and is thus considered as if the channel [*mashpia*] had personally fashioned it and thereby completely attained the level of Universal Intellect by conveying to and actualizing another. In this way a person actualizes complete wholeness unlike anything that could be attained by studying on one's own (Judah Loew of Prague, *Eternal Pathways [Netivot Olam]*, 7 and 8).

Rabbi Loew teaches us that to be a true guide, like Moses, one needs preparation, a generous spirit, and the sensitivity to facilitate individual seekers to grow in the Spirit in ways best suited to them. The last qualification points out the transformations that may occur in the guide through the direction process. Rabbi Loew's younger contemporary, the moralist and mystic Isaiah Horowitz (d. 1630), cited an additional way that the seeker might serve as a "gift" to the guide. He portrayed divine creativity and grace as being inherently reciprocal.

From the very outset of time, taught Rabbi Horowitz, divine creativity was marked by the interplay of opposites that transformed each other.

> with six movements. And behold the existence of Time only occurs through the First Day, which was born of the first movement. It was born with 24 hours divided into two periods, with each of the 12 hours being included in the other 12. For the channel [*mashpia*] becomes the receptor [*mikabel*] and the receptor becomes the channel, the front becomes the back and the back the front, the left becomes the right and the right the left. Accordingly, because the movements [that created Time] only attained wholeness through the 24 hours, the 12 hours of day and the 12 hours of night are considered as equals [completing each other] (Isaiah Horowitz, *The Two Tablets of the Covenant [Shnay Luchot HaBrit], Hullin, Perek Torah Or*, 47).

As the guidance encounter increasingly reveals the hidden Creator of all, a mysterious dynamic unfolds. Many a spiritual director has sensed this paradoxical reality—the guide also derives guidance, the seeker also guides and each is indispensable in forming a grace-filled, creative whole.

In It for God

What lessons might contemporary spiritual direction draw from the Hebrew terms *mashgiach* and *mashpia*? The first is Judaism's challenge to godly action, here embodied in the call to sacred attention. As God is attentive to each detail that unfolds in this world, so are we summoned to be attentive to the external events and inner movements that unfold in our seekers' lives and in our lives as their guides. While we cannot fix their brokenness, we can help them be mindful of God's caring, continuing presence as they experience moments of consolation, desolation, and the interstices that lie between. By mirroring God's loving attention through our attention to their unique sensibilities and God's unfolding revelation as refracted through our own traditions, we can create that "sacred container" through which the Divine can be manifest in great and small ways, in the revealed and hidden aspects of life.

A second and perhaps more uniquely Jewish insight is the reciprocal nature of grace that can be revealed through the spiritual guidance process. By channeling the flow of grace and guidance to another, we recognize that guide and seeker will both convey and receive blessing, and both will be transformed by the experience.

However, as this further quote from Isaiah Horowitz indicates, the third partner in the relationship, God, is also transformed through the direction encounter:

> [B]ecause the human is created in the image of God, human actions channel [*mashpia*] additional divine radiant energy [*shefa*] to the Supernal [worlds] that are configured according to that same likeness (Isaiah Horowitz, A Conceptual Key [*Maphtaychot LaInyanim*]).

Playing upon the kabbalistic notion that what transpires respectively in the divine and earthly spheres affect each other, Rabbi Horowitz conceived of grace as a flow emanating from the Divine, descending to earth and then, through human agency, being rerouted back to its source to help strengthen the Divine itself. Because human reality reflects the image of the Divine, each represents but half of the equation needed to complete the circuit of blessing and life. Unlike the Christian notion that grace is an unearned gift God bestows upon us, the Jewish concept is that human action is indispensable not only to the flow of grace, but also to the actualization of God Godself![4]

This audacious teaching has some radical implications for the work of spiritual direction. Despite its various formulations and guises, the main question of spiritual direction has been, "Where was God in this for you?" Based on the conception that grace flows but one way, this question summons the seeker to look for the providential that might underlie the seemingly coincidental in his life. If, however, grace is reciprocal, then the following question must also be posed: "Where were you in this for God?" This complementary query can add a whole new dimension to the practice of spiritual direction and the way our seekers see themselves. The following is a case in point.

> Sy is an accountant who lives in the southeastern United States. After enduring years of dysfunctional marriage to a gambling addict, Sy moved from his family home and began divorce proceedings. Having shielded his teenage children from their mother's

addiction, Sy bore the brunt of his son and daughter's anger over the breakup. At a spiritual direction session, Sy spoke of his hurt and his attempts to rebuild his life. He described a recent graduation party he had attended as the date of the graduate's mother, herself a divorcee. Even though he played no role in the demise of his date's marriage, he found his attempts at greeting the graduate's father, a long-time acquaintance, cavalierly rebuffed.

Faced with the realities of divorce and the web of small town life, Sy lamented his rather "knotty situation." When asked about his feelings at being rebuffed, Sy was finally able to access the profound sense of hurt and loss he'd been experiencing. He sensed God's presence with him as he walked in this Valley of the Shadow, as his old life was dying and his new life was yet to be born. However, when asked where he might have been for God during this transition time, his mood seemed to lift. He realized that his overture to the graduate's father might have been more than a pleasantry; it might have been a godly, liberating act. "Who knows? Maybe my greeting helped begin God's process of loosening the knots that are so painfully binding us to each other."[5]

God's Partners

Classical Judaism has long understood the reciprocal nature of our relationship with God. The term *brit,* covenant, used to describe God's relationship with Abraham and his descendants and the Revelation at Sinai, implies a mutual set of responsibilities and benefits that flow both to humanity and to God as a result of our relationship. The talmudic Sages called upon us to act in *imitatio Dei* ("as God is merciful, so shall you be merciful") and to remember that we are God's partners in the work of creation.[6]

When it comes to the practice of spiritual direction, Jewish tradition summons us to these same tasks. To be a *mashgiach* means that just as God is attentive and present, so must we be attentive and present. To be a *mashpia* is not only to channel God's guidance and grace to others—it represents our role as conduits channeling our seekers and ourselves to realize our part in both actualizing divine grace on earth and in channeling it back to God.

Notes

A version of this essay initially appeared in *Presence: An International Journal of Spiritual Direction,* 10, no. 1 (February 2004): 28–32. Special thanks go to Barbara Sussman and Rhonda Shapiro-Reiser for their clinical and scholarly insights that have contributed to this work.

1. Gershom Scholem, *Kabbalah* (New York: Quadrangle, 1974), 23–26.
2. On the role of prophet as offering intercessory prayer and guidance on the Sabbath and New Moon, see Genesis 20:1–7 and II Kings 4:17–23. On the clumsy adventures of Eli the High Priest as a spiritual guide, see I Samuel 1:9–17 and 3:1–10.
3. For Moses as the model of a *Moreh Derech,* see Exodus Rabbah 12. On the importance and function of a *chaver,* see *The Fathers According to Rabbi Nathan,* trans. Judah Goldin (New York: Schocken Books, 1974), ch. 8.
4. Moshe Idel, *Kabbalah: New Perspectives* (New Haven: Yale University Press, 1988), chap. 8.
5. Adapted from a group supervision session of Lev Shomea, February, 2003, residency that occurred at Elat Chayyim Jewish Retreat Center in Accord, New York. The names, location, and some details of the session have been altered for the sake of privacy.
6. See Howard Addison, *Shutafo: Partners with God* (New York: United Synagogue Press, 1991).

Rabbi Howard A. Addison is the author of *Show Me Your Way: The Complete Guide to Interfaith Spiritual Direction,* in addition to other books that explore the connection between Kabbalah and personality type. A congregational rabbi for nearly thirty years, he now teaches at Temple University. He is the G. G. Scholem Professor of Jewish Spirituality at Graduate Theological Foundation and is a cofounder of Lev Shomea, the first institute to train spiritual directors in the Jewish tradition.

Practicing Spiritual Guidance

Spiritual Direction as a Contemplative Practice

Rabbi Zari M. Weiss

Achat sha'alti mey'et Adonai
otah avakesh
shiviti b'veit Adonai
kol y'mei chai
lachazot b'noam Adonai
u'l'vaker b'heychalo

One thing have I asked of the Eternal One
This one thing I request
To dwell in the house of Adonai
All of the days of my life
To gaze with pleasantness on the Eternal One
And to visit in God's temple.

PSALM 27:4

To dwell in God's house, to gaze with pleasantness on the Eternal One: These ancient words of the psalmist so beautifully express the longing of the one who desires to live life in the light of God's presence. Not just during those fleeting moments of spiritual inspiration or enlightenment, but indeed, as the psalmist yearns, "all the days of my life." The poet who wrote these words so many years ago knew the feeling of God's presence or nearness; this poet knew the inner stillness and serenity that often accompanies such moments.

In the contemporary literature of spiritual direction, this experience would likely be described as a "contemplative" one. Indeed, much of the literature describes spiritual direction as a contemplative practice, one that is built on the expectation that both director and directee come to the encounter with a contemplative attitude. Furthermore, for those engaged in the ongoing practice of spiritual

63

direction, it is generally understood that contemplation becomes an orientation in life, not just what occurs in the hour-long monthly session with director and directee.

For many Jews, the word *contemplative* may sound foreign, and more descriptive, perhaps, of a religious/spiritual approach found in other faith traditions. For those Jews involved in spiritual direction, the centrality of the contemplative orientation may be perplexing. Always wanting to root our spiritual practices in the past, we may wonder: Are there precedents for the contemplative life within Judaism? What exactly does *contemplative* mean? What does it mean in a *Jewish* context? Is there a particularly Jewish way to be contemplative?

William A. Barry and William J. Connolly, in their book, *The Practice of Spiritual Direction,* speak about the nature of contemplation, specifically as it occurs in prayer:

> Contemplation ... begins when a person stops being totally preoccupied with his own concerns and lets another person, event, or object take his attention. When it is a person who is being contemplated, he lets that person, with his personality, concerns, and activity take his attention. He lets himself be absorbed, for a moment at least, and at some level, in the other person. Contemplative prayer ... means paying attention to and becoming at least slightly absorbed in ... God.... A contemplative attitude can develop from such prayer and, if it does, it allows one to find some ease and spontaneity in paying attention to the Lord as he reveals himself in Scripture, creation, one's own life, and the life of the world, rather than seeing him simply as a background figure for one's own concerns.[1]

They go on to say:

> [O]ne effect of paying attention to something outside ourselves is that it can make us forget ourselves and our surroundings. Contemplation leads to, or rather is an experience of, transcendence—that is, of forgetfulness of self and of everyone and everything else except the contemplated object.[2]

To forget oneself, to have one's own ego-self recede into the background as an awareness of God's presence or reality moves into the foreground: This describes a contemplative orientation in life. Such an experience could not help but, as Barry and Connolly describe, "lead to an attitude of reverence and wonder before the other."[3]

The contemplative approach or orientation in life is found everywhere in Judaism, if one knows where and how to look. Some examples date back to the earliest texts of the Jewish people; others are reflected in the basic practices that frame and punctuate Jewish religious and spiritual life today.

The Foundation: Love of God

Throughout the Torah, the first five books of the Bible, the children of Israel are reminded again and again of the sacred obligation to love the Eternal One, God:

> And now, Israel, what does the Lord your God require of you, but to fear the Lord your God, to walk in God's ways, and to love God, and to serve the Lord your God with all your heart and with all your soul.... (Deuteronomy 10:12–13).

Indeed, for the ancient Rabbis, those who helped transform the biblical form of Judaism into what it has evolved to today; the directive to love God was central. They prescribed that the prayer, now referred to as the *Shema*, be recited twice each day, morning and evening, as well as on one's deathbed:

> And you shall love the Eternal One your G-d, with all your heart, with all your soul, and with all your might (Deuteronomy 6:4).

The obligation to love God was to be remembered at all times: when one sat in one's home or walked out along the road. It was to be passed on from generation to generation (teach these words intently to your children), and it was to be lived out in the world as well as in one's own personal life (inscribe them on the doorposts of your house and on your gates) (Deuteronomy 6:5–9).

Furthermore, the commitment to love God was to be kept at the forefront of one's actions and thoughts (bind them as a sign upon your hand, and keep them visible before your eyes). It was, ideally then, something that should be practiced constantly, at all times and in all places. Doing so could not help but support the cultivation of an awareness of God in everything that one did.

In his commentary on the Torah (Deuteronomy11:22), Rabbi Moses Nachmanides (Ramban), a thirteenth-century mystic and legalist, wrote about practicing the love of God at all times.[4] He writes that such constant love is an essential aspect of *devekut*, cleaving to God:

> Included in *devekut* is remembering and loving Him constantly, your thoughts never leaving Him when you walk, when you lie down, when you rise; so much so, that when you talk to others, it is only with your mouth and tongue [that you talk] but your heart is not in it, for [the heart] is in the presence of G-d."[5]

Nachmanides goes on to describe the experience of those who are able to maintain this spiritual state at all times:

> It is likely that those who have attained this [high] rank partake of eternal life even during their earthly sojourn for *they themselves [thus] become an abode of the Shechinah* [italics mine], as was alluded to [by R. Yehuda HaLevi] in the Kuzari.[6]

But how is it possible to achieve this state? In his book, *Meditation and the Bible*, Aryeh Kaplan cites a teaching by Moses Maimonides, which describes the way that we can begin to cultivate this state of being in our own lives:

> What is the way to love and fear G-d? When a person contemplates [*hitbonen*] His great, wondrous deeds and creations, seeing through them His boundless, infinite wisdom, he immediately loves, exults, and is ecstatic with a passion to know the great Name. This is what King David meant when he said, "My soul thirsts for G-d, for the living Deity" (Psalms 42:3).

> When one thinks about these things, he immediately becomes awed and abashed. He realizes that he is but an infinitesimal creature, lowly and unenlightened, standing with his diminutive, deficient mind before the Perfect Mind. David thus said, "When I see Your heavens, the work of Your fingers … what is man that You consider him?" (Psalms 8:4–5).[7]

In other words, Maimonides suggests, by pausing and seeing *beyond* what appears on the surface, a person can become aware of the various ways that God is or might be present: in any created object, in any event, in any experience of life. When he does, he will necessarily become filled with an awareness of God, and will realize his own minuteness relative to the magnificence of the Great Mystery of the Divine. His sense of self will recede, and his awareness of God will move to the forefront.

Kaplan then expands on the concept of *hitbonenut*, contemplation, by examining the root of the Hebrew word:

> This word, *hitbonenut*, is the reflexive of the root *bin*, meaning "to understand." It is from this root also that the word *binah*, meaning "understanding," is derived. *Hitbonenut* literally means "making oneself understand"; that is, *contemplating something so deeply and completely* that one makes himself understand it in all its aspects.
>
> The connotation of *hitbonenut*—contemplation—is to gaze and stare at something, either visually or mentally, until one understands it thoroughly. We see it in the sense of visualization in such verses as, "I have made a covenant with my eyes, should I then contemplate [*hitbonen*] a maiden" (Job 31:1). It also refers to thinking over a statement, as when Job said, "I have contemplated you" (Job 32:12), indicating that he had contemplated what they had said.
>
> This word is also used with respect to God, and in this sense, it is often a preparation for the mystical state. We thus find such verses as "Contemplate [*hitbonen*] the wonders of God" (Job 37:14), and "Contemplate the love of God" (Psalms 107:43).[8]

Kaplan says that one way to practice *hitbonenut* is to focus on (gaze or stare at) something so intensely that she reaches a state of understanding, what might better be called "an interior state of understanding." This practice, Kaplan states, can also be applied to God. When a person intensely focuses on or gazes at (in her inner mind's eye) so intensely on God (or perhaps, God's manifestations in the world) that her own ego-self recedes and an awareness of God comes to the forefront, she can become, as Nachmanides taught, "an abode of the *Shechinah*." Living in this state, as an abode of the *Shechinah,* was likely what the psalmist described when he wrote the beautiful words of yearning expressed in Psalm 27. It is what we might call a contemplative state of being.

Becoming an Abode of the Shechinah?

Not everyone can become an abode of the *Shechinah,* of course. Even in Nachmanides' day, there were certainly distractions, things that diverted one's attention from living with a constant focus on God. In our day, especially, we are easily distracted: by tasks waiting to be done, by the phone ringing, by children or others needing our attention. We may set aside time for meditation or prayer in the morning, and may even experience—for a moment or two—the bliss that the psalmist described so poignantly. But all too soon, the feeling disappears, and the experience fades and becomes a memory.

One need not become a permanent abode of the *Shechinah,* however, in order to live with a love of God, an awareness of God, in all aspects of life. There are different degrees of intensity, different places along a continuum of experience that reflect the contemplative life.

The practice of spiritual direction supports the cultivation of the contemplative life. The task of a spiritual director is to be present with another person at any point along the continuum. In the spiritual direction session, the directee is invited to reflect on his experiences, and—in the sacred quiet of the session—to consider if or how God might have been present in any one of them. Beyond the individual sessions, however, as the directee continues in the spiritual direction relationship, he begins to learn a new language, a new way of seeing, and his orientation to life becomes transformed. Direction invites a person to become aware of how God is or might be present in each and every moment. Gradually, the directee begins to live a life in which she increasingly "contemplates [*hitbonen*] God's great, wondrous deeds and creations, seeing through them God's boundless, infinite wisdom." This is the path to the contemplative life; a life lived with an awareness of God, a love of God, at all times.

The Role of the Spiritual Director

Not everyone who comes for spiritual direction has known God's presence, of course, nor do they necessarily know how to experience it. But they do come with a longing, a yearning—even if they can't always name it—to dwell in God's house, to bring an awareness of God to every aspect of life. The task of the director is to recognize that longing, to support and encourage it.

In order to do so, the director must spend time cultivating the contemplative stance in her own life. The director does this by tending to her spiritual life and practice and by working with her own spiritual director.

In the direction session itself, the director must also provide a sense of spaciousness. She must make room for the directee's awareness of God to grow and to deepen. The director must constantly practice self-supervision, noticing those times when her own ego or agenda gets in the way, thereby precluding the directee's relationship with God from being at the forefront.

The director offers an encouragement to greater silence and openness, to be receptive to what might emerge in the silence. As Barry and Connolly write:

> Such openness runs counter to much of our usual personal activity. We try to control our perceptions; we are threatened by newness and strangeness. As a result, we often see only what we want to see or what our perceptual and cognitive structures let us see. To try to contemplate means to try to let the other be himself or herself or itself, to try to be open to surprise and newness, to try to let one's responses be elicited by the reality of the other [in this case, God]. So, when we contemplate God, we try to let him be himself and not our projection of him, and to be real ourselves before him.[9]

Directors must be patient. Again, Barry and Connolly write:

> Spiritual directors sometimes must work patiently and creatively if directees are to experience contemplation and see themselves as contemplative people.... Spiritual directors sometimes have to work long and patiently with people to help them reach the point of being able to forget themselves. Self-absorption can even mask itself unconsciously as virtue.[10]

One way of doing this, they suggest, is to invite the directee to become absorbed in something other than himself—music, natural beauty, art, architecture, or anything else that will absorb him.

> They would benefit more from spending time at first in some activity that they enjoy that has a contemplative aspect to it. This might

be anything from birdwatching to admiring the architecture of a city, from listening to the surf to listening to Bach—any receptive experience that helps a person forget himself and become absorbed in something else.[11]

In Jewish practice, one traditional way to do this is by focusing on the *shiviti*. The *shiviti* is a special chart or wall hanging designed for gazing. Based on the verse from Psalm 16:8, "*Shiviti HaShem l'negdi tamid*—I place the Eternal One before me always," the chart contains the Psalm's verse, with emphasis on the four letters of the divine name. Often, there are additional verses from Scripture and from mystical texts. There are various techniques for using a *shiviti*, which are beyond the scope of this chapter. The purpose, however, is precisely the one described above: to help a person forget himself, and become absorbed in something else, in this case, the Divine. By doing so, a person may enter into a more contemplative state, and sense that she is sitting—if but for a few moments—in the light of God's Presence.

Rabbi Abraham Joshua Heschel writes eloquently about the need to forget oneself, to have one's ego needs and concerns recede into the background, particularly during a time of prayer:

> The focus of prayer is not the self. A man may spend hours meditating about himself, or be stirred by the deepest sympathy for his fellow man, and no prayer will come to pass. *Prayer comes to pass in a complete turning of the heart toward God,* toward His goodness and power. It is the momentary disregard of our personal concerns, the absence of self-centered thoughts, which constitute the art of prayer. Feeling becomes prayer in the moment in which we forget ourselves and become aware of God.... The thought of personal need is absent, and the thought of divine grace *[chesed]* alone is present in his mind.[12]

The director helps the directee do this during the direction session by returning again and again to God. (Of course, as explored elsewhere in this book, the word *God* is not always explicitly used. Sometimes the director invites the directee to pay attention to where she feels more energy, called to life, to wholeness; where she has a moment of absolute clarity.) In whatever theological language she discerns is most helpful, the director gently brings the directee back, helping her to see intimations of the Divine. As the director models this in the session, so the directee increasingly learns to cultivate and return to that perspective in the course of her everyday life.

Why Is the Contemplative Life Important?

Most people manage to live their lives without a constant awareness of God. They go about their lives, their work, their social interactions without feeling the bliss of God's light. Perhaps they participate in some form of worship occasionally, or even regularly, and some may even experience moments of transcendence. Their lives are full, meaningful, worthy. What value is there to striving to live a contemplative life? Why is it important?

We can only imagine if or how the world would be different if all people did, in fact, conduct themselves with an awareness of God before them, with a love of God in their hearts at all times. We can only imagine how they might treat the earth differently, how they might treat others differently—their wives, their children, those of different races and classes—how they might treat themselves differently.

Throughout history, a minority of Jews have chosen to live a contemplative life in isolation from others. Most, however, who have been drawn to the contemplative life have done so while being fully engaged in the world. Rabbi Yaakov Yosef of Polennoye, a great Hasidic teacher, once said that one aspect of the excellence of the early Sages was that while they were engaged in mundane work with their physical limbs, their minds and souls were simultaneously attached to God [and God's Torah].[13] For contemporary Jews, living a contemplative life means using our limbs and all the parts of our physical beings to be fully engaged in the world, while having our souls and hearts attached to God. If more of us were to do so, we can only imagine how much better the world would be.

Notes

1. William A. Barry and William J. Connolly, *The Practice of Spiritual Direction* (New York: Seabury, 1982), 48.
2. Ibid., 49.
3. Ibid., 50.
4. "to love the Eternal your God, to walk in all God's ways, and to cleave unto Him."
5. Norman Lamm, *The Religious Life of Hasidism: Text and Commentary* (New York: Michael Scharf Publication Trust of Yeshiva University Press, 1999), 134–135.

6. Ibid.
7. Aryeh Kaplan, *Meditation and the Bible* (New York: Samuel Weiser, 1978), 133.
8. Ibid., 131–132.
9. Barry and Connolly, 51.
10. Ibid., 48–49.
11. Ibid., 52.
12. Abraham Joshua Heschel, *Man's Quest for God: Studies in Prayer and Symbolism* (New York: Crossroads Publishing, 1987), 15.
13. Rabbi Yaakov Yosef of Polennoye, *Ben Porat Yosef,* preface, 8c, cited in Lamm, *Religious Life of Hasidism,* 164.

Rabbi Zari M. Weiss has been at the forefront of bringing spiritual direction to the Jewish community. Trained as a spiritual guide at the Mercy Center in Burlingame, California, she is a pastoral counselor, writer, and a founding teacher of Lev Shomea, the first institute to train spiritual directors in the Jewish tradition. A past copresident of the Women's Rabbinic Network, she serves as chair of the Central Conference of American Rabbis' Committee on Rabbinic Spirituality.

Holy Listening: Cultivating a Hearing Heart

Barbara Eve Breitman

The central statement of the Jewish faith, the *Shema*: "*Shema Yisrael, YHVH Eloheinu, YHVH echad*—Hear Israel, YHVH is Our God, YHVH is One," declares that hearing is the quintessentially sacred act for Jews. Paradoxically, the name for God used in the *Shema* is precisely the one Name that cannot be spoken; it is ineffable. Since YHVH is an impossible declension of the verb *to be*—collapsing past, present, and future tenses into one unpronounceable Name—it is as if Jews are being exhorted to listen for the Presence of Being through infinite forms in time and space, to perceive the Oneness that underlies the diversity of life; to know that alone deserves to be called God; and that Oneness can somehow be "heard," in silence. This is not only *hearing* as we hear sounds with our ears. It is hearing with the heart, with the *lev shomea,* the "hearing heart" (I Kings 3:9). But what kind of hearing is this?

"Hearing into Speech"

In the 1970s, feminist theologian Nelle Morton coined the phrase *hearing into speech* to describe what happened as small groups of women came together to listen to each other's stories, offering "a hearing engaged in by the whole body that evokes speech—a new speech—a new creation."[1] In these feminist spirituality groups, as we shared the stories of our spiritual journeys, women came "to experience theologizing as process."[2] Sitting in such circles, we could sense a palpable presence in the group during and after such sharing. It was a presence of life and energy, of passion and honesty. It was a presence that empowered and emboldened. It was creative and erotic. We felt filled with knowledge and vision. We experienced healing and were pointed toward justice. We sensed that, collectively and in extended community with other women engaged in similar endeavors, we were giving birth to a new vitality, creative and conscious, that had not manifested before in the long history of our people. We tried to name it: *womanspirit, Shechinah, Eyn HaChayyim*. Mostly we could not name it. But we felt the presence and held our experiences with reverence.

At the time, I came to believe that our stories were sacred text, that the narratives of our lives were part of an ongoing textual history of Judaism.[3] The stories we told as we heard each other into speech were *Torah*. We dared to believe that our stories, like the stories of our ancestors, were sacred because our narratives, like theirs, chronicled difficult, inspired journeys of Jews coming into the fullness of being, responding to a mysterious call both within our individual souls and within an inspired, ever-expanding community. If I'd had the talent to draw, I would have sketched a picture in which the paths and roads on which our ancestors journeyed in search of and in response to God meandered off the pages of the Torah, into the rooms in which we sat, under our feet and down the roads we continued to walk.

This was among my first experiences with a form of holy listening: listening with such attentiveness and immediacy that the self of a woman who previously had felt silenced or invisible was enabled to emerge into who she could be and become by speaking into the listening heart of a receptive community. We discovered that when we were able to listen to one another in this way (and we were not always able to do so), we witnessed not only how a person could emerge through speech, but also how she could connect deeply and honestly with others to reveal a palpable, living presence sustaining to us all. In these groups, we experienced what I would call "being-evoked-through-listening." As we sang Debbie Friedman's *Lechi Lach*[4] in community and heard our voices echo in the room with a vaulted ceiling where we prayed, I felt (and I venture to say others also felt) that we were individually and collectively being addressed by a call "to go forth to a land we did not know." We were being called to bring the fullness of our selves and the truth of our lives into relationship with the received tradition, to transform Judaism and the Jewish people for a future we did not know, but trusted would continue to be "shown" to us over time.[5]

Trusting our own experiences of the Holy, Jewish feminists began to transform the language traditionally used for naming and thinking about God. For many women it was the first time we gave primacy to our own experiences of the Holy, rather than ignoring or marginalizing those experiences that did not conform to the received tradition. Granting ourselves the authority to create theologies from our experiences of the Holy was a radical act; certainly the tradition granted women no such authority!

Those formative years spent in Jewish feminist community, which empowered me to trust and give voice to my own experiences of God, remain integral to my interest in developing the contemporary practice of Jewish spiritual direction. Ultimately, this practice reflects the belief that for Judaism and the Jewish people to be vital, contemporary Jews need not only to observe mitzvot and to study the received tradition, but to be in relationship with the living God: with the creating, revealing, redeeming Holy One of Being who ever calls us beyond ourselves and into deeper ethical relationship with all of Creation—with the earth, the stranger, and more familiar others—to a place we do not know.

"... And the Voice Did Not Cease ..."

Early in the Book of Deuteronomy, Moses recounts the giving of the *Aseret HaDibrot*, the Ten Commandments (literally "Utterances"), first depicted in the Book of Exodus. His reiteration is followed by this verse: "These words the Eternal spoke unto all your assembly in the mount out of the midst of the fire, of the cloud, and of the thick cloud, with a great voice: *v'lo yasaf*" (Deuteronomy 5:19). Over the centuries, translations of the Torah, based on a range of commentaries, have differed in their interpretation of the words *v'lo yasaf*. Do the words mean "and God added no more," as the phrase is often translated? Or do they mean "and God did not cease"? As classical a commentator as Rashi interprets the verse to mean "for his voice is strong and goes on forever, God did not pause between words." The Sefat Emet expands on Rashi: "Now Torah has already been given to Israel by 'a great voice that did not cease.' It has never stopped. Each day we say: Hear, O Israel, YHVH our God, YHVH is One, this is the voice saying: I am YHVH your God; it has never stopped. But we have to prepare ourselves to truly hear the Sh'ma without any distracting thought."[6] Abraham Joshua Heschel renders the verse this way: "The voice of Sinai goes on forever: These words the Lord spoke unto all your assembly in the mount out of the midst of the fire, of the cloud, and of the thick darkness, *with a great voice that goes on forever* [italics in the original]."[7] Open a contemporary translation of the Torah, however, and you will often find the narrower interpretation.

Differences in interpretation of this verse highlight a tension that is never resolved within the Jewish tradition: the tension between commandment and spirit, between the exclusive primacy of Torah study and observance as the path of divine service versus direct apprehension of God's presence as essential to the spiritual path. Spiritual direction is a practice that clearly affirms the importance of direct apprehension of God's presence to the vitality of the spiritual life, while upholding the value of more traditional modes of observance. From the perspective of spiritual direction, the voice goes on forever. The question is: Can we hear it?

Contemplative Listening

When I discovered the practice of contemplative listening that is the very heart of spiritual direction, I was already an experienced listener, having been a therapist, a pastoral caregiver, and an educator/trainer in these areas for decades. I was well-schooled in the discipline of clearing my mind of inner noise so I could attend carefully to the person in front of me: listen to what she said and how she said it, follow the flow of feelings, observe how she lived in her body and how she moved. I knew how to listen to my own experience of what it felt like to be in the presence of a particular person and to attend to the interaction between us. I knew how to empathize, how to practice what Freud and Heinz Kohut, the originator of self-psychology, describes using the German word *Einfuhlung*: to feel into another person's experience, to imagine what it is like to be the experiencing subject in front of me, rather than observing her objectively. All of these skills provided a foundation for contemplative listening, but they were insufficient.

Contemplative listening involves cultivating another dimension. We begin in silence. In the silence I go inside, quiet down, wait until I am still and fully present in the moment. With *kavannah,* sacred intention, I open my heart to receive the other. In a sense, I attune to the other person in the silence. After a time, words and images come that I hope will resonate with the other person, connect to the sacred season of Jewish time we are in or to another dimension of the present moment. I speak these words as a prayer into the silence. I always express gratitude that we have lives in which we can make this time to be together, well-nourished and safe, sitting comfortably in silence, with awareness that so many others on the planet do not have this luxury at this very moment. I always ask that whatever wisdom or guidance comes from our time together helps each of us, in our own unique ways, to contribute to healing, peace, justice, creativity, and joy in our troubled, broken world. I imagine that I am connected heart to heart with the other person and with *Mekor HaChayyim,* the Source of Life. Sometimes the seeker also offers a prayer. When we emerge from the silence, sacred space has been created. It is by descending to a place of deep interiority and silence that we create a context for holy listening. This is a place from which we can listen for intimations of the Holy, or *kedushah.*

I begin listening with an attitude of receptivity, with relaxed attentiveness rather than focused concentration, with what Carol Ochs calls a stance of "active waiting."[8] This relaxed attentiveness is very important. Just as I might intentionally relax a muscle in my body, I relax the focused, directive, willful self. As a result, an uncluttered, undirected, receptive, and awake consciousness opens up. I listen for intimations, experiences of Divine Presence. This quiet mind and receptive, patient attitude seem to create the possibility for intuition, for insights to emerge that come not from purposeful reasoning, analysis, interpretation, or meaning-making.

Much depends on the *kavannah,* the intentionality that the seeker and I bring to the listening. We bring ourselves consciously and intentionally before God, "to know before Whom we stand." Our intention is to be fully present, to become more aware of Holiness, Holy Presence, to become more attuned to discerning God's invitations as these reveal themselves in day-to-day life. As I am someone who does not believe in *hashgachah pratit,* a Providential God who determines each detail of our lives, what do I mean by "God's invitations"?

As the seeker unfolds the narrative of her life at a particular moment along the journey, I listen for how YHVH as Being is pressing for full presence, aliveness, expression in this person's life, how Being is moving this person at her depths. I listen for how *Mekor HaChayyim*, the Source of Life, is beckoning, drawing, inviting this person into deeper and more truthful connection with herself, with others, with Creation; how Life is inviting this person into service. Because I believe in the underlying unity of all existence, I listen to the total life field of this person, for how, through whom or what, through which experiences and circumstances the invitation is coming; I listen for where, how, when, through whom or what experiences wisdom or opportunity is being offered in response to a seeker's questions or reflections.

I often bring a person's attention back to places in the narrative where I intuit that he may have moved too quickly past a moment of holiness, *kedushah,* or particular aliveness. Moments, for example, when a seeker has felt fully present, in God's presence, vividly alive, creative or filled with purpose, moments of awe, of compassion or heart-opening, of intense awareness or piercing insight, also moments of anger at injustice that seem fueled by the energy of liberation: such moments are places to dwell longer, to savor. These are moments when, if you will, we might glimpse a "face of God," when we can hear the cry of the psalmist echoing, "Seek My face." These are places in the narrative where I want to encourage a seeker to listen more deeply to what is unfolding in the story of his soul's journey through time, to attend to the mystery of how his soul is or was uniquely connected with the Source of Life at that moment. During these moments, it is the seeker's relationship with the Holy that I support. Just as in any relationship, a sense of intimacy or closeness depends on how much time and how much openness we bring to *being* with that person. The same is true of our relationship with the Mystery we name God. In our very busy lives, we often rush past sacred moments. We allow our attention to be grabbed by the next thing and the next thing. We miss the opportunity not only to savor an experience, but also to deepen our connection with the Mystery within the experience.

Spiritual direction is grounded in the belief that as we expand our awareness of the Holy, deepen our connection with *Mekor HaChayyim*, the Source of Life, we will be changed, not only by taking time to pause and to *be,* but by dwelling consciously within the living Mystery itself. We know that flashes of illumination eventually fade, no matter how meaningful or profound. The purpose of engaging in spiritual practice is to transform flashes of illumination into abiding light.[9]

As theologian David R. Blumenthal has written:

The holy is ... encountered in the wholly other, at the edge of human existence. But the holy is also met in the confluence of the wholly other with the wholly mundane; at the center of normal existence. The holy is ec-static, standing outside; it is also famili-ar, standing within.[10]

In spiritual direction, we practice a form of listening contemplatively for experiences of the Holy in the ordinary and extraordinary moments of life.

Deborah is the mother of a daughter with significant disabilities. As her daughter was turning twenty, about to leave home and live independently, Deborah anticipated having the time and energy she had not had in decades to devote to her own growth and development. A deeply spiritual person and committed Jew, Deborah felt she needed guidance about where next to turn in her life. She didn't want therapy or vocational counseling. She wanted support of a different kind, and her rabbi referred her for spiritual direction.

After hearing some history about Deborah's experiences as a mother and her recently begun studies of Hebrew and Jewish text, I asked her to tell me about moments in her life when she felt in the presence of the Holy—however she understood that. She said there was one huge experience: "When my daughter was eight years old, she had a teacher who did not know how to take care of her. She put her braces on incorrectly. She did not keep her clean. I was infuriated with this teacher for her incompetence and neglect of my child. One day picking up my daughter at school, I saw the two of them coming toward me from a distance. My daughter was disheveled and her braces were on incorrectly. I felt a surge of rage course through my body. But suddenly, the entire corridor filled with light. The light also poured into my chest, and as it did, the rage began to disappear and I calmed down. I looked at the teacher's face and I thought 'I am looking at the face of God.' I thought 'even this person, toward whom I feel such anger, is a face of God.' That moment altered what I felt toward her and how I handled the relationship with her thereafter. This experience changed my life. I realized that if I could see the face of God in this woman, toward whom I felt such rage, then everyone was a face of God."

I invited Deborah to go back into this experience, saying that though it happened many years ago, perhaps she could return in her imagination. I explained that often, even when people have such huge experiences, we don't always savor them, take time to dwell in the Presence and deepen our connection with the Holy. Spiritual direction was a practice that could support her to take more time for such contemplation and reflection. Deborah said the experience was still quite vivid and that she could easily reenter the moment.

After a period in silence, Deborah emerged: "In that moment, there was no time and space. It was timeless. In the light, the features of the teacher's face dissolved. Her face was simply shining. That is how I realized 'this could be anyone's face—all peoples' faces are faces of God.' Since then I have carried that knowing in my heart as a practice. Even in seemingly insignificant encounters, when I do that practice, it can shift what's going on.

"When my daughter became bat mitzvah, one of the men in the congregation said to me: 'I saw the face of God in your daughter today.' I was blown away. I had told very few people that story of my experience with the teacher. What I am realizing now is that part of my spiritual path has been to parent my daughter so that others could see the face of God in her and be transformed. My husband and I have always put our daughter out into the world, encouraged her to be herself, to shine as she is. I think underneath that decision has always been the faith that if people could see my disabled daughter as a face of God, they would be able to see other people with disabilities this way, and be changed as I had been. It is so important to name this, to claim this. That experience in the hallway has guided my life ever since that moment."

Connecting with Jewish Tradition

Holy listening also involves listening to what is evoked in the depths of my own being in response to the question or experience sounding in the depths of the other. Images, passages from Torah or other Jewish texts (ancient and more contemporary), liturgy, Hasidic tales may emerge in response to the seeker's narrative. Part of my desire as a *Jewish* spiritual director is to make connections between a seeker's actual experiences and an aspect of Jewish tradition. When I have been able to make connections to a particular text, liturgy, or ritual, the tradition comes alive for this person. Passages or observances that may have seemed meaningless or confusing suddenly yield their riches. People develop a sense of personal connection with a particular verse, prayer, observance, or holiday. Often a text lends legitimacy to a feeling or experience the seeker may think is not acceptable, not spiritual, not Jewish, or even ugly or shameful. Being able to connect personal experience with an aspect of tradition lends more authority both to the tradition and to personal experience. For example, I've sat with directees who felt ashamed at being angry with God. Telling them that arguing with God, expressing anger at God, is actually a well-worn Jewish path, has been freeing to them. The individual Jew and the tradition are mutually enhanced when these connections can be made.

> Sarah, a mother of two young children, lamented that she had little time to engage in any form of regular or liturgical prayer, and therefore she was concerned that she would not be able to deepen her connection with God or with Judaism, as she desired. Listening to Sarah describe her day, I noticed her face light up as she spoke of sitting or exercising in her den, looking out at a large tree in her yard. I invited her to pause at this recollection of the tree. Sarah began to describe the joy she felt watching the birds in the tree, the wind rustling through the branches, how the tree changed with the seasons. When she looked at the tree, she was filled with a sense of gratitude and sensed God's presence. The verse from the liturgy "*Nishmat kol chai t'varech et shemcha*— Every living breath praises your name" came to mind as I listened to Sarah. This was not a verse Sarah knew. I shared it with her, explaining that breath is often associated in Hebrew with soul and God. "So perhaps," she said, "when I don't have words or time for prayer, breathing consciously can be enough. As I breathe, I can remember my connection to God."

> Libby, a middle-aged, single professional woman, opened the spiritual direction session saying, "I feel really cranky and annoyed today. Impatient. It's not a very spiritual feeling, I'm afraid. I've

done my part all these years, but where are You, God? I've been waiting long enough!" More than annoyance, I heard Libby's deep yearning for God; I was reminded of the verse from *Yedid Nefesh,* "*Eleh chamda libi husa na ve'al titalem*—My heart's desire is to harmonize with yours, do not hide yourself from me," which can also be translated "*Eleh machmad libi*—You, God, are the desire, the yearning of my heart...." I gave Libby's experience a name: *yearning*. This reframing enabled her to embrace her emotion, rather than admonish herself for being cranky. I invited Libby to notice where in her body she might locate the yearning and to open to God from that place.

Libby later wrote down what happened during her prayer: "I invite God into my dark space of yearning, a black suede pouch located in my right lateral stomach. The pouch is dark and empty, surrounded by black space, a hole. At first, a white light appears in front of me, touching my abdomen. The layers of my body darken, become more numerous and further hide me from the light in front of me. I wait. The layers soften, lighten and then brighten. The pouch inside deflates, grows small and moves laterally. The contents of the pouch are sprayed out through the side of my body (my right flank) and look like a spray of white sparkles. The sparkles meet the white light at my right side and my dark inside closes up and becomes nothing. I realize I've been hiding from God."

Libby emerged from the silence and said with surprise and awe: "All along I've been blaming God for hiding from me. But I've been hiding from God. That changes everything."

Kol Adonai Ba-Koach

A midrash on Psalm 29:4 states that each Israelite and every Jew to be born heard God at Sinai according to his or her own strength—*Kol Adonai Ba-Koach* (Pesikta d'Rav Kahana 12:27). One of the most remarkable gifts of being a spiritual director has been the opportunity to hear the incredibly diverse ways people experience, image, and encounter God or the Holy. While there are many different systems and typologies that attempt to identity spiritual types, I have found Tilden Edwards's simple approach incredibly useful for the practice of spiritual direction:

- God may be the Redeemer who urges them to work for social justice and *tikkun olam.*
- God may be the Beloved who inspires devotion (emotion, passion, and yearning are central to their relationship with the Holy).
- God may be the Source of Creativity in nature, art, or healing.
- God may be the Wise, Knowing, Seeing One, most available through the exercise of the intellect and the process of study, or through intuition.
- Any talk of God or naming of God may feel idolatrous, though they have had experiences of ineffable holiness.[11]

As spiritual directors, we need to be able to hear the very different ways people image and experience God. We need to listen for their theologies, and not impose our own. Not all people are contemplatives. Many people are not comfortable using the word God at all. However, most people have a way of expressing connection to *Mekor HaChayyim,* the Source of Life.

Rachel, an artist, has told me clearly she does not believe in God. She sought spiritual direction because the competitive nature of the marketplace and the academy where she taught was killing her. She felt a sense of urgency about deepening her connection with the spiritual dimensions of her life and her work. Over time I began to hear the profound struggle that was taking place within Rachel's soul: "The work I am creating now is disturbing. It makes people uncomfortable. It is organic; sometimes it looks like parts of our insides coming out. I wish I were creating something beautiful. I want people to like me, to like my work. I don't want them to be repulsed by what I create. But I am repulsed by what I see happening now. I am repulsed by what human beings are doing to the earth because we think it is inanimate. In my experience, we *are* the water, the rain, the coal, the sky."

I invited Rachel to bring photographs of her paintings to our sessions so I could learn her language. As she shared her work, I felt the force of what was pushing up through her vision, her hands. But this surge of creativity also came up against Rachel's fears of being rejected, unloved, criticized, shamed for exposing the ugliness she saw and felt inside herself. As I listened, I brought Rachel's attention over and again back to her creativity, to the images she experienced as arising from deep within her, unbidden. I encouraged her to notice the difference in how she felt when she trusted that creativity and when she got caught up in the constricting judgments in her mind. We never used the word *God*.

Spiritual direction can be very helpful in supporting people who are activists to become more contemplative, to draw strength, inspiration, and energy for the social justice work they are called to do.

> Jacob is a young, committed social activist who is clear that his spiritual path is working for social change and economic justice. His mind is often racing and he can get swept up in the busy-ness of work and overwhelmed by the feeling that "Everything depends on me." While in college, Jacob had experimented with mindfulness meditation, but it was at a time when he had stopped doing political work altogether to see what it would be like to be less driven. Back at work full time, Jacob stopped his meditation practice. However, it became clear while in spiritual direction that Jacob needed to resume his practice and strengthen his Shabbat observance. The practice enabled Jacob to quiet his mind, what he and I came to refer to as "parting his mind" so he could be nourished by a deeper source within. Over time, Jacob began to discern the difference in how it felt when his passion and work for social justice were being fueled by a self-punitive, often debilitating perfectionism and when it was grounded in his connection with Life. He began to identify, viscerally, when he was caught up in the "idolatry of believing it is all up to me" and when he was actually more creative, energetic, trusting, knowing he was working in partnership not only with other people, but being sustained by the Source of Life Itself.

For people drawn to traditional Jewish study and halachic practice, spiritual direction can be a support to their deepening observance of mitzvot.

> When Leila entered spiritual direction, she was trying to decide whether or not to apply to rabbinical school. A thirty-something married mother of three children, she felt strongly drawn to advanced Jewish learning; however, the demands of work, home, and

family made such a career change extremely difficult. As time went on, it became increasingly clear that Leila's path, at least for the present, was to deepen her relationship with God through observance of mitzvot and holidays. Not raised in observant homes, Leila and her husband were very intentional about each new mitzvah they took on. As Leila spoke about building a sukkah for the first time and inviting both Jewish and non-Jewish neighbors to share meals with her family, her eyes shone. As she described the joy she felt watching her children's enthusiasm for decorating the sukkah and inviting friends to play with them in the backyard, she spoke of her great pleasure in being able to teach people in her community about Jewish traditions. Becoming kosher, Leila explained that every day as she shopped for food or explained to her children what they could and could not eat in restaurants, she was conscious of choosing life. One day, Leila said: "I don't know what lies ahead, but for the moment, God is in my life through the mitzvot. Following the mitzvot carves a path for me through the woods. It rules out some things and rules in others. This is how God is present in my life daily."

Discerning the "Sparks"

The great medieval kabbalist Isaac Luria imagined creation as the unfolding of a great cosmic drama. According to the Lurianic myth, the world as we know it was created by a catastrophe known as the "shattering of the vessels" or *shevirat hakelim*. To bring about creation, God formed vessels and poured into them divine light meant to take forms appropriate to their function in creation. But the vessels could not contain the light and they shattered. The created world thus became an admixture of divine sparks of the *Shechinah*, the Indwelling Presence, and shards of the broken vessels. Because of this catastrophe, nothing in creation is in its proper place and all of Being is in exile, in need of redemption. This myth sets the stage for how Kabbalah conceives of the sacred purpose of humankind: "To lift up the scattered sparks of light and restore them to the place they were intended to occupy … is the essential task of man."[12] According to the Baal Shem Tov, the founder of Hasidism, God takes care to ensure that in the course of each person's lifetime, we will encounter the sparks that we alone can uplift.[13]

I often share this myth with people because it offers them an evocative way to "listen" to their lives. As seekers unfold their narratives, I listen for where the sparks might be. Based on our gifts, talents, and personal tendencies, in interaction with the historic moment and situation in which we find ourselves, we are each able to glimpse the sparks that are uniquely ours to uplift. The sparks can reveal themselves through both ordinary and extraordinary events.

Ten years ago, when a first cousin of mine was murdered, I felt in the depths of my being that one of the reasons I had been put on this earth was to assume responsibility for the care of her orphaned children at that moment. The inner experience of knowing was clearer and more profound than any knowing I have ever experienced and it enabled me to move through many seeming obstacles. I "saw" the sparks that were uniquely mine to uplift. It feels the same way ten years later. This experience strengthened my belief that it is possible for us to discern the unique tasks of our souls if we are awake and are willing to respond.

> Louis, a middle-aged physician, has told me of his vision for improving care for patients recovering from catastrophic injuries by attending to dimensions of their trauma not currently being addressed in most hospitals. He is aware, however, that his anger at how the medical establishment operates and his tendency to give up too easily when rebuffed have prevented him from fully following this sense of calling. When I share the myth of the sparks, he is very moved. "I'm not interested in listening to the whining of my ego anymore, or even in figuring out where it comes from. I did that in therapy for years. I want to discern the sparks and follow them." It is just about the end of our time together and suddenly his face lights up. "I wasn't going to mention this because I had already decided not to pursue it, but I was invited to interview for a new position in another city. Now I think I ought to go to the interview. If they are interested in me, knowing what I care about, perhaps something I cannot yet imagine may emerge from our discussions." "Discerning the sparks is a process that can take time," I say. "You cannot always know which are your sparks and which are not. Over time, a pattern or path may emerge that you can only see in retrospect."

Rabbi Tirzah Firestone has offered the following translation of the words of the Slonomer Rebbe, Noach Barzovsky of Slonom, commenting on Isaac Luria:

> Indeed, we need extreme clarity to discern *et asher HaShem Elohecha sho-el may-imcha,* exactly what it is HaShem is asking of us, and what path is ours....
>
> Before anything else, a person needs to meditate well and dig deeply into the knowledge of what his/her special task is in the world.... We are given signs by which to discern it, and sometimes we know it because it is the most difficult thing we could ever undertake.... But when we have this clarity about *shlichuto alay admut,* our special mission to earth through which we fulfill ourselves, we no longer get confused about the great work or equivocate about the amount of energy we must invest in it. Nor do we lose hope in life, because we know that our soul's purpose is fulfilled by means of it...."[14]

Listening for Obstacles

Though people who enter spiritual direction bring a desire to develop spiritually, to deepen their connection with the Holy, to discern the path of their souls, we nevertheless have endless ways of avoiding, resisting, and evading spiritual experience. Gerald May, a psychiatrist and pioneer in the contemporary field of spiritual direction, has written. "The human mind is an endless source of inventiveness when it comes to avoiding the implications of spiritual experience."[15] The story of Jonah, the most reluctant prophet of the Hebrew Bible, is probably the most well-known example of such avoidance. But he is certainly not the last! As a spiritual director, I have been awed (and sometimes bemused) to witness the endless repertoire of ways we have of resisting the Mystery we call God, just as I have been awed by the variety and diversity of human experiences of the Holy. As spiritual directors, we need to listen for these resistances just as we listen for God's invitations.

The ego and self, or soul, exist in paradoxical relationship to one another when it comes to spiritual growth. While it is the ego's job to guide the course of our lives, make decisions, make plans, and protect personal autonomy and the separate self, openness to spiritual experience and the possibility of self-transcendence occur when the ego relaxes, surrenders to the unknown, and is willing to let go of habitual or familiar ways of life; that is, when the ego stops trying to direct and control experience. Though we need much willfulness to negotiate life in postmodern America, we also need a willingness to navigate the spiritual journey.[16]

Sometimes people's avoidance or resistance to God can seem almost humorous. On several occasions, directees and I have laughed out loud as they became aware of a particular form of resistance.

> Talya is a rabbi with a strong commitment to observance, including daily prayer. One morning while davening *Shacharit* at home, she heard a still, small voice inside, saying, "Put down the prayer book. All I want is your heart!" "What did you do?" I asked. Laughing, Talya replied, "I didn't listen to it. After all, I had to finish davening!"

Talya was well aware of the tension within the tradition between *keva*, the obligation to follow the fixed liturgy, and *kavannah*, bringing deep intentionality to prayer: "It matters not whether you do much or little, so long as your heart is directed to heaven"(*Berachot* 17a). She was also familiar with the famous words: "*Rachmana liba ba-ei*—God wants the heart" (*Sanhedrin* 106b). For months, she had been getting increasingly clear messages that her attachment to a consistent but rote form of davening was getting in the way of her being open to God during prayer. Yet even when she heard a "still, small voice," she ignored it!

Some resistances are much more complex and result from personal or cultural history, which has been passed down through intergenerational experiences.

> Josh, a widower and the father of five, was terrified of what would be demanded of him if he opened up to God. "I want to stay selfish. I already give an enormous amount to my children; I am always trying to carve out just a little bit for myself. I am scared of what more God will want of me."
>
> I asked Josh if he might be willing to talk with God about that fear. Josh went into silent prayer for a long time. As he emerged, he described seeing images of himself crawling on his belly in the mud around dead bodies—a Holocaust image. I knew

Josh's parents were survivors. "How could God want me to do this? To crawl in the mud under the control of the Nazis? My father never surrendered." Josh began to cry and recount his parents' story of survival: his mother, his father's sister, and a good friend were lined up to be shot. His father was not in the lineup. His father begged the guard to let his wife go, and miraculously, he succeeded. His wife was taken out of the line. "When my father told me that story, he was tormented by enormous guilt that he didn't save his sister or his friend." Josh explained that at a conference he attended once on Trauma and the Holocaust, he heard a researcher say that, for children of survivors, the parents' survival story becomes the centerpiece around which their whole personality becomes organized.

I mirror back to him, "It is true your father didn't surrender, but it was to the Nazis he didn't surrender, to their destructive, overwhelming power. But it sounds like he gave himself completely to life and to love, knowing he could just as well have gotten shot himself for begging the guard."

Josh looks up suddenly, saying "He surrendered to love." Josh realized he had confused opening up to God with surrendering to Nazis. "If I am open to God, I would feel filled, not depleted."

Because one of the primary functions of the ego is to preserve the individual self, people will often resist opening up to a power greater than the self, even when that power is God or the Ground of Being. When people have personal or cultural memories of annihilation, it is much more difficult for them to loosen the grip of the ego and relax the individual will. As we become aware of such histories, spiritual directors do not analyze or interpret them, as a psychotherapist might. Instead, we encourage people to ask God for help, to address God directly, sometimes to get angry directly with God, to break their hearts open, to be vulnerable and honest before God. Whether or not people's theologies encompass the possibility that there is a God who hears such prayers, I have witnessed time and again that when people are able to bare their souls to the Universe and ask for help, they often experience surprising internal shifts and are given access to insight or intuition they did not have before.

A crucial aspect of holy listening is listening for moments in the narrative when a seeker may need to address God directly. The role of the spiritual director is to support the evolving relationship between each soul and the Mystery we name God. Therefore, as people reveal places in their lives where they feel stuck; as they describe emotions they cannot untangle—pain or yearning they have not been able to share with other people, decisions they cannot seem to make on their own—our role as directors is to encourage them to engage in a form of what Rebbe Nachman of Breslov called *hitbodedut*: setting aside a period of time to pour out before God one's deepest longings, needs, and distress. Some might say that such a practice is merely a form of Freud's "talking cure," although it is to God rather than the psychoanalyst that one's free associations are addressed. Yet there's a key difference: where the words are coming from. While Freud's analysands were instructed to follow the associations of their *mind*, the practice of *hitbodedut* involves breaking one's *heart* open, speaking to God from the heart. According to Rebbe Nachman, this is the most essential of all practices, to be placed above all else.[17]

The Place Where Words Come From

While Nachman elevated the practice of *hitbodedut* to the highest importance, the idea that God is near to those who break their hearts open has been central to Jewish thought throughout the ages. The psalmist was the first to declare: "God is close to the brokenhearted" (Psalm 34:19). Later, talmudic sages and Hasidic rebbes understood that there was not only the brokenness that happens when the heart is shattered against one's will, by loss, grief, or trauma. They understood that the intentional act of breaking one's heart open to God, breaking through the hardening of the heart—through denial, avoidance, and self-protection—is crucial to having a relationship with the living God. The following saying is attributed to the Baal Shem Tov, the founder of Hasidism: "In the habitation of the king are to be found many rooms, and there are different keys for every lock; but the master key of all is the ax with which it is possible to open all the locks on all gates. The master key is the broken heart. When a man truthfully breaks his heart open to God, he can enter into all the gates of the apartments of the King above all kings, the Holy Blessed One."[18] When people break their hearts open to God, surprising transformations can occur.

Rebecca explained that over the course of a ten-year marriage, because of countless niggly arguments, petty disappointments, and corrosive bickering, her heart felt closed. "I've been to therapy," she said, "but it hasn't helped. I know I loved my husband Jacob when we got married, but I can't connect to that love anymore. And I can't bear being so hurtful and hardhearted to him anymore."

The spiritual director asked if Rebecca would be willing to address God directly. Rebecca went inside and from the depth of her need, asked for help with what she had not been able to do for herself: to heal her heart so she could love again.

A month later, Rebecca realized that she had gotten a kind of "answer." It came in the form of awareness and tears. "My heart isn't closed or hardened," she said. "As I was praying yesterday, I saw that my heart is actually scarred and calloused. I thought I had become a hardened bitch." Rebecca realized that after the many losses she'd experienced, she'd stopped being able to cry. When she felt hurt or disappointed, she could only get angry.

Several months later, out of the blue, Rebecca was contacted by the first man she fell in love with, at the age of twenty-one, now a fifty-something scientist named Josh, with a wife and two children. He explained that he'd found a software program that enables people to locate anybody in the world with an e-mail address, and he had wanted to find her. They had not seen or spoken to each other in thirty-five years.

Resurrecting memories of their youthful time together and their painful separation, Rebecca was overwhelmed with grief and sobbing. She realized the separation from Josh was the bottommost layer of grief in her heart. But if a therapist had asked her when her history of loss began, she would not have gone back to this relationship; she had lost touch with its significance. Through Josh's mysterious reappearance, Rebecca gained access to a distant past that had been inaccessible.

Rebecca shared with her husband what had been going on with Josh via e-mail. She needed to cry with him. Sensing the emotional significance of what had been transpiring in his wife's life, Jacob offered himself to Rebecca for comfort. The two shared a tender moment of the kind they had not shared in years. Jacob felt he could touch his wife's heart again and they both realized they could begin to heal their marriage. Rebecca's prayer, somehow, had been "answered."

Spiritual directors need to encourage people to speak from their deepest truth, from the place "where words come from." Gerald May, a founder of the Shalem Institute, was known to tell the following story about Quaker pioneer John Woolman. The story is based on a journal entry Woolman made during the years 1761–1762, describing an encounter between himself and an Indian chieftain. Woolman attended a prayer meeting of Indians and English-speaking settlers. Interpreters were necessary, since few of those present were fluent in both the English and Delaware tongues. After laboring for a long time through interpreters, Woolman stood up and declared he wished simply to pray out loud to God from his heart, omitting laborious interpretations. At the end of his prayer, the Indian chieftain placed his hand on Woolman's chest and said, "I love to hear where words come from."

Over time, as seekers become increasingly able to speak from "the place where words come from," they become more aware of the different layers and depths of their inner experience. They cultivate interiority, *penimiyut*. Addressing God directly from the depths of feeling and heartfelt truth enables people not merely to utter the words of prayer, but, as Psalm 69 intimates, to become our prayer, *va' ani tefillati*. Ultimately, spiritual direction is a practice that seeks to support us to live our whole lives as prayer, as Ann Kline has said, "as a radically involved dialogue with the Holy."

"If You Truly Listen to the Voice of the Eternal One …"

The Book of Deuteronomy rings with calls to the Israelites to listen to the voice of the Eternal. The second paragraph of the *Shema*, the biblical passage (Deuteronomy 11:13–21) we read after reciting the *Shema*, is a powerful exhortation: If you truly listen, loving and serving Your God with all your heart, with every breath—then the eternal circle of life, of this wondrous and abundant creation, will continue to provide sustenance and nourishment to you and your offspring. But if you stop listening to the living God, you will no longer be nourished. Place these words on your heart, into your life-breath. Bind them as a sign upon your hand and let them rest before your eyes. Teach them to your children. Remember them always.

Spiritual direction is a practice for deepening our capacity to listen to the voice of the Eternal.

Notes

1. Nelle Morton, *The Journey Is Home* (Boston: Beacon Press, 1985), 128.

2. Ibid., 82.

3. Rebecca Alpert, "Our Lives *Are* Text: Exploring Jewish Women's Rituals," *Bridges: A Journal for Jewish Feminists and Our Friends* 2, no. 1 (Spring, 1991/5751): 75. See footnote 37.

4. Debbie Friedman, *Songs of the Spirit: A Debbie Friedman Anthology*, CD (Studio City, CA: Jewish Music Group, 2005).

5. *B'not Esh* is a Jewish feminist spirituality collective, founded in 1981. Since that time this ever-evolving community of Jewish women has been meeting annually, supporting each other's work in envisioning and creating feminist Judaism(s).

6. Arthur Green, *The Language of Truth: The Torah Commentary of the Sefat Emet, Rabbi Yehudah Leib Alter of Ger*. Translated and interpreted by Arthur Green (Philadelphia: Jewish Publication Society, 5759/1998), 90.

7. Abraham Joshua Heschel, *God in Search of Man: A Philosophy of Judaism* (New York: Harper & Row, 1966), 138. In his footnotes, Heschel cites his own sources: "According to the Aramaic translation of Onkelos, and Jonathan ben Uzziel and to the interpretation of Sanhedrin, 17b; Sotah, 10b; and to the first interpretation of Rashi."

8. Carol Ochs and Kerry Olitzky, *Jewish Spiritual Guidance: Finding Our Way to God* (San Francisco: Jossey-Bass Publishers, 1997), 68.

9. Roger Walsh and Frances Vaughan, *Paths Beyond Ego: The Transpersonal Vision* (Los Angeles: J. P. Tarcher, 1993), 113.

10. David R. Blumenthal, *Facing the Abusing God: A Theology of Protest* (Louisville, KY: Westminster/John Knox Press, 1993), 27.

11. Tilden Edwards, *Spiritual Friend: Reclaiming the Gift of Spiritual Direction* (New York: Paulist Press, 1980), 112–116.

12. Gershom Scholem, *The Messianic Idea in Judaism and Other Essays on Jewish Spirituality* (New York: Schocken Books, 1972), 186.

13. Ibid., 189.

14. From a handout by Rabbi Tirzah Firestone of her own translation.

15. Gerald May, *Care of Mind, Care of Spirit: A Psychiatrist Explores Spiritual Direction* (HarperSanFrancisco, 1992), 85.

16. Gerald May, *Will and Spirit: A Contemplative Psychology* (San Francisco: Harper and Row, 1982), chs. 1 and 2.

17. Arthur Green, *Tormented Master: A Life of Rabbi Nahman of Bratzlav* (Tuscaloosa: University of Alabama Press, 1979), 145.

18. Martin Buber, *Tales of the Hasidim: Early Masters* (New York: Schocken Books, 1972), 64.

Suggested Reading

Guenther, Margaret. *Holy Listening: The Art of Spiritual Direction*. Cambridge, MA: Cowley Publications, 1992.

Barbara Eve Breitman, MSW, LCSW, is a psychotherapist, teacher, and writer. She has been at the forefront of the contemporary field of Jewish spiritual direction. A cofounder of Lev Shomea, the first institute to train spiritual directors in the Jewish tradition outside a rabbinic seminary, she teaches spiritual directors at the Reconstructionist Rabbinical College, the rabbinical seminary of Hebrew College in Boston, and the ALEPH rabbinical program.

Berur: *How Do You Know If It's God?*

Rabbi Howard Avruhm Addison

Divine Inquiry

"… and she went to inquire of God. And God said …" (Genesis 25:22–23).

After nineteen prayerful, tearstained years our mother Rebecca finally conceived. Growing larger each day, Rebecca nonetheless felt that the joy of her impending motherhood was becoming tainted. Two competing forces seemed to be wrestling within her, tearing her apart physically and emotionally. Wracked with pain and existential doubt, she cried, "If this be the case, then why do I exist?" Moved by distress and an intimation that something larger was at play, Rebecca went "*l'drosh et Adonai*—to inquire of God."

But what does this mean, "to inquire of God"? Three classical biblical commentators offer different insights into this curious phrase. Abraham ibn Ezra (d. 1164) claims that Rebecca sought divine guidance from a prophet, probably her father-in-law Abraham, who was still alive at the time. Solomon ben Isaac (d. 1105), popularly known as Rashi, states that Rebecca searched for divine counsel at the *Beit HaMidrash,* the mythical House of Study, of Shem, Noah's son.[1] A final interpretation is asserted by Moses ben Nachman (d. 1270), more commonly referred to as Nachmanides or Ramban. Citing verses from Scripture, Ramban indicates that the phrase *to inquire of God* means to pray.[2] Thus, when faced with radical feelings of discomfort, Rebecca prayed and then paid attention as divine guidance manifested in her consciousness, revealing the potential implications of her difficult pregnancy.

More than competing commentary on a single verse, these interpretations represent three classical Jewish approaches to discerning God's word, each with its own warrant from the Torah. The path described by

Ibn Ezra is well known from biblical times: When seeking divine guidance, ask a prophet. Deuteronomy 18 cites God's promise to raise up prophets after Moses who would speak God's word to the people. Although our tradition claims that, as a means of determining normative Jewish practice, prophecy ceased in the early Second Temple period with the death of Malachi, classical Jewish sources still speak of gaining insight through other levels of divine inspiration.[3]

The avenue described by Rashi is that of normative rabbinic Judaism: If you want divine guidance, you will find it in the *Beit HaMidrash,* the House of Study. Deuteronomy 33 states that Moses commanded us to follow the Torah, as "the heritage of the congregation of Jacob." To find God's word, then, is to immerse oneself in that heritage, the teachings and observances of our people, that these might guide our personal and communal lives. Thus *l'drosh et Adonai,* the "inquiring of God," cited in Genesis, is realized as *l'drosh et Torat Adonai* (Ezra 7:10), as studying, interpreting, and applying the insights and dicta of Torah. And if a particular matter is too difficult to discern, Deuteronomy 17 bids us to go to a Jewish, or halachic, legal authority, who will instruct us as to the Torah, the divine guidance, we should fulfill.

The third path, cited by Ramban, does not begin with external authority, be it a person or text. Instead, God's word becomes manifest through feeling and cognition, prayer, contemplation, and inner discernment. This path, though not recognizable to some as authentically Jewish, does have substantial grounding in our tradition. Deuteronomy 30 states that God's word is not external to us, but "within our mouths and hearts to enact it." Psalm 40 speaks of coming before God with a "Scroll inscribed upon me" and "Your Torah implanted in my viscera." Here *l'drosh et Adonai,* "inquiry of God," involves prayer and attentive silence, so the "Interior Torah" may rise from our innermost being to the level of articulation, and we may act according to its wisdom.

Seeking God Today

The approach cited above by Rashi has remained predominant since the destruction of the Second Temple in 70 CE. Those within the contemporary Hasidic and Sephardic communities may still seek divine guidance from wonder-working rabbis with ascribed prophetic powers. However, normative Judaism continues to place near exclusive emphasis on Torah, *halachah,* and communal authority as the arbiters of God's will. Faced with religious inquiries, Orthodox rabbis prescribe a *p'sak halachah,* an appropriate, binding legal imperative; cognizant of *halachah,* many liberal rabbis suggest guidance based on the wisdom and examples gleaned from traditional practice and lore. Although disagreeing on the authority of Jewish law, both groups share a sense that the sacred is primarily conveyed to the individual by Torah and/or *halachah,* as mediated through the collective experiences of the Jewish people. While taking into account the concrete reality of the individual seeking counsel, neither Orthodox nor liberal rabbis consider the experiences or the inner life of the seeker as valid coindicators of divine guidance.

In this era of growing spiritual hunger and the desire for a more personal connection to the Holy, many contemporary Jews wonder why God directly guided our biblical ancestors but seems consigned to silence or mere echoes today. Even those committed to normative halachic practice recognize that Jewish law might not cover some of the most important aspects of our lives. *Halachah* describes in minute detail how a divorce document, a *get,* should be written. It offers little guidance, however, as to whether, even in the face of overt abuse, it is the time for my partner and me to divorce. If Psalm 23 promises us a divine immediacy beyond the application of communal norms, that God "guides me" and "stands by me," how shall we sense that Presence and intuit its guidance?

The contemporary practice of Jewish spiritual direction seeks to answer that question, in part, by recapturing the sense of divine inquiry explicated by Ramban. Any authentic model of Jewish spiritual guidance must begin with Torah. However, there is a definite strain in our tradition that indicates that the Torah might address each of us differently in our own particularity and uniqueness:

> When the Divine spoke, each heard according to his or her capacity. Thus David said, "YHVH's voice comes in strength" (Psalm 29); not in "divine strength" but in the strength to be heard by each [listening] individual. Thus the Blessed Holy One said to them: It is not that these you hear are many different voices; know that I am the One [from Whom it all derives]. I, YHVH [the Source of All Being], am your [individual] God (Pesikta d'Rav Kahana 12:27).[4]

However, this leads to an irreducible dilemma. If the path of divine inquiry, as interpreted by Rashi, may create an externally imposed formalism, that proposed by Ramban may devolve into sheer subjectivity. How can we know that the voice we intuit is God's? Might it not be an expression of our own desires or a self-serving rationalization? Perhaps we're simply deluded. Even among biblical prophets, only Moses is said to have received direct, unambiguous divine instruction. The rest of us need a process to help distinguish between the authentic and the delusional, between true guidance and wish projection. In the world of spiritual direction, this process is known as discernment.

The Language of Discernment

To better grasp how Judaism understands discernment, it is helpful to look at some classical Hebrew terms used to denote this process. Foremost among these are *berur* and *mishkal hahasidut*.[5]

The etymology of *berur* stems from the process of smelting metal. *Bor,* meaning potash or lye, was used to help purge the dross so that only the pure, strong metal element would remain. *Bar* or *barah* in biblical Hebrew connotes that which is pure, lucent, or clear.[6] As we shall see, rabbinic texts use the word *berur* to indicate choices that lead to integrity.

The kabbalists gave the term *berur* a new theosophical twist. Their basic understanding of our physical world is that everything and every situation is an admixture of spirit and the physical, of *netzotzot*, divine sparks that form the essence and life force of everything, encased in and obscured by *kelipot,* shells of matter and bodily desire. Thus *berur* is a process of clarification and extraction, of recognizing and freeing the sacred embedded in the mundane husks of everyday busy-ness as well as in the darker shells of our compulsions and self-serving choices. On a deeper level *berur* calls us to acknowledge the potential sanctity present even in the *kelipot* themselves, for "no place is devoid of the Divine Presence."[7] Therefore *berur* both clarifies the path to personal sanctity and aids in the ultimate redemption of our world. Isaiah Horowitz, a seventeenth-century moralist and mystic writes:

> Before Adam sinned and the shells *(kelipot)* were revealed they existed in potentia like the dregs that are interlaced with the wine

while both are contained within the prior actuality of the grape. When Adam sinned the light was hidden, the shells were actualized, revealed and dispersed.... The ascending level of our perception should be to discern *(l'barair)* the inward *(netzotzot)* from the externals *(kelipot),* to consume and be nourished by the inner and to discard the shells. But in the future, that which is as dark as night will shine as brightly as day *(Torah Or,* The Light of Torah, on Genesis, *Parshat Chaye Sarah).*

In his eighteenth-century moralist text, *Messilat Yesharim, The Path of the Upright,* Moshe Chayyim Luzzatto offered insight and guidance to those wishing to pursue a holy life. Chapter 20 prescribes a discernment process called *mishkal hahasidut* for those who have embarked upon the path of spiritual refinement. The word *mishkal,* "Scale," summons images of a person carefully weighing all relevant external factors, inner dynamics, traditional wisdom, and religious imperatives until perfect balance is achieved. *Hasidut,* "saintliness," connotes a level of spiritual trust, intentionality, and behavior that goes beyond perfunctory observance and the baseline requirements of Jewish law. For Luzzatto, *mishkal hahasidut* is a process of prayerful analysis and consideration whose initial motivation and ultimate goal are the same: heightened God consciousness and pious, loving conduct.

Discernment is not just a matter of disparate choices; rather it is an attentive way of living. Thus the Hasidic master, Mordechai Yosef Lainer of Isbitza (d. 1854) distinguished between two radically different religious personalities. The first he associated with the character of Joseph, who withstood Mrs. Potiphar's advances in Egypt, and his son, Ephraim, leader of ancient Israel's Ten Northern Tribes. In line with Rashi's interpretation of the Rebecca story, this personality type seeks God through the dictates of the *Beit HaMidrash,* zealously follows the letter of Jewish law, and may castigate those who don't. Juxtaposed against the Joseph personality is the integrated, redemptive personality of Judah, leader of the Southern Tribes, forebear of King David and the Messiah. In words that amplify the Ramban's approach, the Isbitzer Rebbe wrote:

> The root of life for Judah is to look to the Blessed God regarding the course of every action. Even though he sees where the judgment (applicable precedent in Jewish Law) leans, still he looks to the Blessed God to see the depth of the truth of the matter ... not to act

in a way that is simply habitual. Even though yesterday he acted in such a way, yet today he doesn't want to rely on his former response, only that the Blessed God should illuminate God's will into him anew (*Mei HaShiloach, Living Waters, Parshat VaYeshev*).

Going beyond the notion that we each receive Torah differently, the Isbitzer Rebbe asserts that we each might receive our own Torah differently from one day to the next. External circumstances change, the nature of our relationships changes, and we ourselves change. What seemed obvious yesterday might not be so clear today. Therefore Judah will not merely rely on halachic precedent, but will prayerfully place each deliberation before God to seek deeper insight and divine confirmation before acting.

The Discernment Process

How might we, who lack the immediate divine awareness of a Judah, place our deliberation before God? What may be construed as legitimate markers of sacred illumination? As mentioned above, chapter 20 of *Messilat Yesharim* describes a three-phase process, which I offer here with some elucidation from the other classic and contemporary Jewish spiritual sources.

Timimut HaMashavah: Prayerful Purity of Intention

"… that one's heart might be upright" (Luzzatto, *Messilat Yesharim*).

Since the boundary between legitimate self-interest and harmful self-centeredness is thin and porous, discerning God's will must begin with the dedication to achieve *timimut lev,* a simple purity of heart untainted by self-serving motives. One's sole desire must be *la'asot nahat ruach l'fanav yitbarach,* to comport oneself in a manner pleasing to the Blessed One as a devoted child would seek to please an honored, beloved parent.

The following *kavannot,* meditations, can help prayerfully open our intention to actualize *timimut lev.* They can be recited aloud, repeated mantralike to oneself, or chanted slowly and quietly in English or Hebrew:

- Show me Your way, O God, teach me Your path, guide me in Your truth *(Drachechah Adonai hodee-aynee, orchotecha lamdaynee; hadreechaynee ba-ameetechah)* (Psalm 25:4–5).
- Let Thy will be my will, that my will be Thy will *(Aseh ritzono ritzoncha ... sheya-aseh ritzoncha kirtzono) (Pirke Avot, Ethics of the Fathers* 2:4).
- I act from no intention other than to please the Creator of Blessed Name *(La'asot nahat ruach laBoray baruch Shemo) (Tzavaat HaRibash, The Testament of Rabbi Israel Baal Shem Tov,* chap. 46).

Iyun Analysis

"... analyze one's actions that they be brought into conformity with the purpose [of pleasing God]" (Luzzatto, Messilat Yesharim).

If the goal of discernment is to choose that which is "pleasing to God," the prophet Micah offers three behavioral criteria to help us judge what this might mean:

It has been told to you O Man what is good and what YHVH requires of you. To act justly *(asot mishpat),* to love kindly *(ahavat chesed)* and to walk modestly *(hatznaya lechet)* with your God (Micah 6:8).

The following twentieth-century commentary provides insight into Micah's message:

In regard to justice it is sufficient to carry out its behests; but in regard to mercy the deed alone is insufficient, even when done from a clear sense of duty. Love is an essential accompaniment of every kind deed of mercy (Hermann Cohen, d. 1918). To walk humbly ... [i]n fellowship and communion with God means not ostentatiously but with inward devotion and noiseless acts of love (Max Margolis, d. 1932). *Tziniyut* denotes modesty, decency, chastity, personal holiness, purity (J. H. Hertz, *The Pentateuch and Haftorahs,* pp. 684–685).

How can we discern if a choice might be pleasing to God? By considering its effects on our behavior. First, will it lead us to be more just, to act with greater fairness, integrity, honesty, and sense of justice? Will it promote faithfulness to our legal, financial, and moral obligations, particularly if we feel called to withdraw from a relationship or a previous commitment? Second, will it impel us to greater acts of compassion and charity, performed not grudgingly, but with grace and care? Third, will it lead to greater humility and modesty, to less ostentation, vulgarity, and acquisitiveness, to live more simply and purely? Such are the behavioral markers that can help us discern whether our "actions are pleasing to the Creator—*oseh nahat ruach laBoray baruch Shemo.*"

As we know, however, balancing justice, compassion, and humility is not always simple. In the real world these virtues can be at odds with one another, making it difficult to know which course of action to choose. The extent of this difficulty is highlighted by a rabbinic tale concerning a criminal who sought refuge from a Roman legion. Having traced their prey to a nearby town, the Romans demanded that he be handed over or else they would burn down the town and kill its inhabitants. The dictates of Jewish law allowed the resident rabbi, Yehoshua ben Levi, to surrender the criminal and save innocent lives. Having done so, however, his revelatory visitations by Elijah the prophet temporarily ceased. When Elijah finally reappeared, the rabbi was perplexed.

> "Had I been asked to hand over random, innocent individuals, I would have refused and suffered martyrdom. Here the law was clear."
>
> "True," replied Elijah, "you acted according to *Mishnah,* the ruling of justice. But in what way was *chesed,* pious kindness served? Maybe you should have found another way" (Bereshit Rabba 94:9).

At moments when principles conflict, the accumulated wisdom of Torah can prove invaluable to the discernment process, attuning our minds and souls to hear God's voice amid the static of current circumstance. Therefore the Baal Shem Tov stated: "Something may come your way and you may not know whether to pursue it or not. If you've studied Torah that day, you will be able to discern your course of action from the material that you learned" (*Tzavaat HaRibash, The Testament of Rabbi Israel Baal Shem Tov,* chap. 31).

Bitachon: Trust in God

" ... cast one's lading with God ... " (Luzzatto, *Messilat Yesharim*).

If justice, kindness, and humility are the behavioral markers of discernment, what might the affective markers be? What are the "soul states" that might confirm if our actions are pleasing to God? In chapter 20 Luzzatto quotes Psalm 86 when referring to one who has successfully navigated the aspects of *mishkal hahasidut:* "Fortunate is the person whose strength is in You.... Good will not be withheld from those who walk with integrity" (Psalm 86:6, 12).

While not explicitly defining there the *good* to which he's referring, Luzzatto does give an indication of what he means in his Introduction to *Messilat Yesharim*. Based on Deuteronomy 10:12–13 he lists those traits that God "commands you today for your good." These include: awe, love, walking in God's ways, and wholeheartedness.

Awe

The Hebrew word *yirah* connotes reverence, wonder, and fear. Rather than the dread of punishment, however, it is a sense of finitude in the presence of majesty, of personal smallness and surprise, a recognition that one could not have arrived at a given conclusion or insight unaided. Almost every guide and seeker has experienced in a session that moment when reflection and prayer lead to an insight or a connection that takes our breath away, when, bursting with gratitude, we say, "This didn't come from us alone; let's give thanks to God!" Other times one might even burst into tears when realizing that one is being called to give up a behavior, a job, a position of status, or even a relationship that has provided security, comfort, and a sense of identity. As Shneur Zalman of Liadi, the founder of Chabad Hasidism noted, these tears of trembling and renunciation are, however, the prelude to even greater joy that comes with drawing closer to God.[8]

Love

Ahavah impels us to instinctively act in ways that gratify God. Conversely, one naturally recoils from the thought of disappointing God through unworthy action. Feelings of enthusiasm and deep, abundant joy, even if preceded by tears of renunciation, are reflections of choosing a path that is "pleasing to God."

Walking in God's Ways

Halicha b'drachav includes all the behavioral elements encompassed by Micah's dictum. But even more than outwardly affecting what we do, they affect the state of our souls. Not only do we act more justly, we feel instinctively alert to matters of integrity and justice. Injustice, dishonesty, and indifference seem inherently repugnant. Not only do we perform charitable acts gracefully, we feel expansively able to give and receive love. Feeling humble and modest as we consciously cleave to God *(devekut),* our tolerance for vulgarity, excess, and ostentation, even in matters of religious observance, proportionately shrinks.

Wholeheartedness

Shelemut halev allows one to give oneself over completely to the discerned course of action. It is marked by simultaneous feelings of certainty and surrender, of freedom from resistance or hesitation, of conscious awareness, not mere force of habit. With feet firmly planted on the right course, one will successfully navigate this next stage of life's journey with God's help, despite any apparent difficulty. Luzzatto alternatively refers to *bitachon* as *mashlich yehavo al Adonai*—casting one's lading with God. Having borne the cargo of our external reality, feelings, deliberations, attentiveness, and clarification before God, we now feel divinely assisted in bearing what might be a heavy but precious burden. With a new sense of lightness, we feel accompanied and supported as we embark on our path.

Bitachon, trust in God's guidance, is therefore marked by feelings of wonder, awe, reverence, surprise, humility in the face of majesty, joy, enthusiasm, integrity, love, modesty, certainty, support, and *devekut,* cleaving to God. Conversely, feelings of self-inflation, sadness, anger, hostility, boredom, antipathy, hesitance, uncertainty, and disconnection might well be signs of what the psalmist referred to as *to-ay levav,* errant heart, a characteristic of those "who do not know My ways"(Psalm 95:10). In Deuteronomy 30:19 God places before us life and blessing, death and curse. God's call is that we "Choose life," that which is life-giving, through which we grow in integrity, love, and humility, and that which enlivens rather than deadens our souls.

Hazarah: The Return Loop

Though *hazarah* is not formally included as an aspect of *mishkal ha-hasidut,* Luzzatto states in chapter 20, "An act should not be judged by the first impression that it makes on the mind." Discernment involves a repeating cycle of prayer and intentionality, attention to external consequences and inner affect, "trying on" provisional choices and testing the results. Such discernment emerges gradually, as distinguished from snap decisions and the desire for instant resolution.

Among the reasons for a gradual discernment process is our penchant for self-deception. A decision might initially evoke within us the joyous, enthusiastic feelings of *bitachon.* The Isbitzer Rebbe warned that these moments born of *gadlut,* spiritual expansiveness and exuberance, warrant *berur (Mei HaShiloach, Living Waters, Parshat VaYigash).* Is the joy I'm feeling emanating from my desire to please God or my desire to please myself? Affectively, it is crucial to note whether the buoyancy we experience is also accompanied by the other feelings of *bitachon:* wonder, reverence, integrity, and humility in the face of Majesty. If not, then chances are what we are feeling is closer to self-inflation than to *bitachon.* On a practical level, the Baal Shem Tov counseled as follows: When discerning a course of action, mentally strip it of every shred of profit, pleasure, or self-satisfaction *(hana'ah).* If that path still seems right, then pursue it *(Toldot Yaakov Yosef, VaYikra).*

Another reason for gradual discernment is the way our quirks of ego can contaminate even the most purely motivated acts. Overflowing with devotion, you might decide to expand your observance of kashrut as a means of coming closer to God. If over the next months you find that perfectionism is robbing the observance of all joy, leaving anger and disconnection in its wake, then you need further *berur.* What is driving me to be more punctilious than *halachah* requires? Am I serving God or just providing a religious cover for my own compulsions? The Baal Shem Tov envisioned the *yetzer hara* as a cat burglar. If you think you've overwhelmed it with zeal or scared it away by stringencies, you always run the risk of it sneaking back where and when you least expect it. Better, he said, to capture it and keep it under observation over time to more fully recognize its potential impact.[9]

Conversely, there are situations that require difficult, even wrenching, first steps, but whose ultimate outcome will be for good.

You might continually avoid hurtful issues in the workplace or at home, thinking it's more loving or humble to be patient and keep the peace. The thought of confrontation feels as painful as death. However, as time goes by, a pattern may reveal itself. Due to pent-up frustrations and new irritants, situations that could have been resolved become untenable. Rather than actually keeping the peace, you express your discontents indirectly through passive-aggressive behavior, sarcasm, or even withdrawing from what were otherwise positive relationships. By recognizing these self-subverting tendencies over time, you might discern that it is actually more "life giving" to take the hard step and confront difficult issues head on, to recognize, as Shneur Zalman of Liadi taught, that needed resolution can lead to more lasting, "God-pleasing" joy, even when its path leads initially through tears of consternation.

Barah: *Pure, Lucent, Clear*

Among the main tenets of Jewish covenantal theology is the notion that we humans are God's partners in the work of creation. This principle can well be applied to the work of discernment. The sections above described the human elements of the *berur* equation: purifying our intentions, scrutinizing our deeds, noticing changes in our affect, monitoring the consequences of our choices over time, all done in prayerful openness to God. However, as the Isbitzer Rebbe taught, "… the Blessed God warns Israel to always be in a state of *kedushah* [sanctity] and thus always ready, expecting at all times the salvation of the Blessed God Who will illumine their eyes …" *(Mei HaShiloach, Living Waters, Parshat Kedoshim)*. Having done our work, we prayerfully offer our efforts, our intentions, even our confusion to God, and, like our mother Rebecca, hopefully wait for God's guidance to break through. Sometimes soberly, sometimes with broken hearts, we echo the sentiments of Eliezer Azikri's love poem to God, *Yedid Nefesh*, "God, these are the desires of my heart; You are the desire of my heart; be merciful and don't hide."[10] Then we await God's guidance, knowing that the moment can't be manufactured, yet trusting in Scripture's promise: "Those who hopefully wait for God find their energy transformed"(Isaiah 40:31).

Perhaps the most important rabbinic statement on discernment is found in the second chapter of *Pirke Avot, Ethics of the Fathers*:

> Rabbi (Judah the Prince) said: What is the straight path [*derech ha-yashar*] that one should discern [*she-yabor bo*]: that which is beautiful [*tiferet*] to the one who enacts it and is recognized as beautiful [literally, "brings one beauty"] from [other] human beings [*ha'adam*].

While offering a fairly deliberative interpretation of this passage, Judah Loew of Prague actually intimated how each word of this aphorism can help us recognize when a flash of insight might be true divine illumination (*Derech Chayyim, The Way of Life,* chap. 2). He points out that in response to most life situations, we can undertake several alternative paths with full integrity. More problematically the power of rationalization is so strong that at times we can justify almost anything to ourselves. Therefore, true guidance is more than *hagun,* honest; it is *yashar,* straight, not *m'ukam,* crooked or bent. Like Occam's razor it cuts through the Gordian knot of both our well-intentioned yet circuitous designs and our more self-serving, even devious schemes. In addition, this straight path is not something we have formulated or designed; it is something we discern, *she-yabor bo.* Like the desert well from which Hagar quenched her son Ishmael's thirst (Genesis 21), its wisdom was always there but obscured by external circumstance and/or our own inner conflicts. Suddenly, a flash of illumination smelts away the dross, and the insight revealed is *barah:* pure, lucent, and clear.

Beyond the assent of our speculative and moral reason, the "straight path" evokes a deep, aesthetic sense of appreciation within ourselves and others. Devoid of self-serving motives and the desire for acclaim, it is acknowledged as life-enhancing and enlivening, even when requiring difficult sacrifices. When seen through the lens of our full humanity *(ha'adam)* instead of the narrow scope of our creaturely concern for self-preservation *(ha-briyot),* this path is recognized as *tiferet,* beautiful, that which later kabbalists understood to be the point of symmetry and perfect connection among all divine traits, the figurative "heart-space" of God. If, as Abraham Joshua Heschel taught, we should approach our lives as works of art, then walking the "straight path" will ennoble our own lives and may offer a model for others to appreciate and emulate.

An example of this dynamic is found in the deliberations of a woman charged with the ongoing care of her aged mother.

For fifteen years a daughter had managed her Alzheimer's-stricken mother's affairs, ensuring that the mother could continue to live in her own home with the finest round-the-clock care. Given her mother's relative physical health and the longevity of her illness, the daughter could foresee that the combined family resources would not allow the status quo to continue indefinitely. She consulted financial advisors and researched fine private and institutional living options, many of which she could have chosen with full integrity. She also prayed a great deal. In the midst of her exploration and planning, the daughter went on retreat. During group spiritual direction, a voice broke into her consciousness, cutting through the thicket of her dilemma: Care for your mother as she would have cared for you. Reduced to tears she immediately discerned that in its commanding beauty and simplicity this was the *derech ha-yashar,* the "straight path" of divine guidance. While this flash of illumination neither rendered her previous investigations vain nor obviated the need for careful planning, it gave her a touchstone to guide her efforts. Above any financial or logistical concerns, every decision about her mother's future would have to pass a single litmus test: Would it provide her mother with the kind of attentive, loving care that her mother would have provided if she, the daughter, had been incapacitated and defenseless?

When Observing the Mitzvah Isn't the Most Godly Choice

Among the marks of *bitachon* that Luzzatto derived from Deuteronomy 10:13 is the commitment to observe all of God's commandments. However, he and other Jewish spiritual teachers pointed to those occasions when deviating from halachic convention might be more pleasing to God. Already embodied in the system of *halachah* is the notion of *pikuach nefesh,* that one may disregard any mitzvah to save a life, except acts of public idolatry, incest, and adultery or murder. Some Hasidic masters, however, pointed to Yael, wife of Hever, who seduced then killed Sisera, a Canaanite general who had attacked Israel during the period of the Judges, to indicate that one might even transgress those bounds if it means saving the Jewish people.[11]

Luzzatto also indicated that what often passes for halachic observance are really additional strictures that go beyond what *halachah* requires. In chapter 20 he counsels that if such punctiliousness leads to strife and hard feelings, it is better to forgo exaggerated piety. His wisdom is exemplified by the story of a highly observant Jew who had been recently widowed. Invited by his brother to come for a Shabbat dinner, the widower arrived with his suitcase and a bag containing a chicken from the only kosher butcher in town he trusted. His brother refused to serve that chicken because he only trusted a different butcher. At a time that called for comfort and togetherness, the two brothers ate dinner at the same home that *Erev Shabbat,* one at the table with his wife, the other from a bag on the porch by himself.

While these responses to dire emergencies or additional stringencies might seem obvious to many, there are other times when the path to discernment might point toward potentially more dangerous territory. This is especially true in our time, when choice and individual autonomy reign supreme, when only a relative few take the parameters of *halachah* seriously. When a disregard for the validity of external norms is combined with our human propensity for rationalization, one can begin to slide down a slippery slope that can justify almost anything by labeling it "God's will."

One such set of circumstances is what the Baal Shem Tov calls the "semblance of transgression." While the act being considered might not in itself be a sin, the trappings of the act can be seductive and lead to misinterpretation. Such was the case of an extremely devout father who had a ne'er-do-well son. Despite the father's best efforts, the son only showed passion for one thing—playing poker. At wits' end, the father finally asked his son to teach him how to play. Surprised, the son agreed and soon the father began accompanying him to his games. When asked by friends how a devout Jew could enter such profane environs, the father replied, "I'd go to Hell itself to save my son." Through their gambling excursions, the father was able to build a new rapport with his son, which in turn provided the son with a bridge back to a more responsible, productive life. Although gambling is not totally forbidden by Jewish law, given the risk of financial loss, gambling addiction, and possible association with unsavory characters, the father's path certainly was fraught with danger. Only ongoing discernment, combined with strength of purpose and character, allowed him, with God's help, to bring his son back toward the father's ways, rather than the other way around.

Beyond the "semblance of transgression," there might be times when answering a higher spiritual or moral call might summon us outside the bounds of convention or *halachah*. Such instances of apparent antinomianism recur in the Bible, including Judah's fulfillment of the levirate marriage with his daughter-in-law, Tamar (Genesis 38), and Boaz's marriage to the Moabite woman, Ruth (Ruth 4). Both of these seem to violate scriptural law (Leviticus 18:15; Deuteronomy 23:4), and yet these two unions set the stage for the birth of King David, forebear of the Messiah. How might we distinguish between, on the one hand, a sacred response that recognizes both the general validity of religious law and its inability to subsume all imperatives of the Divine; and, on the other hand, an urge to fulfill our inner desires that can devolve into uninhibited libertinism? Although he did not present these in a systematic manner, the Isbitzer Rebbe did prescribe *berurim*, asceticlike discernment practices, to aid us when we face what have been called "insuperable urges."

- Particularly when faced with untoward sexual involvement, distance yourself from the situation by ten degrees of separation. The Isbitzer Rebbe implies that this is what the Simeonite prince, Zimri, did before entering into what seemed to be illicit sexual relations with the Midianite princess, Cozbi, whom Lurianic sources claim was his hidden soul-mate *(Mei HaShiloach, Living Waters, Parshat Pinchas)*.
- When discerning the purity of a given option, consider its potential benefits, losses, and impact on the honor of oneself, the community, and God. This mirrors the statement of Rabbi Judah the Prince in *Pirke Avot*, chapter 2, that discernment is found at the intersection of that which is beautiful to oneself, others, and, by extension, God *(Mei HaShiloach, Living Waters, Parshat Kedoshim)*.
- During moments of exaltation, if not actual self-inflation, the following four steps might be undertaken to assess the purity of one's motives:

    1. Similar to Buddhist prescription, remember that life and its desires are ephemeral. Question whether it's worthwhile to engage in what might well be personally defiling and provide but fleeting enjoyment.

2. Study Torah. Its teachings might offer salvation from unto-ward craving or insight into legitimate ways to fulfill one's desires.

3. As a hedge against arrogance and the illusion of human self-sufficiency, recite the *Shema.* This is a reminder that all is in-terconnected and in the hands of the One true God. The Isbitzer Rebbe cites a statement in the Talmud indicating that at the end of time God will invite the righteous into a circle dance. Some contemporary Jewish spiritual directors have suggested that, when faced with an insuperable urge, one should envision that urge surrounded either by the words of the *Shema* or by a circle of contemporary and past righteous people whose wisdom and examples would be in-vited to help illumine this difficult situation.[12]

4. If all these fail, then envision the actual day of your death, an occasion where lust and desire have no place. Looking back over your life, consider if you'd like to be remembered as having committed the act you're considering *(Mei HaShiloach, Living Waters, Parshat Vayigash).*

Given the Isbitzer Rebbe's deterministic theology, he contended that if one's desire remained after all these practices, then "This must be from God and will endure."[13] While few of us would be willing to make such a categorical assertion, we can be fairly sure that after such intensive discernment practice and its concurrent lapse of time, an issue that continues to call us "outside the lines" must run deep and demands further exploration. Even if the pursuit of "doing justly, loving kindly, and walking humbly" might, heaven forbid, lead us to act wrongly beyond the accepted norms, we can still find hope in a God for Whom "Nothing is too wondrous" (Genesis 18:14), Who can ultimately write straight with the crooked lines of our lives.

God Is Guiding Me

How do we know if it's God? The truth is that we can't. Discernment is much like sailing a boat. Initially, the wind fills your sails only to die down somewhere midcourse. You then need to tack, adjust your bearings to regain the wind, and then repeat the process through calm and storm until your "zigzag" route successfully leads you to harbor.

Consider Abraham's situation in the *Akedah,* the binding of Isaac. Initially, he is sure that God's word, "Take him up to the sacrifice" (Genesis 22:2), means that Isaac is to be sacrificed. During the journey to Mt. Moriah, Abraham first responds to Isaac's inquiry concerning the absence of a sacrificial lamb and later hears an angelic voice of restraint as he lifts the knife over his son. Seeing a ram caught in the thicket, Abraham finally discerns that it is not God's will that he sacrifice his son on the mountain, but that he and his son worship God on the mountain by together sacrificing the ram.

Like the journey of the *Akedah,* the process of *berur* is filled with uncertainty. It also reinforces a truism that my coeditor, Barbara Breitman, wisely and repeatedly affirms: God's time and ours aren't the same. Yet despite the perils and sacrifice, discernment over time can be a transformative, sanctifying experience, as the following vignette shows.

> After several years of marriage, Sherry's husband informed her that their relationship was over. Since they had two small children, she implored him to join her in counseling. However, months of futile therapy sessions and sleeping in separate rooms led Sherry to realize that her husband's decision was irrevocable. "Should I stay or should I go? That is the question."
>
> Each morning Sherry quietly recited Psalm 25, "Show me Your way ... " as a prelude to meditation. As a trained Jewish educator, traditional Jewish sources began to break into Sherry's consciousness. First she heard, *"Shev v'al ta'aseh,"* a Jewish legal dictum to "sit still and not act." Although it would have been less painful for her to leave, Sherry remained at home. While her husband was consumed by work and enrollment in professional training, Sherry adjusted her schedule, spent more time with their children and strengthened her relationship with their younger child.
>
> After many weeks, the message received during her meditation shifted. *"Ki krova yeshuati lavo*—For My redemption is soon to come" (Isaiah 56:1). "When?" Sherry would cry. However, she gradually noticed fresh opportunities unfolding as she formed new friendships that held promise for her future.

Nearly a year and a half had elapsed since her husband's fateful announcement when Sherry heard different guidance as she meditated: "*Koom, lech, alay*—Arise, go forward, and ascend." Her husband was about to finish his training, and Sherry realized that it was time to begin her life's next chapter. Sadly, it would include divorce. However, her transformed priorities and deepened relationships gave her a hopeful if not entirely clear vision of what might lie ahead.

Can discernment become innate? While no one can live in exact alignment with God's will, the ongoing practice of discernment can help us develop ever-greater attentiveness and responsiveness to the Divine. Through repetition, we can internalize the steps of *berur* until purifying our intentions, monitoring our affect, scrutinizing our acts and their consequences over time, and "casting our lading with God" become a way of life. More cognizant of the nuances of God's voice emanating from our own "Interior Torah," we, as the Isbitzer Rebbe claimed of our father Jacob, might also say, "I am ever aware that the Blessed Holy One is guiding me."

Notes

1. Genesis Rabbah 63.
2. Psalm 34:5.
3. Among the terms used for this level of divine revelation are *Gilui Shechinah* (Revelation through the Divine Presence), *Gilui Eliyahu* (Revelation from Elijah), *Ruach HaKodesh* (the Holy Spirit), and *Bat Kol* (a Heavenly Voice).
4. The word *Elohecha,* "your God," in the first of the Ten Commandments (Exodus 20:2) is expressed in the second person singular.
5. Other terms used to connote discernment include *havdalah,* "separating" the sacred from the profane and mundane, and *havchanah,* to distinguish between the authentic and the false. While some texts refer to more mystical forms of discernment, like the posing of "dream questions," such approaches lie beyond the purview of this essay.
6. Francis Brown, S. R. Driver, and Charles A. Briggs, eds., *A Hebrew and English Lexicon of the Old Testament* (Oxford, UK: Clarendon Press, 1968), 140–141.
7. This insight is most often cited in Aramaic *(Leyt atar panui minei)* and attributed to its kabbalistic source, Tikunei Zohar 122b. However, its Hebrew precursor *(Ayn makom she'ayn bo Shechinah)* is found in connection with God's appearance to Moses in a lowly, burning thornbush (Exodus Rabbah 2:5) and seems axiomatic to normative rabbinic theology.
8. Shneur Zalman of Liadi, "Tanya," cited in chap. 26, Norman Lamm, *The Religious Thought of Hasidism: Text and Commentary* (New York: Michael Scharf Publication Trust of Yeshiva University Press, 1999), 392–393.

9. From *Likutim Yekarim*, in Isaiah and Joshua Devorks, eds, *Tractate Avot with the Commentaries of Rabbi Israel Baal Shem Tov* (Hebrew) (Jerusalem: Institute for Mishnaic Research, 1988), 91.

10. There are two different *girsa'ot,* versions, of the concluding phrase of *Yedid Nefesh*'s third stanza. The one most commonly found in Ashkenazi prayer books, "*Eleh chamdah libi,*" means "These are the desires of my heart." That found in Sephardi siddurim and considered by many to be Azikri's original is "*Eli machmad libi*—My God is the desire of my heart."

11. Rabbi Zadok ha-Kohen of Lublin in Lamm, *Religious Thought of Hasidism,* 593.

12. This observation was offered by a group of Jewish spiritual directors who had attended a class I taught on this material during a Jewish Spiritual Direction Advance Practice Seminar, held at Elat Chayyim, the Jewish Retreat Center, in Accord, New York in July 2005.

13. On the deterministic theology of Mordechai Yosef Lainer of Isbitza, see Shaul Magid, *Hasidism on the Margin: Reconciliation, Antinomianism, and Messianism in Izbica/Radzin Hasidism* (Madison: University of Wisconsin Press, 2003), chap. 4.

Suggested Readings

Baal Shem Tov, Israel. *Tzava'at HaRivash: The Testament of Rabbi Israel Baal Shem Tov.* Translated by Jacob Immanuel Schochet. Brooklyn: Kehot Publications, 1998.

Lainer, Mordechai Yosef of Isbitza. *Living Waters: The Mei HaShiloach: A Commentary on the Torah.* Translated by Betsalel Philip Edwards. Northvale, NJ: Jason Aronson, 2001.

Luzzatto, Moshe Hayyim. *The Path of the Upright.* Translated by Mordecai M. Kaplan. Northvale, NJ: Jason Aronson, 1995.

Wolf, Pierre. *Discernment: The Art of Choosing Well.* Liguori, MO: Liguori Press, 2003.

Rabbi Howard A. Addison is the author of *Show Me Your Way: The Complete Guide to Interfaith Spiritual Direction,* in addition to other books that explore the connection between Kabbalah and personality type. A congregational rabbi for nearly thirty years, he now teaches at Temple University. He is the G. G. Scholem Professor of Jewish Spirituality at Graduate Theological Foundation and is a cofounder of Lev Shomea, the first institute to train spiritual directors in the Jewish tradition.

Spiritual Types: One Size Doesn't Fit All

Rabbi Shohama Harris Wiener

Introduction

There is an ancient rabbinic story I call to mind when I think of spiritual typologies. When sovereigns want to mint a coin, they put a face on it, and the face is identical on each and every coin. When the Holy One creates a human, however, no two faces are exactly the same. Each and every person is unique (*Sanhedrin* 4:5).

While it may be true for ponchos, that "one size fits all," it is not valid for giving counsel. This is particularly true in the sacred work of spiritual direction. It is necessary to see the individual before us, and to remember that no one quality, or type of personality, in and of itself, is spiritual. The question is this: In what way do given traits bring us closer to God, or further away? Every quality can have an elevated aspect, which helps us manifest the Divine; each also has a shadow aspect, which clouds our ability to do so.

During my twenty years of study and practice as a *mashpia,* a Jewish spiritual guide, I have studied many systems of spiritual typology, both Jewish and secular. Each has added to my understanding of how people grow spiritually in different ways. Insights, gleaned from these systems, combined with practical experience, have helped heighten my instincts so I can work intuitively when guiding seekers and be "present in the moment."

The spiritual typology I find most helpful comes from Kabbalah, as embodied in its teachings concerning the *Arba Olamot,* the Four Worlds, or Realms of Spirituality, and the *sefirot,* divine energies. They help me in intuiting which questions to ask, and assessing what avenues of growth might be most beneficial to an individual. They also give the people I work with a framework and a set of categories for understanding their internal struggles, as well as their issues with other people.

What follows is a presentation of the Four Worlds seen as personality types and a system I have derived, based on Kabbalistic teachings,[1] which sees the lower seven *sefirot* as qualities that each of these types, in their own way, will need when confronting seven basic issues along the path of life. Interspersed are examples of how these categories have been helpful in my spiritual direction practice. To ensure each person's privacy, the seekers' names and the exact details of their stories have been changed.

A word of caution: In our study and our practice we must be mindful not to "mistake the map for the territory." As will be discussed below, few of us, if any, manifest pure type; rarely does anyone confront the seven basic life issues in a neat sequential order. Since all systems are constructs of the human mind, they are but partial representations of ultimate truth, even if divinely inspired.

The Four Worlds

Jewish mystics have perceived four basic modalities of being spiritual: *Atzilut,* immersion in the Divine Spirit; *Briyah,* thought or intellect; *Yetzirah,* feeling and emotion; and *Asiyah,* doing and action. There is a teaching that each of us is "hard-wired" to prefer one modality over the others, in the same way that we favor our right or left hand. Given the hundreds of people I have worked with, this seems to be an exaggeration with a large kernel of truth. In my experience, many individuals have one or two nearly equal core modalities, and at different times in their lives may be drawn to the spirituality embodied by any one of the worlds.

We can learn which world(s) lies at the seeker's core through careful inquiry. While various spiritual inventories and questionnaires are available, I usually ask about those states that feel most natural, and the activities that bring the greatest joy. No matter which are dominant in our earliest years, the process of maturing in God calls us to broaden our spiritual horizons, and to take on the challenge of growing in different worlds, until we feel some facility in all of them. Perhaps this is what the psalmist meant by the words: "From narrowness and constriction I call 'Yah, God'; You answer me with *Merchav-Yah,* spacious freedom divine" (Psalm 118:5).

The Wheel of Spirituality

Although no diagram can fully represent the Four Worlds and their dynamic interaction, certain visualizations can prove useful. The Wheel of Spirituality, developed by the Christian pastoral counselor Corinne Ware, is based on the work of Urban T. Holmes.[2] Though Ware is not a Jewish mystic, and does not use kabbalistic terminology, her two-dimensional diagram does offer helpful insights into the Four Worlds metaphor.

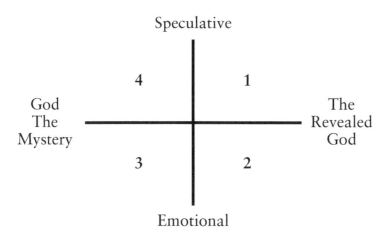

The vertical axis of the wheel is a continuum of the Speculative/Intellectual (top) to the Emotional (bottom). The horizontal axis links the Revealed God (right) to God the Mystery (left). In Judaism, God is revealed through the verbal images of the Divine found in the Torah and our classical texts. God the Mystery, perhaps identified with *Ayn Sof* of Kabbalah, would be the Presence we encounter in meditation and personal prayer.

The Wheel of Spirituality visually depicts how our spirituality manifests itself through four quite different modalities. It also offers insight into why it is difficult for synagogues to meet the needs of all current and potential members. The formal service, with fixed prayer and Torah study, is most likely to attract intellectually focused, *Briyah*/Quadrant 1 individuals while the emotionally expressive *Yetzirah*/Quadrant 2 types would be more drawn to an informal, spirited service. Those in *Atzilut*/Quadrant 3 would prefer to meditate, and those in *Asiyah*/Quadrant 4 might find greatest fulfillment through social action, by physically connecting with nature, or by creating works of art.

What this simple diagram also illustrates is that Quadrants 1 and 3, *Briyah*/Intellect and *Atzilut*/Spirit are oppositional, as are Quadrants 2 and 4, *Yetzirah*/Emotion and *Asiyah*/Action. When someone is exceptionally strong in one of the quadrants, the natural way to find balance is to grow first in the qualities represented by the opposite quadrant. For example, those in Quadrant 2, whose emotion-charged religious fervor might dull their sensitivity to the needs of the world, can grow through the godly serving of others, represented by Quadrant 4. Conversely, those engrossed in the social activism of Quadrant 4 can find their personal connection to God revitalized through an infusion of Quadrant 2 religious zeal. Expanding into the adjacent quadrants can then facilitate further spiritual growth.

Spiritual Direction Issues and the Four Worlds Typology: Initial Steps

Discerning the Core World

Frequently, the primary roles people play are at odds with their core strengths, thus alienating them from their true selves. They may have chosen a career in response to pressure to acquire income or status; family or social expectations may be forcing them to function in capacities at odds with their true dispositions and talents. This is particularly true in Western culture, which traditionally assumed that men would exhibit strength in *Briyah* or *Asiyah,* Intellect or Action, while *Yetzirah,* Emotion, was to be the natural and perhaps exclusive province of women. The situation of Bob, presented below, is representative of the conflicts many people experience, and the healing that can come by identifying and aligning oneself with one's core spiritual world.

From *Briyah* to *Yetzirah*, Thinking to Feeling

Bob was a successful business executive in his fifties, capable of conceiving complex strategies and negotiating any deal with acumen. He came to spiritual direction because he had to force himself to go to work in the morning; at the same time his involvement as a member of his synagogue board was expanding. He was curious to see if spiritual direction could offer him insights that would make his life more fulfilling.

The process of discernment took about a year. Through guided meditation, he began to access the true self of his dreams. To better sense his own spiritual core, I taught him to meditate and urged him to attend a weekend retreat. I also suggested that he take up a *hitbodedut* practice by daily talking aloud to God and keeping a spiritual journal.

These exercises, together with our regular guidance sessions, helped Bob discern the emotional and spiritual worlds that reflected the person he felt "Life" was calling him to be. He realized that what was most important to him at this point was to have work that helped people. In line with his newly found access to the world of feelings, he decided to train as a life coach. It took him another year to transition out of his business, and enter a training program for this new career. However, he experienced joy and renewed energy as he moved toward a goal along what he felt to be his true path.

Encouraging the Gifts

Having helped the directee discern his core spiritual world, it is then important to see where that directee's gifts lie, and to encourage expression of those gifts within a spiritual context. For example, a person with an intellectual gift might study Torah, Jewish thought, or Hasidic commentaries; a person with emotional wisdom might take on the mitzvah of visiting the sick; someone with a vibrant sense of connection to the Holy might consider beginning a Jewish meditation practice; and those with a gift for art or a penchant for social justice might learn to do Hebrew calligraphy or champion the cause of the oppressed.

Understanding Other Worlds

God has created us all with unique gifts, yet called us to be *aravi'im zeh ba-zeh,* to be connected with one another. This means we must appreciate and value those who differ from ourselves. On Sukkot the lulav and etrog comprise three diverse tree branches and one fruit.

Each stands for a different type of Jew, and it is only when all four are held lovingly and waved together that we can be redeemed.

It is a kind of *avodah zarah,* idolatry, to think that the limited scope one's mind perceives can encompass all divine truth. Therefore, one role of the spiritual director is to help directees see beyond the limited framework of their own primary worlds and appreciate the spiritual paths of others.

> As a rabbi, I am often called on to provide spiritual counseling for couples. Jack came with his wife, Sarah, because they were drifting apart over differences in their spirituality. Jack had attended synagogue regularly for many years, and enjoyed a traditional service and a good sermon. Sarah, though uncomfortable in synagogue, felt a close, less mediated connection to God. She complained that Jack couldn't understand or support her belief in personal, intercessory prayer. "Sarah nearly died a few years ago," Jack told me. "The doctors held out little hope, but she and her friends prayed for her recovery. She has regained her health, but I don't believe it was because of the prayers. It was a happy coincidence."
>
> It was clear that Jack, who received his spiritual sustenance through formal services and Torah study, was most comfortable in the realm of *Briyah,* approaching God rationally with his mind. Sarah, on the other hand, had her primary connection to God through the realm of *Atzilut,* Spirit, and possibly *Yetzirah,* emotional fervor. In those realms of more immediate divine connection, the miraculous that underlies "coincidence" is reality. I've often seen such spiritual pairing among partners, especially those who have been together for several decades.
>
> I explained to Jack that, like wearing eyeglasses with different-colored lenses, people of different spiritual types actually "see" the world differently. God has created us all, and all types are needed to compose the "Face of God" here on earth. No matter what our primary view, there are ways we can expand our vision. The challenge for all of us is to appreciate and honor each other in our differences, to grow in areas where we are limited, and to work together for the common good.
>
> I urged them both to go to a Jewish retreat center where Sarah could be in workshops on mysticism in prayer and Torah, and

Jack could learn Jewish meditation and chanting. They followed my suggestion, and came back with new appreciation for each other's path.

Ongoing Issues: Levels within Worlds

Another key aspect of spiritual direction is guiding people toward the more elevated aspects of their primary world. As mentioned above, there are no traits that are inherently spiritual; each has its own light and shadow side. We can think of each world as containing three levels: The *tzaddik* or upper level, is the most evolved, manifesting the full wisdom and compassion inherent in that realm's gifts; the *benoni* or average level is where most of us function, being neither saints nor sinners; and the *rasha* or lower level contains the shadow dimensions with which we all must contend, including fear, hate, envy, and greed. To achieve holiness we must recognize our flaws so we might wrestle with and transform them. People whose strengths are in different worlds face different kinds of challenges. As mentioned above, the *tikkun,* or corrective, for those challenges usually lies initially in accessing the spiritual strengths of the world represented by the diagonally opposite quadrant on the Wheel of Spirituality, followed by cultivating aspects of the adjacent two worlds.

Atzilut

The *tzaddik* aspect of *Atzilut* is manifested in the peace, equanimity, and joy that comes from direct experience of the Divine. Its compassion, vision, and deep wisdom can raise the spiritual level of others. Stories of the Hasidic rebbes often refer to their uncanny ability to see into the essence of a Hasid's soul, and offer just the right insight and counsel.

The *rasha*, or shadow side, of *Atzilut* is detachment and subjectivity, which can lead to disconnection from community, family, objective standards of judgment, and even one's own physical health. For example, one of my early teachers of Jewish mysticism was a gifted young rabbi who later became so entranced with the Upper Worlds that he lost interest in eating. Tragically, he died from complications of anorexia.

Tikkunim, or correctives, for the excesses of *Atzilut* spirituality may include the study of Jewish texts and communal liturgical worship as objective touchstones to one's personal experiences of the Divine; ecstatic communal prayer; connection to others through deeds of loving-kindness; and grounded activities through which we steward God's creation, like gardening, cooking, and cleaning.

Briyah

The *tzaddik* level of *Briyah* can promote healthy intellectual curiosity—the hunger to explore traditional and contemporary sources of wisdom, fresh insights, and innovative formulations of ritual and practice. The Sages who formalized the structure of Jewish life and prayer were, no doubt, strong in this quadrant.

The *rasha,* or shadow side, of *Briyah* can lead to both arid scholasticism and empty formalism. Study of increasingly intricate and obscure topics may stimulate the mind without touching the soul; going through the motions of observing mitzvot may allow one to be *yotzei,* to have fulfilled one's religious/legal obligations, but do little to arouse the spirit and heart.

Tikkunim, or correctives, for the excesses of *Briyah* may include contemplative activities, such as meditation and chanting, or creating sacred art forms, which help the intellectual type expand beyond mind and connect experientially with the realm of Spirit. Ecstatic singing, dance, and direct service to others can also help them move beyond their heads into their hearts and bodies.

Yetzirah

The *tzaddik* aspect of *Yetzirah* is passion and enthusiasm in service of others and God, called *hitlahavut* in Hebrew. People in this quadrant are in touch with their emotions, feel them strongly, and can offer them up as gifts to God.

The *rasha,* or shadow side, is an overemphasis on the ecstatic that can lead to self-absorption in one's own fervor. One may find it hard to function in family and community life, which requires planning, patience, and sensitivity to others' needs.

Tikkunim, or correctives, for the excesses of *Yetzirah* may begin with *tzedakah* projects that involve community, whether it be *hachnasat orchim* (inviting guests), a political action project, or raising funds for a charity. To move further beyond the subjectivity and upheaval of their own emotions, study of texts and contemplative activity may also be of help.

Asiyah

The *tzaddik* level for the world of action includes service to others through the many acts of *tzedakah* that directly help individuals or worthy social causes. We give through our money and our deeds. Judaism places great emphasis on the importance of *ma'asim tovim,* good deeds.

The *rasha,* or shadow side, can initially be seen in a compulsive busy-ness as a way to escape introspection and honest emotion. It can further descend into the realm of addiction in any number of areas— eating, substance abuse, gambling, shopping, anything to find temporary comfort and joy while anesthetizing one's inner pain.

Tikkunim, or correctives, for the excesses of *Asiyah* include first opening the heart in surrender to God. Next comes the building of legitimate self-esteem by engaging the body, mind, and soul. This is often accomplished within the context of ongoing, spiritually oriented support groups. The Twelve-Step Movement offers support groups for every kind of addiction. In a Jewish framework, the study and practice of *Mussar,* ethicist texts, and behavior-modification exercises can help identify and address compulsive, ungodly behavior.

The Seven Sefirot and Life Issues

While the Four Worlds are helpful in assessing a person's strengths and areas in need of spiritual growth, I find the *sefirot* useful in identifying the major life challenges people encounter, and the divine qualities needed to address them. In most systems there are ten *sefirot.* Because the upper three *sefirot* are considered by many kabbalists to be beyond our comprehension, for our purposes we will focus only on the lower seven. There is wide disagreement among Kabbalists on the descriptions of the *sefirot.* Below is a system that I have adapted, based on categories provided in *Sefer Yetzirah.*[3]

Chesed: Life and health versus death
Gevurah: Peace versus war
Tiferet: Wisdom/heart versus foolishness

Netzach: Grace versus ugliness

Hod: Abundance versus poverty

Yesod: Generativity/children versus desolation

Malchut: Sovereignty versus subjugation

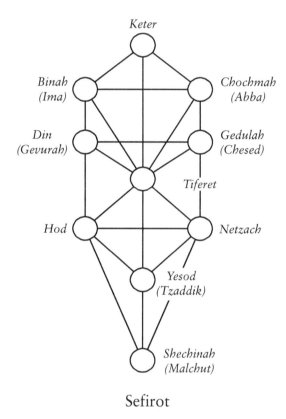

Sefirot

To illustrate each *sefirah*/life struggle, I will share vignettes from the spiritual journey of Louise, whom I companioned over a period of seven years. When Louise first came to me, her immediate life situation had her mired in the practical, emotional, and intellectual challenges represented by the worlds of *Asiyah* (Doing), *Yetzirah* (Feeling) and *Briyah* (Intellect). As we shall see, her path led her through a series of the above-mentioned life struggles to the greater spiritual connection of *Atzilut,* her primary world, one that she had yearned for, at times unknowingly.

Chesed and *Gevurah*

Louise was a forty-year-old wife and the mother of three teenagers when she first came to spiritual direction. She taught in an adult education program part-time, but most of her energy went into being a homemaker. She had come because her husband was physically and emotionally ill; she loved him and wanted to keep the family intact. Although she had been an agnostic for many years, she hoped that there was a God, and that perhaps God could lessen her distress. Having spent her life pleasing others, she was seeking the courage to reach out to a God she didn't believe existed.

In my opening prayer, I asked that our visit be graced with God's presence and guidance, and that she be given the strength to allow God in. Louise, in her prayer, asked that God manifest to her, and said that she would be willing to follow whatever would be asked of her. After a period of silence, Louise reported that she felt as if a flame lit up in her heart, and that she felt an unseen, but loving Presence surrounding her.

I encouraged her to dialogue with this Presence daily, to meditate, and to keep a journal. As our sessions continued, her spiritual practice increasingly drew her toward Jewish learning and observance, interests she found the strength to maintain despite her family's resistance.

Chesed and *Gevurah* are usually paired as two poles of a dyad in the sefirotic system. *Chesed* is an expansion from the place of love and can serve as a focus when struggling—literally or figuratively—for life and health in the face of death and dying. When people are afflicted, as both Louise and her husband were in different ways, self-love and love of others can help bring healing of soul, if not of body. For the wounded and their caregivers *chesed* can represent the drive to embody our highest abilities and visions in our lives.

Gevurah, on the other hand, is the power of discriminating judgment and the ability to set life-maintaining boundaries, especially amid hostile circumstances. Being raised under emotionally or physically difficult, if not abusive, conditions, can have an enormous impact on spiritual development. In particular, children of Holocaust survivors, one generation away from the original trauma, share an ingrained sense of fear and lack of trust. As adults, many need to reenvision their understanding of God, and reclaim their sense of value. As Louise experienced, *Gevurah* can provide the courage to open oneself up to the unknown and to struggle to maintain one's own path of integrity.

Tiferet, Netzach, and Hod

Over the course of our time together, I learned more about Louise and her life story. A much-loved child, she had always done what her parents wanted. As she became overly dependent on external validation, she tended to let others unduly influence her decisions. This included becoming a traditional wife and mother. At twenty-one she married a brilliant man who was a secular Jew, and shortly thereafter began to teach part-time and raise a family.

Although she deeply understood others and had a great capacity for love, Louise lacked the assurance to rely on her intuition and feelings when making decisions. Her interior wisdom, competence, and even sweetness were eclipsed by her lack of sense of self. Due to her husband's illnesses these issues came to a head as Louise grew deeply concerned about her family's financial security, as well as her own.

Her daily dialogues with the Divine Presence, as well as meditation, journaling, and increased Jewish observance, led her to experience a growing sense of God's love. She became more confident in relying upon the true wisdom of her heart and began to reevaluate the arrangements to which she had acceded as a young adult. Experiencing herself as worthy of receiving God's guidance in her life, Louise shined with an enduring inner grace that was clearly visible. Despite the passage of years or what others might think, Louise felt herself growing ever more beautiful.

In response to her growing financial concerns, I showed Louise that praying for *parnassah,* livelihood, was a legitimate Jewish practice, and that became part of her daily prayers. As time went on, her interest in learning Hebrew and studying Jewish texts became a passion, and she began to teach in local synagogues. This didn't immediately solve her financial problems. However, rich emotional and spiritual arenas began to open up to her as she felt less dependent on her husband's income and sensed her own growing competence.

Tiferet symbolizes the "heart space" of the sefirotic system. Poised between the preceding *sefirot* of *Chesed* and *Gevurah*, it represents the emotional wisdom that derives from properly balancing love and judiciousness. As Louise discovered, overdependence on external validation can obscure both self-reliance and true empathy. The clouding of our emotional intelligence can lead us to unconscious choices, compromised arrangements, and potentially unhealthy relationships. Some people seem more naturally endowed with emotional intelligence, which may facilitate more expansive spiritual development. Like Louise, however, we all may gain greater access to the power of *Tiferet* through regular spiritual practice.

Netzach and *Hod* are also paired *sefirot;* together they represent the aesthetic and practical issues stemming from *Tiferet. Netzach* symbolizes an enduring sense of inner grace, reflecting healthy self-esteem. Our society places enormous pressure, particularly on women, to appear young and thin. These artificial standards of beauty have led to increasing numbers of people struggling with anorexia and bulimia. Expectations set by our family of origin can establish ingrained patterns of self-perception and response that can only be interrupted later with great difficulty. By learning to experience herself as worthy of God's guiding presence, Louise was able to sense the grace of *Netzach* and reflect it with growing consistency in both her inner and outer life.

In spiritual guidance, even financial circumstance can become a foreground issue. Those facing loss of income or poverty will have far different concerns than the comfortable or the affluent. As Louise discovered, beyond the financial, *Hod* embodies intellectual, emotional, and spiritual wealth. More than prosperity, it represents an attitude of appreciation and abundance, which can help endow us with feelings of competence and confidence in the face of uncertainty.

Yesod and *Malchut*

After three years, Louise returned to graduate school to train as a Jewish educator. With her children almost grown and out of the house, she was looking for a way to continue to nurture the next generation, Jewishly and spiritually. While she had begun as a teacher, she soon rose to be educational director of a synagogue school. She claimed the dormant leadership gifts that had always been hers and used them to satisfy her spiritual longings. Louise introduced meditation and personal prayer into the school curriculum, and began to lead workshops in these areas as well. Her growing connections within the Jewish world helped her build a network of like-minded friends.

By this time Louise's husband was in better health. Still a secular Jew and frustrated by Louise's newly committed Jewish lifestyle, he asked for a divorce. Of course, they felt sadness and regret at the breakup of a long-term marriage, but they were able to maintain a respectful relationship that allowed for mutual support of their now adult children. Louise's earnings, combined with alimony payments, enabled her to support herself with dignity.

Others of differing primary worlds might have been drawn toward areas of increased academic exploration *(Briyah),* communal service *(Yetzirah),* or social activism *(Asiyah).* Louise found her life illumined by the light of her primary world, the world of Spirit, *Atzilut,* as she developed her practical, emotional, and intellectual strengths.

Yesod and *Malchut* are the last two *sefirot,* linked together along the central axis of the *Etz Chayyim,* the Tree of Life. They represent the focusing and conveying of divine energy to the world. *Yesod,* generativity, symbolizes the nurturing of life and the passing on of heritage. People involved in child rearing can find spiritual growth within the context of family. In both teaching and learning from their children, they begin to actualize previously unrealized qualities. As Louise found, such growth can also occur outside the home through teaching and mentoring those who come after us.

On a personal level, *Malchut,* sovereignty, represents being in charge of our own lives rather than living the life someone else has envisioned for us. It also concerns issues of leadership, or the suppression thereof, due to gender, birth position within the family, or the mores of the society in which one lives. Through her own spiritual growth, Louise was able to access her connection to *Malchut* and step into leadership roles neither she nor her family had previously thought possible.

Tikkun Olam

As part of spiritual guidance, it is important to help people look beyond the immediacy of their own lives, to see their struggles within the larger picture of human society. Taking an active role in changing our environment for the better is the essence of *tikkun olam*, Judaism's imperative to repair the world.

Let me cite but a few examples. *Chesed* calls our attention beyond self-love and love of those within our circle to concern for issues of life and death, health and disease around the earth. As our world becomes an ever-smaller global village, attention to the environment, the purity of the water we drink, and the suitability of food we eat has a great effect on our vitality as individuals and as a family of humanity. *Yesod* summons us to expand our vision so that we look beyond the walls of our homes, classrooms, and offices. It calls us to see ourselves as nurturers for all living creatures—human, animal, and plant—and for our planet earth as well. This perspective is reflected in our ancient Jewish texts, particularly in the words of the prophets. *Malchut* reminds us that people in a democracy have freedom to grow in ways that are difficult for those living in political dictatorships or those whose social conditions prevent them from attaining full autonomy. Therefore, we are bidden to have greater awareness of the oppressive forces at work in the world and the roles we might play to promote the liberation of body, mind, and spirit. This core message of Judaism lies at the heart of the Passover *Haggadah* and the entirety of our Pesach observance.

Final Thoughts: A Bead and a Prayer

In using the Four Worlds in spiritual direction, it is important to realize that the diagram of quadrants is only one way to visualize their interconnectedness. Alternatively, Rabbi Elie Kaplan Spitz has likened the Four Worlds to a three-dimensional bead, with the three colored rings of the bead representing the Intellectual *(Briyah)*, the Emotional *(Yetzirah)*, and the Physical *(Asiyah)*. Spirit *(Atzilut)*, is visualized as the energy pulsing through the void at the bead's center.[4] To the extent that we have strength in a particular world, that ring will be fuller. To the extent that we function at the more morally elevated levels in a given world as we meet the life challenges symbolized by the *sefirot*, the color of the ring will be brighter and clearer. In this visualization, it is easy to see that Spirit is not a separate world in the way that the others seem to be. Rather, the essence of divinity lies at the core of everything, binding the disparate aspects of reality together and permeating all.

As we serve as companions to seekers along the way, may the Four Worlds typology help us and them identify their core spiritual strengths and those areas that summon them to further growth. May the unfolding of the life challenges represented by the *sefirot* give us greater awareness of the struggles we encounter along life's path and the divine energies we can access to help us successfully negotiate these tasks. May the rings of our worlds shine ever more vibrantly and may the Divine that lies at our innermost core grow ever more expansive.

Notes

1. Aryeh Kaplan, trans. and ed., *Sefer Yetzirah: The Book of Creation,* rev. ed. (York Beach, ME: S. Weiser, 1997).
2. Corinne Ware, *Discover Your Spiritual Type: A Guide to Individual and Congregational Growth* (Bethesda, MD: Alban Institute, 1995), 131. Based on the work of Urban T. Holmes.
3. Kaplan, *Sefer Yetzirah, The Book of Creation,* see pp. 164 and 287. For a spirituality guide based on this work, see Melinda Ribner, *Kabbalah Month by Month: A Year of Spiritual Practice and Personal Transformation* (New York: Jossey-Bass, 2002).
4. Elie Kaplan Spitz, *Does the Soul Survive? A Jewish Journey to Belief in Afterlife, Past Lives & Living with Purpose* (Woodstock, VT: Jewish Lights Publishing, 2000).

For other approaches to the *Olamot, Sefirot,* and differing spiritual typologies see:

Addison, Howard Avruhm. *Cast in God's Image: Discover Your Personality Type Using the Enneagram and Kabbalah.* Woodstock, VT: Jewish Lights Publishing, 2002.

———. *The Enneagram and Kabbalah: Reading Your Soul.* rev. ed., Woodstock, VT: Jewish Lights Publishing, 2006.

Edwards, Tilden. *Spiritual Friend: Reclaiming the Gift of Spiritual Direction.* New York: Paulist Press, 1980.

Gafney, Marc. *Soul Prints: Your Path to Fulfillment.* New York: Pocket Books, 2001.

Rabbi Shohama Harris Wiener is *rosh hashpa'ah,* director of spiritual direction and development for the ALEPH: Alliance for Jewish Renewal *smicha* programs, and president emerita of the Academy for Jewish Religion.

Spiritual Direction:
No Inside, No Outside

Rabbi Sheila Peltz Weinberg

I was hiking with a dear friend before breakfast. We were part of an interfaith contemplative retreat for religious leaders pursuing social justice. We had been spending our time talking about injustice, poverty, war, and racism. It was a diverse and dynamic group of people. It was fall in northern New Mexico and the scenery was breathtaking. The aspen trees were a translucent gold in motion. The sky was infinitely clear. It was so quiet you could hear your own breath. As we climbed up the mountain, the views kept widening, becoming ever more spectacular.

Kate turned to me at one point and said, "You don't know how good it is until you know how bad it is and you don't know how bad it is until you know how good it is." I stopped short. Is it true? When we face pain squarely and fully, do we become more open to life's glory? And when we touch the fragile joyous beauty of being alive, do we enter more deeply into the suffering of this world? I think it is true. I think this is the trajectory of a life of faith, a pulsation between the gratitude and praise for every moment of life and a call to express this love in work for healing, justice, and peace.

The way this works speaks to the heart rather than the head. The human heart is only one muscle. When it opens to grief, it also opens to love. You can't divide the heart without closing it down. A spiritual life must participate in the whole of life, which includes the golden aspens on the mountain as well as the hungry children in the inner city.

Faith has become a very popular word lately. Everyone is trying to figure out what it is and how to get it or use it. Many of us are trying to understand the relationships between faith and action; between private spiritual practice, religious community, and public activism; and between religion and state. This essay is an extended reflection on this subject, which is both very new and very old.

Back in 1948, the great American Jewish teacher Rabbi Mordecai Kaplan wrote: " ... the crisis in human affairs in our day has led many people to feel a deep need for religious faith. They are profoundly disillusioned with the materialistic outlook on life. Their reliance on the scientific control of natural forces as a solvent of all human ills has turned out to be illusory. Their expectation that out of contending social forces there would evolve a program of universal welfare has proved will-o-the-wisp."[1]

Another rabbi, Jonathan Sacks of Great Britain, writing over a half-century later puts it this way: "Civilizations at the height of their powers have found it hard to maintain a sense of limits. Each in turn has been captivated by the idea that it alone was immune to the laws of growth and decay, that it could consume resources indefinitely, pursuing present advantage without thought of future depletion.... The great faiths teach a different kind of wisdom: *reverence* in the face of creation, *responsibility* to future generations, and *restraint* in the knowledge that not everything we can do, should we do."[2]

The words of these two esteemed rabbis fall a few years short of spanning my lifetime. It has been a time that has witnessed the withering away of old certainties and the grasping for new certainties. We are part of a profound encounter with all kinds of limits—especially those of knowledge, power, and resources. Precisely in responding to those limits, however, we continue to experience that which is beyond our categories and ability to control, the place where faith is born.

Questions abound: How do we find balance in a world off balance? How do we integrate our personal spiritual lives and our public lives? How do we allow ourselves to know how good it is and how bad it is, and allow the knowledge of each to penetrate the wisdom of each? What is the inner work and what is the outer work that grows faith? How do we mobilize the courage it takes to face the other in ourselves and ourselves in the other? How do we become willing to risk being uncomfortable? How do we learn to rest in the unknown? These are our questions. They are questions of faith.

No Inside, No Outside—Toward an Integration of Spirit and Action

I had an amazing opportunity one summer to go kayaking in Tebenkoff Bay in the Tongass Forest in Southeast Alaska. It is a pristine wilderness. We were the only kayakers. It was so clear that we were visitors, sojourners passing through. There were plenty of residents, from the eagles and starfish to the otters, whales, and salmon, to the little critters that had a full civilization going in each tidal pool. The Sitka spruce stand alive for five hundred years, they stand for another five hundred years after they die, and, once they fall, they decompose on the forest floor for yet another five hundred years. That takes us back to the completion of the Babylonian Talmud. That is residency. We are sojourners but we are made of the same stuff as the trees and the critters that will become the rocks. Like the ebbing and flowing of the tide and the rising and setting of the sun, our breath, our moods, our energy come and go. We too are limited. We too are connected. We too are being born and dying in every moment.

Our Rabbis knew this truth. It is written in Avot d'Rabbi Natan (31): "Whatever the Holy Blessed One created in the world, God created in *Adam* [humanity], God created forests in the world and forests in *Adam*. God created a wind *(ruah)* in the world and a wind in *Adam*." My friend, Nancy, who paddled in the bow while I paddled in the stern made up a little song to keep us moving through the water: "No inside, no outside; no inside, no outside," she sang.

I think there is a clue in this song to the work of faith that we need to do. I think we need to keep looking in and keep looking out, and learning from each turn the truth about the other. Suffering is of a piece. So are violence, hatred, greed, joy, love, and generosity. They are inside and outside.

The view of nonseparation—no inside, no outside—abounds in poetry and testimonies of mystics across all religious boundaries. It is a view that can be cultivated in contemplative practice and in dialogue among people of diverse backgrounds. It is the view that makes for inclusivity, nonviolence, gratitude, and service that does not demean or belittle. It is the essence of this Australian aboriginal saying: "If you have come to help me, you are wasting your time. If you have come because your liberation is bound up with mine, let us work together."

In the Talmud there is an image of the world as a wheel that keeps turning around and around (*Shabbat* 151). External conditions keep changing. The wheel is in motion. Today one person or group or nation is on top; tomorrow another. A true reflection of the way things are, the underlying unity and interdependence of all beings, the no

inside no outside view, would have us all engaged in creating conditions that benefit the common good. We would know that we are all
sojourners but no one would be a stranger. Moreover, as we became
more aware of the inner obstacles to freedom and peace, we would be
more able to work for our ideals without falling back into patterns we
are trying to change.

Abraham Joshua Heschel, a man of faith and action, a brilliant
teacher, a mystic, and a social activist, had a career as a Yiddish poet
as a teenager in Vilna. In one poem, called *"Ich un Du"* (I and You),
Heschel presents a dialogue between the human being and God in
which it is impossible to tell where one begins and one ends. It is a reflection of this truth and ideal of unity that resonates among all mystics. Here are two stanzas:

> I live in me and in you.
> From your lips flows a word from me to me.
> From your eyes drips a tear—whose source is me.
>
> When a need springs in you, it's in me.
> When you crave a human presence
> Tear at my door.
> You live in yourself, You live in me.[3]

This poem points to a unified consciousness through which we see the
Divine in our love and pain and in the love and pain of others. There
is no separation. We are not the finite aspiring to the Infinite; rather
we are the Infinite expressed as finite.[4] Closeness to God is closeness to
God's creatures and creation. Love is One. It could mean nothing less.
I think this is the central understanding that makes spiritual direction
possible. As Rabbi Joshua says in *Ketubot* (68) in the Talmud,
"Anyone who shuts his eyes from the obligation of charity is like one
who worships idols." This means that there is no spiritual dimension
that does not have a social component. To the extent that we hide or
run away from our interconnection, we have lost a relationship with
the whole.

And who among us does not hide or run? Is not the truth of our
human experience closer to separation and fragmentation than union?
Don't we spend a lot of time thinking about being different, standing

apart, being afraid, judging, doubting? All are stances of separation. We are living in the age of multitasking. We are having one conversation and thinking of another while dialing our cell phone. This is our state of affairs. We are distracted. There seems to be so much to do all the time that it is hard to get things done. It is a struggle between the things and us and we are in a grand campaign to subdue all of them, but they keep gaining momentum. A "thing" mentality—a materialistic worldview—is all about separation.

In a recent critique of the environmental movement, called "The Death of Environmentalism," authors Michael Shellenberger and Ted Norhaus detect the mentality of fragmentation working to undermine the campaigns to reverse climate change. They write, "Environmentalism is today more about protecting a supposed 'thing'—'the environment'—than advancing the world view articulated by Sierra Club founder John Muir, who nearly a century ago observed, 'When we try to pick out anything by itself, we find it hitched to everything else in the Universe.' "[5]

This is our state of affairs. We know fragmentation, but we intuit unity. We know spirit split from action and we have heard about leaders, movements, and moments in which justice and love truly kissed. When we enter the gate of contemplative practice, such as a relationship of spiritual direction, we are calling ourselves out of fragmentation and pointing toward unity. This is much the same as the moment in prayer when we gather the fringes from the four corners of the tallit prior to calling out God is One.

At Riverside Church in New York City on April 4, 1967, the visionary spiritual social activist, Rev. Martin Luther King Jr. spoke these words: "I am convinced that if we are to get on the right side of the world revolution, we as a nation must undergo a radical revolution of values. We must rapidly begin the shift from a 'thing-oriented' society to a 'person-oriented' society. When machines and computers, profit motives and property rights are considered more important than people, the giant triplets of racism, materialism, and militarism are incapable of being conquered."

I am inspired to use the rubric of the three "grant triplets" for our exploration. Each one—materialism, racism, and militarism—is a form of fragmentation and "thing" orientation. Each is an "ism" that obscures the human ability to experience love and connection with each other, the earth, and ourselves. Each of the triplets manifests in global structures as well as in the recesses of our own hearts and minds. Throughout this journey we will be looking at the role of contemplative practice, spiritual direction in particular, and we will be asking again and again: What does this tell us about faith?

Materialism as Idolatry

Let's begin with materialism. Jonathan Sacks has a good working definition: "Advanced consumer cultures," he writes, "are built on a rapid succession of artificially induced and temporarily satisfied desires. When the market becomes not a mechanism of exchange but the guiding paradigm of life, then meaning itself is undermined."[6] We are all familiar with materialism. How often do we walk into a store for one thing and suddenly find that we *need* something else. How often is it easier to buy a new one than fix an old one? How long does the excitement of shopping last? Does it go past the checkout line? How often have we wondered, "What will they think of next?" How much of our self-worth and respect for others is governed by the stuff we possess or do not possess? How hard is it to break a dependency on some thing? How easy is it to develop a dependency on some thing? How much of our time and our physical, emotional, and mental energy do we spend in relation to money and things? How satisfied are we with our things? How much guilt is elicited by the fact that we have so many more things than the vast majority of people on this planet?

Of course, materialism is a spiritual issue. In the Bible, materialism is called idolatry. When items of limited value are given more status and attention than God—who is limitless—then we have idolatry, the ultimate sin. What happens when we look inside? When we are quiet enough to notice the stirrings of our heart and the stories of our minds, what do we see? We see constant craving. We see the tendency to place our faith in the next minute. We are longing to get *there* but when we do, we realize that *there* is now *here* and there is always a new *there*. We are internally more often dissatisfied with what is, waiting for this to pass so that we can get to the next thing—the next report, meeting, service, dinner, day, year, job, friend. In this circle of dissatisfaction, there is never enough time. So we get more things and find that we have less time.

The spiritual life is a path away from materialism. First we become aware of the truth of dissatisfaction. We see its roots in our own greed and desire, which are never sated. We seek to fill up on things because we are empty inside, disconnected, lonely, lacking in a sense of blessing and goodness. We are in exile. It takes time to see this. These patterns are revealed to us when we stop rushing and sit still. We see both how dissatisfied the mind can be in its craving and how content we can be to just be present. When we calm down a little bit, we begin to see how wondrous everything is when we pay attention to just this moment.

The spiritual direction relationship allows for time to slow down. Two people face each other. There may only be an hour, but there is all the time in the world. Nothing needs to be fixed. Nothing needs to be accomplished. Two people are attending to what is present in this moment. Two people are recognizing what is already present. The process itself is the antithesis of materialism.

I think of a directee I once worked with who was immersed in a million projects. At the beginning of each session I would just listen as she talked, and talked and talked. Inevitably, there would come a moment when time opened up. She stopped racing. She noticed her breath and the pounding of her heart. She became aware of the seduction of all the things in her life. And in the pause, in the gap, in the space, another awareness arose to the surface. It was quiet and pure and still and felt sacred. It was always there of course, but we needed to make the gateway of practice, just sitting together, for it to enter consciousness.

The verse from Psalms, *Ashrei yoshvei veytecha*, is found three times in the daily Jewish liturgy. "Happy are those who dwell in your house," it says. It is the spiritual antidote to materialism. When I was on a three-week silent retreat, I wrote this poem about the *Ashrei*.

> We are practicing happiness here.
> The happiness of peace and contentment,
> The happiness of feeling connected,
> The happiness of greeting the sun in the morning
>   or just taking another breath,
> The happiness of knowing that this bad mood will
>   pass and this harsh thought has no substance,
> The happiness of letting go of ill will for this
>   moment,

The happiness of allowing desire to come to its
    natural end in the mind,
The happiness of growing still,
The happiness of seeing life and death in
    everything and not being afraid.
Is this political? Well, I think it is.
This happiness doesn't hurt people we do not
    know.
This happiness doesn't tell us to be ashamed of
    growing old.
This happiness doesn't tell us we aren't okay but
    can fix that if we try hard enough.
This happiness doesn't attract a lot of buyers and
    sellers.
It calls for careful cultivation like a field of precious
    jewels.
Moment after moment.
It calls for dedication and community and
    willingness and faith.
It calls upon wisdom and courage.
It is itself a child of goodness.
So simple.
So huge.
But it is the only happiness there is.

Contemplative practice helps us alter our relationship to time. We learn how to dwell more fully in the house of time. This fills up the inner emptiness in a way that no thing can. When we are more peaceful inside, we are less vulnerable to the lure of the mall. Jewish religious life is anchored in this enterprise. What else is the celebration of Shabbat and the festivals but a program to establish meaning, connection to God and other people? It is the giant anti-materialism practice.

Shabbat as Spiritual Practice,
Shabbat as Social Justice

The first time the Sabbath is introduced in the Torah as a noun is in the section on manna. It is six weeks after the Exodus and the newly freed slaves are complaining already. They don't trust Moses. They don't like the whole situation. And they are hungry. They miss the bread in Egypt. It is here that God tells Moses that God will rain down bread from the sky. It is fitting that bread is connected with the Sabbath. *Lechem* is "bread" in Hebrew and comes from the same root as *milchama,* which, paradoxically, means "war." Bread is a product of human effort in partnership with the earth. The effort can lead to struggle when we fear that we don't have enough and fight each other for ownership of the land or the other resources so bountiful on this earth.

So this amazing substance—this manna—rains down on the people. And it tasted like wafers of honey or some say it tasted like anything you wanted it to taste like. And the only condition was that the people had to eat each portion on the day it appeared. They couldn't hoard it. And on the sixth day a double portion came so that on the Sabbath, when there was no manna to gather, there was no need to gather it. This continued for forty years.

This text teaches us about Shabbat as a spiritual practice. Forty years of living with trust that each day you will receive the manna might truly transform the fearfulness of slavery into the steadfastness needed for freedom. The Sabbath comes in the manna story as a special case of living with an open heart in the midst of not knowing. The Sabbath is a defragmentation practice. Can we take a day off and not be too worried that things won't get done? Will we be too stressed to simply allow what is to be for one day? What could we let go of for a day? Using money? Driving? E-mail? Which of our innumerable daily habits could we let go of? Could we allow creation to feed us for one day? What would that be like? Shabbat is manna practice. We intertwine one day of wilderness in a week of living in civilization. To what end? To the end of remembering our Source and our destiny; to the end of purifying our hearts of self-centered fear and greed; to the end of knowing sacred time; and to the end of feeling blessed.

Sabbath is the quintessential spiritual practice. We are practicing Sabbath in an hour of spiritual direction, in twenty minutes of meditation, or in a momentary pause before we say that hurtful word to our child. We have to suspend the habitual in order to see something new, in order to be released from our sleepwalking state of self-centered separation into a worldview of connection and wholeness.

Of course the Sabbath is political. It is a day of rest for everyone— boss, hired hand, even the animals. It leads to Sabbath economics, which mandates a sabbatical year for the land, giving the bondsmen a chance to be free, and a jubilee year for the remission of debts. The Sabbath commemorates creation and liberation. As we reflect on creation, we realize that we are connected to all other beings. Our freedom depends on everyone else's freedom; our well-being depends on our striving for the well-being of others.

We are living in a time that George Soros calls "market fundamentalism," which is itself a form of idolatry—taking a manmade artifact and endowing it with transcendental value. The market is a means, let's remember, not an end.[7] We know, too, that we cannot experience Shabbat and be fully present to creation unless we are free people. It is very hard to rest on Shabbat if certain conditions aren't fulfilled. If we are hungry or homeless or at war, it is very hard to relax into the spacious, trusting mind of Shabbat. Our spiritual practices inevitably challenge us to consider a range of social issues from resource allocation, employment, and education to war, foreign policy, and human rights.

What does this all tell us about faith? The transformation of materialism into spirituality is an act of faith. It is also the core of faith. It is our eternal struggle against idolatry and the embrace of the living and invisible God. When we face the power of desire and division—whether in our own bloated and frantic appetites or in the distorted priorities of our government—we are humbled. We look into the face of desire and see fear. We look into the face of our craving and see our loneliness and disconnection. We see exile. And it is faith that says, "Things can be different." It is faith that leads us to a vision as old as Isaiah and as new as today. It is faith that assures us that generosity and gratitude are not impossible dreams. They can be realized in any moment. It is faith that is a call to stillness and activism. Faith does not separate into *either/or*. Faith unifies in *both/and*. Faith moves us away from the thing orientation of materialism toward a sustaining wholeness that is able to love and to serve.

Do We Need Wars to Unite Us?

Whether it is $12,000 a second or $1 billion a week or the preponderance of each tax dollar, the sums being spent by the United States on war defy the imagination and indicate one thing: War is the number one priority of our nation. Since our enemy is not another nation but a vague, potent, and omnipresent threat, there is no promised end to this state of war. In order to sustain the massive effort and expenditure, certain ideas and viewpoints must be taught and learned. This is what King meant by militarism. When we wage war, we must experience extreme separation from the other. Our unity as a people emerges from our separation from our enemy. Chris Hedges, who served as a war correspondent for many years, wrote a book, called *War Is a Force That Gives Us Meaning,* on the phenomenon of militarism. He suggests that the cultivation of victimhood is essential fodder for any conflict.[8] In a state of war, "All cultured life," Hedges writes, "is directed to broadcast the injustices carried out against us." The self-absorption of victimhood engendering both fear and self-righteousness is profoundly alienating. One must separate oneself from the humanity of the enemy—the opposite of empathy—in order to be effective as a warrior. Hedges describes this well: "To achieve corporate action, self-awareness and especially self-criticism must be obliterated. We must be transformed into agents of a divinely inspired will, as defined by the state, just as those we fight must be transformed into the personification of unmitigated evil."[9]

How high the stakes of war have become in our time! The last century saw more bloodshed than any other in history and the new millennium has not gotten off to a good start. Now is the time to confront the human capacity for hatred, violence, and destruction with a new and greater urgency. Could there be a more important challenge?

Jews have spent nearly two millennia as bystanders to the militarism of the great powers. We have a literature and liturgy rich in images, teachings, prayers, practices, and promises of peace. Now we are back in the fray. As a people with a state, we are struggling with the boundaries between the excesses and distortions of militarism and the real needs of self-defense. We are grappling on the ground with the intricate balance of justice and peace. What are the spiritual tools that can guide us now? What can we learn about war when we go inside? What is the nature of hatred, anger, fear, and violence? What do we see when we have the opportunity to shine the light of awareness on this mind, the one right here, the only one we can truly know?

Just as the obliteration of awareness is the key to militarism, so the liberation of awareness is the source of a path to peace. How does this work? What happens when something arises that I do not like? It might be a person who just reminds me of an unpleasant moment in my past. It might be a character trait that I would prefer not to acknowledge was still part of my makeup, like envy or impatience. It might be the way things are going—the traffic, the weather, the lecture, the tone of voice or the whining of a coworker. It might be a physical sensation, a sense of inadequacy, or a fear. It might be anything at all that I do not like in the moment.

In the normal course of events when my capacity to pay attention is reduced, I will take this dislike personally. I will see the object of my dislike as a thing that I should get rid of because it is unpleasant. I might get angry or judgmental at someone else or myself as a way of pushing the irritant away. Or I might try to get distracted, get something to eat or drink or smoke or watch. I will see the object that is in my way, so to speak, as a solid and fixed entity separate from myself that I can vanquish in one way or another. I will see myself as a victim of this mood or situation.

Out of a Narrow Place

One primary purpose of spiritual practices, including spiritual direction, is the expansion of awareness. We observe this in Jewish prayer. Rabbi Michael Strassfeld translates the Hebrew word *shevach* (praise) as "expansion of consciousness." We say words of praise to God, not because God needs our praise, but because the very act of praising opens our perspective, like the wide-angle lens on our camera. Our all-important sense of self becomes smaller. We lighten up. This is tremendously helpful.

In embodied spiritual practices, like yoga, one experiences the body lengthening, making more room between the vertebrae, the literal growing of the physical container of consciousness. Tension is contracted energy in the muscles and tissues of the body. When that tension is released, the vital energies of the body—fluids and breath—are free to flow and fully enliven the whole of one's being. A flexible, supple spine facilitates clearer thinking and acting.

In spiritual direction, consciousness shifts because of the intention we bring to the meeting. Seeker and guide agree that the time together will be dedicated to a greater vision, a deeper, clearer understanding. Each partner yields control to something greater than himself or herself. That greatness is itself in the process of emerging. Often this is called seeing from the perspective of God or Spirit. In the act of holy listening, in Hebrew *Shema Yisrael,* self-preoccupation is transfigured into identification with the greater unity of being, which we may call God.

When we engage in spiritual practice (whether it is spiritual direction, meditation, or prayer), we learn to pay attention to the content of our minds. We learn to notice what happens when we struggle. We notice how when something unpleasant arises and we are afraid or angry, we can bring our attention to the energy moving in our bodies. We can become aware of the stories we are rehearsing in our minds, the views, prejudices, and stereotypes that we tell ourselves. We develop a steadiness of mind that witnesses without judging. Awareness illumines these thought patterns. We notice, too, that when we struggle to stop feeling a certain way, we tend to lock in that feeling. Let's say I am hurt by something someone says. If I start to tell a story about how bad that person is or how I am always getting hurt or how I am overly sensitive or this person is overly mean, I will stay stuck and in pain. If, however, I shift my attention to the energy of hurt arising and watch it move through my system, I will be freer to determine what would be a wise response rather than a reflexive and possibly hostile reaction.

Developing awareness expands my choices. If I am less certain of what is true, I am more open to new ways of seeing, thinking, and acting. Spiritual practices aim to teach us—body, heart, and mind—to see movement, dynamism, possibility, and energy instead of static concepts. Awareness reveals interconnection and continuous change. It touches the realm of unity and nonseparation and has the power to heal division and abate struggle. It discloses the illusion of any form of absolute or inert view of reality. It reveals to us the kind of thinking that induces violence and builds the myths that lead to hatred and finally to war.

I worked with a young man in spiritual direction who easily flew into a rage when he was displeased with what was going on. We sat together and I invited him to feel his rage. (At another time I might have suggested that he allow God to be present in his anger.) He was willing to stop and direct his gaze to the rage. My role was to provide safety and companionship. He knew I would not judge him or reject him because of these emotions. He could feel how much pain he was in. The story that was fueling his anger loosened its grip on his mind. He saw the energy of hatred move through his body and grow smaller. He was free in that moment to think clearly about what had happened and to respond in a thoughtful and measured way. He had avoided war.

Of course, war cannot be stopped by spiritual practice alone. However, each person's consciousness impacts the collective consciousness. Our becoming more able to live in peace in our own minds can be part of the collective effort to dismantle militarism as the habitual reaction to conflict in our world. Abraham Joshua Heschel speaks of this hope when he writes: "Prayer takes the mind out of the narrowness of self-interest, and enables us to see the world in the mirror of the holy.... However, prayer is no panacea, no substitute for action. It is, rather, like a beam thrown from a flashlight before us into the darkness. It is in the light that we who grope, stumble, and climb, discover where we stand, what surrounds us, and the course, which we should choose. Prayer makes visible the right, and reveals what is hampering and false."[10]

Liberating Our Energy

Spiritual practices of meditation, prayer, yoga, contemplative study, and spiritual direction promote the expansion of love, abundance, and unity. Wars are fought over perceived scarcity and the threat to one's security, prosperity, or self-image. Humanity is already facing the prospect of resource depletion in land, water, oil, essential minerals, and timber. The human toll will be immeasurable if we rely on war as *the* mode of settling disputes. Reason calls for the establishment of a global system of resource conservation and collaboration.[11] This approach seems to me to be the communal manifestation of our inner work.

The call to develop alternative energy is a serious alternative to militarism. It should not be confined to one nation. It needs to be international. The sun, like the earth, is no one's possession. As the child of one of the early astronauts said to her father when she saw the picture of the earth from space: "Daddy, who drew the lines [on the globe]?" It is not surprising that energy is central to both inner and outer work. It is not surprising that a willingness to stimulate global creativity and cooperation around energy is one way of working toward peace.

How do we connect all this with faith? Faith is commitment to practice. It is the willingness to sit with the painful and the uncomfortable without running away or lashing out. Faith is being willing to not know. Faith is not the opposite of doubt but rather the opposite of being absolutely certain. Certainty closes us off and faith opens us up. Faith requires strength. Faith is not afraid to fail and not afraid to appear weak. But it is not easy to reach by oneself. That is why we need teachers, models, and communities to support us as we grope our way into faith. Faith is breathing into the back of the body, a leaning into the whole that is greater than the sum of its parts. Faith is falling down and getting up again and again and again. Faith is not worrying so much about how silly you look or how smart you sound. Faith is realizing that you are not the only one who is suffering or confused. Faith is the willingness to seek new ways that have never been tried before because we know that violence really has not made things better. Faith is the choice of life, creativity, and possibility. Certainty is the choice of hatred, violence, and war. How certain do you have to be to use a nuclear weapon?

Jonathan Sacks has a beautiful statement in his book, *Dignity of Difference,* about Jewish suffering and the tears that are written into the very fabric of Jewish memory. He asks: "How can I let go of that pain when it is written into my very soul?" And he answers himself: "And yet I must. For the sake of my children and theirs, not yet born. I cannot build their future on the hatreds of the past, nor can I teach them to love God more by loving people less.... The duty I owe my ancestors who died because of their faith is to build a world in which people no longer die because of their faith. I honour the past not by repeating it but by learning from it ... by refusing to add pain to pain, grief to grief. That is why we must answer hatred with love, violence with peace, resentment with generosity of spirit and conflict with reconciliation."[12] This is faith.

Seeing God's Image in One Who Is Not in Our Image

The third of King's "giant triplets" is racism. Racism shares with militarism and materialism a "thing" rather than a "person" orientation.

It is both the product and the creator of division and separation. When we speak of racism, we include other forms of oppression as well, such as classism, sexism, homophobia, and anti-Semitism. All these structures of thought, speech, and behavior diminish human dignity. They also diminish God's image, since, as we learn in Genesis, every human being is created in the Divine likeness, and is endowed with infinite value. Rabbi Sacks speaks to this moment in history. He calls for a paradigm shift through which we can be enlarged, not threatened, "by the presence of others who think, act and interpret reality in ways radically different than our own." He goes on to say: "The challenge to the religious imagination is to see God's image in one who is not in our image. That is the converse of tribalism. But it is also something other than universalism. It takes difference seriously."[13]

How does racism grow in the mind? When we sit quietly, even for a few minutes, we notice how busy the mind is. We notice how the mind makes up things. It doesn't like not to know. The mind likes to make sense of things and put things together. It prefers any explanation to being uncertain. How quickly does your mind jump to conclusions when you are waiting for a friend who is late? Or when someone doesn't return an e-mail or a phone call? Or when someone criticizes you for something? Of course, stories are essential. We exist through our narratives in many ways. And stories help us understand things so that we can take effective action when, for example, a doctor gives us a diagnosis of a particular illness and we then can find the right treatment. The problem is that stories, like names and labels, can also imprison us. We tend to think that we are our thoughts. We are in love with the way we see things. We are sure it must be the truth.

Enchanted by Our Own Thoughts

An example of how we tend to get entranced by the names we give to reality was the reaction when the Old Man in the Mountain collapsed. The Old Man was a rock formation in the White Mountains of New Hampshire that was beloved by many and even graced the New Hampshire license plate and New Hampshire state quarter. There was quite a debate about whether or not to try and rebuild it, and the site where it had once been became a memorial. People left flowers and even notes saying, "We will miss you." The human mind works like that. We think we see things and then, when they are no more, we grieve their loss.

This tendency of mind allows for the growth of the great myths of separation. Often tales that disdain the other are systematically taught because they serve the needs of those in power. Pharaoh tells the Egyptians that the Hebrews are a dangerous people; therefore, they must be taken under the control of the state. The Exodus narrative is a paradigmatic story of racism and oppression.

The moment-to-moment power of awareness is the beginning of liberation—whether it is personal or political. The bedrock of our spiritual practice is our ability to see how our minds construct reality, erecting snares designed to keep us safe, snares that we fall into again and again. This point is illustrated in Martin Buber's *Tales of the Hasidim:* "Rabbi Rafael of Bershad, the favorite disciple of Rabbi Pinhas told: 'On the first day of Hanukkah, I complained to my teacher that in adversity it is very difficult to retain perfect faith in the belief that God provides for every human being. It actually seems as if God were hiding....' The rabbi replied, 'It ceases to be a hiding, if you know it is a hiding.'"[14] A young woman in spiritual direction is telling me about her fears. She is recounting the way she constructs stories that then frighten her. She recounts the stories. They are scary, and it is also clear that they have no basis in fact. There is space. We have agreed to allow the sweet air of God's love and truth to fill this small room for this brief hour. She laughs. I laugh. We see through the illusion. It is actually funny that the imagination is so fertile. It is clear to her that the stories are a chimera. The only things that are real between us are the almost audible sound of two hearts beating, the lilt of our laughter, and the sense of God's loving presence in our lives. God is out of hiding.

Together and alone, we practice seeing how fluid reality is. We practice seeing how easy it is to make a box around something, anything—a physical sensation and call it a pain, or a series of thoughts and call it a view or an opinion. We see how easy it is to ascribe blame and judgment and how quick we are to generalize about people we do not know. I am sitting at a meeting where everyone around the room takes a turn reading. When it comes to Phil's turn, I notice how I bristle and contract. He is a middle-aged man who does not read well. He mispronounces many words and doesn't ever seem to recognize punctuation. I become impatient and judgmental when he reads. I begin to suffer. I become aware of my thought patterns—"We shouldn't let him read. He is wasting our time. Why doesn't he just pass when his turn comes around?"

I know I have separated. I know that he is diminished in my eyes because of my judgments. I invite God into this moment. I recognize that there is some space between my thoughts and feelings, and my awareness. I relax. I let go. I am able to see Phil's sweetness, his beautiful eyes, his bravery, his dignity, his radiant soul. I have returned from exile. God is no longer hiding.

Our spiritual practices bring us out of exile. They expand our options and release us from the safety of our delusions. They necessarily undermine our views and prejudices. We simply can't take them at face value. We know how unreliable the mind is. We know how dynamic every category is. We are not prepared to stop investigating for ourselves the ever-alive flow of life. For one who is in a more awakened state of consciousness, every encounter is new; every person is utterly unique. Life is more risky on this edge of existence but every meeting is filled with an infinity of possibility rather than prejudgments of racism and other forms of oppression.

Religion as Verb Not Noun

Imam Feisal Abdul Rauf, leader of a mosque a few blocks from Ground Zero in New York City, has written a book called *What's Right with Islam*. In it he cites the late professor Wilfred Cantwell Smith of Harvard's Center for the Study of World Religions, who challenged the way we use the term *religion*. "As Professor Smith liked to say, Judaism, Islam and Christianity are in reality verbs, not nouns."[15] Semitic languages like Arabic and Hebrew are built around verbs, or dynamic actions, in contrast to Greek and Indo-European languages, which gave the noun—the object—much higher status. The use of terms such as *Judaism, Islam,* and *Christianity* to refer to systems of observance and beliefs did not really appear until modern times, and Rauf summarizes the implications of this shift: "… religions, which once referred to acting piously, became known instead as an identity. Religion changed from something you *did* into something that you *were*. Instead of you owning your religion (as an act that you do) and being responsible for your religion (your acts of religiosity), you instead belonged to your religion; it became something that owns you."[16]

If we could speak to each other across our differences about what we *do* and why, not who we *are,* the conversation would really shift. We would not have to defend the structures that define who we are. We would not have to hold up the Old Man in the Mountain. We could speak from the heart of our understanding of the spiritual enterprise, about our values and commitments, the narratives, practices, ceremonies, teachings, models that support those values. We could ask each other: What are you trying to achieve as religious people for your own souls, the community, and the world? We could turn inside first and then turn to each other and ask: What are the obstacles to realizing your intentions? What separates you from yourself, each other, and us? What are temptations that lead you astray? How do you let go of ego, pride, and fear? How do you work with the tendencies of the mind to become enchanted by their own fabrications? What really hurts you? What do you truly love? What are your dreams? What are your nightmares? We might sit together as seekers of the One—each with the treasures of our ancestors and each wanting to find a path to heal and help. We would need to be willing to allow a lot of silence to surround us. We would need to be willing to really be humble, rather than recite verses that praise humility. Confronted by globalization, we come to realize that one cannot fully understand and appreciate one's own faith until one knows another and one must truly know one's own faith in order to know another. In this process we begin to liberate the universal spiritual virtues of reverence, restraint, humility, prophetic vision, compassion, and justice from the deep wellsprings of wisdom and experience.

In Genesis 12:2, God calls Abram and says: "I will make of you a great nation and I will bless you and will make your name great. I will bless those who bless you and I will curse those who curse you. All the families of the earth will find blessing in you." These words indicate that the personal spiritual journey of Abram—that ultimately became the source of three religious civilizations—was intended for the blessing of all the earth. It is the journey of the soul—personal, private, quiet, and deep—and it is the service of the community of all who dwell together on this fragile and sublime earth. These twin tasks are truly one.

And this is our faith. We need to keep seeing where we are blind, and we cannot see that alone. We must join with others who can give eyes to our blindness as we give ears to their deafness. One stops and is quiet for a while to begin to see with new eyes. But one is not meant to withdraw into solitude or to retire into the stillness. Shabbat is one day out of seven. There is work to be done. Our faith brings us out of Shabbat into the week. And our faith takes us back to the rest of Shabbat. Our faith brings us out of our interior into connection and sends us back into our interior. Our faith brings us out of our comfort zone and into the conversation with someone who is hurting in ways we must understand and it can be frightening. Our faith lets someone else see that we are hurting in ways we hope they will understand. We are called out again and again *"Lech lecha"* (God's first words to Abram)—"Go out and go into yourself," meaning go into yourself by going out and go out with the wisdom you receive by going into yourself.

Replacing Both/And for Either/Or

I have a young friend, Jane, who is very bright, and filled with a great desire to make the world better. She is a graduate student, and the more she learns about the giant triplets of materialism, militarism, and racism, the angrier she gets. She has suffered a lot in a painful and deprived childhood. She has been introduced to various spiritual practices and comes back frequently to the same question: "How can I act for justice when I am practically consumed by my anger at the corrupt systems of power, and how can I allow myself to be spiritual if that means acceptance? I don't want to accept and I don't want to burn out. Help!"

"What are our choices, Jane?" I said, while moving my left hand to one side of the dining room table and my right hand to the other side. "On this side, you have a spirituality that says everything is fine as long as I am fine. As long as I take care of myself and can be peaceful, I do not need to engage with the rest of the world. This can't be right. It doesn't see the truth of interconnection. It is self-centered and weak. On the other side we are called to right every injustice and are overwhelmed by hatred at the powers arrayed against us. There is no respite, or relief. It is impossible to carry the burden. So," I said, bringing my hands together, "we have to do both. We have to do the work of justice and remember that it is not all up to us. Look at Abraham and Moses, who carried promises given by something beyond their comprehension that would not be realized in their lifetimes or, perhaps, ever. They still carried the promise and we have that promise today. We act, but we remember it is not just up to us. We act but we are cognizant of our limitations because we exist in a context that is so much more vast, free, and completely loving than anything we can know."

My hands were together on the table. Palm to palm. I was reminded of the first time in the Bible that the word *emunah* appears in Exodus 17:12. *Emunah* is usually translated as "faith" but it can also mean trust, truthfulness, faithfulness, security, and stability. In this verse, *emunah* means "steady." Moses is leading the Israelites in battle shortly after leaving Egypt. He is God's servant and it is really God doing the work, but Moses has to keep his hands up. Moses' hands get tired. So, he sits down on a stone and then Aaron and Hur, one on each side, support his hands and his hands are steady *(emunah)* until the sun sets.

At first I thought that this story would be a perfect ending for these ruminations. On a second reading I was taken aback by the fact that I was drawing spiritual imagery from the battlefield. In truth, the Bible is filled with scenes of battle and can be read to prove that God is on our side—whatever side that is. In my view, each of our traditions must confront the imagery of war in our sacred texts and recognize the dangers, in our nuclear age, of reading these texts literally. The battles are less about us against them; they are more about how we embrace life itself. And, that is a real struggle. We know how hard it is to remain steady in the face of suffering and what it takes to see through the corruptions of militarism, materialism, and racism as they permeate our minds and our culture. We know how the inside and the outside reinforce each other. We understand how the distortions of racism and materialism lead to militarism and how each is entwined with the other. How challenging it is to truly disengage the old when the new is scarcely born!

This is a story of faith. As we peel away the layers of dead skin and lifeless form of the giant triplets that Rev. King thundered against, we see revealed the unity that we come from and the harmony that we are. Sure, we are easily tired. It is simply too hard to keep our hands up all the time. So, we rely on each other for the steadiness we need, the *emunah*. We hold each other's hands. This, in fact, is the center of the practice of spiritual direction in my understanding. It is the act of forming sacred community. And we begin to open circles: circles of contemplation, circles of silence and circles of song, circles of action, circles of justice and law, circles of truth, circles of faith, circles of memory and imagination, circles of kindness, circles of love—ever-widening and including neighboring circles into the great circle of the One.

Notes

1. Mordecai Kaplan, *The Future of the American Jew* (New York: Reconstructionist Press, 1981), 256.
2. Jonathan Sacks, *The Dignity of Difference: How to Avoid the Clash of Civilizations* (New York: Continuum, 2002), 172.
3. Abraham Joshua Heschel and Morton Leifman, *Ineffable Name of God: Poems* (New York: Continuum, 2004), 7.
4. Beatrice Bruteau, *Radical Optimism: Practical Spirituality in an Uncertain World* (New York: Crossroads, 1996), 63.
5. Michael Shellenberger and Ted Norhaus, "The Death of Environmentalism: Global Warming Politics in a Post-Environmental World," Hawaii: Environmental Grantmakers Association Conference, October 2004.
6. Sacks, *Dignity of Difference*, 76.
7. Ibid., 159.
8. Chris Hedges, *War Is a Force that Gives Us Meaning* (New York: Anchor Books, 2003), 24.
9. Ibid., 74.
10. Abraham Joshua Heschel, *Quest for God: Studies in Prayer and Symbolism* (New York: Crossroads, 1987), 7–8.
11. Michael Klare, *Resource Wars: The New Landscape of Global Conflict* (New York: Metropolitan Books, 2001), 226.
12. Sacks, *Dignity of Difference*, 190.
13. Ibid., 23, 60.
14. Martin Buber, *Tales of the Hasidim: The Early Masters* (New York: Schocken Books, 1991), 122.
15. Imam Feisal Abdul Rauf, *What's Right with Islam: A New Vision for Muslims and the West* (HarperSanFrancisco, 2004), 115.
16. Ibid., p. 115.

Suggested Readings

Gottlieb, Roger. *Joining Hands: Politics and Religion Together for Social Change.* Cambridge: Westview Press, 2002.

Hanh, Thich Nhat. *Creating True Peace: Ending Violence in Yourself, Your Family, Your Community, and the World.* New York: Free Press, 2003.

Matt, Daniel C. *The Essential Kabbalah: The Heart of Jewish Mysticism.* New York: HarperCollins, 1994.

Thurman, Howard. *The Search for Common Ground: An Inquiry into the Basis of Man's Experience of Community.* Richmond, IN: Friends United Press, 1973.

Wallis, Jim. *God's Politics: Why the Right Gets It Wrong and the Left Doesn't Get It.* HarperSanFrancisco, 2005.

Rabbi Sheila Peltz Weinberg serves as outreach director of the Institute for Jewish Spirituality. A pioneer in the field of Jewish mindfulness meditation, she is the author of several essays on Jewish feminism and spirituality and was a contributor to the Reconstructionist prayer book, *Kol Haneshama.*

Chavurat Ruach (A Fellowship of Spirit): Community for Spiritual Direction

Ann Kline

> If I am not for me, who will be?
> If I am for myself alone, what am I?
> If not now, when?
>
> HILLEL (*PIRKE AVOT* 1:12)

While Hillel did not realize it, he was talking about the experience of spiritual direction—the claim and expression of our spiritual yearning—as it happens in a group. In group spiritual direction we come with our own seeking, our own desire to deepen our connection with the One that is the Source of our being. There we find others sharing the same sense of "something more" being possible in this enterprise called living. In being present with others in that shared desire to deepen our awareness of God, however we name that sense of the transcendent—Truth, Reality, Love—we experience ourselves in a deeper way, inseparable from that which we seek. Together we hold ourselves true to our purpose, to love and to serve this Truth in the whole of our lives.

Spiritual direction in a group is a unique process, distinct from one-to-one spiritual direction, in that it provides for a broader experience of interconnection and community. There are many different ways groups can come together around their spiritual desire: for example, to explore different prayer forms, to meditate, or for text study. Group spiritual direction is a kind of text study, but the text is the Torah of our lives. In group spiritual direction, we are standing together again at Sinai, each experiencing the living word of God as it is revealed uniquely within us. The deeper stirrings and invitations inherent in daily life, and our response to them, are the black fire of God's urgings against the white fire of our being. Just as text study can be prayer, so is the way we listen to the undercurrent of holiness within

154

the context of our lives. We do not come together to understand; we come together to touch the mystery of our lives. As Lawrence Kushner has recognized, "Spiritual awareness is born of encounters with the mystery."[1]

Just as at Sinai, even though we hear the voice of God in our lives each in our own way, in group spiritual direction we know ourselves to be joined together in one united expression of God's continual creative longing. Just as at Sinai, it is that awareness that gives rise to spiritual community. In group direction we can sense the immediacy of God's presence asking us, If not now, when? The moment for opening to God is now. The group supports our willingness to be present to God, now, in the midst of, and at the core of, our lives.

Overview of the Group Process

"[W]hen two persons meet and exchange words of Torah, the Shechinah hovers over them, as it is written, 'Then those who fear the Lord conversed with one another; the Lord listened and heard....'" (*Pirke Avot* 3:3).

Group spiritual direction is a small group of people meeting regularly to share their desire for God in the whole of their lives. The practice, like all spiritual direction, is at heart a prayer practice. Prayer is the willingness to open oneself up to a sense of deeper reality, what Abraham Joshua Heschel called the "holy dimension of living." In group spiritual direction, people come to together to look at their lives through that lens, and to do so in an atmosphere of trust and reverence
Several elements nurture that atmosphere:

Self-revelation. The content of group spiritual direction is each person's life and one's unique response to God, or the Holy, within our experiences. Our joys, sorrows, questions, celebrations, choices, and challenges in life can all provide the text that focuses the group prayer. Therefore, people must be willing to share the particulars of their lives, most particularly their inner lives, with others.

Mutuality. Everyone engaged in a spiritual direction group must be willing to open their experience to the others in the group.

Sharing exposes the heart of each person to the other. That is very risky business. For each person to feel safe enough to open up his fears and desires, every other person must be willing to take the same risk. This means that each person in the group participates in the sharing equally.

Shared ownership. Shared ownership also nourishes trust. While groups may have designated "facilitators," those people serve to support the group rather than "lead" it in the usual sense of that word. All group members must offer their willingness to assume equal responsibility for the whole of the group if the true potential of group direction is to be realized. This means praying for others outside group meetings and contacting members when they miss a meeting. It also means taking equal part in holding the sacred space of the meeting through one's own sense of "prayerful presence"—openness to deeper listening—within the group. Each person in the group is a vital component of the group.

Commitment. Commitment to the group means showing up and taking our places in the circle. It means holding each other to our intention in being together—not to knowing each other better but to knowing God, holiness, in our lives better. It means holding the group in our hearts between the times of meeting, understanding that the prayer that is shared in the group is part of God's ongoing revelation from Sinai. We are always there standing and receiving the expression of God's covenant with life. Most of all, however, it means commitment to one's own spiritual life and desire for a deeper relationship with the Divine in daily living. This means that participants in a group are committed to some sort of intentional spiritual journey and honor that in ways outside the group.

Confidentiality. What happens in a group stays in a group. We might find ourselves in groups with people whom we see in other parts of our lives. When we meet in the grocery store or at the Oneg, we do not go up to a group member and ask about the family situation they shared at the last group meeting. We do not call a group member between meetings to share the great insight or inspiration we had for that person. We trust that what happened in the time of the group was enough. We recognize that prayer, ours and God's, is active and present and ongoing in the times between meetings. Often a person has moved on so that what has become so vital to us, the receiver of the story, is no longer as vital to the person who shared it. We trust that God is at work in each person's life and that she will find what she needs through God's activity more than our own.

Structure. Spiritual direction happens in a group the same way that it does in one-to-one direction relationships: People meet to listen together to where they are experiencing the opportunity and invitation to deepen their heart's response to life, to make choices that reflect their desire for alignment with their sense of God, and to appreciate the "holy dimension" of living. While that kind of radical listening can happen anywhere, anytime, it helps to have a structure that supports it.

There are many different group direction formats. What follows is a basic structure for group spiritual direction adapted from the guidelines developed by Rose Mary Dougherty and the Shalem Institute for Spiritual Formation:

A group of three to five people meet regularly (typically, once a month).

Each group meeting is facilitated, either by a specifically designated person who serves the group by modeling the process and keeping the group on track (but does not share his own journey) or by each member of the group rotating the responsibility.

Each meeting begins with a time of silence (as much as twenty to thirty minutes), which can include a brief reading or *niggun* to nurture the interior stillness or *dumiya.*

The facilitator moves the group through the process, and begins by inviting a person to share what she wants to look at from her life experience.

After the sharing, two to three minutes of silence ensue.

The facilitator opens the group to assisting the presenter's reflection on the undercurrents of meaning and mystery in what has been shared.

After this reflection, the facilitator returns the group to silence for two to three minutes.

The process of sharing, silence, reflection, silence, is repeated until everyone has shared.

Time is reserved at the end for the group to reflect on how it has felt to be together as a group and where it may have strayed from its intention to listen to God together.

A group of three to five people will take two to two and a half hours for this process. (With this process, a group of six could choose to meet every two weeks, with three people sharing each time so that everyone shared in each month.)

This is one model, the one with which I have particular experience. Like sonatas, there can be many variations within the form. Just as there may be different ways of approaching spiritual direction, there may be many ways to approach a group process for spiritual direction. I use the model that I know as a base for examining, and developing an appreciation for, the elements that make for group spiritual direction.

Understanding the Group Process

"Torah is acquired through [many] virtues: ... By attentiveness ... by a perceptive heart, by patience.... By knowing one's place...." (*Pirke Avot* 6:6).

Everyone engaged in group spiritual direction plays several roles. All are "presenters," bringing their life stories into the shared light of the group. Each person is a spiritual "director," listening to God with and for the presenters. Each person shares responsibility for honoring the intention of the group in coming together, keeping the group "on track" and contributing to the group an open, prayerful willingness to listen. The most significant role, however is God's, the *Ruach HaKadosh*, the One in whose presence the group meets and who is the true facilitator of the group process. In this section we will look at each of these roles in more detail.

The Role of Silence

By attentiveness ...

Spiritual direction is a prayer practice, a place of encounter and response, not so much to each other as to the divine Source within us.
When we share, we are not just speaking the bare facts of our lives. We
are also listening to and for the undercurrents of meaning, mystery,
possibility, and wonder in our experiences. We are listening for the
ways we are being asked to choose life in its deepest sense in the whole
of our choices.

Silence encourages that listening. It is silence that enables the
group to receive what the presenter shares, to listen *with* rather than to
the presenter. Silence helps to free us from the need to know, understand, explain, interpret, or rewrite another person's text. Silence en-
genders appreciation and opens us all to the deeper movement of grace
in our lives. When God spoke from Sinai, God's first utterance was
aleph, a silent letter.[2] If we are to stand together as witnesses to each
other's Sinai, we must listen together from the same place of receiving
from the silence.

Silence, in effect, makes room for God to be a more conscious
presence in the circle. The opening silence before the group sharing begins helps to orient us toward the deeper Source of our being, the unit-
ing creative Breath of Life. To step into that silence is to immerse, as in
a *mikvah,* in a sense of wordless creative potential, always active and
present. It is to remember who we are and who God is and why we are
coming together in the group. We come together not to hear what we
each have to say about our particular situation or experience, but to
hear what God has to say, how God is speaking to us through the circumstances and choices of our lives. Mahatma Gandhi said, "God
speaks to us all the time, but we do not know how to listen."[3] Silence
teaches us how to listen.

Silence also teaches us how to speak. The group process is a
rhythm of silence and speaking, like the breath flowing in and out of
our body. Before we speak, whether to share our own experience or to
reflect on another's, we listen in the silence. From this *makom,* this
grounding in silence, we enter the *Makom,* the presence of God. This
is the stance of Elijah at the cave, finding God in the "still, small
voice" (I Kings 19:12)—literally, "the thin voice of silence." From that

place of deeper listening, not to each other but to God, the Holy, the deeper inner wisdom of our souls, we find the words that encourage each other to claim the truth and mystery of our lives.

What "trains" us to be spiritual companions for each other? The silence.

The Role of the Group

By a perceptive heart ...

The role of the group in spiritual direction is similar to that of an individual spiritual director: to pray with and for the person who is receiving the spiritual direction. In a group, each person will be both the "directee" and a "director" at different times in the process. The group listens with, not for, the person presenting her story. Often when we listen, we sit outside a person's story, as distant observers or from the other side of the desk. From that vantage point, we comment, interpret, and advise, telling another what we think is really happening, telling our story in response, or trying to "help" a person figure out what to do. Group spiritual direction, however, does not allow us to be observers. Rather it situates us right there next to the presenter.

> A man was on his knees, searching for something.
> A neighbor came along and saw him, so he asked:
> What are you searching for?
> My key. I've lost it.
> His neighbor got on his knees, too, and both men
>   searched for the lost key.
> After a while, the neighbor asked: Where did you
>   lose it?
> At home.
> Then why are you searching for it here?
> Because the light is better here![4]

This story illustrates how we can frustrate our own desire to enter more deeply into our experiences by staying where it is most comfortable and familiar. Sometimes it takes another, looking *with* us rather than *for* us, to ask the right questions and to help us to see where the key to our experience lies—often in the darkness.

Like the neighbor in the story, the group is there to be with the presenter, helping in the search by steering from the literal events (the light in the above story) to the truth that may have no "light," or easy answers, but may well be found in the very darkness of not knowing. From that willingness to share in another's journey, the group supports the presenter by helping her to identify her own questions and honor the mystery, wonder, and potential of her own experience. The group affirms the presence of God by being present to God with the presenter. It leaves the presenter free for her own discernment.

This is a counterinitiative way of being and it can take some time for a group to feel comfortable with such a stance. The group may find it hard to let go of needing to "do" something with what a particular presenter has shared. It is challenging to ask questions that invite reflection rather than to provide answers to another, or to ask questions to which we do not know the answers—especially when those questions may serve to guide a person deeper into a desert rather than out of it. We cling to our roles of helping, caring, experienced, competent, knowledgeable people. To step out of our "self" and enter into the experience of another, just as it is, places us in the same stance of unknowing. This takes faith: that God is, indeed, active and present and the true guide.

It also takes faith and the willingness to accept that the desire for God is in itself an answer. Our desire for God, the deepest wisdom of our hearts, can be so obvious it takes another to help us see it. Our role in the group is to be true lights for each other, to help us find and touch the desire for God that we may have lost amid life's clutter of experiences. In *Pirke Avot*, it is written,

> When one gives priority to reverence over wisdom, his wisdom will be enduring; but when one gives priority to wisdom over reverence, his wisdom will not be enduring (*Pirke Avot* 3:11).

Reverence is the freedom to appreciate without the need for understanding. The primary role of the group is, in effect, to reverence.

The Role of the Facilitator

By knowing one's place …

The dictionary defines the word *facilitate* as "to make easier or less difficult" *(New American College Dictionary).* The facilitator of a spiritual direction group helps to make the process of listening to God together less difficult. The facilitator may be a person who assists the group, but is not a participant in the sense of sharing his own faith journey (but does share in all other parts of the process). Or she may be a participant in a group where each person takes turns serving in that role. If a primary *middah* (soul quality) of a group is faith, a key *middah* of a facilitator is humility.

The facilitator is not the group's spiritual director. She holds the space for the prayer of the group. The facilitator does this by providing the structure that allows for listening and sharing without the facilitator taking center stage. It also asks that the facilitator take her place in the group by modeling the process of group spiritual direction through honoring silence and participating as a "prayerful presence," offering the kind of responses that invite the presenter's reflection and deepening appreciation of his experience.

One does not need to be a trained spiritual director to facilitate a group. What one needs, however, is an appreciation of spiritual direction that comes from personal experience of that process, and the experience of one's own attentiveness to God in prayer. From this inner sense, a facilitator can draw the willingness to hold a group true to its intention in coming together: to honor and support each person's desire for a deeper relationship with God or the Holy. This may mean calling a group back into silence if it has strayed too far into problem solving or analysis. It may require encouraging the group to use the processing time at the end of the meeting to take an honest accounting of how the group worked together. One does not learn how to do this the same way one learns how to sew a button. Primarily, we are taught how to do this through our own listening to God in the group.

A facilitator (who serves only this role in the group) is someone who is working himself out of a job by promoting shared ownership of the group. This is done by having the group take responsibility for such things as contacting absent members, designing its own "rituals" for closing group meetings, and addressing problems or issues that arise in the group by drawing on members' own sense of discernment. The facilitator serves the group by progressively stepping out of the way and then taking her place within a circle of equals.

Time

By patience ...

A group needs enough time to get comfortable with a process that may at first feel like a pair of tight new shoes or an oversized coat with too-long sleeves. Spiritual direction groups are not "drop-in" groups. It is helpful to designate a specific period of time for the span of a beginning group (at least six to nine months, meeting once a month). Whatever the length of commitment, it needs to be long enough for a participant to get a sense of the process and for trust to develop within the group. (It is also helpful to plan the meetings so that the first few are closer together, so that people can develop familiarity with process.)

Meeting once a month can be a challenge. People may feel that there is not enough connection with the group when the meetings are so infrequent. It is important to remember that the focus of the group is not the group; it is the desire for God. The group process supports a person's ongoing spiritual practice and living out of his intention to become close to God. The time *between* meetings is where the spiritual "work" occurs. While it does not necessarily need to be a month, enough time needs to elapse between meetings for life and practice to happen. People may also find that it is hard to keep focused on the group in the times between meetings. Praying for members of the group between meetings is an essential part of the process.

At the end of a "season" of group spiritual direction, a person may look back and say, Nothing happened. Just as Moses could not see God until after God had passed and Moses could see where God had been, it takes patience to stay faithful to a process long enough to be able to look back and see what may (or may not) have been happening. If one is looking for evidence of change, growth, or transformation as a result of the group, a person may be disappointed. If a person looks back at her time in the group and says, "My intention to live my life in relationship with God has deepened and I felt supported in that by the group," then the group fulfilled its hope in coming together.

There is no optimum length of time for a group to stay together; it lasts as long as it lasts. I have known groups that have stayed together for over fifteen years. That is wonderful, as long as the group continues to feel that the process supports their desire for God and has not become an end in itself.

Starting a Spiritual Direction Group

"When a person's good deeds exceed his wisdom, his wisdom will be enduring...." (*Pirke Avot* 3:11).

What does it take to start a spiritual direction group (besides *chutzpah*)? Once a person has found within himself and the community a nudge to start a spiritual direction group, how does he go about putting it into place?

Telling people about group spiritual direction. Finding the right language for speaking to others about spiritual direction, including spiritual direction in a group, is more art than science. It comes from knowing your audience and knowing yourself. There is no right or wrong way to phrase things, or particular words or phrases that will somehow "open the door" or flip the switch of understanding for others. As at Sinai, people will hear the same words differently. It is important to find your own language, your own words—to be communicating your own truth. This can only happen through your own experience. To talk about group spiritual direction, you need to have experienced it—or at least to have experienced spiritual direction and have some sense of what the process might be like in a group. Once you have your own experience, your words will have the clarity and authority of truth. Those who understand and are moved by what you share are the ones whom you are called to be with in this *avodah* (service).

Determining who participates. Not everyone will be "right" for group spiritual direction; by that I mean looking for a community to hold them to their intention to explore the holy dimension of their lives. People seek out groups for many reasons. For group spiritual direction, people must want God to be the primary focus of their concern, rather than the focus being therapy, healing, support through crisis, or simply the companionship of friends.

Selection works best when it is self-selection. In congregational settings, where people expect to be able to sign up for whatever the synagogue offers, it may be difficult to refuse someone the opportunity to participate in a group. It is important to provide enough information for people to understand what the process entails: silence, self-revelation, silence, listening to others, prayer, silence. Hearing the specifics of the group process may be enough for people to know whether or not it is the kind of experience they are looking for. One way to ensure that people understand the process is to talk to them personally. I asked everyone registering for group spiritual direction to call me so that I could provide more information than what I could include in a flyer. In some settings it may be appropriate to ask people to answer a few written questions that encourage them to reflect on what draws them to group spiritual direction. Another way to help people understand the process of group spiritual direction and encourage self-selection is by providing an initial orientation, discussed below.

Another concern in group participation is the freedom that the group feels in being together. The makeup of particular groups can affect a person's willingness to entrust the group with the details of her spiritual life. Particularly in congregational settings, people may know each other in parts of their life outside the group. The question to ask of potential participants is this: Would you feel free *enough* to share the particulars of your spiritual journey within this group? What is essential is enough of a sense of openness within the group that a person feels he can meaningfully participate, even if there are some aspects of his life that he may choose not to share with the group.

Providing orientation. The process of group spiritual direction may be quite unfamiliar to people. People may be curious, but not know whether it is the kind of experience they are looking for. Before launching into a group, it is good to provide a foundation of understanding and commitment through an orientation. This orientation should include an introduction to the underpinnings of group spiritual direction: silence, prayerful listening, and the nature of spiritual direction and spiritual community. It should also include some opportunity to experience the kind of self-disclosure that group spiritual direction asks of participants before people are asked if they would like to commit to a group.

Providing an encouraging environment. Pay attention to where group spiritual direction will take place. When I started my first group, we initially met in a classroom with fluorescent lights and chairs that had immovable desks attached. Needless to say, the environment did not promote freedom for intimacy and interior reflection. (We quickly moved to the rabbi's office.) People have met in libraries, chapels, and in people's homes. I know of groups that have met on the *bimah*. Sitting in front of the open ark can be a powerful reminder of the group's intention, and in whose Presence they are sitting. The Torah's detailed instructions for construction of the *mishkan* (Tent of Meeting) itself is a testament to the significance of creating sacred space. Sacred space is created by the trust and prayer of the people who occupy it. Attention to details such as lighting, beauty, symbolism, and comfort are, as Torah shows, part of the prayer.

Taking the first step. You do not need to have all the answers, to see each step before you take the first one. Like anything else, putting together a spiritual direction group is itself a prayer practice, a journey of faith. Lighten up, and let yourself learn in the process. You do not need to be perfect, only faithful to your deep inner listening. If not now, when?

Is It Jewish? (Why Group Spiritual Direction?)

"Do not look at the flask but at its contents" (*Pirke Avot* 4:27).

I confess that it is with some trepidation that I approach the question, What makes group spiritual direction "Jewish"? A better question in my mind is this: "What does group spiritual direction have to offer the Jewish community? In other words, why do it?"

Arthur Green, in his book *These Are the Words*, defines a *chavurah* as "a group of friends joined together for the purpose of spiritual quest."[5]

As he notes, such groups have existed throughout Jewish history. In *Pirke Avot*, we are told that one of the forty-eight virtues for a life of Torah is to "cleave to colleagues." Jewish life is nothing if not communal.

There is a Hasidic story about a young man who goes to visit his rebbe. They sit together before the fire as the young man describes how sad he feels. "Rebbe, I cannot find my way to God." As they talk, the fire begins to die out. The rebbe says nothing but starts poking at the fire, gathering the scattered embers together. As the embers meet and touch, their inner heat is released and the fire blazes again, renewed.

We need each other to keep the flame burning. I have been both saddened and inspired by the stories I have heard again and again from men and women of various ages, backgrounds, and denominations. With variations, the punch line of the stories is always the same: I do not feel that I can talk with other Jews about my personal experience of God. This was my experience. I needed to go outside the Jewish community to find those with whom I could share my life at the heart level. I, too, have felt the loss of not being able to connect my deepest experiences to the community that supported and sustained my Jewish life intellectually, ritually, and culturally. Group spiritual direction is part of my—and many others'—response to that (ever-closing) gap in Jewish experience. With the same creativity, spiritual longing, and inspiration that has embroidered Jewish life for centuries, people are borrowing old and developing new "tents of meeting" where people can come together and share the way they hear God speaking *to them* from Sinai.

Group spiritual direction is not a substitute for Jewish community; it is a potential way to deepen the experience of Jewish community. Participants in spiritual direction groups have shared how seeing members of their group scattered throughout a crowded sanctuary grounded them in a sense of worship deeper than the liturgy alone. They became, in a sense, a living liturgy that helped to breath life into what had been inert words on the prayer book's pages.

Spiritual community is not a group of people who share a theology, a tradition, or a practice. It is a group of people with whom the "desire for God comes alive" and who support one another in honoring that desire.[6] A spiritual direction group can be such a community for each other, if (to paraphrase Parker Palmer) what they want is not community but God.[7] In opening up our desire for God with others who share that same desire, we can find a sense of community that extends beyond the time of the meeting, beyond the particulars of the group members, beyond the walls of a synagogue or even the confines of any particular faith tradition. This sense of community draws us into the larger sense of connectedness, where all life becomes *chavurat ruach*, a community of spirit. This is the true gift and blessing of group spiritual direction, that we can come to know in a deeper, stronger, more committed way that we all are truly one. The deeper we know this through the prayer and listening that happens within a group, the more we begin to live the whole of our lives aligned with that truth.

The experience of group spiritual direction threads us together with God in a tapestry of interwoven meaning. Our lives become joined through our shared desire to live from the ground of that meaning. As our lives are strengthened by that shared fabric of hope and possibility, we are part of bringing the torn pieces of this world together in new patterns of healing and renewal.

Notes

With deep gratitude to Sandy Jardine, for her support with this chapter and for the "perceptive heart" (and mind) that she brings to this *avodah*.

1. See Lawrence Kushner, *Honey from the Rock* (Woodstock, VT: Jewish Lights Publishing, 1995), 34.
2. See Lawrence Kushner, *The River of Light: Jewish Mystical Awareness* (Woodstock, VT: Jewish Lights Publishing, 1993), 59.
3. See R. K. Prabhu, ed., *Truth Is God* (Ahmedabad, India: Navajivan Publishing, 1955), 34.
4. Midrash. From Rabbi Chaim Stern, *Day by Day: Reflections on the Themes of the Torah from Literature, Philosophy, and Religious Thought* (Boston: Beacon Press, 1998), 136.
5. Arthur Green, *These Are the Words: A Vocabulary of Jewish Spiritual Life* (Woodstock, VT: Jewish Lights Publishing, 2000), 154.
6. Rose Mary Dougherty, *Group Spiritual Direction: Community for Discernment* (Mahwah, NJ: Paulist Press, 1995), 13.
7. Parker Palmer, as quoted in *Plain Living: A Quaker Guide to Simplicty* (Sorin Books, 2001), 143.

Ann Kline has helped pioneer the introduction of group spiritual direction to the Jewish community. A teacher, writer, and spiritual guide, she is a cofounder of Lev Tahor: A Center for Jewish Soulwork in the Washington, D.C., area.

The Jewish Path

Spiritual Transformation: A Psychospiritual Perspective on Jewish Narratives of Journey

Barbara Eve Breitman

Rabbi Bunam used to tell the story of Rabbi Eisik, son of Rabbi Yekel in Cracow. After many years of poverty that had never shaken his faith in God, he dreamed that someone bade him look for a treasure in Prague, under the bridge that leads to the king's palace. When the dream recurred a third time, Rabbi Eisik prepared for the journey and set out for Prague. But the bridge was guarded day and night and he did not dare to start digging. Nevertheless, he went to the bridge every morning and kept walking around until evening. Finally the captain of the guards, who had been watching him, asked in a kindly way whether he was looking for something or waiting for somebody. Rabbi Eisik told him of the dream that had brought him here from a faraway country. The captain laughed: "And so to please the dream, you poor fellow wore out your shoes to come here! As for having faith in dreams, if I had such faith, I would have gotten going when a dream once told me to go to Cracow and dig for treasure under the stove in the room of a Jew—Eisik, son of Yekel, that was the name! I can just imagine what it would be like, how I should have to try every house over there, where one-half of the Jews are named Eisik and the other half Yekel." Rabbi Eisik bowed, traveled home, dug up the treasure from under the stove and built the House of Prayer that is called "Reb Eisik's Shul."[1]

This simple Hasidic tale captures many of the paradoxes of the spiritual path: There is both nowhere to go and someplace to "get to." The treasure is very close, "in our mouths and in our hearts" (paraphrase of Deuteronomy 31:14), yet we often have to undertake long, arduous journeys to discover it is at home. Like Reb Eisik, who circled the bridge every day, we need spiritual practice, liturgy, and ritual to help us attune to the rhythms of day and night, the seasons of nature and of our individual and communal lives. Ultimately, however, the encounter with Divine Presence comes as an unexpected gift. Though the treasure is always accessible, it seems hidden as if guarded by a sentinel who keeps it secret. Though the treasure is within the self, the key to finding it lies in the discovery of a dream we share with others. Though the treasure is of immense value and belongs to everyone, only some choose to search for it. While the willingness to embark on the journey and to exert the effort "to wear out one's shoes" may be necessary for spiritual growth, ultimately, transformation does not come through strenuous acts of will but through subtle, effortless, and often surprising shifts in awareness. Though we set out on the journey motivated to find the treasure for ourselves, after discovering it, we want to share the riches, to serve and guide others, as Reb Eisik builds a House of Prayer for his community.

In the Jewish textual tradition, the dynamics of the spiritual life are often described, as in this tale, through narratives of journey. Jewish Sages and mystics are famously unsystematic in describing discrete stages of spiritual development. Nevertheless, the tradition is rich with wisdom about spiritual transformation. This essay is an attempt to see what can be learned from the master story of the Bible, the Exodus journey, about the process of spiritual transformation. It is also an initial effort to articulate how Jewish narratives and imagery can be used to describe the dynamics of spiritual growth by looking at the many stories and metaphors of journey that suffuse the tradition. I focus here on the Exodus narrative because, as our master story, it has so deeply shaped Jewish self-understanding. But there are many more narratives of journey to be found in the Bible, in Midrash, in the Zohar and Hasidic tales; there are many journey metaphors in the kabbalistic and Hasidic traditions.

Before turning to the Exodus narrative, however, there are two paradoxes hinted at in this deceptively simple story about Reb Eisik that I want to explore more fully.

Willfulness and Willingness: Ego and Soul

The first paradox has to do with the tension or balance between effort and effortlessness, willfulness and willingness that we can see illustrated in Reb Eisik's journey. Willfulness involves the assertion of the individual to achieve personal mastery and autonomy; it involves the effort to plan, strategize, even attempt to control, and negotiate the complexities of living through assertion of the individual will over the mystery of life. Willingness involves a receptive attitude or stance, a letting-go, an opening to the Mystery, or, in the words of the Kotzker Rebbe, "letting God in." Rather than striving for the autonomy of the separate self, an attitude of willingness enables us to realize our rootedness in God and relatedness in creation.[2]

As God's covenantal partners, Jews are commanded to actively, purposefully, and intentionally engage in specific observances, practices, and behaviors to foster ethical and spiritual growth. As Max Kadushin has said: "*kedushah* [holiness] is now something that must be achieved through effortful personal conduct...."[3] Therefore, a stance of willingness may seem uncomfortable, even un-Jewish. However, as the above Hasidic tale illustrates, Jewish mystics were aware that experiences of spiritual transformation often come unbidden, by surprise, after human beings exert effort to do what they can do, but then are mysteriously "met" and taken the rest of the way through no exertion of their own. Jewish Sages often describe this experience as a form of reciprocity within the Divine-human relationship.

This is perhaps no more poignantly expressed than when Sages describe the process of *teshuvah,* or repentance: A king had a son who had gone astray from his father and took a journey of a hundred days. His friends said to the young man, "Return to your father." He said, "I cannot." Then his father sent word to say, "Return as far as you can, and I will come to you the rest of the way." So God says, "Return to me and I will return to you" (*Pesikta Rabbati* 184b). Using a metaphor of journey, the Sages point to the subtle dance between the soul and God: A human being must begin the process of *teshuvah* by making a decision to repent, by searching his soul, making amends, seeking forgiveness. Often, however, human effort is insufficient to create a full healing of heart, a transformation of self or other. Time and again, people have the experience of doing what they can do, then letting go. And somehow, after letting go, they are changed.

Nowhere to Go and Someplace to "Get To"

The second paradox is that there is both nowhere to go and someplace to get to. Despite differences in belief, theology, and approach, theorists of spiritual development seem to agree that growth involves an ongoing process of self-transcendence: a continual de-centering of the previous center of self and a movement toward identification with increasingly expanded senses of self, until one comes to experience the individual self or soul as rooted in God or bound up in an "inescapable network of mutuality."[4] Using a distinctively Western philosophic and theistic vocabulary, James Fowler, the pioneer of faith development theory, eloquently describes a point toward which self-transcendence can lead:

> a relinquishing of self in the ground of Being, a kind of reversal of figure and ground in which the person of faith now participates, albeit as a finite creature, in a kind of identification with God's ways of knowing and valuing other creatures ... This kind of transvaluation gives rise to strategies of non-violent opposition to entrenched evil in hearts and societies. It gives rise to activist efforts, through pouring out of the self, to transform present social conditions in the direction of God's commonwealth of love and justice.[5]

Sylvia Boorstein, a Jewish teacher of mindfulness practice and author of the book *Don't Just Do Something, Sit There,* is quite adamant that though the path may be "just sitting," there *is* someplace to get to. In her keynote address to the Jewish Meditation Conference in 1999, Sylvia recounted the story of how a pugnacious journalist had questioned her about the desired effects of spiritual practice. Sylvia fairly exploded with incredulity: "What is supposed to *happen*? What is supposed to happen is that when we see clearly the confusion in our own minds and the suffering it causes around us, and the confusion in other people's minds and the suffering that that causes, and when at the same time we see the extraordinariness of life itself and the marvelousness of life constantly recreating itself and the amazing way that the cosmos is held together in this lawful way and everything conditions everything else and impacts everything else and every single thing we do matters and makes a difference; when we see clearly we are really inspired to engage ourselves in compassionate and helpful responses to the whole world. That's what's supposed to happen!" Sylvia concludes: "Jewishly, we say it: *"Taher libenu l'avdecha b'emet*—purify our hearts so that we can truly serve."[6]

Abraham Joshua Heschel uses the language of holiness to describe the process of self-transcendence at the heart of Judaism:

> What I have learned from Jewish life is that if a man is not more than human, then he is less than human…. Israel was made to be a "holy people." This is the essence of its dignity and … of its merit. Judaism is … kinship with ultimate reality…. A sense of contact with the ultimate dawns upon most people when their self-reliance is swept away by violent misery. Judaism is the attempt to instill in us that sense as an everyday awareness. It leads us to regard injustice as a metaphysical calamity, to sense the divine significance of human happiness, to keep slightly above the twilight of the self, ready to perceive the constant dawn in our souls.[7]

The idea that there is "someplace to get to" raises questions about whether there is, indeed, a discernable process of change people undergo on the spiritual path. Many spiritual directors believe that developmental schemas that outline predictable and sequential stages of growth cannot account for the complex vicissitudes of human transformation, the unexpected shifts in awareness that suddenly transform people's lives, or the cultural differences between faith traditions. Nevertheless, I do believe spiritual directors need a vision of the direction in which we are headed, just as our ancestors wandered, not aimlessly, but toward the Promised Land. Though the Torah narrative is propelled forward by the promise of settling in the Land of Israel, the people who journey for forty years are left on the east bank of the Jordan, never able to enter the land of their yearning. The Torah seems to be saying: the journey itself *is* home, but a journey "with no direction home," will not lead us toward the Mystery we name God.

The Longer Way Around

The first question God addresses to humankind in Torah is *"Ayeka? Where are you?"* According to Reb Shneur Zalman of Liadi, God addresses this question to us every day. The question invites us to locate ourselves again and again on our journeys through time. It beckons us to a life of awareness and response. Yet, as we learn from the story of Eden, it is only too human to hide when so addressed. Much as we might wish it were otherwise, the spiritual path is not an easy or direct route, even when we cultivate attentiveness and commitment. There are ups and downs, tortuous twists and turns.

The road is a highly evocative image: " 'Here time ... pours into space and flows through it.... ' "[8] The road or path speaks of movement—through time and space, away from and toward. Always there are junctures, intersections, and turning points along the way."[9] While the journey is a universal metaphor, it has particular resonance for Jews. The Hebrew Bible is among the earliest human documents to describe spiritual transformation through narratives of journey. The very meaning of the word "Hebrew, *Ivri,*" in the Hebrew language is "one who journeys or passes over." The core biblical mythos of the Jewish people is the story of the Exodus and the wandering through the wilderness toward Sinai and the Promised Land. This metanarrative is presaged by the wanderings of the patriarchs and matriarchs of Genesis. The wisdom writings that form the last section of the Bible are rich with stories of famous journeyers, like Jonah, the unnamed lovers of Song of Songs, Ruth, and Naomi.

The story of the people who will eventually become God's covenantal partners begins with an invitation to journey into the unknown. After the flood, despairing of humanity as a whole, God turns to Abram, a single individual, and speaks these famous words: *"Lech lckha m'artzecha....*—Go forth from your native land, from your father's house to the land that I will show you" (Genesis 12:1). Unlike Adam and Eve who had to be cast out of Eden, or Noah who was forced by flood to board the ark, Abram willingly leaves what is familiar and follows God's call into the unknown. It seems to be precisely this willingness to let go of familiar or habitual forms of security and the illusion of control, to open to uncertainty that initiates the spiritual journey.

As God shall learn, such willingness is not an inherited trait. Generations later, Jacob's offspring settle and eventually become enslaved in Egypt. Unwilling to break his promise to Abraham, God must lead an entire nation out of slavery, despite their reluctance to leave. But miraculous liberation is not enough to prepare the Israelites to be covenantal partners. To accomplish such a profound transformation, God draws the people into a forty-year journey through the wilderness. In Exodus 13:17, we learn that God intentionally chose to lead the Israelites on a longer, more arduous route, though there was a shorter route available through the civilized land of the Philistines. This teaches that the longer way around, despite its disadvantages, was to be preferred.

The theologian Belden Lane asserts that much wisdom about the life of the spirit can be learned from God's preference for long journeys through fierce landscapes. The God of Sinai is a God who forces God's people into wild and wretched climes because this is where trust must be absolute; this is where surrender is learned; this is how the people come to understand who they are. "In stretching the self to its edges, the geography helps in forcing a breakthrough to something beyond all previously conceived limits of being." By journeying through the austere, unaccommodating landscapes of desert and mountain, human beings can experience the smallness of the self and the majesty of Being. Such "threatening places [are] a way of challenging the ego and leaving one at a loss for words. If we cannot know God's essence, we can stand in God's place."[10]

Like the journeys of our ancestors, the journeys of contemporary seekers also take the longer way around. Are there identifiable moments, movements, or stages through which the Israelites pass that could illumine our own journeys? Mindful of my earlier caveat, I would answer, yes. Interweaving our ancestors' story with vignettes from the lives of contemporary seekers, I hope to describe a process of spiritual transformation that emerges from the Torah narrative.

Exodus as Paradigm of Individual Transformation

Although the Exodus narrative describes a journey of national liberation, as the story is retold annually at the seder, the *Haggadah* (the traditional text read during the seder ritual) declares that it is incumbent on each Jew to look upon herself or himself as if she or he had come forth from Egypt. The Maggid of Koznitz, an early Hasidic master, taught that not only on Passover but each day Jews should look upon our lives as if God were helping to liberate us from Egypt.[11] It is possible, therefore, to read the Exodus story both for its powerful message of societal liberation and for wisdom about the individual spiritual journey. Within Judaism, individual spiritual transformation is ineluctably linked to social transformation. As I read the story of the Israelites' journey from being slaves to becoming a holy people, I see four phases that will be discussed below: Awakening: Responding to the Call; Strengthening through Doubts, Trials, and Signs; Deeper into the Wilderness; the *Mishkan*: Knowing God's Presence Dwells within Us and All around Us.

Awakening: Responding to the Call

"An angel of God appeared to him in a blazing fire out of a bush…. 'Moses! Moses!' 'Here I am' " (Exodus 2:5).

"Moses said to God, 'When I come to the Israelites and say to them, "The God of your fathers has sent me to you" and they ask me, "What is His name?" what shall I say to them?' And God said to Moses, 'Ehyeh asher Ehyeh.' He continued, 'This shall you say to the Israelites, "Ehyeh sent me to you"'" (Exodus 3:13–14).

Tradition tells us that as God addressed Moses out of a scraggly bush of desert tumbleweed, so a moment of illumination can come in the humblest of circumstances. According to the text, the name of God revealed to one being invited to journey is *"Ehyeh asher Ehyeh—I will be what I will be."* Often when God addresses characters directly in the Bible, the text records such moments as "calls from the future": Characters are beckoned to a distant time or place they cannot foresee, catalyzed to action as a destiny is revealed or a disaster foretold. Though we might read these passages as unique products of ancient prophetic imagination, contemporary people, as we shall see, have comparable experiences, though we rarely imagine them as invitations from the Mystery we name God.

For the Israelites, the awakening occurs after many years of enslavement, when their suffering has become intolerable. "A long time after, the king of Egypt died. The Israelites were groaning under the bondage and cried out; their cry for help from the bondage rose up to God. God heard their moaning, and God remembered His covenant with Abraham and Isaac and Jacob. God looked upon the Israelites, and God took knowledge of them" (Exodus 2:23–25). A *midrash* suggests that this was the first time the people petitioned God for relief. Previously, they had believed their enslavement to be the work of one man, trusting that when he died, they would be freed. However, when they saw that the new pharaoh effected no change in policy, their illusions were shattered. Crying out for help, the Israelites wake up.

Suddenly or gradually, a person can arrive at a turning point when everything known seems alien, when a previously comfortable way of being is experienced, perhaps for the first time consciously, as suffering. Sometimes the call is faint and comes as a gnawing sense of unrest. At other times, the call is a shofar blast, a shocking or disturbing change in circumstances, a sudden realization, an unexpected invitation, a shattering cry, or the wailing of another whose suffering we can no longer ignore. Awakening can be a "push" arising from circumstances we can no longer tolerate, or a "pull" summoning us to a new reality. A person may or may not have faith in God. What she recognizes is that life cannot go on as it has been going, or that something has happened that has changed her life forever.

This call can be alluring or terrifying. Numbness, illusion, complacency, or grim endurance is pierced. A person might suddenly acknowledge the entrapment of addiction, the desolation of a troubled or neglected marriage; a person might be shocked by the onset of illness, the loss of a job, or realize that she can no longer stay "in the closet" about a core aspect of self. When awakening comes as a diagnosis of serious illness, the illusion ruptured is the one most of us live with all the time: that our lives are permanent. We gaze into the void and see how little control we have over what matters most.

Rebbe Nachman of Breslov understood that the greatest enemy of the true seeker is the belief that one has finally arrived at a place of adequate understanding. "At such times the seeker must call out to God, hoping that his heart-rending cries will pierce the walls confining his mind.... " From such outcry, a new perspective can be born. Nachman, who "depicted spiritual growth as an ongoing chain made up of challenges, resolutions, and higher challenges," cautions that any form of complacency is a dangerous illusion from which we need to continually wakeup.[12]

But awakening does not come only through distress. Sometimes it comes as an exciting invitation to new life, to expanded creativity or work, to a new mission or sense of purpose; sometimes through encounters with other people, through exposure to new experience, through a dream; sometimes as a surprisingly welcome intrusion into a stable but humdrum life. Sometimes a vision of new possibility appears with clarity and sometimes with only a hint. Always, it will require a letting-go of old habits or familiar ways of being.

When Moses is addressed at the Burning Bush and told that he will be God's instrument for the Israelite people's liberation, he is a humble shepherd in Midian (Exodus 3). He is shocked by the divine announcement of his new role in history and cannot imagine how he will become the leader of a nation. A close reading of the text amplifies the call that Moses heard. As he approaches the bush, God commands Moses: *"Halom she-naalecha m'al raglecha ki hamakon asher atah omed alayv admat kodesh who,"* usually translated, "Remove your sandals from your feet because the place on which you stand is holy ground" (Exodus 3:5). This verse can also be understood as "You must step out of your old habits in order to stand on holy ground."[13] Though Moses cannot imagine what lies ahead, the language of the text hints at the future. In Hebrew, the word for *bush* is *"sne."* These are the same letters that make up the word *Sinai*. The revelation of the bush points Moses toward Sinai.

Contemporary Jews are not accustomed to thinking of God as calling us to "wake up" or pointing us toward the future. However, as people engage in the practice of spiritual direction, they begin to notice moments when the energy of life, love, creativity, or the call for justice seems to be drawing them forward with more intentionality than can be explained by the ongoing thrust of maturation or even self-willed moral conviction. People notice moments of alert recognition, intuition, or yearning; inner urgings that seem to be saying their life's purpose can only be fulfilled by making sometimes radical choices; people "hear" the cry of the wounded earth or the outcry of others whose suffering requires a response. People recognize opportunities, even demands to use their unique abilities, talents, and gifts in service to others. Upon reflection, people recognize treacherous junctures when they had to choose whether or not to proceed down a path that would lead to the deadening of self, creativity, authenticity, or integrity. We may not previously have thought of these as "callings" from God. These are moments in which we can hear ourselves being addressed: "I put before you [this day] life and death, the blessing and the curse. Choose Life—if you and your offspring would live … " (Deuteronomy 30:19). These are moments when the vital self or soul, understood within Judaism to be a spark of the Divine within each of us, is quickened to awareness.

> Rachel entered spiritual direction, saying, "I am here as a matter of life and death. I often feel anxious. I've been in therapy for years and it has been very helpful. But I cannot find peace. I don't believe in God. But I know I need something spiritual. If I don't pay attention to this feeling, I will die." After listening to Rachel pour out her heart, the spiritual director invited her into a moment of silence, simply to be aware of her breath. She emerged a few moments later in great distress. "I don't feel like I have a right to exist" and burst into tears. Although an accomplished person, Rachel had been raised by parents who admired only her achievements. She had become a talented "doer," motivated by success; but at midlife, she felt a gnawing emptiness inside. Rachel intuited that if she did not discover her connection with the Source of Life, her long-deadened spirit might actually die. As she stopped crying, Rachel was invited to go back into silence while the director "held" her prayerfully. After a while, Rachel emerged, calmer. She had found a place of inner stillness. The spiritual director encouraged Rachel to savor the palpable presence of stillness a few moments longer, to experience the difference between "being" and "doing."
>
> At the end of the session, the spiritual director wrote out the Hebrew letters for the ineffable name of God and showed Rachel the relationship between God's name and the verb *to be*. Rachel was amazed to learn that the God she had been taught to think of as "Lord" was actually the mysterious YHVH, a name that if pronounced, might sound more like breath than speech. Over the course of the next weeks, Rachel began a practice of sitting silently, breathing into her heart. She began to cultivate a deepened

interiority and to discover an inner stillness and peace she had not experienced before.

———————————

Joseph, a rabbi who had been in spiritual direction for several years, returned from a trip to Israel, saying, "I witnessed a group of Jewish Israeli and Muslim Palestinian children in dialogue, struggling through their grief and pain to understand each other, and also joyous to be playing and learning together. At that moment, I knew I could never turn back. I have ignored the call to work for peace in the past because it seemed overwhelming. But it is as if I felt personally addressed this time. I was filled with a sense of purpose and inspiration. I was also filled with dread at the possibility the war will go on endlessly. I was standing on holy ground and I could no longer ignore the call to work for peace. I am ready to say *Hineni.*"

Strengthening through Doubts, Trials, and Signs

"[The foremen of the Israelites] left Pharaoh's presence, and came upon Moses and Aaron standing in their path, and they said to them, 'May the Lord look upon you and punish you for making us loathsome to Pharaoh and his courtiers—putting a sword in their hands to slay us.' Then Moses returned to the Lord and said, 'Oh Lord, why did You bring harm upon this people? Why did You send me? Ever since I came to Pharaoh to speak Your name, he has dealt worse with this people, and still You have not delivered Your people' " (Exodus 5:20–23).

Hearing the call can be awesome and exhilarating, but it can also be terrifying. The status quo is disrupted. Rarely does one have sufficient faith in oneself or God to let go of stability or familiar identity and venture into the unknown. Faith grows by being tested over and over through trials, false starts, doubts, failures, and finding hope again.

This process is vividly illustrated in the story of the Exodus. Though they can no longer bear the oppression of slavery, the people require signs and miracles before risking liberation and the unknown (Exodus 4:30). Even after witnessing signs, their confidence is short-lived. When Pharaoh makes their work harder, the people complain bitterly (Exodus 5:19–23). God multiplies the signs and sends the plagues not only to frighten and weaken the Egyptians, but also to strengthen the Israelites' faith (Exodus 7ff). Not until they witness God's overwhelming power, in slaying the Egyptians' firstborn while shielding the Israelite children, are the slaves willing to venture out of Egypt (Exodus 14–15). And not until the miracle at the Red Sea does the people's newly found faith rise up as a "Song of Thanksgiving" to their Redeemer.

Even after their liberation, the people need evidence of God's steadfast presence and so a Pillar of Cloud by day and Fire by night appears to guide them. Sustained by manna, thirst quenched by miraculous waters, they continue to murmur about the Egyptian threat, complain about the absence of water and the lack of food. They defy God and challenge Moses. Just as the Israelites are, perhaps, on the brink of surmounting their inner demons, they are attacked by the Amalekites. Learning to work together, Moses, Aaron, Hur, Joshua, and the people find the strength to overwhelm this attack from without (17:8).

The plagues and miracles necessary to lure the Israelites away from Egypt and sustain them in the desert are powerful images that bespeak the enormity of what it takes for us to break through habit and repeatedly open ourselves up to the unknown. There is a well-known midrash that proclaims that the sea could not part until at least one person, Nachson, prince of the tribe of Judah, was willing to walk into the waters up to his nose. The midrash alludes to how death defying initial steps may seem.

It also captures symbolically the degree of threat perceived by the ego when a person is called to surrender to a power greater than itself, even when that power is Ultimate Being, God. Protecting and preserving the integrity and safety of the separate self are among the primary tasks of the ego. Therefore, people will almost automatically resist what is perceived to be the experience of self-annihilation necessary to draw closer to God. However, as an individual relaxes, lets go of this fear, and opens up to the Mystery, she can, like the Israelites, receive a first glimpse of revelation.

Standing at the foot of the mountain while Moses is on high, God speaks directly to the people. The mountain aflame and trembling, God thunders down the Ten Commandments. Its message lies at the heart of the covenantal relationship.

I am the Creator of all Life, known by My actions in history as One who liberates and frees human beings from falseness, idolatry, and oppression. As My covenantal partners, you must have ultimate reverence for life. You must choose always to embody that reverence in ethical behavior toward others. I give you a holy day each week, a time to pause and remember: The Source of all life alone deserves to be called God.

These ethical imperatives impel the Israelites to behave as if the other is as sacred as the self; behave with awareness that to harm the other is to harm the self. What is revealed are the bedrock principles of behavior required to preserve the Holy interconnectedness of all life.

Unfortunately, however, even this revelation does not necessarily clarify for individual seekers which path will be most life-serving at any particular juncture. People need to engage in an ongoing process of discernment. As spiritual directors, we can notice flashes of insight, moments when life is beckoning and inviting seekers into the fullness of themselves; we can notice resistances to awareness of and response to the calls people have discerned. But as we do, we must always honor the mystery that is transpiring between this unique soul and God. If we listen closely, we will be as surprised as he is by the unpredictable transformations that happen along the way.

> Not long after Joseph's trip to Israel, his adult daughter was diagnosed with a serious illness. This was an enormous blow, not only because of his fear for his daughter, but also because caring for her meant postponing once again his work for peace. Joseph wondered whether he would ever regain the sense of inspiration he'd felt in Israel, whether it had even been real. He was filled with doubt and fear. The spiritual director did not offer reassurance, but encouraged Joseph to continue to listen for how he was being called.
>
> After several months, Joseph revealed: "Through this ordeal, I've been cultivating the capacity to hold my center in the face of doubt, sustaining my daughter and myself through times of anger, fear and despair. I don't believe in a God who intended any of this, but before my daughter's illness, I didn't understand what parents go through who lose children. I had a commitment to peace, but not enough empathy to help me understand what people really ex-

perience when they lose beloveds to war and violence. Coping with my daughter's illness has deepened my empathy for everyone who loses a child. I believe it will help me hear the rage and fear of people on both sides of the conflict." After his daughter's health returned, Joseph realized his commitment to working for peace had been strengthened, not derailed.

Deeper into the Wilderness

"Then the Lord said to Moses, 'Set out from here, you and the people that you have brought up from the land of Egypt, to the land of which I swore to Abraham, Isaac, and Jacob.… I will send an angel before you … but I will not go in your midst, since you are a stiff-necked people, lest I destroy you on the way.' When the Israelites heard these harsh words, they went into mourning, and none put on his finery … and the Israelites remained stripped of their finery from Mt. Horeb on" (Exodus 33:1–3).

Even the overwhelming power of divine revelation is not enough to fully transform the people. If the Israelites are to be changed from slaves into a holy people, they must let go of previous ways of being; old identities must die away. They must face their true vulnerability and dependence on the Source of Life. They must confront their capacity for idolatry: the belief that any form of materialism can ever provide real security in the face of Life's mysteries. They must learn the difference between worshiping God's gifts and *Mekor HaChayyim,* the Source of Life itself. During the episode of the golden calf and the *teshuvah* that follows, the Israelites strip away idolatry and illusion and are transformed into more trustworthy covenantal partners.

The stripping away of old identities can happen through soul-searching and voluntary acts of *teshuvah*. It can also come through the path of silence and regular contemplative practice. For many people, however, it is the shattering wrought by trauma, loss, and grief that initiates the wilderness journey through which an old self dies. As people lose faith in God and in the meaning and purpose in life, they bring their desolation and sense of estrangement into spiritual direction.

When Laura's young husband died suddenly, she felt the fabric of her life viciously ripped to shreds. For months afterward, she roamed her empty house screaming, "Where are you? Where are you?" unable to believe that her husband was gone forever. Seeing the postman still delivering letters and the newspaperman still on the corner, she was enraged at God. "How can everyone else go on as if it is business as usual, when my life has been utterly shattered? There is no meaning in life, and no God."

Staring into the void, smashed by the implacable indifference of the universe, the one who grieves is forced to let go of the ego's most precious illusion: that the individual self is permanent and we are the center of the universe. Many people are overwhelmed by bitterness, fear, despair, or stagnation when this illusion dies. But the shattering of the illusion of the separate self can also serve as an opening to greater compassion and deepened empathy for the suffering of others. It is this opening of the self to the experience of the other that leads to self-transcendence and the intuition of the interconnectedness of all life.

During the initial days, weeks, months after significant loss, people are in so much personal distress that the spiritual director, like everyone else who cares and comforts, can only console them with compassion. But sometimes, as a seeker struggles to understand or encompass the experience of loss, he discovers one of the great mysteries of life: Loss and suffering can be powerful engines of spiritual growth precisely *because* grief destroys the ego's illusions of autonomy, dominance, and control. Those who are able to let an older version of self die, so a newly enlarged sense of self can emerge, undergo a profound transformation.

A teaching of the Maggid of Mezerich points to this mystery: "For in the case of an earthenware vessel, its breaking is its repairing [Shabbat 16a]. That is, man, who is an earthenware vessel made of shards of soil, is purified by his breaking—that is, the breaking of his heart; but it must be broken so that it is no longer fit for its original use."[14] When the heart breaks open, it can encompass more of the world within it, and a person can discover new meaning and purpose through serving a larger circle of life. Not every seeker will be able to open up to the experience of self-transcendence available during grief. But some will be able to. As spiritual directors, we must listen for the emergence of a larger narrative, the story of an expanding sense of self.

In the biblical narrative, the wilderness experience is envisioned as God's distance and absence. Moses leaves the people to commune alone with God at the summit of the mountain and the Israelites feel abandoned, by both Moses and God. They build the golden calf. When Moses discovers the people engaged in idolatry, he hurls the first set of Tablets at the foot of the mountain and they shatter against the rock. As punishment for their idolatry, God threatens the people with complete abandonment, "I will not go in your midst" (Exodus 33:3). It is this threat of utter abandonment that finally causes the Israelites to let go of the last remnants of their previous lives, rending their garments, stripping themselves of their finery, and repenting.

The narrative of the people's *teshuvah* is remarkable for its wisdom about how the felt experience of alternating periods of God's absence and God's presence catalyzes spiritual transformation. Moses pitches the Tent of Meeting at quite a distance from the encampment. When Moses goes out to the Tent, the people leave their dwellings and gaze after him. When Moses enters the Tent, the Cloud descends and the people bow (Exodus 33:7–11). No longer is the Pillar of Cloud immediately before them, as it had been at the start of their journey. Now they must pay close attention to when the Cloud descends and when it lifts. Repeatedly rising and bowing, sustaining their faith during God's absence and opening to the Presence when it can be apprehended, the Israelites begin to internalize their relationship with God. Through this process, they break open their hearts and learn to "let God in."

After the period of *teshuvah,* Moses ascends the mountain a second time and returns forty days later with the second set of Tablets. According to tradition, the day Moses reascends is the first day of Elul and the day he returns with the Tablets is the first Yom Kippur (Eliyahu Zuta 4:2). This association, of course, establishes a deep resonance between this stage of the people's journey through the wilderness and the practice of *teshuvah.*

According to many Sages, *teshuvah* is *the* engine of spiritual transformation. *Teshuvah* involves soul-searching, repentance, and reorienting ourselves to be in harmony with the Web of Life. According to the Rabbis, *teshuvah* is one of the seven things established before the creation of the world and the only one that requires human participation for its ongoing existence. *Teshuvah* is a building block of creation, woven into the very fabric of the universe. "Great is *teshuvah* for it brings healing to the whole world, and an individual who repents is forgiven and the whole world is forgiven" (*Yoma* 86a). The Rabbis state over and again that God prefers the repentant sinner to one who has not sinned at all: "Even the utterly righteous cannot reach the place occupied by those who have repented" (*Berachot* 34b). How can that be? Wouldn't God prefer the utterly righteous?

The wisdom of the tradition is that it is precisely through acknowledging our true vulnerability and imperfection that we can draw closer to each other and to God. Looking honestly at how we have harmed others, asking for forgiveness, and making restitution requires breaking open the small self and enlarging the capacity for empathy; *teshuvah* requires self-transcendence, opening the self to include the other.

> For many years Rebecca had been involved in a Twelve-Step program. Recovery eventually motivated her to seek spiritual community with Jews. She'd had an adult Bat Mitzvah and entered spiritual direction to continue deepening her relationship with God and Judaism. After several months, as her conversations with God became more regular, Rebecca realized that she had been in denial about her husband Jonathan's sexual addiction, his compulsive use of Internet pornography, and his demanding sexual interactions with her. She decided to confront him about his behavior and seek therapy for herself. Her husband did not respond well to the confrontation. Gradually, Rebecca realized that she might have to leave her marriage. But the prospect of divorce and single parenting was terrifying.
>
> Rebecca was a physical therapist who hadn't worked in years. Her children were still young. As her husband's refusal to face his addiction persisted, Rebecca broke her heart open to God: "Is this really what you want? I waited so long for a partner and spent so many years alone. Have I come so far, become a happy wife and mother after years, only to leave it all behind?" She raged at God and was filled with dread.
>
> Then on Simchat Torah, Rebecca heard the words of the Book of Joshua read: "Be strong and resolute; do not be terrified or dismayed, for I, your God, will be with you wherever you go" (Joshua 1:9). This became Rebecca's prayer as she separated from her husband.
>
> Shocked by Rebecca's leaving, her husband entered therapy and a recovery program.

During the separation, Rebecca struggled inwardly and financially. She found part-time work and rediscovered how much she loved being a physical therapist. As her husband's recovery deepened, he realized he could no longer work at a job he found deadening to his spirit. He longed to change careers. As Rebecca saw her husband recovering from addiction and coming back to life, she realized she also had *teshuvah* to do. She had refused to heed her husband's cries of distress about work. Wanting to remain at home with her children, she had not paid attention to what this arrangement was costing him. With deepened faith in herself and God, Rebecca made a remarkable decision. She would support her husband so he could change careers. "I cannot choose Life for myself, without choosing Life for him as well. If this relationship is a sacred covenant, I must care about his relationship with God as well as my own."

———————————

Responding to a call to engage in interfaith work, after his daughter's recovery, Joseph attended a workshop of Jews, Christians, and Muslims in New York. His desire was to meet Muslims from the Middle East because his primary concern was the conflict between Israel and the Palestinians. Though he did not say so, he was disappointed when all the Muslims were African-Americans, Nation of Islam. Joseph was stung by the words of an African-American imam, who expressed much hurt and rage that, since 9/11, there were many more white Jews and Christians seeking to dialogue with Muslims than in the past, but that when African-American Muslims came to the table, they were not considered "real Muslims." Joseph saw himself in the mirror held up by the imam, who labeled this attitude for what it was: American racism. Joseph saw how his ethnocentric viewpoint had blinded him. Although his desire to work for peace between Israelis and Palestinians remained strong, Joseph saw the need for *teshuvah*. His heart expanded to begin to encompass the reality of African-American Muslims: how 9/11 had suddenly brought them to the table with white people who would not have been sitting with them before, bringing their ongoing struggles with poverty and racism into greater visibility. Joseph saw clearly that the world in which he needed to struggle for peace was already in the room.

Rav Abraham Isaac Kook, the modern mystic and chief rabbi of Palestine prior to the establishment of the State of Israel, understood *teshuvah* to be far more than individual efforts to redress particular transgressions. For Rav Kook, individual acts of *teshuvah* enable human beings to participate in a great cosmic drama. He saw Life as seeking ever-higher levels of development, and individual acts of *teshuvah* sustained by a vast interconnected web of life:

> Penitence *(teshuvah)* emerges from the depths of being, from such great depths in which the individual stands not as a separate entity, but rather as a continuation of the vastness of universal existence. The desire for penitence is related to the universal will.... From the moment the mighty stream of the universal will for life turns toward the good, many forces within the whole of existence are stirred to disclose the good and to bestow good to all.... In the great channel in which the life-sustaining force flows, there is revealed the unitary source of all existence, and in the hovering life-serving spirit of penitence all things are renewed.... Penitence is inspired by the yearning for all existence to be better, purer, more vigorous and on a higher plane than it is. Within this yearning is a hidden life-force for overcoming every factor that limits and weakens existence.[15]

The Mishkan: *Knowing God's Presence Dwells within Us and All around Us*

"When Moses finished the work, the Cloud covered the Tent of Meeting, and the Presence of the Lord filled the Tabernacle. Moses could not enter the Tent of Meeting because the Presence filled the tabernacle. When the Cloud lifted from the Tabernacle, the Israelites would set out on their various journeys, but if the Cloud did not lift, they would not set out until such time as it did lift. For over the Tabernacle a Cloud of the Lord rested by day, and Fire would appear in it by night, in the view of all the house of Israel throughout their journeys" (Exodus 40:34–36).

The day after Moses returns with the second set of Tablets, God reinstates the command to build the *Mishkan,* the Tabernacle or portable sanctuary in which God's Presence will dwell. All the Israelites contribute to this effort, either through material donations or labor as craftspeople. Only Moses does not participate, until the very end. By this point in the narrative, Moses knows that a sanctuary for God on earth can only be built by a people who both work together intelligently and stand in direct relationship to the Holy, without an intermediary. The sanctuary is built by willing hearts, people employing their skills and giving freely of themselves (Exodus 25:2).

Recapping and tracing the path of the gold from the moment of leaving Egypt to the building of the *Mishkan* highlights the psychospiritual journey the people have thus far undergone: As the final plague against the Egyptians approached, God advised "the people to borrow, each man from his neighbor and each woman from hers, objects of gold and silver" (Exodus 11:2) to take on their journey. Some of this gold was used to build the golden calf (Exodus 32:3). When Moses destroyed the calf, he ground the idol into bits, mixed the gold dust with water, and forced all the idolaters to drink the potion (Exodus 32:20). Finally, the remaining gold is transfigured a third time when Bezalel, the sculptor, fashions moldings, overlays, rings, fire pans, lamps, and other furnishings to adorn the portable *Mishkan* that holds the Tablets of the Covenant (Exodus 35:4–35).

Just as God instructed the Israelites to stock up on gold before heading into the wilderness, we need strength for the challenges and risks involved in embarking on a spiritual journey that will be fraught with doubts, pitfalls, and obstacles. But our individual gifts and resources are to be used in service to God. If we believe they are purely for individual benefit; if we worship the work of our hands, or use the fruits of success purely for selfish ends, we engage in idolatry, just as the precious metal is used to construct the golden calf. As flawed human beings, we will inevitably fall into such temptations. Engaging in *teshuvah,* we acknowledge and repent for our capacity to harm others, just as the Israelites must drink the crushed gold. Through this process, by integrating the shadow, we are transformed. Then our individual gifts, talents, abilities, and strengths may be brought into divine service as we become vessels in which Holy Presence can dwell, as the Israelites fashion the *Mishkan* from the remaining gold.

Moses writes the second set of Tablets in his own hand, perhaps indicating that, as a leader, he now experiences God within himself, no longer solely as a force intervening from outside and beyond. Both the shattered Tablets and the whole Tablets are preserved by the Israelites and placed in the Ark of the Covenant. Holding symbols of both wholeness and shatteredness, the *Mishkan* becomes a manifestation of God's Presence dwelling *b'tocham,* literally in their midst.

> Following his interfaith work in the United States, Joseph did indeed enlist in the Compassionate Listening project in Israel. In a letter to his spiritual director, written while in Israel, he wrote: "I am on the verge of tears every day. Sometimes filled with hope and joy, sometimes with agony, but always with the sense of being more alive than I have ever been. I have had to listen to words that hurt. A member of Hamas described how he watched his father being killed by Israelis when he was a child and how he had been tortured in jail. An elderly Israeli couple, survivors of the Holocaust, were members of the Irgun in 1948 and now are in favor of a two-state solution. My teacher says, 'Some people think because there is a conflict, they have to choose sides. We are trying to say there is a third way. There's a way to stand for both sides.' Everybody I speak to sees themselves as victims. Though this kind of person-to-person diplomacy is incredibly slow, it is very deep. I believe that the heart of peace is hearing how violence springs from the roots of suffering. If we will ever have peace, we must have compassion, even for our enemies."

The Pillar of Cloud or Fire that at an earlier stage had guided the people through the wilderness, is no longer in the lead. The Luminous Presence descends only to tell the people when it is time to rest (Numbers 9:15ff). When it lifts, the people discern on their own in which direction to journey, guided by the Indwelling Presence. Moses can no longer enter the Tent as he had in the past because "the Presence of the Lord filled the Tabernacle" (Exodus 40:35). Although Moses continues as their leader, both he and the people now understand that the Presence dwells within them and all around them.

Living daily with awareness of God's presence can be nourishing and joyful. We are aware of the miracles of life. We can celebrate; we are able to give and receive love; to be grateful for creativity, for our temporary health, for opportunities to work and share our gifts with others. We have peace of mind. But sometimes, people who felt closest to God in the wilderness find the experience of simply dwelling in God's presence disorienting and confusing. They may interpret the comfort of this phase as distance from God, although they are happy and content in their lives.

> Batya was a survivor of childhood sexual abuse who struggled through years of deep darkness. Her most profound experiences of holiness had been discovering God in the darkness. After years of heartbreak, she found a fitting partner, a man who loved her and whom she loved deeply. In group spiritual direction, she admitted with confusion: "I am lonely for God. I felt closer to God when I was suffering. What face of God is available at times of abundance? I don't know. I should feel gratitude. Actually, I do feel grateful, but I am still dissatisfied because I don't feel close to God." As the group reflected with Batya, she came to a new realization: "If I stop looking so hard, I'll notice more. Sitting across the table from Jacob in the morning, drinking coffee, his sweet face and the aroma of coffee at dawn, planting in our garden. I haven't had a garden in years. Putting in the bulbs, smelling the earth. This is a time for me to find God through physicality, through my body."

This is a time when the ego is comfortable; life feels good. Spiritual directors need to support people to savor the holiness of these times, to deepen their connection with the Holy through the small and large wonders of embodied life. This is a time to deepen and expand one's capacity for love and creativity. The primary danger for one on the spiritual journey is complacency, to stop listening to how we are being called. If we keep listening, we will hear *"Ayeka?"* and perhaps be called to journey again into the unknown. After the dedication of the *Mishkan* and the observance of the second Passover, the Israelites resume their pilgrimage toward Holy Land.

In Conclusion

As the Israelites continue on their journey toward the Promised Land, there is more backsliding. As in Torah, so in life, challenges and temptations continue; even after undergoing profound spiritual transformations, people can slip into idolatry, small-mindedness, and unconsciousness. Personal suffering and the experience of multiple losses can become overwhelming, and the sense of self can constrict rather than expand. We do not make the journey—down into slavery, up from slavery, and through the wilderness to revelation, eventually learning to dwell in God's presence—once and for all. Both on our individual life journeys and on our journeys through the annual cycles of holidays, we make this journey many, many times.

The Hasidic rebbes coined the phrase *"yeridah l'zorech aliyah—* descent for the sake of ascent." As Degel Mahaneh Efrayim says: "... no one can stand on one rung forever, but everyone is constantly going up and down. The descent is necessary in order to ascend.... [T]he very descent by which one becomes stuck to the ground is itself a ladder by which one can reach a higher rung than before...."[16] This powerful metaphor of journey recognizes that the process of spiritual growth and transformation involves repeated journeys of descent into darkness and through wilderness as we continually integrate more and more of what lies hidden both within our own psyches and within the world; then bringing it into consciousness and the light of day. There are many more narratives and metaphors of journey to explore within the Jewish tradition: in addition to the biblical stories of Jonah, Ruth and Naomi, and the lovers in Song of Songs, mentioned above, there are rabbinic midrashim, the Zohar, Hasidic tales (especially the stories of Nachman of Bratzlav), and kabbalistic myths of the soul. As the field of Jewish spiritual direction continues to evolve and we develop Jewish vocabularies for spiritual growth and development, there are rich veins to mine.

Let me conclude this chapter as the traditional *Tefillat HaDerech* or Wayfarers Prayer concludes, with a verse taken from Exodus 23:20. The one who journeys repeats three times:

> Behold I send an angel before you to protect on the way and to bring you to the place that I have prepared for you. Behold I send an angel before you to protect you on the way and to bring you to the place that I have prepared for you. Behold I send an angel to protect you on the way and to bring you to the place that I have prepared for you.

May we recognize the "angels" and be protected on the way as we and those we companion continue to journey toward those places that yet await us.

Notes

1. Martin Buber, *Tales of the Hasidim: The Late Masters* (New York: Schocken Books, 1948), 245.

2. For a fuller discussion of these concepts, see Gerald G. May, *Will and Spirit: A Contemplative Psychology* (San Francisco: Harper & Row, 1982), chaps. 1, 2.

3. Max Kadushin, *Worship and Ethics: A Study in Rabbinic Judaism* (Evanston, IL: Northwestern University Press, 1964), 224–225.

4. Martin Luther King Jr., as quoted in Roger S. Gottlieb, *Spirituality of Resistance: Finding a Peaceful Heart and Protecting the Earth* (Lanham, MD: Rowman & Littlefield, 2003), 28.

5. James W. Fowler, *Faith Development and Pastoral Care* (Philadelphia: Fortress Press, 1987), 75–76.

6. Sylvia Boorstein, Keynote Address: "The Importance of Intuitive Mind." The First Jewish Meditation Conference, sponsored by Elat Chayyim, April 9, 1999, New York City.

7. Abraham Joshua Heschel, *Moral Grandeur and Spiritual Audacity: Essays* (New York: Farrar, Straus and Giroux, 1996), 7.

8. M. M. Bakhtin, "The Forms of Time and the Chronotopos in the Novel: From the Greek Novel to Modern Fiction," *PTL: A Journal for Descriptive Poetics and Theory of Literature* 3 (1978): 516.

9. Ora Wiskind-Elper, *Tradition and Fantasy in the Tales of Reb Nahman of Bratslav* (Albany: State University of New York Press, 1998), 51.

10. Belden C. Lane, *The Solace of Fierce Landscapes: Exploring Desert and Mountain Spirituality* (New York: Oxford University Press, 1998), 39, 53, 65.

11. Martin Buber, *Tales of the Hasidim: The Early Masters* (New York: Schocken Press, 1972), 290.

12. Arthur Green, *Tormented Master: A Life of Rabbi Nahman of Bratzlav* (Tuscaloosa: University of Alabama Press, 1979), 295.

13. I thank Rabbi David Ingber for this insight, included in a Dvar Torah at Elat Chayyim, summer 2005.

14. Rivkah Schatz Uffenheimer, *Hasidism as Mysticism: Quietistic Elements in Eighteenth-Century Hasidic Thought* (Princeton, NJ: Princeton University Press, 1993), 217–218.

15. Abraham Isaac Kook, *The Lights of Penitence, Lights of Holiness: The Moral Principles, Essays, Letters and Poems,* translated by Ben Zion Bokser (Mahwah, NJ: Paulist Press, 1978), 56.

16. From a translation by Arthur Green, in a handout prepared by Elliot Ginsburg for a course we taught at Elat Chayyim, August,1998.

Suggested Readings

Cronk, Sandra. *Dark Night Journey: Inward Re-patterning toward a Life Centered in God*. Wallingford, PA: Pendle Hill Publications, 1991.

Fowler, James. *Stages of Faith: The Psychology of Human Development and the Quest for Meaning*. New York: HarperCollins, 1981.

Goldberg, Michael. *Jews and Christians: Getting Our Stories Straight*. Philadelphia: Trinity Press International, 1991.

Greenspan, Miriam. *Healing through the Dark Emotions: The Wisdom of Grief, Fear, and Despair*. Boston: Shambhala, 2003.

Heschel, Abraham Joshua. *God In Search of Man: A Philosophy of Judaism*. New York: Harper & Row, 1955.

Kegan, Robert. *The Evolving Self: Problem and Process in Human Development*. Cambridge, MA: Harvard University Press, 1982.

Wilber, Ken. *The Eye of Spirit: An Integral Vision for a World Gone Slightly Mad*. Boston: Shambala, 1997.

Barbara Eve Breitman, MSW, LCSW, is a psychotherapist, teacher, and writer. She has been at the forefront of the contemporary field of Jewish spiritual direction. A cofounder of Lev Shomea, the first institute to train spiritual directors in the Jewish tradition outside a rabbinic seminary, she teaches spiritual directors at the Reconstructionist Rabbinical College, the rabbinical seminary of Hebrew College in Boston, and the ALEPH rabbinical program.

The Siddur: A Guide to Jewish Spiritual Direction

Rabbi Amy Eilberg

The Siddur, the traditional Jewish prayer book, represents our people's collective expression of the universal yearning for God. It gives language to our awe, need, and thanksgiving, helping us to speak of the stirrings of the heart, and reminding us to turn our hearts toward the One in prayer. It offers words when our own words fail, and inspires us to open more fully to our experiences of Mystery. Compiled over two millennia, it is the record of one side of the Jewish people's eternal conversation with the Holy One of Being, in which we may join at any moment.

In the corpus of Jewish classical texts, there is no single work consciously written as a handbook for the practice of Jewish spiritual direction. However, as the basic Jewish manual for personal and collective prayer and a daily course in cultivating relationship with God, the Siddur can serve as such a guidebook, on at least three levels.

First, as the daily guide for all Jews seeking deepened awareness of Divine presence and more consistent connection with the One, the Siddur serves as the quintessential book of Jewish spiritual direction, for directors and directees alike. Second, the Siddur serves as the Jewish spiritual director's comprehensive source for prayer texts that may prove helpful to directees in deepening their spiritual work and grounding it in a Jewish context. Third, the Siddur can serve as a manual for how to conduct a spiritual direction session, by teaching directors how to cultivate qualities of soul, such as reverence, humility, and radical trust, and how to increase attentiveness to God and openness to divine guidance.

In this single brief essay, I will offer reflections on ten subjectively chosen texts from the Siddur that illuminate aspects of Jewish spiritual direction.[1] I have chosen prayers that have played a crucial role in my own spiritual development or in the lives of people whom I companion, or that illustrate key themes in spiritual direction.

I also focus particularly on prayers that lend themselves to a prayer technique that has been helpful to many spiritual seekers. Often called Centering Prayer in Christian literature, the practice involves reciting a sacred phrase or sentence synchronized with the breath; for example, reciting the first half of a verse on the in-breath and the second half on the out-breath. When a prayer is "breathed" in this way, it can serve as a powerful anchor and source of comfort, strength, or wisdom.[2]

Awakening to the Moment: Modeh/Modah Ani L'Fanecha *(Thank You, God, for Life)*[3]

Many years ago, during a dark period in my life, I spent many hours in my therapist's office, pouring out grief, confusion, fear, and self-blame. One graced day, I was suddenly filled with a new sense of possibility about my life. When the session neared its close, my therapist offered words that I could only call a benediction. He said, "Amy, it's a miracle that there is so much vitality in you."

I left his office and drove to one of my favorite pilgrimage sites, a lookout point just north of the Golden Gate Bridge. Gazing out over the brilliant blue water, a prayer arose in me, unbidden: "*Modah ani l'fanecha, Ruach chai vekayam….*—Thank You, God, You have lovingly returned me to life; Your faithfulness is very great.[4]

I had experienced a moment of awakening, a sense of the God-given life-spirit returning to me after a long dark night. This prayer, of course, is not only about physical awakening from sleep. It expresses what Abraham Joshua Heschel calls "radical amazement," the essence of religious consciousness, the awareness that every moment of life is itself a wonder.

As spiritual directors, we commit ourselves to sustaining this kind of radical awakeness to the miracle of each moment of life every time we speak and listen with another. Thus, spiritual directors practice and model what all spiritual seekers strive for—a strengthened capacity to recognize the possibilities for renewal and re-creation that exist in every moment.

Recently, a seeker came into my office, reflecting deeply on the last two words of this prayer, "*Rabba emunatecha*—Your faithfulness is very great." A person with tremendous compassion for others, she was being led to claim a new level of love and compassion for herself.

She now heard the prayer as God's words to her, affirming her own trustworthiness and essential value. She was moved to respond in kind. "If God sees me as worthy, how can I see myself otherwise?"

The words became her mantra during a wondrous two years of awakening to her own giftedness and capacity for love. In moments of doubt, again and again, she would tune in and listen for God's words to her, "*Rabba emunatecha*"—*you* can trust yourself greatly, as I do.

This loving voice of the Divine is often drowned out by louder, nastier voices within us. It often requires a descent into deep quiet to hear this voice and to recognize it as the voice of Truth. The spiritual direction encounter serves as the sacred container within which this voice can be heard.

The Soul's Pure Essence: Elohai Neshama (The Soul You Have Given Me Is Pure)[5]

For many of us afflicted with self-doubt, it is much easier to see our flaws than our intrinsic beauty, goodness, and giftedness. This prayer, in remarkably few words, helps us to restore clear seeing. "*Elohai neshama*" asserts unequivocally that our lives are not our own, and all that we are is a gift from God. The prayer insists that our essence is pure, that we carry in the center of our being a part of God. Surely, we make many mistakes every day. We stumble and fail miserably, betraying the divine essence planted deeply in our being. Yet we are exactly who we were created to be: frail, finite beings containing the spark of the Infinite.

The spiritual direction hour is filled with reflection on the real stuff of our lives. Each month we bring ample evidence of our frailties, speaking of our broken relationships, our doubts, and our failures. Yet we also bring our longing to live with more mindfulness, connection, and faith. In our pain over our flaws and in the tiny steps we take to be true to our divine nature, the purity of the soul and its Creator shine through.

Constant Awareness of the Divine: Avar'cha et Adonai Bechol Eit (I Will Praise God at Every Moment)[6]

My training as a spiritual director included two ten-day retreats, time that was suffused with holiness. Our days were filled with classes about the theory and practice of spiritual direction, punctuated by periods of prayerful silence. It came to feel as if we were spending entire days in prayer.

In one of the most powerful exercises of my training experience, we were invited into silence and directed to bring our attention to the presence of the Divine within us. The direction was offered simply, expressing the belief that the Divine is present in all of creation, including ourselves. As the exercise deepened, to my own surprise, I began to feel a palpable sensation of Presence in the center of my chest. The sensation did not leave me when the session ended. A sense that I can only name "God" continued to occupy that space at the center of my being for the rest of the week. On the last day of the retreat, a prayer emerged from that space: "I want to live *here* for the rest of my life."

Finding my own sacred center, an almost physical sense of the Infinite within, opened up the possibility of moving beyond the goal of finding many intermittent experiences of God throughout my day (as in the Rabbis' instruction that we are to find one hundred opportunities each day to invoke God's presence in "ordinary" sights, sounds, and events). I now yearned for a seamless awareness of divine Presence in my life, for the constancy described powerfully in the prayer, "*Shiviti Adonai l'negdi tamid*—I place God before me always."[7]

This is the essence of the prayer: "I will bless God at every moment; let praise of God be always on my lips,"[8] along with its corollary, "I will praise God with my very life; sing to my God with all that I am."[9] The desire is to have my every word, act, and intention dedicated to the Holy. The spiritual direction relationship supports us in making our very lives into psalms of praise.

God's Love: Karov HaShem Lechol Kor'av (God Is Near to All Who Call, to All Who Truly Call on God)[10]

Rabbi Dan Alexander, a gifted congregational rabbi, now in training as a Jewish spiritual director, recalls being asked by his spiritual director at an eight-day silent retreat at a Catholic retreat center to contemplate the question, "What do you desire from God today?" He recalls the following sequence of thoughts and feelings:

1. Those Christians always ask the wrong questions! I should not ask about my desires vis-à-vis God but God's vis-à-vis me.

2. But, hey, I am here at this Jesuit place, so I may as well play along. So, what *do* I desire from God?

3. All of a sudden, a floodgate opened and a wave of emotions gushed forth: sadness, anger, worry, and longing.

4. When the wave of emotions passed, I knew exactly what I wanted from God that day: I wanted a hug. To be blatantly anthropomorphic, I wanted God to hug me the way my mother did when I was little.

5. I began to daven *Shacharit* (pray the morning service), highly aware of my heart's desire, highly appreciative of the natural beauty surrounding me, grateful for the rare opportunity for spacious contemplation in silence. I had not gotten far into my davening when one line in *Ashrei* stopped me short. "*Karov Adonai lechol kor'av, l'chol asher yikra'uhu be'emet*—God is near to all who call upon God, to all who call in truth." It was God's hug, as delicious in its own way as the hugs of my dear mother, full of love and compassion and affirmation.[11]

While the liturgy is replete with descriptions of God's tender care for us, we post-Enlightenment Jews have, for the most part, lost our ability to ask for such closeness, or to recognize it when it is offered. The spiritual direction relationship may serve as an incubator, helping us to open to a sense of God's loving presence in our lives.

God in All Things: Shema Yisrael *(Hear, O Israel, Adonai Our God, Adonai Is One)*[12]

Some years ago, I had the privilege of studying Hasidic texts with Arthur Green, a master scholar and teacher of Hasidism. One of the texts he taught changed my life.

> The intention of *echad* (one) in the affirmation of Oneness of the Recitation of the *Shema* is that we should have the intention that in all the worlds, there is nothing but the Blessed Holy One, Who fills the whole universe with Presence.... Our essence is the soul within us, which is a part of the Godliness above, so we see that

there is nothing in the universe but God. And the essence of the intention of *echad* is for us to see that the fullness of the universe is
God's Presence, so that no thing is empty of God....

We should cleave so much [to God] that the essence of our
vision be the Blessed Creator—not that the essence of our vision be
the world, to which we add the Creator. It is not so. Rather the
essence of our vision becomes the Blessed Creator.[13]

The theology embedded in this text asserts as a matter of fact that God
is present in all things—in every living being, in every human experience, in every moment of life. Each aspect of existence contains the
Divine, for each is a part of God, and God a part of all.

Perhaps most difficult to absorb is the implication of this teaching
that every feeling, thought, and desire within us also contains the
Divine, sometimes in hidden or distorted forms. It is a lifetime's spiritual work to cleanse the accretions of pain and conditioning that may
obscure the divine sparks buried within our thoughts and feelings, so
that their sacred essence may shine in our lives.

This theology offers an all-encompassing statement of faith, expressed as a constant refrain in the Hasidic writings that "*Melo kol
ha'aretz kevodo*—The fullness of all the earth is God's Presence."[14]
This suggests that all of existence is itself a seamless manifestation of
God, awaiting our recognition. This is the essence of the *Shema*, the
affirmation of God's oneness.

I have come to think of this theology as the foundation of Jewish
spiritual direction. From this perspective, the metaquestion of the spiritual direction encounter—"Where is God in this?"—is perhaps tauto-
logical, and easily misunderstood. The question may seem to imply
that God is in some aspects of an experience but not in others (e.g., in
joy, inspiration, and selflessness, but not in cruelty, confusion, and terror). Rather, from this point of view, "Where is God in this?" must be
understood as a rhetorical question, whose answer is always, as the
kabbalists loved to put it, "*Leit atar panui minei*—There is no place
empty of the Divine" (*Tikunei Zohar* 122b). The only questions are
these: Can I see it? Can I let it in, even embrace it? How must I respond to it? Thus the spiritual direction encounter itself serves as a reminder, an invitation to drop into the omnipresence of God, and invite
us to turn our hearts toward this truth.[15]

Speaking Less and Praying More: Yihiyu Leratzon Imrei Fi *(May the Words of My Mouth and the Meditations of My Heart Be Acceptable to You)*[16]

One of the more difficult aspects of the discipline of spiritual direction is the art of speaking less and listening and praying more. Many teachers of spiritual direction recommend that a director wait until a particular reaction repeatedly knocks on the door of her awareness before even considering saying it aloud to the seeker. It is essential to the practice of spiritual direction to leave as much space as possible open to the presence and guidance of God. This is a lesson not easily learned.

But of course, what spiritual directors practice while in session is only a focused version of what all spiritually attentive people seek. Thus, the spiritual direction session, with its emphasis on attentiveness to silence and the experience of the Holy that underlies our usual narratives, serves as a challenge to the excessive wordiness of our everyday lives, an avalanche of words and thoughts that leaves little space for the Divine. The process of the spiritual direction session trains us in the discipline of pausing before speaking, asking throughout our lives, "Would God desire that I say this right now?"

The Practice of Peace

Most Jewish prayer services climax in prayers for peace. Such prayers are found at the end of every *Amidah* (Standing Prayer), every full *Kaddish* (Mourners' Prayer), and *Birkat HaMazon* (Grace after Meals), to name just a few. The Rabbis tell us that peace is the container for all other blessings, and that God's very name is Peace.

Spiritual direction is itself a practice of peacemaking. Generally offered for the sake of supporting another's unfolding connection to the Divine, this kind of nonjudgmental, trusting listening to another lies at the core of all peace and reconciliation practices. In the reverent quiet of the spiritual direction session, the seeker practices listening to herself with gentle, nonjudgmental awareness. For this hour, internal warfare quiets down, as the sacred space shared by seeker and guide inspires acceptance of all parts of the seeker's experience. Listening with gentle acceptance to all that life presents, seeker and guide listen ever more deeply to the reality of human life, in oneself and in the other, until there is no "other"—only a single human family, struggling together to find the peace that all beings desire.

Not Knowing: Va'anachnu Lo Neida Ma Na'aseh *(We Do Not Know What to Do; Our Eyes Look to You)*[17]

As I prepare to teach a class or address a group of people, I am often nervous. I have worked on this reaction in many ways over the years, in the hope of healing it or simply accepting it. One of my favorite strategies is to evoke the presence of my teacher, Sylvia Boorstein, who tells the story of going into the ladies' room prior to addressing an intimidating group of people. In the privacy of the rest room, she said to herself, "There is no way I can make myself any smarter than I am between now and the start of my talk five minutes from now. This is who I am; I'll give what I can give."

Another thing I have tried is to call to mind the words, "*Va'anachnu lo neida ma na'aseh*—We do not know what to do; our eyes are on You." When I am able to do this, I am admitting that I cannot be as smart or wise as I would like to be, and I cannot even know what would be most helpful to the people in the room. I can only give what I have, and trust that this is enough.

A remarkable text in the Exodus story brings us a similar piece of wisdom. In the midst of the plague of darkness, Pharaoh agrees to allow the Israelites to leave, insisting that they leave behind their flocks and herds. Moshe refuses, saying that they must have all their livestock with them, for "We shall not know with what we are to worship God until we arrive there."[18]

It is always so. We can never know which of our gifts, experiences, or insights we will need in a particular moment, so all of our planning and worrying is both futile and faithless. What we can do is to bring all of who we are to each moment, trusting that, when the time comes, we will have what we need.

This consciousness lies at the core of the spiritual direction encounter. There is no planning and no agenda, and to the extent that we are open to divine guidance, we are richly satisfied, and nearly always surprised. With God's help, touching this experience of trust month after month in spiritual direction, we learn to approach more of the moments of our lives in this way.

Dancing with God: Hashiveinu Adonai Eilecha Venashuvah *(Return Us to You, O God, and We Will Return)*[19]

The opening words of this verse are deceptively simple. But reflection on this brief phrase reveals a wealth of rich spiritual imagery.

The first word, *hashiveinu* ("return us"), is in the *hif'il* form, the verb conjugation indicating causal action. The prayer assumes that we cannot return to God, to the true direction of our lives, of our own accord. Everyday life relentlessly draws us away from our center. According to the prayer, only God can cause us to return, but first we must ask for God's help. The prayer thus suggests a grace-filled partnership, including our calling out, God's gracious response, and our return.

This is the dance of faith. We yearn for deep connection, yet we cannot do this without God's calling us home from all that draws us away. Our lives are a continually unfolding reciprocal exchange of our prayerful initiative, God's loving invitations, and our movement toward the Holy.

This alternation between our own efforts and divine grace is continually observed in spiritual direction. In the sacred time and space of the spiritual direction encounter, we recognize the mysterious interplay of our longing and the presence of the Divine, the places where things happen because of our own hard work, and the times when we are moved beyond what we could have done on our own. Again and again, we observe the dance, trusting our Partner ever more.

The Practice of Trust: Beyad'cha Afkid Ruchi Be'eit Ishan Ve'a'ira *(In Your Hand I Place My Soul, When I Wake and When I Sleep)*[20]

For ten years (which are, thankfully, behind us), my husband and I commuted between two homes, two thousand miles apart. I was an unlikely frequent flyer, for, although I like to travel, I am quite frightened of turbulence in flight. One terrifying night, flying over Chicago, we encountered severe turbulence. Other passengers continued to eat their dinners. I began to pray the last line of *Adon Olam*, half the line on my in-breath (*Beyad'cha afkid ruchi*—In Your hand I place my soul), and half the line on my out-breath (*be'eit ishan ve'a'ira*—when I wake and when I sleep).

The plane continued to pitch and rock for what seemed like a long time. Occasionally, I wondered at what point I should switch over to saying the *Shema,* to be recited just before the moment of death. I would then bring my attention back to the calming rhythm of prayer and breath. My fear did not leave me, but my breathing slowed, and I was able to dip into a place of deep prayer. For a moment, I considered what would happen if I died that night. I mentally checked on my loved ones, knowing that they were all safe and happy. I touched a place of deep calm about where I was in my own life. For a moment, it was OK.

The turbulence passed, as do the large and small storms of doubt, fear, sadness, and anger that blow through my mind on a regular basis. At such times, I frequently reach for this powerful prayer. As I grow older, I increasingly believe from my own life experience the oft-re-peated truth that every experience of life eventually passes. Every joy and every sorrow, every delight, pain, and conflict eventually shifts on its own, despite my own best efforts to manage things through force of will. The challenge of life is not to finally learn how to fix the things that plague us, but how to survive them gracefully. We must learn to breathe through the periods of turbulence until the air grows smooth again.

Fundamentally, we know what our spiritual director will say in response to any life challenge that we bring to the session. When her loving, prayerful presence meets our yearning for the sacred, we come to remember that all we need to do is turn to God, access the Holy that lives deep within us, even now, in the midst of whatever plagues us. We need not believe that God literally has a hand to hold us, or even specific intent for us, to be able to tap into the ever-present rise and fall of the breath, the bedrock of existence, our Source.

Conclusion

We have seen in this small sampling of texts three ways in which the Siddur may serve as a manual for the practice of Jewish spiritual direction:

1. The Siddur gives both directors and directees a rich tapestry of theological reflection, describing the way the world works, reflecting on the nature of our connection to God, and offering us a portrait of who we were created to be, as human beings and as Jews.

2. The Siddur contains an inexhaustible repository of texts for prayer and reflection, which directors may offer to directees, to connect an individual's experience to the collective Jewish context, to offer the knowledge that others have taken similar journeys throughout the ages, and to support an individual's desire to live a more holy life.

3. These texts, a manual of Jewish connection to God, illustrate and describe what happens in the spiritual direction hour. These sacred images highlight how the director may best serve as a vessel for divine guidance, and they demonstrate the plethora of ways in which the Divine may manifest in human life.

In a word, the Siddur serves as the Jewish explication of the fundamental instruction to spiritual directors, to remember that God is the director of the spiritual direction encounter, indeed, of our lives, moment by moment. May we see the day when more Jews will open to this truth.

Notes

1. In this, I follow the example of my friend Rabbi Simkha Weintraub in his beautiful chapter, "From the Depths: The Use of Psalms," in Rabbi Dayle Friedman's anthology, *Jewish Pastoral Care: A Practical Handbook from Traditional and Contemporary Sources* (Woodstock, VT: Jewish Lights Publishing, 2005), 161–182.

2. For example, a basic breath prayer might be to focus on the last verse of the book of Psalms: "*Kol haneshama tehallel Yah*—Let all that breathes praise God," on the in-breath, and "*Halleluyah*—Give thanks," on the out-breath. Or breathing the *Shema* deep into one's being by silently praying the words, "*Shema Yisrael*—Hear, O Israel," on the in-breath, "*Adonai Eloheinu*—*Adonai* is our God," on the out-breath, and "*Adonai Echad*—*Adonai* is One," on the in-breath, then beginning again.

3. Found early in *Birkot HaShachar*, the Morning Blessings, at the start of every Morning Service, *Siddur Sim Shalom for Weekdays* (New York: Rabbinical Assembly, 2002), 2–3.

4. The traditional language of the prayer refers to God as "*Melech chai vekayam*" (ever-living King). Since the image of God as king is problematic for me, in my

personal prayer I substitute the language *"Ruach chai vekayam"* (ever-living Spirit).

5. Found early in *Birkot HaShachar,* the Morning Blessings, *Siddur Sim Shalom*, pp. 8–11.

6. Psalm 34:2 and in *Pesukei Dezimra*, Psalms of Praise, section of the Morning Service for Shabbat. Ibid., pp. 62–63.

7. Psalm 16:8.

8. See note 6.

9. Psalm 146:2. *Siddur Sim Shalom,* pp. 82–83.

10. Psalm 145:18 and in the *Ashrei* prayer in *Pesukei Dezimra*, ibid., pp. 82–83.

11. From a student paper submitted to the Morei Derekh Training Program for Jewish Spiritual Direction, sponsored by the Yedidya Center for Jewish Spiritual Direction (www.yedidyacenter.org).

12. Deuteronomy 6:4 and *Siddur Sim Shalom*, pp. 100–101.

13. *Likutim Yekarim,* edited by Rabbi Meshullam Feibush Heller of Zbarasz, 1792, p. 53b #161 and p. 10b #54; translation by Rabbi Jacob Staub (adapted) (Jerusalem: Kolel Mevakesh Emunah).

14. Isaiah 6:3 and quoted in the *Kedushah* of every *Amidah* prayer, e.g., *Siddur Sim Shalom,* pp. 108–109.

15. I explore this idea in greater detail in my article, "Jewish Theologies of Spiritual Direction," in *Presence: An International Journal of Spiritual Direction*, 11, no. 3, (September 2005), 26–32.

16. Psalm 19:15, placed at end of every *Amidah* (Standing Prayer), *Siddur Sim Shalom*, pp. 120–121.

17. II Chronicles 20:12, and at the end of *Tachanun* service. Ibid., pp. 136–137.

18. Exodus 10:26.

19. Lamentations 5:21, and at the end of Torah service. *Siddur Sim Shalom,,* pp. 150–151.

20. Adapted from Psalms 31:6 and incorporated into the end of the *Adon Olam* prayer. Ibid., pp. 6–7.

Rabbi Amy Eilberg serves as codirector of the Morei Derekh training program of the Yedidya Center for Jewish Spiritual Direction. A long-time leader in the Jewish healing movement, she is now involved in the work of peace-making, particularly in connection with the Israeli-Palestinian conflict.

Live with the Times: Spiritual Direction and the Cycle of Holy Time

Rabbi Marcia Prager

Hints of Adventure: Sensing God's Pulse

"*Kol dodi dofek pitchi li....* The voice of my beloved is a beating pulse, calling: Open to me, let me in!" (Song of Songs 5:2).

How are we to feel the pulse of God calling us every moment, beating, open to me, let me in?

We pray, do mitzvot, and learn holy Torah that we might open our hearts to the pulsing flow of God within us and around us. As Jews we also live within flowing cycles of holy time, bathing our lives in the rhythms of holy days and sacred seasons.

For many of us these holy days, paved over by the highway of the secular calendar, emerge erratically, if at all. They seem random; like blips on a screen, they appear and then recede. They may evoke nostalgia, or even vague recollections: Yes, isn't there a Jewish holiday called Sukkot this week?

Others among us, having more access to spiritual resources or more supportive families and communities, make concerted efforts to celebrate. We may live in quite observant communities, in which the Jewish calendar and the secular calendar intertwine, an uneasy dance at times, but regular, familiar. Some of us may even live in Israel, where the Jewish calendar is the normative calendar, and the rhythms of the Jewish year are woven directly into the fabric of everyday life, even for secular Jews. But, sometimes, wherever we are in this spectrum, we want to go deeper.

This chapter offers a hint of a road map for that adventure. A hint because no brief essay could pretend to do more than that; an adventure, because the soul's journey through the deepest revelations of the

Divine that flow within the cycles of the year couldn't be less than that. As both seekers and spiritual guides, we must embark on the journey ourselves. There is a substantial literature on the cycles of the Jewish sacred year. By all means we should read, but then we must immerse ourselves deeply, living the energetic rhythms of the sacred year. There is a surrendering, a willingness to be carried and held by the cycles of new moons and full, holy times and holy days, which then schools the soul. The soul finds itself at home within the narrative of these holy cycles and times. The journey of the soul is guided by the sensation of traveling through the spiral of the years, and by repeated exposure, with ever-increasing maturity and depth, to their inner lessons.

In his preface to a paper on the Hasidic master Tzvi Elimelech Shapira of Dinov (d.1841), often called the *B'nai Yissasschar*, my colleague and friend Hillel Goelman wrote:

> We often conceive of the Jewish year as a progression, a sequence of holidays/Holy Days ... tied to historic episodes in our past ... [or] tied to the seasonal periodicities of the earth.... [C]ertain Holy Days seem to stand alone, not tied to either....
>
> What [may be less evident is] ... the placement ... of the Holy Days throughout the year is a manifestation of an underlying Divine intention to make the Divine Presence manifest to our human understanding.
>
> ... [T]he days themselves are not isolated oases in barren stretches of emptiness. They are heartbeats in an endless, continuing, rhythmic, pulsating flow that accompanies the breathing of the Divine Name in every moment of existence.... Cosmic time, in the Jewish sense, is not a linear sequence of moments strung together.... Time is a pulsating energy that ebbs, flows, and manifests in different ways ... [and we] can attune to the divine energy suffusing time."[1]

Not every person engaged in the art of Jewish spiritual direction will aspire to the level of a Tzvi Elimelech Shapira of Dinov. However learning to walk the divine, energetic rhythms of the Jewish year and attuning one's own inner rhythms to the cycles of sacred time can be of great value in growing our own souls. That attunement, in turn, can provide a precious dimension of sensitivity that we can bring into the relationship of spiritual companionship, *hashpa'ah*.

As a *mashpia,* I am alert to how these themes emerge in my own soul-story, in the larger story of my people, and in the yet larger stories of this planet and cosmos that shape me. I try to refrain from superimposing any simplistic template onto the experience of the seeker, but I do listen for echoes of the great cycling themes that I have come to know in myself. I "listen" energetically, not just to the words but also to the larger communication conveyed through gesture, tone, posture, breath, evidences of tension or other heightened emotions that, with permission, may be explored. I listen inside myself for the voice of God within me, to guide me in discerning which questions to ask and which observations to share. I always request permission to speak, as a question that arises within me may belong only to me. No matter how attuned my "listening" or how gentle my questions and observations, they might be my own projections. So the seeker must be the ultimate judge of her own inner truth.

Each month and each holy day calls on the soul to respond and take new risks, to feel the pulse of Divinity more strongly and open up to new possibilities. There is no preprinted set of good questions for spiritual directors to ask when approaching a given season, like the customs questionnaire at an airport. But there are palpable ways in which our souls feel the subtle shifts in the "temperature" of the divine flow and we can learn to bring these to awareness in spiritual direction.

New Moons and Full

New moons and full. Full moons and new. The cycle of the year carries us. Months are, as we see, quite literally tied to the moon. Each new moon inaugurates an energy shift we can learn to feel, which is encoded in the very language we use. In Hebrew all letters correspond to numbers. When one spells, one also counts. This is the art of *gematria.* The word for month, *chodesh,* has the numerical value of 312, which is 12 x 26. Twenty-six, in turn, is the numerical value of YHVH, the sacred unpronounceable Name of God. So, the "month, *chodesh*" = "Divine Name" x 12! Each of the 12 months is infused with the power of the Divine Name.

Further, the four individual letters of the Divine Name can be arranged in twelve different ways. From this we learn that there are twelve unique ways that Divinity flows through the year. Each month inaugurates both a new quality and a new experience of God to influence our actions. Each month manifests the Divine Name anew, bringing a new infusion of divine intention into the world. Perhaps this is why the word for "month," *chodesh,* derives from *chadash* meaning "new."

As we shall see below, the progression of months and their holy days are anything but arbitrary. Each new moon and each full moon invites us to address particular ways in which the *shefa,* the flow of the Divine into the world beckons our souls.

Summer into Fall

Themes for a *Mashpia*

Heat, danger, destruction, exile, alienation, pain, grief, consolation, longing, hope, promise, return, forgiveness, reunion, compassion, love, lovemaking, consummation, ecstasy, celebration, fertility, quickening, deepening, introspection, concealment, gestation, and rebirth to come.

Tammuz to Cheshvan

"Where does the circle start? When does the year begin?" asks author and educator Arthur Waskow. As with many Jewish questions, he notes, "There are at least two answers—and both of them are right. The year starts twice."[2] The month that Torah itself calls the New Year is Nisan, the month of Aviv, of spring, rebirth, and new life. The new moon closest to the spring equinox is the new moon of the earth softening, opening, birthing. When it waxes full, our people, Israel, are again birthed from the tight places of Egypt into a new existence as a free people dedicated to serve only the One God.

Since the time of the Talmud, however, we have celebrated Rosh Hashanah not in Nisan, but on the new moon of Tishre, the seventh month that brings us the cooling, introspective turning of fall. Like Shabbat on the seventh day, the seventh month calls us to rest and renewal, to a time of inner reflection and return. The now-ripened fruit will plant its seed in the earth's womb anew to gestate and await the "birth-time" of spring.

The renewal-time of fall emerges out of Tammuz and Av, months of scorching heat, severity, and danger. The Roman siege of Jerusalem that breaches the walls in Tammuz ends with the burning of the *Beit HaMikdash,* the Holy Temple, on the ninth of Av—a time of pain and grief. At this time of sorrow, dispersion, and exile we grieve. We come to understand that exile is not merely a political condition but a spiritual condition as well; to bring healing to the world we must each mend our own internal exile. We understand that the human being is also a temple of God in need of restoration and repair. Alienation is our exile as layers of rage and unhealed grief obscure the *netzotzot elohut*, the holy sparks alive in our hearts.

However, in the most painful experience lies great potential. By allowing ourselves to feel pain and grief we are drawn toward healing along the path of redemption. We have inherited an extraordinary tradition: the ninth of Av will be the birthday of *Mashiach*, the Messiah, the time of whole-earth transformation, renewal, and hope.

On the fifteenth day, *Tu b'Av,* at the full moon, the rhythm begins to shift. Songs of consolation comfort us as deep mourning is transformed into joy and sadness into rejoicing. In ancient times this was a day of romance and courting. The new moon that next arises marks the arrival of Elul, the month of return to the Divine Beloved. Elul is the month whose letters spell as an acronym *"Ani l'dodi v'dodi li*—I am my beloved's and my beloved is mine," from the most sensual of biblical love poems, the Song of Songs (6:3). Our hearts open in love and longing. In Elul we begin to sound the shofar that awakens the soul to the approach of her Beloved, and calls the soul to *teshuvah*, return.

Elul is the month in which the rabbis teach us that Moshe received the second set of Tablets that he would later bring to us, suggesting further that the energy of Elul is one of receptivity and embrace. The divine desire turns toward us in love; the desire for union is very strong. The energy of Elul also points to the act of creation, which arose in the divine mind before creation's onset and rises anew each year.

In the Rosh Hashanah *Musaf* service we say, "This is the day of the beginning of Creation." As the new moon of Tishre rises, *ratzon*, divine desire, increases further. On Rosh Hashanah we link our souls again to God's creative will, God's desire to emanate goodness into the unfolding creation. It is a time pregnant with potential for goodness, for mitzvot and acts of *chesed*, loving-kindness. In Tishre we call out to God: *"Hashiveynu eylecha v'nashuva, chadeysh yameynu k'kedem*—Return to us and we will return to You! Renew our days as they were *k'kedem*." *K'kedem* is a curious phrase. It carries the dual meanings of "as once long ago" and "as yet to be." This is the "once-and-future promise"—that we will be held in such love and delight in the heart and mind of God, that the mere thought of us would be enough to trigger the creation of time and space.

On Yom Kippur, dressed in a *kittel,* a clean, white penitential robe reminiscent of burial shrouds, we step beyond life itself to atone and return, that we may live and not die, that we may be worthy of the love that creates and sustains us. With the full harvest moon of Tishre in the sky, we rejoice in the leafy harvest in the *chuppah*-like structure of the sukkah, joining the etrog with the lulav in trembling embrace to celebrate the consummation of this celestial/terrestrial love. As the new moon of Tishre swells, it is *Shechinah,* the divine Presence herself, Who comes near. Each night the moon brings Her closer, as it were, to her *chuppah,* for the kabbalists envisioned the moon as the "feminine face of God" coming to cosmic union. They also identified the *Shechinah* with us, *Klal Yisrael,* the people Israel, opening our hearts to the Beloved in rapturous joy.

The moon of Tishre wanes and the harvest is done. Fields are bare, seeds hidden away in cellars and earth. The rains of winter and a time of inward gestation begin. In ancient times when the Holy House still stood, three pilgrimage festivals drew us to Jerusalem, one to anchor each season. But the torrential winter rains that flood the roads make a winter Temple festival in the Land of Israel impossible. Yet to dispense with a ritual marker of winter's onset—also impossible! So Shemini Atzeret was carefully tucked in at the end of the seven days of Sukkot, for we had not yet departed Jerusalem and could still initiate the onset of winter together. The expansive *simcha* of Sukkot concludes with chanted pleas for life-giving rains that will continue until Pesach, and echoes of Yom Kippur as we offer culminating prayers for repentance and forgiveness. Then it is time to parade and dance joyously with the Torah, to formally end one Torah cycle and begin anew. Simchat Torah marks one final burst of celebration before winter, a time of inwardness and restraint.

Life Reflecting Time

Sam has taught in the same school system for several years. No matter how hard he worked with his disadvantaged students he felt unappreciated and stymied by an administration intent on maintaining appearances and "covering its backside." At a spiritual direction session, Sam complained about always feeling in the doldrums during the summer. Divorced for many years, he felt more alone than usual, despite having good relationships with family and friends and a variety of communal and cultural interests. Although on vacation, the combined weight of his personal and work situations seemed more crushing than normal. "I just feel like reading and being by myself; I keep wondering if I should even go back."

During the session, Sam discovered that the month of Av had just begun, a time of alienation and exile during which we grieve for the destruction of the Holy Temples. We spoke about how the Rabbis correlated the architecture of the Temples and the inner architecture of the temple of the heart. He reflected that his mood mirrored the emotional quality of the month. Learning that this time represented not only loss, but also the possibilities of renewal that come with "breaking down walls," Sam reflected on new ways he could mark the blessings of even his students' small achievements. He noted that his grief and frustration had actually pushed him to break through some entrenched inhibitions by dancing with surprising abandon at a year-end faculty dinner. Finding his own internal condition mirrored by the sacred rhythm of the month, Sam felt validation and a call to more deeply experience and learn from his sadness, rather than dismiss it. He left with a new openness to possibilities for renewed fulfillment in the fall months ahead.

Winter into Spring

Themes for a *Mashpia*

Pregnancy, incubation, inwardness, expectancy, anxiety, darkness, lights into the darkness, illumination, lighting the soul's lamp, hope, softening, inner fire rising, longing, end of dormancy, risk, stepping beyond alienation and separation, Divinity concealed, God working below the surface, the hidden is revealed.

Cheshvan to Adar

As the days grow shorter and the nights lengthen, a quiet settles upon us. The mood is inward and reflective. The new moon of Cheshvan ushers in no festivals. There will be no holy day until Chanukah, the twenty-fifth of Kislev, the darkest time of the year, when the moon wanes and the sun flees into winter solstice darkness. Will the light return? We light piercing flames into the darkness. Eight candles for eight nights. Night after night their light increases, guiding us into, through, and past the darkness.

Proverbs 20:27 states: "*Ner YHVH nishmat adam*—The human soul is God's lamp." As we light the menorah, we ourselves can reflect the flow of God's light into the world. By its nature our physical world is a place of separation, of fragmentation tinged with confusion and alienation, as evidenced by *Asarah B'Tevet*, a half-fast following on Chanukah's heels, marking the beginning of the Babylonian siege of Jerusalem. Yet each of us can be a menorah radiating the enlightenment of *Or HaGanuz*, God's treasured primordial light of creation's first days, into an all-too-darkened world.

When the new moon of Shevat rises in the night sky, she brings a hint of spring. The winter rains still soak the Land of Israel, but a blush of warmth smiles shyly through. Days are lengthening, earth softening. The time of dormancy is ending.

Rabbi Solomon ibn Gabriol teaches: "The world is a tree and we are its fruits." When the moon of Shevat is full, sap begins to flow in the earliest of the trees to blossom with fruit in Israel. The Hebrew word for sap, *saraf* (literally, "fire" or "burning energy"), can allude both to the divine creative energy that fills the trees and their fruit and the initial flames of yearning that rise within us with the first intimations of spring. Therefore, the fruits we eat on Tu B'Shevat can stir our souls to identify with creation and reconnect with its Divine Source.

Mi sheh nichnas Adar marbim b'simcha! When Adar enters, joy increases! And much hoped for, too! The new moon of Adar ushers in the final stretch of winter. Weary of the lingering rain and cold, the full moon brings a festival of release: Purim—a time for merriment, parody, rule breaking, even socially sanctioned inebriation. As we read the Megillah, clacking groggers drown out the name of the evil Haman whose plot to murder and pillage our people is foiled by the wise Mordechai and his heroic young cousin, Esther. Costumes, noisemakers and street parades accompany the general revelry.

Clearly, Purim serves a valuable social function: release of potentially harmful, pent-up, late-winter frustration into a bust-loose festival in which good triumphs over evil. Yet under the surface lie Purim's deeper messages. What can it mean that we are encouraged to become so "drunk" that we cannot distinguish between *Baruch Mordechai* and *Arur Haman,* Blessed be Mordechai and Cursed is Haman? Would we ever want to so numb our consciousness that we could not discern good from evil? And why, in the entire scroll of the Megillah, does no reference to God ever appear?

During Pesach God blazingly reveals God's Self to us as the ultimate liberating power, bringing us out of *Mitzrayim,* Egypt, and on to Sinai to forge a covenant with us as a nation. So why does God not appear in the Purim Megillah? We chant the story and can feel God working. God is the hidden actor, whispering the stage cues from behind the curtain, the main character who never gets a line or a curtain call. Yet at Pesach, God reveals God's Self to each of us in acts and visions so compelling that our entire national consciousness is restructured. What then is the message of Adar? Hidden or revealed, God is always present. The name *Esther* echoes the Hebrew word *nistar,* "hidden." *Megillah* sounds like the Hebrew for "revealed," *nigleh.* So on Purim we read the "Megillah" of "Esther" in order to begin revealing what is hidden! God moves in the world from *nistar* to *nigleh,* from the hidden to the revealed.

As alluded to above, the kabbalists often describe our world as *olam ha-p'ridah,* a world of separation and opposites—of good and evil, right and wrong, blessing and curse. Yet they point out that the numerical value of *Baruch Mordechai,* Blessed be Mordechai, and *Arur Haman,* Cursed is Haman, are the same. This does not mean there is no difference between good and evil, but rather calls us to a deeper understanding of how seeming polarities might actually intertwine. Walking beyond *olam ha-p'ridah* is a journey toward *yichud,* the Divine Unity that underlies and transcends the apparent contradictions of our world, where even polarities like *Baruch Mordechai* and *Arur Haman* merge. This is Esther's walk, and ours. Esther's brave walk from *purdah,* her separate women's abode, to approach the king reminds us what a risky venture it is to leave the comfort of our certainties and aspire, through heightened consciousness, to experience, however briefly, the expanse of Infinite Oneness, the chamber of *yichud* where false perceptions fall away. As we celebrate Purim, the very costumes we wear remind us how the gaudy garments of our habitual assumptions mask deeper, hidden truths.

Life Reflecting Time

Sarah came into our monthly spiritual direction session bitter about how her family had suffered from her father's drinking. The legacy of his defeatism and withdrawal had left its mark on her family in so many ways. A family gathering would soon be bringing the whole extended family together, and she dreaded the embarrassment. Everyone would compare him to her uncle, his brother, a smashingly successful attorney, always articulate, always competent and in charge. Why had God so favored him and his family and so shamed her father and his? With Purim arriving in only a few days, we began to reflect on Esther's risky venture of walking past old assumptions to discover new truths.

As we explored her family story in greater depth, we discovered that her grandparents had tried to shield their children from terror, by keeping them ignorant of their Holocaust tragedies. The two brothers had grown up in the shadow of terrible trauma in a home filled with unspoken fears. Sarah began to see how her father's retreat from the world and her uncle's aggressive style could be viewed as two sides of the same coin. Looking deeper, she observed that, despite his drinking, her father never became unkind, whereas her uncle's "workaholic" success had some severe emotional costs. Each brother, she saw, was still living with the secret terrors of his own childhood.

Sarah was able to move past her assumptions about both her uncle and her father to a deeper level of compassion. This, she saw, was how God was working toward healing. She began to understand how she and her cousins could use the family gathering to share their parents and grandparents' stories in a way that would bring them and their children to a new appreciation of compassion and God's healing power. Sarah left highly motivated to love her father in a renewed way, and be an agent of rapprochement in her family.

Spring into Summer

Themes for a *Mashpia*

Labor pains, birth, liberation, freedom, telling the story, questions, bondage, illusions, trust and faith, hunger, fulfillment, obstacles, courage, purification, refinement, realignment, ripening, opening to receive, commitment, holiness, deep encounter, wisdom, transformation, insecurity, wandering, danger, destruction leading to renewal, and rebirth.

Nisan to Tammuz

The new moon of Nisan ushers in the month of Aviv, spring, bringing liberation from the constrictions of winter and the promise of rebirth. In the mystical tradition, Nisan is called the month of "speaking." The Hebrew verb *sach* means "to tell"; *peh* is "mouth." Thus *Pesach*, Passover, summons each of our mouths to be a "mouth that tells!" The *Yitziyat Mitzrayim*, the Exodus from Egypt, the Place of Constriction (Hebrew, *tzar*), is one of the great tales of human history. So central is its telling, that the text we chant to relive our liberation is simply called *Haggadah*, the "Telling."

And what a tale! Upon entering *Mitzrayim* we are a small clan, protected by Joseph, living in a most fertile land. We grow and grow; as we swell, the environment seems to shrink around us. Restrictions tighten until our once hospitable home becomes an enslaving prison. We long for escape, but the time is not ripe. Plagues will yet shake the land, waves of contractions that culminate only when the full moon of Nisan rises. Our birth as a people begins; we start to move. Soon waters of the Red Sea break apart, opening like a birth canal. We pass through and embark on our journey outward to Sinai and *Eretz Yisrael*.

Interestingly enough, the "Telling" begins not with narrative but with questioning, "Why is this night different from all other nights?" and with encouragement, "Whoever enlarges upon the telling is praised!" Why? So that each of us can experience the telling as a personal reliving, not as something that happened to someone else. We are invited to reenter, reenact, and expand upon the telling, until our lives and this narrative become inextricably intertwined.

Karen Roekard, with her now famous *Santa Cruz Haggadah*, introduced me to the extraordinary range of soul-searching questions that can be evoked by the ritual elements of the seder. Every year I refine my own adaptations of those questions so that our seder becomes an opportunity, not only to feast and sing, but to further our inner work. In turn these questions find their way into my own practice of *hashpa'ah*, spiritual direction.

What forces now imprison us, that seemed so hospitable and have become so lethal?

Come learn! The word *pharaoh* can be compared to the Hebrew word *oreph,* which means the back of the neck—near that part of the brain that controls imagination. Bondage to the "Pharaoh Within" is bondage of illusions, when we imagine that we are powerless, and become alienated from our true selves. How do we become enslaved to such false and limiting ideas? And when we think we have left that Pharaoh behind, external obstacles, like the Sea of Reeds, may also block our path to freedom. What are some of these obstacles in our lives and what support do we need to dissolve them that we might walk forward?

What old fears and insecurities might we need to rinse away?

The first hand-washing is called *ur'chatz.* In Aramaic this word means "trusting." We ask: What do we need to wash away so that inner trust and faith can flower? The bowl of saltwater on the table represents not only our Israelite ancestors' tears; they are tears we have cried throughout this year. We ask: Can we speak about what some of those tears have been, that we would now like to sweeten with the green parsley of rebirth and hope?

For what do we hunger this year?

At the seder table we call out "Let all who are hungry come and eat with us." But sometimes hunger is not only for food. What do we each need to ask for, in order to feel full and filled? Matzah is called *"lechem oni*—the bread of poverty." We break the middle of the three matzahs on the seder table and hide the larger piece, symbolizing the Great Redemption to come at the end of time. The broken, smaller piece remains on the table. Perhaps it is a reminder that, while our awareness of God often focuses on the transcendent and great, God is also present in the poorer, broken "small pieces" that can sustain us in the here and now and point us toward the redemptive work ahead.

How might we broaden our perspectives?

We sing *"Avadim Hayyinu b'Mitzrayim*—We were slaves in Egypt, the Constricted Place," acknowledging that sometimes we see our lives through the narrowest of lenses, and thus lose sight of the big picture. Unable to see alternative possibilities and other points of view we are enslaved to the narrowest understanding of things. What might look different if we broadened our perspective? Moshe argued that his speech defect was an impediment to leadership. Yet with God's grace and the support of Aaron and Miriam, Moshe's words have inspired countless millions. What have we each defined as impediments that needlessly hold us back?

What have we wrought that calls for repair?

The plagues can be understood as a "karmic backfiring" to the unrepented, oppressive actions of the Egyptians. The Nile in which they drowned the Israelite baby boys ran red during the plague of blood; their inability to see the Israelites as their brothers and sisters presaged the plague of darkness. Misdeeds not rectified through *teshuvah* often boomerang and cause real suffering both to their victims and to their perpetrators.

The moon of Nisan brings questioning and speaking, the shedding of old paradigms and the birthing of new, liberating possibilities. The Nisan moon wanes, and by the new moon of Iyar we are already two weeks out of Egypt, two weeks into the seven-week journey to Sinai where heaven and earth touch and we experience the most compelling collective revelation of God's presence in our history as a people.

The journey out of *Mitzrayim* takes seven weeks, just like the seven weeks from the ripening of spring barley to the harvest of the early wheat. When we become a settled agricultural nation in *Eretz Yisrael,* this seven-week journey is linked to the agricultural *Omer* season in the land. Gratitude for the ripened barley at Pesach-time brings us to the Holy House, the *Beit HaMikdash* in Jerusalem, with offerings of thanksgiving: an *Omer* of newly harvested grain. These are also an anxious seven weeks. Will the wheat harvest too bring prosperity and abundance? Every day brings us one day closer to the hoped-for harvest. Every day we walk one day closer to the God-encounter of Sinai. Seven weeks of seven days.

Over the centuries, even as our living connection with the agricultural rhythms of the land was lost, our spiritual connection with this time of preparing to receive Torah grew. Kabbalists introduced the spiritual practice of using these seven weeks as a time of intensive inner work, spiritual refinement, and preparation. A unique "spiritual inventory" emerged, based on the sefirotic map that details the flow of divine energy throughout the universe. In the Jewish mystical tradition, the drama of creation is depicted as the emanation of ten shimmering pulsations of Divinity, *sefirot,* flowing outward from *Ayn Sof,* the

Unfathomable Beyond, into the unfolding cosmos. These interactive energies organize the flow of "God-ness" into and within the world. As creatures made in the image of God, we humans are uniquely gifted to sense these energies and use them to connect with our source in the Divine.

Equating the last seven of these emanations with creation's first "seven-day week" in the Torah, great kabbalistic teachers used this rubric to fashion a day-by-day spiritual practice for the seven-weeks-times-seven-days journey from *Mitzrayim* to Sinai. Abundant versions of this *Omer*-counting practice are available today.[3] Each of the forty-nine days we purify and refine the ethical/spiritual qualities of soul that correspond to the sefirotic energy-combination of the day. On the second day we consider whether our love is disciplined, *Gevurah she-b'Chesed,* whether we love others selfishly or respectfully; on the eighteenth day we explore *Netzach she-b'Tiferet,* whether our compassion is reliable and enduring or inconsistently felt and expressed. Integrating this *Omer* practice can offer us an evocative path to self-exploration and serve as an aid to our practice of *hashpa'ah,* spiritual direction, alerting us to the subtle movements of spirit and possible spiritual tasks appropriate to those we companion during this season.

It is this inner work, this "soul chiropractic," that spiritually realigns us and prepares us to receive Torah. The aforementioned *B'nai Yissasschar,* Tzvi Elimelech Shapira of Dinov, reminds us that the period of the *Omer* is the time of the "Good Heart," for *lev tov* has the same numeric value in *gematria,* forty-nine, as the number of days of the *Omer.* As we progress on this path of refinement, the heart opens and we see more deeply and clearly. We are walking toward Sinai, toward the possibility of seeing the Divine face-to-face. When we see deeply, we realize that "No place is devoid of God" (Exodus Rabbah 2:5; Tikunei Zohar 122b), that we are part of the divine ocean of Being. The key is a good, open heart. The new moon of Sivan brings us almost to the mountain. In the land of Israel, the ripening wheat is bursting with readiness for harvest. Fifty days after *Yetziyat Mitzrayim,* our escape from Egypt, we are camped in the foothills of Mt. Sinai. An iridescent cloud engulfs the mountain. Rolling thunder, bolts of lightning, and the piercing call of the shofar greet Moshe, who ascends to receive Torah. Together we hear the unutterable sound, the timeless reverberation of the infinite "Aleph," the first exhale of *Ahhh* in *Anochi*, *"I am,"* and our very souls begin to faint (*Pesikta Rabbati* 20:4). We call out *"na'aseh v'nishma*—We will do and we will hear (better: comprehend)," and seal our relationship with the One. We become a covenanted people. Of this we read in Song of Songs (8:8): "I rose to open to my Beloved."

Centuries later, in the Land of Israel, with great celebration, we'll bring the first fruits of our harvests to the *Beit HaMikdash*, the Holy House, to reaffirm this covenant and our enduring partnership with God. Although the destruction of the Temple ended the first fruits offering, Shavuot remains our sacred time to stand again at Sinai, to open the innermost chambers of the heart to the *I am* of the universe, and again receive Torah.

The festival of Shavuot is one culmination of the process of liberation begun at Pesach. Here at Sinai, freedom from servitude to any temporal power finds completion in a new understanding of freedom: freedom as commitment. We will serve no ruler but the Infinite Eternal One. We hear the One call to us: "Be holy, for I, the One Power that 'Gods' you, am holy" (Leviticus 19:2). We commit ourselves and all future generations to this striving: to be a holy people in a living, committed *brit olam*, an eternal covenant with the One Sourcing Power, Creator of the Universe.

Rabbi Meir Alter of Ger asks, "Why is the festival of Shavuot called 'the time of the giving of our Torah' and not the time of the receiving of our Torah?" He answers: "Because the giving of the Torah happened at one specified time, but the receiving of the Torah happens at every time and in every generation." Opening the heart to this deep encounter is the gift and challenge of this time.

New moons and full, full moons and new. The cycle continues. From Sinai we travel on toward the Land of Promise, but the challenge of entering exceeds our courage, and we turn away. Even this turning away becomes part of the journey, accompanied by growth and losses. Aaron will die, and Miriam too. Even Moshe must pass before a new generation can enter the land. We relive these stories as the heat of Tammuz and Av, the months of summer, pierces us. A time of danger and destruction again yields to hope and rebirth.

Life Reflecting Time

Terri felt imprisoned by the unfolding drama of her life. After many years together, her husband indicated that their marriage was through. Not wanting to tear her family apart, she asked him to join her in counseling, which proved of no avail. Simultaneously, she discovered that her contract was not going to be renewed at work. However, to fulfill her contract's terms, she would have to stay another year and a half to receive her severance.

> Usually you are told to find solace in work when you have trouble at home, or comfort at home when you are troubled at work. But what do you do when both places are oppressive and you can't find haven or respite in either?

Soon after the observance of Pesach, Terri reported a transformative experience to her spiritual director.

> This year at the seder, we each took turns passing the plate of matzah over our heads, symbolizing the Angel of Death passing over the Israelite houses in Egypt. When my turn came, I felt a profound sense of relief, as if the burden of these last months were being lifted and all the life-deadening forces I've been enduring were beginning to pass on. I'm not sure what these intimations of liberation mean yet, but I felt a shifting quite unlike anything I've recently experienced.

Moving into silence, Terri and her director offered thanks for the blessing of this season. They then began to explore how Terri could ready herself spiritually to discern the new revelations concerning her life that might lie ahead.

Connecting to God through Time

In his essay titled "The Tree of Life of Sacred Time," Rabbi Zalman Schachter-Shalomi asks:

> How are we to understand the process of engaging in *d'vekut,* of connecting with God, on the level of time ... [seeing that] we find ourselves in bitter exile from our soul in the realm of time? Instead of living in "organic time," natural and healthy and under the eyes

of the Divine, we live in a kind of time where any activity which is not productive appears to be a waste of time. All of the holiness, which the Creator imparted within time, specifically the long view of patience and the quality of compassion through which we change the texture of time, is lost to us. Thank God, we have the order of the sacred times of the year. Whoever holds on to them holds on to the tree of life."[4]

In a world that treats time as an economic commodity, living in the sacred cycle offers both a soul-nourishing refuge and a radical affirmation of the liberating potential of holy time. Each season offers its blessings and challenges to us as individuals and as a community. Living inside the rhythms of holy times requires that we allow the sacred story of the year to be an active, transformative agent in our lives. In this way we school our souls in what is ultimately a redemptive process for each individual, for the community, and for the planet.

The story is told that Shneur Zalman of Liadi, the great founder of *Chabad* (Lubavitch) Hasidism, told his Hasidim to "live with the times." His startled followers pondered what to make of this astounding suggestion in light of their commitment to a most traditional lifestyle. Could their beloved rebbe be suggesting that they read newspapers, adopt modern dress, go to theaters? Finally they prevailed upon his son, Dov Ber, to ask his father what he meant. He returned with this explanation: "Live with the times, you know, understand what the Torah teaching is for the week, what is the import of the month and season of the year, and how the Torah parasha and holy days affect the times!"

My *bracha* to all of us in our work: May we live well with the times! May the blessings and challenges of the seasons inform our souls' journey and bring ever greater depth and insight to all who come to us for spiritual guidance, for *hashpa'ah*.

Notes

1. Hillel Goelman, *Selections and Commentary of the B'nai Yisssasschar*, unpublished paper, 1989.
2. Arthur Waskow, *Seasons of Our Joy: A Modern Guide to the Jewish Holidays* (Boston: Beacon Press, 1991), 1.
3. Among the more popular is Simon Jacobson, *A Spiritual Guide to the Counting of the Omer* (Brooklyn: The Meaningful Life Center, 1996).

4. Zalman Schachter-Shalomi, "The Tree of Life of Sacred Time" (Philadelphia: ALEPH Publications Pamphlet Series, 1997).

Suggested Reading

Roekard, Karen G. Rosenfield. *The Santa Cruz Haggadah*. Berkeley, Calif: The Hineini Consciousness Press, 1991.

Rabbi Marcia Prager is director and dean of ordination programs for ALEPH: Alliance for Jewish Renewal, and rabbi for the P'nai Or Jewish Renewal communities of Philadelphia, Pennsylvania, and Princeton, New Jersey. Author of *The Path of Blessing: Experiencing the Energy and Abundance of the Divine*, she codirects the Davvenen Leadership Training Institute at Elat Chayyim Jewish Retreat Center, and teaches widely in Jewish and interfaith settings.

Spiritual Companionship and the Passages of Life

Anne Brener

To celebrate Aviva's entrance into her ninth month of pregnancy, our community of women met in my backyard. I provided a giant cauldron in which countless pots of soup had simmered. These chicken, split-pea, red-bean, and other concoctions had been offered as nourishment to those joining me for Shabbat and holidays, as well as to new mothers, mourners, people who were ill, and others at times when the sustenance of community was called forth by personal need and traditional Jewish injunction. For Aviva's fete, the cauldron would hold the ingredients brought by each woman to be added to the pot I would put on the stove and boil as she and her firstborn began the labor that would bring a new soul into the world. Each ingredient of that soup, which would feed Aviva and her husband during the first week of their newborn's life, represented some aspect of wisdom that the women were eager to pass on to the young family as they traversed this new threshold.

As spiritual directors, we provide the cauldron, holding the medium in which the labor to create new life can take place. We are called to offer spiritual counsel to individuals as they undergo the various life passages that appear—sometimes of their choosing, often unbidden, in the course of their lives. We are the midwives—present at these significant turning points in the life cycle—both the joyous and the tragic. It is our task to gently raise the sparks under the pot that cause the simmering that will melt the separate ingredients into a uniform, flowing broth and transform uniqueness into oneness, connecting individuals to *Adonai Echad,* the One God. As spiritual directors we have the privilege of midwifing our directees as they find God in the midst of their individual life stories.

Jews believe in marking turning points. Traditionally, we pray three times a day: at the onset of morning, afternoon, and evening. We have rituals for the significant life-cycle events that mark important moments in individual and communal life. We celebrate each new month with special songs, prayers, and practices. Every time a Jew passes through a doorway, he is instructed to pause, raise a hand, and plant a kiss on the mezuzah that hangs on the doorposts of our houses. This affectionate pause reminds us that every coming and going is a moment of awe. We learn that a wise person stops to mark such moments, reflecting on the transition and reaching up to connect with what is holy before stepping into the unknown.

Breaking the glass to conclude a wedding is another ritual of protection as we greet the awesome unknown that accompanies turning points. One reason given for this practice is to remind us that the Holy Temple in Jerusalem remains in shards. Another is the superstitious belief that demons lie in wait, like bandits on the road, during times of profound transition. The loud noise made as the glass is shattered is said to scare those demons away. This magical interpretation of a ritual enacted at a joyous celebration acknowledges that even times of delight have their share of emotional and spiritual challenges.

As Jewish spiritual directors we are called to be present for those on the threshold of new life experiences. It is our role to marry the miraculous to the mundane, finding in each passage a portal for the Holy. We know that Holiness Itself is healing. Therefore we facilitate, encourage, and support its presence in the cauldron of change, as we create the place, *HaMakom,* where Holiness is joined to the life-cycle events our directees face.

HaMakom

HaMakom is a name of God. It is the name of God invoked at turning points from ancient times. This understanding of God, which describes the cauldron of comfort created in spiritual direction, was summoned on behalf of people facing life-altering challenges, including grief, illness, or changes in financial or community status in the time of the Temple. We use this name of God in the Mourners' Blessing today. *HaMakom* literally means "the Place." That conflation of holiness and space beautifully describes what each of us creates for our directees in the container provided by spiritual direction.

There are many names for God in the Jewish tradition and many of them describe Divinity through divine qualities or attributes. We speak of *HaRachaman,* God the Compassionate; *El Emunah,* God the Faithful; or *Dayan HaEmet,* God the True Judge. These are only three of many on the long list naming God through descriptive epithets. But *HaMakom* is different.

HaMakom is a name for the Holy One that is not descriptive. *HaMakom* embraces without defining the nature of the embrace. It provides a context without a prescription for behavior. It neither describes the face of Holiness whose presence is invoked nor refers to the behavior of the one who is encouraged to find Its Holy Presence. By invoking this name of God, the Mourners' Blessing instructs us to hold the place for transformation and healing without intruding—a place for doing the work, which, in the words of Psalm 30, "turns mourning into dancing." This cauldron, *HaMakom,* whose name is God, perfectly mirrors through its nonintrusive embrace the kind of safe attention that spiritual directors provide to those who are journeying across a threshold of change.

Just as the name of God that was used in the Temple's blessing for mourners nourishes us with wisdom regarding the needs of mourners, so, too, does our ancestors' understanding of who constituted a mourner. For, as I stated above, it was not just those who grieve a death who received the Mourners' Blessing. As it says in the talmudic tractate *Semachot:* Those who were consoled in this way included "those who grieved a death, those who had someone sick at home, those who had lost a significant object, and those who had been excommunicated." This understanding of the commonality of experiences of loss is of particular relevance to spiritual directors because it reminds us that the qualities of attention and presence that undergird our work and are implied in the blessing that invokes the word, *HaMakom,* apply, no matter what the nature of the life passage that is faced.

Engaging the Unknown

When we create a place for transformation and name that place God, we acknowledge the mysterious nature of healing and the fact that healing comes from some place of soul beyond our understanding or control. Like so many others, Dennis came to me with the conviction that he could not heal after the tragic death of his son. He said to me, "I am only here because my friend made me come, but there is no way that you can help me. I will never get over this horror."

After a short silence, in which I took a deep breath and prayed that the right words would come, I replied, "Dennis, you may be right. Given what you have known and experienced up until now, it is unlikely that you have the tools that could prepare you for this unfathomable loss." I rephrased my words and continued. "It is not likely that anything that you know up until now can give you a vision of healing." As I paused briefly, Dennis looked surprisingly relieved. Here was someone telling him that there was truth to his understanding of the boundaries of the world he knew, giving him permission to feel the desperation and hopelessness that engulfed him as he mourned what was inconceivable. He felt validated in his experience of his son's loss and accepted in the torment of it. He felt safe that I would not try to take away a pain that connected him to his beloved son. And yet he was curious. Wasn't I supposed to be the one who could help? Hadn't he been encouraged to think that I could provide the answers to the unbearable questions and restore him to the world of the living? How could I concur with his belief that his situation was hopeless?

It was to Dennis's curiosity that I was directing my words. The parable is all wrong. It was curiosity that saved, not killed, the cat. The certainty that convinces us that we know what something is about—that's what holds us back. The greatest obstacle to healing is the certainty people have that healing is impossible, and the rigid pictures that they carry about what healing should look like.

I gently raised the temperature under the cauldron, as I continued my response to Dennis, reiterating my validation as I inserted one word, addressed to his curiosity, almost as an incantation to summon the possibility of the unknown. "You may be right, Dennis," I continued, "given what you have known up until now, you may not have the information you need to allow you to pass through this terrible loss." I continued, slowly adding more words of possibility. "However," I said, "have you considered the possibility that there may be something that you don't know? Perhaps there is some unknown bit of information that is, as yet, beyond the world you have lived in up until now that might give you the tools to come through this and embrace life again, despite the knowledge of this terrible tragedy?"

With each *maybe, however, perhaps,* or other word of uncertainty, the heat under the pot was raised another notch until the temperature was at the boiling point and Dennis's curiosity was engaged to the extent that the boundaries of certainty were beginning to dissolve. As the pot simmered, I could see Dennis opening up to the possibility of the unknown.

I spoke again. "Healing comes from the place we do not know. If we are willing to admit that there are things that we may not know, there is a possibility that the unknown can reach out to us and carry us to a promised land of healing. Healing will not look the way you envision it from the land in which you currently stand, but if you can open yourself to the possibility of the unknown, there is a possibility of healing."

Katnut *to* Gadlut

I spoke the words *the place, unknown, promised land,* and *healing* in the way I wrote them above, in lowercase letters, but in my heart they were written in boldface and capitalized, as one would write the names of God: **The Place, The Unknown, The Promised Land, Healing.** It is the work of spiritual direction to marry individual stories of change and challenge to the Unknown Mystery, facilitating a transformation, which kabbalists conceived of as moving from our understanding with *mochin de katnut* (the contracted mind) to *mochin de gadlut* (the expanded mind). These concepts are well described in the familiar Hasidic story that tells us that every day we should wear a garment with two pockets, and that in each pocket should be a note. The first note should have the message, "The universe was created just for me today," an example of *mochin de katnut* and the second should include the message, "I am but a speck of dust in the universe," representing *mochin de gadlut.* Our lives and our individual stories are the garment on which the divine story is embroidered. As spiritual directors, we help those who come to us decipher that story.

When our lives are changing, we contract around the uniqueness of our story. Our world narrows, just as when we are kicked in the stomach, all of our awareness goes to the experience of our pain. *Katnut. Katnut* is holy. It allows us to treasure our own individuality. Intimacy with the size and shape of our distinctive experience allows us to know our own story fully. But *katnut* is not the end point. Solipsism and narcissism would be the result if we only valued our unique experiences. Paradoxically, it is through embracing our individual stories that we begin to see what is universal in them. The deeper we go into our own experience, intimately mining our personal stories, the more we are able to reach out to others. Spiritual directors have the task of facilitating that transition, whereby *mochin de katnut* becomes a vehicle toward *mochin de gadlut*.

God: The Goal and the Stumbling Block

Those seeking spiritual direction during their liminal moments frequently come in spiritual crisis. While some people are sustained by their faith during these times, many find that as their world changes, so does their understanding of God. In difficult times people may experience a sense of abandonment by the God who has nourished them in the past. The image of God that may have been the bedrock of their lives may have been shattered. And they are further bereft.

Dennis admitted that he had always felt that he lived under God's protection. Although he had faced challenges in the past, including his mother's illness when he was a child, financial reverses in his professional life, and a divorce, he had come through those hard times, felt he was a better person for the struggles, and thanked God for the blessing. Now he felt that he had been abandoned completely by God's caring wing. "I even feel foolish," he confessed with some embarrassment, "for laboring under the illusion, all these years, that there was something out there paying attention to me." Dennis began to weep. And I once more marveled at the wisdom of the Jewish mourning rituals, which exempt mourners from reciting certain prayers and fulfilling specific mitzvot (commandments) shortly after a death. This acknowledges that the alienation from God, which Dennis was experiencing, is one of the steps in the dance of mourning.

As the tears fell, I sat with Dennis in silence. I prayed that he would feel comfort in my presence. I prayed that I would have the ability to listen to his pain with a pure heart of compassion. I prayed that my own sadnesses over my own losses would not cause me to withdraw from the heartbreak I was witnessing or cause me to shut down any parts of my listening heart. Gazing across the space between the chair in which I sat and Dennis's place on my office couch, I invoked the presence of *HaMakom* in the place between us. I looked across that Place into Dennis's watery eyes and silently said, "The God in me salutes the God in you."

After a while, I broke the silence, not with words, but with a box of tissues. I handed Dennis the entire box, allowing him to choose when he might want to pluck one to dry his tears, rather than force a tissue on him and risk giving him a message that I wanted his tears to stop. In a moment I said, "This box is not what you think. It is a lacyrmonium, a holy vessel for catching tears." After a pause, I added, "It is our holy tears that soften our hearts and remove the dust of our experience that keeps us from being able to see something new." Silently I added, "... and obscures the face of God."

One of the ways we enable our directees to move from the pocket of *katnut* to the more expansive pocket is by using image, ritual, and metaphor. These engage the processes of change in an embodied way, which can often give us more effective means for transformation than addressing the stumbling blocks of change with the tools of emotions or intellect.

As it turned out, Dennis had not availed himself of many of the Jewish mourning rituals. His pain had been so great that he had not allowed himself to yield to their support and comfort. I encouraged him to begin saying *Kaddish* for his son, starting in my office. When he recoiled at the words, too angry with God to want to utter words of praise, I validated his saying the words in tones that were angry and even sarcastic. I directed him to stand, stamp his feet, and raise his fists at the heavens as he uttered the ancient words of mourning. As Dennis embodied his grief with movements that were initially quite grotesque, he began to work through some of his anger. Reverentially, I witnessed as his cadence changed and the sounds of the *Kaddish* became a comforting lullaby, to which Dennis swayed back and forth like a child being rocked to sleep in the arms of a nurturing parent. After some time, I asked Dennis if it was possible to hold two paradoxical images of God at once, God as both the demon who had taken his son and the comforter of shattered hearts. Dennis's ritual dance had opened a door to a much larger sense of God than he had known before. Image, ritual, and metaphor more tangibly equip us to fulfill the words of the psalmist, who said, "You have turned my mourning into dancing."

Mourning into Dancing

Another treasure from the time of the Temple, when the Mourners' Blessing was directed to those facing life-altering challenges, this line from Psalm 90, chanted by the Levites, indicates mourning as the common process that signals all turning points. It prescribes dancing as the common palliative. At first glance, the phrase *mourning into dancing* sounds like a promise that pain will magically be replaced with celebration, the instant healing for which those who come to us for spiritual direction yearn when they face the unknown, unmapped path of change. It is the work of the spiritual director to help them understand that what the psalmist's words really mean is that mourning itself is a dance. It is an ancient dance that has been choreographed over the millennia by all those who have passed through this world. It contains the accumulated wisdom of all the generations. Like many dances, it has steps, which may follow a predictable pattern. At the same time each dancer—each mourner—must discover her unique rhythms and forms within the greater dance.

The steps of the dance of mourning are revealed in the panoply of emotions that accompany our turning points. These might appear as trickster demons that scare mourners into thinking that when they are caught in the midst of fear, anger, tears, anxiety, or another "demon," this malicious entity will trap them forever. But each demon has a size and a shape, a beginning and an end. These demons loom large when our directees meet them on the mourners' path. We need to remind them that all a demon is really asking for is the chance to have its voice heard, so that it can be transformed into an angel and restored to its primary task: singing God's praises—the point of healing in the dance of transformation.

Surprisingly, the demons Dennis faced in grieving over the loss of his son were not unlike those faced by people approaching apparently joyous passages, such as marriage or birth. For all of us contemplate new worlds with preconceived ideas, anxieties, and questions. If we conceive of the challenges at turning points as demons that wish to be redeemed, we can embrace these demons in the holy dance in order to make them allies in the soul work that needs to take place as we help our directees marry their stories to Holiness.

These demons along the path to healing can be likened to the first four steps of Dr. Elisabeth Kübler-Ross's stages of grief: Denial,

Bargaining, Depression, and Anger. Dr. Kübler-Ross articulated the process of change as a predictable, normal, and transformative process. Her path provides a recognition of the universals of change. She teaches us, too, that transformation can be seen as a series of temporary steps, reminding us that none of the experiences that must be encountered will last forever. Hopefully, this will encourage those exploring turning points in spiritual direction to take the time to explore each aspect of growth and change fully, to see what can be learned about being human at each stage.

As a model, Dr. Kübler-Ross's stages of grief have provided a therapeutic paradigm that has given countless individuals a context for understanding their experiences of profound change. As spiritual directors, we can build on her work to de-pathologize the process of change, remove the shame from the necessary stages through which those who face change inevitably pass, and provide a context that will allow them to face and come to terms with the deepest and most meaningful aspects of mourning. As spiritual directors we can use this schema to encourage our directees to savor each state, to find what is holy in each step along the way. While denial, bargaining, depression, and anger don't sound like appealing places to be, each of them can be a dwelling place for God. Each stage can be a profound teacher regarding the nature of being human and confronting change. Viewing each in this way lifts the struggle from *katnut* to *gadlut,* as we seek to find the presence of God in the midst of these challenges. In so doing we make each step on Dr. Kübler-Ross's path a place for discovering God, just as Jacob found God unexpectedly in the places where he encountered angels. For in each of these places our directees can learn what they need to know about the turning point they face, about being human, and about God.

Witnessing Dennis's dance of *katnut* on the path to *gadlut* required my patience and permission, as he courageously encountered the demons that lay in wait for him on his mourner's path, allowed them their voice, and began an intimate dance with them, which transformed them into angels, bringing him closer to God. Dennis stopped seeing himself as a solitary victim, singled out for the terrible curse of losing his son. He began to experience his loss as the universal struggle to come to terms with what it means to be a human being on a planet where people die. He had made the transition from *katnut* to *gadlut.*

Letting God in, in Times of Joy

The face of God can be obscured, not only in times of tragedy, but also in times of joy. Just as spiritual directors may make the valleys high in times of tragedy, there are times when we are called to make the mountains low, helping our directees, who may be intoxicated by joy, to hold on to their spiritual practices and sense of awe. Jane, a long-time directee came to me, exhilarated by her new relationship. She was filled with details about places she had been and things she had done with the wonderful partner who had entered her life. She told me of their compatibility and how this differed from other relationships she had had, upon which we had reflected in the past. Breathlessly, she shared with me her sense of having triumphed over her past.

Breathlessly is a key word here. While I was delighted with Jane's news, I observed that she was neglecting her spiritual practices. She was not meditating regularly and was skipping Torah study and some of the other activities that had comforted her at times when her life had felt like more of a struggle. In her joy, Jane was isolating herself from the person she had been in the past and some of the sources of nourishment that enriched her life before this relationship. In some ways, she was making an idol of her joy; placing it on a mountaintop and assuming that it would be invulnerable.

The truth is that we can contract around joy as much as we can around grief. When good things happen to us following a period of struggle, we often want to declare ourselves "cured." We not only dis-tance ourselves from the difficult experiences of our past, but also from the wisdom gleaned from them. We are prone to hold onto the good thing with the same *katnut* that we often bring to our sense that we have been singled out as victims in a tough time.

While I did not want to deflate Jane's joy—certainly not!—I wanted to bless it in a way that would encourage her to tend to what was holy both in her current joy and in her past vulnerability. I wanted her to be able to bless the miracle of healing and renewal, while re-maining mindful of the need to nurture the flame that sustains us in good times and in bad.

For me, one of Judaism's most profound teachings comes at Sukkot, when we are commanded to dwell in temporary and fragile dwellings, while celebrating *zman simchateynu,* the time of our joy. This paradox of embracing vulnerability encourages us to hold onto the things we love, but not so tight as to make them into idols. As Jane and I spoke about the joy of her new relationship, we were both moved to tears, as we remembered how certain she was that she would never love again. In remembering the certainty around which she had contracted in the past, she acknowledged the fragility of this new relationship, committing herself to tend it with reverence.

Dr. Elisabeth Kübler-Ross's concept of stages is relevant not only to grief, but also to joy. She taught us to recognize that feelings are transitory. We experience them and then we move into another place. Like the teaching of Sukkot, we learn to embrace each place on the path, learning what we can as we dwell in the sukkah, the temporary dwelling place in which we find ourselves, embracing what is holy therein, while preparing to meet whatever will be coming.

Several years later, what was coming for Jane was a baby. Again, the excitement of anticipation and the details of preparation had Jane moving at an accelerated pace that did not allow room for the sacred. We were able to use her childbirth exercises as the entry point for Holiness into an event that was clearly a sacred passage for Jane and her husband (not, incidentally, the person about whom she had been so exhilarated and so certain several years before). As Jane and I worked together, in anticipation of the birth of her child, we reflected on the Hebrew words for *breath* and *soul,* which are cognates. Knowing that Judaism teaches that life begins with breath and that upon birth, God breathes souls into bodies, Jane was able to bring this understanding into the breath work she was practicing to ease her childbirth process, drawing on all her experience with meditation as she approached this new and exciting life passage.

Connecting her breathing to Holiness helped Jane to engage God as a partner in creating the soul that would be entering the life she shared with her husband. It helped her to conceive of her infant child, not just in terms of the physical being for whom she and her husband would be responsible, but also as a soul entrusted to their care. It also enabled Jane to feel that God was with her, the Ultimate Midwife, nurturing and protecting her as she went through this ultimate life passage.

In the Song of Songs (8:8–9), the question is asked,

What shall we do for our sister
On the day that she will be asked for?
If she is a wall
We will fashion for her a silver skirt
But if she is a door
We will plank her with cedar.

The question of whether we face a wall or a door on the day that we are asked to confront profound turning points is one we must ask our directees as they face the existential challenges that arise at these significant moments. Holding onto a fixed set of beliefs, an idealized past, or a present joy makes our lives opaque, a kind of wall, which is impenetrable and cannot be breached. Here sparks of Holiness are often inaccessible. It is our holy task, as spiritual directors, to show those we serve the door, opening them up to the multitude of possibilities that are always present at thresholds—especially the possibility of God's presence.

Anne Brener, author of *Mourning & Mitzvah: A Guided Journal for Walking the Mourner's Path through Grief to Healing,* is a psychotherapist and rabbinical student at Hebrew Union College. She teaches at the Academy for Jewish Religion, Los Angeles, and is on the Morei Derekh faculty. A New Orleans native, she spent three months doing relief work in the Gulf South following Hurricane Katrina.

Soul-Traits in Classical Mussar and Contemporary Jewish Spiritual Direction

Alan Morinis

Introduction

The challenge that confronts the spiritual director, as I have come to see it, is to be in the presence of another person with such openness, such openheartedness, such authenticity, such clear immediacy, that the spirit of the moment yields up a secret. This secret is something unattainable through the plodding dissections of the mind, something as unscripted as to be expressible only in metaphor, as the Jewish tradition does when it speaks to us of *Ruach HaKodesh* (Holy Spirit), prophecy, and the *Shechinah* (not that these equate exactly to the spiritual direction experience).

When you are familiar with encounters of this sort, in which one heart through its openness serves as a key to unlock another heart, then you will know that what is in question here is spiritual art, not science.

My exposure to spiritual direction has come about exclusively through the Morei Derekh program of Yedidya, in which I have taught since its inception.[1] As a consequence, the style of spiritual direction with which I have become familiar centers on the practice of contemplative listening. The deliberate interaction between and among people that takes place in the context of this sort of spiritual direction has at its heart the practice of listening deeply, often in mutual silence, with the intention of becoming sensitive and attuned to the sacred dimension that lies beneath the surface of ordinary life. The goal is to open the channels to receive and perceive as much as possible of the Divine Will, as it applies to an individual and to specific situations.

The assumption and the hope in this method of spiritual direction is that more of the Divine Will can be discerned by means of supportive and shared listening for the still small voice within, and that this method will turn up the surest guidance one can hope to have in any life situation.

Anyone who wants to practice spiritual direction in this way is challenged to discover the path that will lead him or her to *become* the heart that opens the way to this encounter. Few are born with this capacity. The rest of us must learn and cultivate the qualities that carry us in that direction. For that, the Jewish tradition does offer a path of preparation, which is known as the *Mussar* tradition.

It is because I have background and training as a student and teacher of *Mussar*[2] that I inadvertently find that my discipline has something to offer in the endeavor of spiritual direction. It turns out that the perspectives and methods developed by the *Mussar* teachers in the thousand-year history of this discipline seem to be entirely applicable to the training of Jewish spiritual directors and the practice of contemporary Jewish spiritual direction[3] for reasons and in ways that I hope to make somewhat clear here.

The Middot *Perspective*

Mussar needs to be explained to some extent because it is almost certain to be unfamiliar to many readers. Although *Mussar* is a venerable tradition of introspection and self-development that has evolved in the Jewish world over the past millennium, it has never been known outside the world of Orthodox Judaism, which spawned it and nurtured its development. And even within the Orthodox world, *Mussar* is not much in evidence today, and certainly not in the full-blown expression that the tradition has been given in previous generations.

The thought and practice of *Mussar* are developed and encompassed in a body of written works, including *Chovot HaLevavot (The Duties of the Heart)* by Rabbi Bahya ibn Pakuda in the eleventh century, *Orchot Tzaddikim* in the sixteenth century, *Messilat Yesharim (The Path of the Upright)* by Rabbi Moshe Chayyim Luzzatto in the eighteenth century, and even relatively recent works such as *Michtav mi-Eliyahu* (translated as *Strive for Truth!*) by Rabbi Eliyahu Dessler and *Alei Shor (Branches Over the Wall)* by Rabbi Shlomo Wolbe, among many others. These texts have defined *Mussar* perspectives and practices. In nineteenth-century Lithuania, a movement based on *Mussar* thought was founded and guided by Rabbi Israel Salanter (1810–1884), in which much of the thought and many of the practices we now associate with *Mussar* were innovated, and older thought and techniques were elaborated and enhanced.

Mussar is no different from any other broad tradition within the Jewish world in that there is not a singular and monolithic theory to which all who align with the rubric subscribe. Even direct disciples of Rabbi Salanter, who built their own schools of *Mussar* in the nineteenth and twentieth centuries, interpreted and articulated *Mussar* in their own unique (though compatible) ways. In presenting a brief overview of *Mussar* in contemporary language, I offer a synthesis of some essential themes and focuses. A great deal is left out that the reader is encouraged to pursue elsewhere.

The Soul

The starting point for an understanding of *Mussar,* especially in relation to Jewish spiritual direction, is the soul. This is *Mussar*'s starting point because it is nothing less than our own starting point as human beings as well. When God created the first human, the Torah records that *HaShem* "breathed into his nostrils the breath of life; and man became a living soul."[4] We have been that way ever since.

It is interesting and important that the Torah says that "man became a living soul" rather than something like "man was given a living soul." This difference shows up in our own thought today as well. We tend not to see ourselves primarily as souls, and even if you are someone who does acknowledge the reality of soul, you are nevertheless much more likely to say that you *have* a soul than that you *are* a soul. When you put things that way—that you have a soul—the implicit message is that the soul is somehow a possession or an offshoot of your identity. That way of seeing things suits the ego just fine because it confirms our identity as the central feature of our inner being. But despite the ego's insistent and noisy protests to the contrary, it just isn't so. The primary reality of a human being, and what makes us human, is that we *are* all living souls, as the Torah says.

It may take a profound reorientation to look beyond the material and the psychological to see that we are all souls, and that soul is the fundamental and primary ground of our human existence. From that perspective, however, our lives can be seen to be, primarily, as soul journeys on which the ego is a great assistant and a terrible *chef de mission.*

Tradition teaches that there are three primary aspects of the soul, though I need to underscore that this is just a way of talking so we can describe the subject. In reality, the soul is an undivided whole. At the level of soul, there is no break between heart and mind, emotions and intellect. All embody faculties of the soul.

The Torah also tells us that we are made *b'tzelem Elohim*[5]—in the image of God. It is at the very core of the soul that we find an inner dimension shaped in the "image and likeness" in which we are created. Because of its divine antecedents, this essential kernel within us is inherently holy and pure. It isn't possible to taint this deep aspect of soul, no matter what evil deeds a person may do. It glows with a warm and steady flame, and its light is constant. This spiritual nucleus is called *neshamah,* and it is the source of all the holiness and completion we seek in our lives. It exists within us now, though the way to it may not be very clear. The *neshamah* is also the place where spiritual connection takes place, to other people and to the Divine.

The next dimension of the soul is that aspect that is the source of animation and vigor or, alternatively, depression and lethargy—no more, and no less, than the "spirit of life." This is called *ruach*.

The third aspect of the soul is the one that is most visible and accessible to us. Here we find all the human traits we see in others and ourselves, like the emotions and thought, desires and talents. This dimension of soul—called *nefesh*—interacts with this world and is the home of the traits of personality, identity, and character with which we tend to identify ourselves and others in this life.

With only limited exceptions, all the familiar features of our inner world are aspects of the *nefesh*-soul. Emotions, desires, conscience, wisdom, and all our capacities of one sort and another are traits of the *nefesh*. Even the faculties we ordinarily allot to the "mind"—like thought, logic, memory, and forgetting—are all powers of the *nefesh*.

The *Middot*

The catalogue of traits that are housed in the *nefesh*-soul features very prominently in the discipline of *Mussar* and provides the practical link between *Mussar* and spiritual direction. Recall that the light of the *neshamah* burns constantly and radiantly at our core, and that this is the locus at which spiritual connection takes place. The poet Moses ibn Ezra writes:

In my body He has kindled a lamp from His glory;
It tells me of the paths of the wise.
It is the light which shines in the days
Of youth, and grows brighter in old age.

Were it not derived from the mystery of His light
It would fail with my strength and my years.
With it I search out the chamber of wisdom,
And I climb with no ladder to the garden of
delights.[6]

He writes here of the *neshamah*. The *Mussar* teachers tell us that we are all repositories of that holy light—the lamp kindled from God's glory that reveals the chambers of wisdom—and yet in the condition of our actual lives, the reality is that some measure of that holiness is almost always obscured behind a veil. The single factor that determines the extent to which the *neshamah* and its holy light are opened or closed off to us, our experience, and our lives is the state of the inner qualities that are located at the level of *nefesh*.

To avoid any possibility of misunderstanding, let me clarify here that what I am *not* saying is that certain inner qualities, which we might want to call "vices," are obstructions to connection to deep soul. The *Mussar* view is that all human qualities—even traits we might conventionally conceive to be undesirable, such as anger, jealousy and lust—are not to be seen as intrinsically "bad." *Mussar* offers us the insight that each of us is endowed at birth with every one of the full range of human traits, and this is as it should be. Every trait has its role and the potential to be either a positive or a negative inner influence. This is one of the messages of the Psalms when taken in the aggregate, where every emotion and human state is poetically depicted and none does not have a place.

What sets one person apart from another, then, is not whether one has a trait that the other does not—that's actually not possible because we each have them all—but rather the degree or level of the traits that live within each of our souls. It is the measure of our traits that creates our distinctiveness and, when the measure of a trait turns out to be problematic in ways I will soon describe, it is the level of that trait (and not its intrinsic nature) that causes it to function as an obstacle that occludes the light of the *neshamah*.

In Hebrew, the collective word for these soul-traits is *middot*. That word is almost always translated into English as "traits of character," but literally it means "measure." This etymology confirms what the *Mussar* teachers teach, which is that the differences between people, and also what separates us from our own inner spiritual source, is not whether a trait is present in us, but rather the *level* of each trait. It's easy to see how anger, greed, or jealousy, for example, can become obstacles to the inner light but this view of our interior lives tells us as well that even so-called virtues, like kindness, trust, and generosity, can equally become inner impediments. How does that happen?

The Veils and Their Roles

In his book *Eight Chapters* the Rambam (Maimonides) provides us with a good image for understanding how the holy inner light gets blocked. He writes there specifically about prophecy, though what he says applies to any efforts to open the inner channels to the divine Source and its Will:

> In the Midrash and the Haggadah as well as in the Talmud, it is often found that some of the prophets saw God from behind many veils, while others saw Him from behind a few veils, depending upon their closeness to God and their level of prophecy. They [the Sages] said that Moses, our master, saw God from behind one diaphanous veil (Maimonides, *Shmoneh Perakim*).

The Rambam then asks the critical question: What are these veils? He answers:

> Moral habits ... are the veils of the prophets, peace be upon them. Thus, whoever has two or three moral habits not in the mean ... is said to see God from behind two or three veils (Maimonides, ibid).

What Maimonides calls "moral habits" I follow the *Mussar* teachers in calling *middot ha-nefesh,* or soul-traits (at the level of *nefesh*-soul). He gives a short list of examples of some problematic, veil-inducing traits, including lust, arrogance, irascibility, rage, impudence, love of money, and similar things. He identifies for us that these are the veils that separate us from the holy.

Notice that the Rambam says *lust* and not *desire, arrogance* and not *pride, rage* and not *anger,* and so on. He is clearly pointing to traits that are operating at extreme levels within us. As I have said, the issue the *Mussar* teachers see and want us to address that applies so directly to spiritual direction is not the traits themselves but rather their level, whether happily near the mean or in the problematic range, which could be either too high or too low.

The measure of our soul-traits is set at birth, and then, as we go through life, every deed and every thought—whether from experience or, more deliberately, from behaviors we have chosen to engage in—come to be "inscribed" in the *nefesh*-soul. In consequence, the levels of specific soul-traits get raised or lowered. It is when soul-traits are not in the median range that they come to function like inner veils that prevent the full light of the holy *neshamah* from shining through. They are then not in their proper alignment, which is how they come to be obstructions to the light, like veils.

The greater the number of misaligned soul-traits, the greater the number of veils and the more cut off we are from the *neshamah*. Our lived experience in that situation is to feel separated from holiness and from God, and to feel isolated in our world. In the place of inner illumination, we perceive darkness. These veils prevent us from feeling our holiness, from being able to offer our holiness to the world, from being able to sense any aspect of or connection to the Divine in the world. The greater the number of veils, the more this is the situation of our lives.

Recognizing these veils and how they function is very important in the context of spiritual direction because these veils stand as the primary hindrances to the emergence of the contemplative, communion-like experience upon which the process of spiritual direction relies. A person who would be a spiritual director needs to be concerned about the veils to holiness that populate his or her own inner life, which he or she will inevitably be bringing into the work of direction, and which will clutter the channel he or she seeks to open. When acting as a spiritual director, awareness of the veils that separate another person from his or her own access to the divine sources is a different and related concern.

Once a soul-trait is identified to be functioning as a veil, there are prescribed steps for bringing the trait back into balance *(tikkun ha'middot)* in order to raise the veil. We will return to this subject below, but first, more on the traits themselves.

A Short List of Essential Traits Every Spiritual Director Needs to Have in Balance, Whether by Nature or Cultivation

It is excellent and, I would argue, necessary, for a spiritual director who wants to be a catalyst for the experience of open encounter with seekers to prepare himself or herself by identifying and working on his or her own *middot* (soul-traits). This self-knowledge and commitment to re-balancing of inner qualities is a way to clear the path to encounter, though I must stress that no one should think that they have to be per-fect (as if they ever might be) before getting started. What is most im-portant is that the spiritual director embrace the orientation toward recalibrating his or her own obstructive (that is, extreme-tending) soul-traits, and to endeavor to do so. Growth and change will come in time as a result of the practice and the doing. As you lift the veils to the holy in your own life, you prepare to accompany others as they walk the same path in their lives.

In turning now to look at certain traits that I suggest are univer-sally important to the practice of spiritual direction, we will see that applying *Mussar* to spiritual direction begins with spending time learn-ing. The focus of this inquiry is to discover the nature of the inner traits as revealed by the Sages of *Mussar* through their acute observa-tion and insightful analysis of human life. We must first understand the traits themselves as a step toward perceiving accurately how they function in our own lives.

Anavah (Humility)

One of the essential skills of a spiritual director is the ability to listen, and while "listening" is not a soul-trait in itself (being an action), there are *middot* that will impinge on or, alternatively, facilitate the ability to listen deeply and with concentration. Foremost among these is humility. Humility is indeed a *middah*, and a very important one. To be an effective spiritual director you have to have a well-developed sense of humility.

In Jewish terms, humility is not the utter and complete debase-ment of the self that a common (largely Christian-derived) understand-ing of the term *humble* might connote. The *Mussar* teachers tell us that humility is not an extreme[7] but a mean or midpoint between the traits of debasement and arrogance. In fact, the word *humility* does not fully coincide with its closest Hebrew equivalent, which is *anavah*. It says in the Talmud that a person who sits in the same place in the synagogue every time is an *anav* (a humble person).[8] That idea doesn't make sense if seen through the lens of an ordinary understanding of humility as meek reticence and contraction, but it is indeed a major clue to the distinctively Jewish view of this quality. The Jewish understanding of humility has to do with how much space you occupy.

To be humble is to occupy an appropriate space, whether that is actual physical space, or "space" as it applies in psychological, emotional, environmental, financial, and other arenas. A person who sits in the same place in the synagogue occupies his or her own appropriate space and leaves room for others to occupy their spaces. Since all soul-traits can be out of balance toward excess or deficiency, for some people the work of becoming humble means growing larger and moving out of a negative self-image to occupy more space, while for others contraction would be the appropriate goal.

This Jewish redefinition of humility helps us see why this quality is so crucial to the spiritual director. A person with an overblown sense of self (i.e., who occupies an inappropriately large volume of space) will crowd and perhaps even suffocate the directee with his or her ego. Conversely, a person who is too reticent to occupy space will have a hard time mustering the (healthy) presumption to take the risks of offering suggestions and providing guidance. In either case, access to the Holy will be impeded.

Bitachon (Trust)

A second crucial soul-trait the spiritual director needs to have in good measure is trust, called *bitachon* in Hebrew. This term refers not to just any kind of trust but specifically to trust in God. A person who has strong *bitachon* (whether by grace or by dint of hard work) is capable of acceptance, and so is less susceptible to responses of anxiety or judgment, which will inevitably interfere with the real connection and communication upon which spiritual direction depends.

Trust may not come easily because placing our trust in God can seem like a very difficult and maybe even irrational thing to do, in the midst of this unreliable world in which hurricanes, earthquakes, tsunamis, and other natural disasters can and do strike at any moment. A life can be suddenly overturned by illness or accident. And then there is the unaccountable cruelty, incompetence, and stupidity of people to take into account.

I tend toward a *Mussar* orientation that sees in the trait of *bitachon* an attitude of resting in the trust that things will work out just as they should, although that might not be exactly (or perhaps even remotely) how we would want. To worry and fret about what will result from our actions reflects too little trust in God, and puts too much focus on the self as actor, which drops a veil over the soul. At the other end of the spectrum, although some *Mussar* teachers have said that trust means putting full expectations on God to take care of our needs, that strikes me as an excessive reliance on divine intervention and an almost complete abrogation of our own role in our lives. A person ought not be passive or fatalistic, which is the situation of too much *bitachon* that will also create an inner veil. We are meant to make every effort to improve the world in ways that matter to us but once we have made that effort, then we are wise to relax into acceptance, since it is indisputably true that we do not control the ultimate outcome of almost anything we do in our lives.

Activating the trait of trust is important to the spiritual director because it is the quality most effective for loosening the grip of anxiety and fear on the one hand, and indifferent resignation on the other. Trust makes it possible to become a more open, accepting, and yet active being. If you are able to accept that the world is not always nice, comfortable, certain, or easy, but it is the ideal training ground for the heart, you render yourself able to trust in God, and you will have given yourself the capacity to be more open, and openness is essential to the work of spiritual direction.

Kavod (Honor)

The third of the traits essential for the spiritual director is honor, or *kavod* in Hebrew. Too often we judge others harshly (reflecting an excess of the trait of *ha'arachah*—evaluative judgment). Too often, doing so is simply a reflexive response. Rabbi Shlomo Wolbe, a contemporary *Mussar* teacher, points out that our impulse to judge is prior to our impulse to understand, as is true of babies, who know what they like and don't like, even if they don't know what it is. Any tendency to rush to appraise others that remains in the heart of the spiritual director is going to taint the moment.

Earlier I discussed the perspective that *Mussar* offers of seeing everyone as a soul. Once you have internalized this soul-perspective, it becomes possible to peer beneath the surface of any human being to perceive the soul that radiates from within. Developing this skill transforms the person in front of you from a messy, incomplete, disappointing being (as we all are) into a radiant, precious soul who is infinitely and inherently worthy of honor (as we all are, though at a different level). Whatever a person may say, no matter how disjointed or clumsy or distasteful his or her story, no matter how lost or confused he or she may be, no matter how tainted his or her deeds, when he or she is approached and held with honor by virtue of his or her deep soul-natures, harsh and hasty judgment is impossible and that makes openness and connection entirely possible.

It should be self-evident why the ability to honor the soul of another is a necessary quality for the spiritual director to develop, in the face of the opposite and remarkably common tendency to stand in judgment of others.

A Personal Spiritual Curriculum

We have been looking at a short list of *middot* that are universally important for spiritual directors to have in balance. Beyond these necessary traits, the director who sees the value in *Mussar* needs to identify and pursue his or her own personal spiritual curriculum.

We each have our own distinctive spiritual curriculum. What that means is that at this particular moment in your life, there will be one, two, three, or more traits that are tending toward the margin, far from the median, whether by being too strong or too weak. The essential traits identified above may or may not already have a place on your personal spiritual curriculum. Through introspection and paying attention to the feedback received from life, you can become quite astute at identifying the traits that are present on your own spiritual curriculum.

Whether it is humility, trust, generosity, or honor, or perhaps impatience, rashness, or laziness that dominates your list of target traits, understanding and identifying those traits is only part of the *Mussar* approach. Once identified, the next phase of *Mussar* work kicks in, which is to do the work required to recalibrate the level of that *middah* within yourself.

It is beyond the scope of this essay to discuss the variety of *Mussar* methods that have been developed over the centuries for the express purpose of helping the arrogant person achieve humility, for the frantic worrier to develop genuine trust in his or her heart, or for the hyperjudgmental person to offer up honor to another. Suffice it to say that making change is the real focus and identifying the elements of the curriculum is only one step along the way.

It is a central aspect of *Mussar* as well as crucial in applying *Mussar* to spiritual direction to affirm that inner change of this sort is possible. It may not be an exaggeration to say that making those sorts of changes—the angry person learning calmness, the miser learning generosity, the ditherer becoming decisive—is the actual core track of all human lives and the primary spiritual work each of us is in the world to do. We are bolstered in seeing the possibility of change by the Rambam again, who asserts strongly that our inner character is not preordained:

> Let it not pass through your mind like the fools of the non-Jews and most of the *golem*-like Jews that God decrees from the time a person is created whether [that person] will be a holy person or an evildoer. That is not correct. The person could be wise or stupid, or merciful or cruel, or cheap or generous, and so all the other qualities (Maimonides, *Mishneh Torah, Hilchot Teshuvah*).

The inner traits are not predestined, nor are they unchangeable. They can change. They do change. And we can make them change. By our conscious actions, we can lift the veils, and once a person who aspires to be a spiritual director has identified which veils curtain off the light of his or her own *neshamah,* then it requires disciplined effort to bring the soul-trait more toward greater alignment with the healthy, unobstructing mean of the range.

A Final Word on Transforming Our Inner States: Why Spiritual Directors Need to Be Attuned to Soul

The primary reason why it is important for a spiritual director to be attuned to soul and do the work of lifting his or her own inner veils is as preparation to become a clear vessel for the experience of immediate connectivity with another soul and with God, in the hope of perceiving as clearly as possible the will of God. As one Jewish spiritual director trained in *Mussar* put it, "By examining certain qualities within ourselves and being conscious of how we are manifesting them in our lives, we can more directly attune ourselves to God's will."

Secondly, the soul-perspective provides the spiritual director with a lens through which to bring into focus the soul-nature and soul-journey of the other person. Another spiritual director expressed it like this: "*Mussar* has given my work as a spiritual director a 'Jewish ethical compass.' It has also given me great language to use and specific areas to focus on with a directee, if needed, with practical exercises. Even if I don't use the word or the Hebrew terminology with a directee, it comes into play as a way for me to focus on certain areas that I want the directee to consider."

To "become" a spiritual director is much more than a matter of pouring certain prescribed information into neural storage. There is inherent in the notion of "becoming" a reference to the deep level of transformation that is meant to come about. In practice and in particular, this process of transformation can focus on the specific soul-traits that are central features of the director's spiritual curriculum. In addition, this perspective can inform how the director sees the directee and his or her life. A spiritual director trained in *Mussar* reports putting to use *middot* concepts such as humility and others as guidance tools, but also has invoked these without bringing up directly the source of these ideas, that is, *Mussar.* "Because *Mussar* has influenced my thinking so pervasively, it has impact throughout my work," she notes.

It would likely be an error for a spiritual director to use knowledge of the soul-traits or the *middot* perspective as a diagnostic tool or in an instructional way with directees. *Mussar* can play a positive role in the direction process by providing the director with a framework for understanding human life in general, from which will come connections and suggestions that can be used to guide the directee in particular. Let me give one example to illustrate how this can work in practice.

It wouldn't be uncommon or surprising to find a directee expressing anger, or maybe even concern over the way anger is playing a role in his or her life, since anger is such a widespread issue. Study of *Mussar* would reveal something that virtually all Mussar teachers take as axiomatic: A link can often be drawn between anger and our old friend humility. Don't anger statements almost always begin with "I"? Isn't it the ego that takes offense at the behavior of others? And so we read in the Ramban's famous letter to his son *(Iggeret ha'Ramban)*: "Once you have distanced yourself from anger, the quality of humility will enter your heart."[9] The converse is also true: To distance yourself from anger, cultivate humility.

The director who is aware of *Mussar* and who finds himself or herself confronted by a directee who is relating tales of anger will instantly find that considerations of ego and humility will come to mind. That connection may provide the director with suggestions to make to the directee of where to look for insight and what to consider effective factors that the directee is likely not to have thought of on his or her own.

Mussar as a discipline is focused on giving us tools with which to bring about deep and lasting inner change. The agenda is defined as raising or lowering the levels of our soul-traits, although another way to express the same idea is as a process of bringing our heart and our heads into closer alignment. Often the ideals we hold for ourselves are strongly held as intellectual ideas but they are not necessarily reflected in the same form in our lived experience. The *Mussar* teacher Rabbi Elya Lopian (1872–1970) wrote eloquently about closing that gap. He defined *Mussar* as "making the heart understand what the mind knows." Spiritual direction is a very idealistic enterprise; *Mussar* complements that idealism by taking a practical interest in how those ideals are going to become the embodied truths of the individual, as characteristics of his or her soul.

As you can imagine, the sort of change *Mussar* is meant to bring about is a long-term process. One of the primary disciples of Rabbi Salanter, who founded the *Mussar* movement, was Rabbi Yosef Yozel Horwitz (1848–1919), whose school of *Mussar* is called Novarodok (named after a town in Eastern Europe). "The problem with people," Rabbi Horwitz said, "is that they want to change overnight and have a good night's sleep that night too."[10] Change of the kind that will prepare an individual to become an effective spiritual director, or will liberate the directee to move to the next phase of his or her life, can be disruptive, and the process may be lengthy. So much so that another of Rabbi Salanter's disciples, Rabbi Simcha Zissel Ziv (1824–1898), who in his own time founded the Kelm school of *Mussar* (of which the above-cited Rabbi Lopian was one product) said about *Mussar* and, by extension, about the work of recalibrating the inner traits that each of us has on our personal spiritual curriculum, "It is the work of a lifetime." Then he added: "And that is why you were given a lifetime in which to do it."[11]

Notes

1. I acknowledge my great debt to Anne Brener, Amy Eilberg, and Linda Thal, my coteachers in the Morei Derekh program, who have taught me a great deal about spiritual direction, spiritual life, and friendship.
2. See my *Climbing Jacob's Ladder: One Man's Rediscovery of a Jewish Spiritual Tradition* (New York: Broadway Books, 2002).
3. Rabbi Rami Shapiro recognized the fit between *Mussar* study and practice and Jewish spiritual direction, and invited me to teach in the Morei Derekh program, for which I am grateful.
4. Genesis 2:7; the Hebrew term used for *soul* here is *nefesh*.
5. Genesis 1:27.
6. Moses ibn Ezra, "The Sources of My Being," in *The Jewish Poets of Spain 900–1250,* trans. David Goldstein (New York: Penguin, 1965), 107.
7. There is no universal consensus on this point. I follow the majority opinion here.
8. *Brachot* 6b.
9. Moses Nachmanides, *A Letter for the Ages,* trans. Avrohom C. Feuer (New York: Art Scroll, 1989), 16.
10. Adapted from Meir Levin, *Novarodok* (Jason Aronson, 1996), 126.
11. Ibid.

Alan Morinis, DPhil, was a Rhodes Scholar, and is currently pioneering the interpretation of the insights of the Mussar tradition to the Jewish community. The author of *Climbing Jacob's Ladder: One Man's Rediscovery of a Jewish Spiritual Tradition*, he is the principle teacher of The Mussar Institute.

New Dimensions in Spiritual Guidance

From My Flesh I See God: Embodiment and Jewish Spiritual Direction

Rabbi Myriam Klotz

The practice of Jewish spiritual direction supports the opening to God's unfolding presence in our lives. This practice seeks to cultivate our ability to listen deeply to the movements of our spirits, and of God's movements within us and within our world. Through the different seasons and textures of a moment, a day, a lifetime, we pause to pay attention to what we are experiencing in our inner lives. This deepening attentiveness toward the inner worlds we inhabit encompasses our emotional and intellectual bodies, even as we focus on the spiritual body. And, none of these dimensions of lived experience can be separated from the physical body we inhabit. What we experience in our inner worlds cannot be separated from the physical dimension of our experience any more than we could say that we live separate from the grace of breath, each moment we are alive. The "material" we have at our disposal to help us discern God's unfolding presence in our lives, is none other than the gritty, sometimes pleasurable and sometimes painful lived experience of our physical existence. "From my flesh I see God,"[1] says a voice in scripture. The "flesh" of direct experience is a lens through which we indeed "see" the Divine manifest in this world, through our own selves.

Since we experience God in our lives through our flesh, our lived physical experience, and if perhaps our very fleshiness—our embodied existence—is in itself a manifestation of the Divine,[2] then when we practice Jewish spiritual direction, we aspire to listen as deeply to what our bodies tell us about God's unfolding in our lives as we listen to any other dimension of our experience.

As Jewish spiritual directors, we can support our directees to listen to, and experience, their bodies as sacred and wise sources of meaning. We can practice being a welcoming presence for the physical dimensions of our directees with the same intentionality as we do for their hearts and their souls. In so doing, we embody the mitzvah, or holy action, of *hachnasat orchim*, welcoming strangers into our spaces with warm hospitality. For some directees, having a safe and welcoming place to "be" in their bodies may be a profound experience, regardless of whatever else unfolds in the direction relationship.

Similarly, we can be intentional about being fully present in our own bodies as we engage in the direction relationship, so that we pay attention to the sensations and truths of our own bodies as we practice. We will *feel* our work with directees not only in our emotional and cognitive realms and in the awareness of our souls, but also physically, if we let ourselves be open to this dimension of our experience. As the Kotzker Rebbe says, "Where is God? Wherever we let God in." Sometimes, God's presence may enter through a sigh; a release of tension in the back; a noted quiver of the lip, a smile, a groan; a moment of eye contact that releases emotion or shares a knowing recognition; a touch of hand upon hand that evokes memory, or that evokes a sense of God's presence in that very moment. These moments may be consciously experienced by the directee, the director, or shared by both. It matters, then, to reflect on how we relate to our own bodies. Are we a clear channel physically that helps to open the relationship between the directee and his sense of God's presence, or are there "blind spots" or other ways in which areas of the director's physical pain, tension, or fears about the physical experience of embodiment might bleed into the director/directee relationship and get in the way of the directee's experience of God's unfolding presence in his life?

In this essay, we explore the complicated, sensitive, and vastly sacred process of embodiment as it anchors the practice of Jewish spiritual direction in the present, unfolding moment. We begin by considering a Jewish approach to embodied spirituality that may be helpful in thinking about the sacredness and spirituality of our bodies, and how tending to our physicality is not a matter of hedonism or avoidance of more "important" matters, but rather is a vital grounding for the life of the spirit in the context of Jewish spiritual direction.

We then will "flesh out" in more detail how we might incorporate somatic awareness into our practice of Jewish spiritual direction. The arena of our bodies and the process of embodiment is vast— touching on nothing less than every realm of our lived experience! In this essay we will focus our exploration on three fundamental areas of bodily experience that underlie every moment of our existence, including our experience of Jewish spiritual direction, in a most basic way: body awareness, breath, and gestured movement.[3]

Exile: Disembodied Spirituality in the Jewish Experience

Eventually our physical bodies will die. According to many strands of Jewish belief, our souls, by contrast, are eternal. What does this distinction mean for the spiritual life while we are alive physically? Does eternality reside in mortal flesh? How do we, human beings, embody this tension between the mortality and eternality that both comprise who we are? We "hold" this tension each moment we are alive.

Human beings from all cultures must wrestle and dance with this dynamic. The cultural forces that contain various communities indeed impact how individuals understand themselves within that context,[4] and impose a structure within (or against) which an individual grows along the spiritual path. The Jewish tradition is no exception. Historically, Jews as a people have often had traumatic physical experiences in, and of, this world. The rupture of Jews from their land; the sensual, immediate sense of relationship to God exemplified by Temple worship; and the personal experiences described so vividly in the Psalms and elsewhere in biblical literature—all this comes to a jerking halt with the destruction of the Second Temple and the displacement of the people to other lands. Centuries of being outside the Land of Israel have perhaps contributed to a collective withdrawal of the Jewish psyche from the earth, the body, and the concomitant sensibilities that can flower when an organism senses that it is safe to "be" in the world, and lives in regular and conscious connection to it.

It is perhaps no coincidence that the Jewish people have been deemed the "people of the book" for centuries. And, while a brilliant survival strategy for a context of exile, a side effect of drawing awareness out of the physical senses and into the life of the mind in a state of exile from its sacred physical grounding, is that the body itself becomes less and less a safe "place" to inhabit. The intelligence of the somatic consciousness becomes narrowed. Sometimes the body's needs are ignored, overridden, or simply not perceived. Over time, from generation to generation, there become fewer ranges of movement accessible, dreamt of in the body's imagination. Intelligence itself, a component of wise discernment, can diminish.

Further, the impact of the Holocaust on the body of the Jewish people in the last century has been made clear in so many arenas. One area that spiritual directors may encounter is the way in which Jewish directees might find the experience of being in the physical world, in their bodies, to be terrifying. While rationally, one may "know" that it is now safe, relatively speaking, for a Jew to fully inhabit the physical world, the visceral, instinctive body may yet still "know" in cellular memory that it has been anything but safe to do so. As a result, adaptive behaviors to compensate for not fully "feeling" into one's physical, sensual self may emerge. There might be a desire to drop into the body, and one may perceive a vague longing or impulse to more fully "taste and see" the sensuality of one's existence. Yet, sometimes without support and help, this urge can be left to wither on the extremities of awareness as a plant dries up when left untended.

The disembodied nature of the collective Jewish experience, as a result of the traumas and displacements of the Jewish people for centuries, contributes to the ways in which one might come to her relationship with God. How one is able to listen deeply to what movements of the Divine are within, calling one forth, happen in the body one inhabits. When intuitions and perceptions, discernment, of God's unfolding presence are constricted as a result of an aversion to noticing and feeling what one physically registers and communicates, there can be a split, a chasm between the egoic self, the conscience, and the soul. If, in a Jewish spiritual direction relationship, a director is able to notice the possibility that the collective Jewish experience might be impacting the experience of an individual, there might be opportunities for the person to open to God's presence as she begins to find, or re-find, safe haven in the home of the body as a home where God, too, lives.

Each spiritual direction relationship is as unique as a snowflake, no two the same. Yet, keeping in our awareness certain operative paradigms that have given shape to the collective Jewish experience in our bodies can perhaps help us in service of the intention of Jewish spiritual direction, discerning the movement of God's presence *in* the lived, sensual world we inhabit. As a result, perhaps, we can have the privilege to help midwife a different kind of integrated relationship between the soul and the body.

Return: A Jewish Approach to Sacred Embodiment

The Bible offers many examples of individuals and the Israelite collective body discerning God's presence in physical and immediate ways. There are also some strands of later Jewish spirituality that affirm this connection. It may be helpful in the course of Jewish spiritual direction for the spiritual director to have a sense of such paradigms of an embodied Jewish spirituality. This foundational approach might be useful information to share with a directee in his search for reconstructing an authentic and holistic relationship with the Divine that is body-based.

In the Bible, the first human being created is named *Adam.* In Hebrew, the word *Adam* is composed of the Hebrew letters *aleph, daled,* and *mem.* If we separate the *aleph,* which the mystical tradition understands to represent the purely spiritual innermost realms that lie outside the physical dimensions of God's essence from the *daled* and the *mem,* which together form the word *dam,* which means "blood," we have before us the biblical view of human existence: the archetypal human is composed of both spirit, and blood—flesh and blood.

Our witnessing to the sometimes harmonious, sometimes volatile coupling of our spiritual and fleshy selves is in part what Jewish spiritual direction is about. What movements of flesh, of spirit, seem to bring us closer to God's presence in our bodies, in our lives? How might different physical states or choices we make regarding our bodies set us into greater harmony, or more dissonance, with God's unfolding presence within or before us? What do we notice about what happens to ourselves when we are "out of balance"? What holds us in balance physically, spiritually? These basic kinds of inquiries inform the work of Jewish spiritual direction, and are given shape by the Jewish view that we are in essence both eternal and temporal, both spirit and matter— and that our spiritual growth is connected to how we learn to cultivate awareness of the sacred as it dwells in our flesh each day.

Similarly, one kabbalistic understanding of a central rabbinic image of God as *Melech,* King, might help us to relate to this "face" of God in an embodied way, and shift a focus from controlling our bodies in service to the spirit, to invoking the sacred wisdom inherent in the soma itself as it lives in partnership with Divine Consciousness. The kabbalists suggest that the letters of the word *Melech—mem, lamed,* and *chaf*—are an acronym referring to parts of the body: *moach*—brain; *lev*—heart; and *k'layot*—kidneys! So, this view implies, the divine "king" whom we might "serve," or open up to, is none other than the Divine Mind, Heart, and Kidneys of the Universe![5]

There have been many symbolic representations of God in the Jewish imagination over the centuries; this one invites us to relate to God's ruling presence not as a ruling power above and separate from humanity. Instead, perhaps, this sovereign existence might refer to the Divine Consciousness that exists *in* the wisdom of the physically manifested world, and within our own bodies, as we are made in the image of God, *b'tzelem Elohim.* Our own bodies and their physical processes mirror the Divine in the unfolding process of creation intrinsically, each breath we take.[6] The human body is thus understood by some in the Jewish spiritual tradition to be a direct channel through which one can discern God's unfolding presence, embedded *in* the very body of one's life.

Given this conceptual foundation for an embodied approach to the Jewish spiritual journey as our base, we will now explore several ways in which it might manifest in a Jewish spiritual direction relationship and how a spiritual director can help integrate body awareness and movement into this practice.

Felt Sense:[7] Feeling Our Souls on the Earth

In the Book of Exodus we learn of Moses' dramatic adventures, which in part are a chronicle of this spiritual leader's sense of the unfolding revelatory presence of God in his life. While Moses is still young in his spiritual development, he is in the wilderness, tending a flock of sheep, when he notices a bush that is burning but not being destroyed.[8] This strange sight gets his attention. When Moses turns aside and contemplates this bush, he hears the voice of God. God instructs Moses: "Take off your shoes, Moses, because the place on which you stand is holy ground *(adamat kodesh)*!!" Moses does take off his shoes, and then God speaks in intimate, revelatory detail with him. Moses learns a great deal about the unfolding presence of God, and about himself and his destiny, in that revealed moment.

A prerequisite for this divine encounter is that Moses take off his shoes, conscious of what posture his body is holding, and, on just what he is standing—holy ground. He has to shed a layer of covering that, while serving as protection from the elements keeps distance between Moses' body and the ground upon which he walks. The text does not tell us exactly what Moses does when he removes his shoes. We might imagine that he spreads his toes, stands on his heels and the balls of his feet, perhaps lifts the inner and outer arches of his feet. Maybe he feels rocks and sand and the hotness of the ground beneath him and it is uncomfortable. Or perhaps it is a relief to have his feet unbound from the thick leather that covered them. Somehow as his bare feet touch the earth he becomes more aware of the sacredness of that ground and of the encounter to which he is becoming alert. God asks of Moses to remove the protective layers that distance Moses from his own perceptions and sensitivity. In order for there to be the greater intimacy of God's revealed presence, Moses has to be able to feel directly the truth of his experience in the moment.[9]

In Jewish spiritual direction, a similar kind of shedding is often necessary to enable a director and a directee to drop into the potential for sacred encounter that the Jewish spiritual direction session presents. A directee—and a director—come to a direction session with all the protective layers of clothing that keep us safe from the elements and discourse of daily life. Yet when the sanctuary of the Jewish spiritual direction space is entered, cloaks can be put aside, perhaps shoes removed, ties and belts loosened. The body can begin to relax and settle, and the mind and heart can then more easily still the business of habitual thoughts and feelings. There is perhaps more spaciousness in which to begin to feel, and register, what is actually happening in that very moment.

On a deeper level, it is important to take some moments to remove the "shoes" that might keep oneself protected, but a step removed, from the immediate sensitivity that comes from direct encounter of the felt senses of the body. As we begin to let go of the protective layers of thought and habit that can keep us from feeling directly the sensations and information that our bodies experience and our hearts feel, we become more receptive to the presence of God that is perhaps waiting for moments of encounter with us.

For one example, I share from a direction relationship with

Melanie, a rabbi with substantial congregational responsibilities. She fills her days and many evenings doing what she feels is God's work, yet she sometimes doubts her sense of call to this vocation. Melanie arrives for spiritual direction month after month harried from the fullness of her activities. She is so very busy and brings with her into the direction session the stimulated sense of an active life. One day, Melanie came to her session very energized and eager to begin. She also said, casually, that she felt tired, but quickly returned to her desire to reflect on some work she had been doing with her congregation. In that moment, I sensed that there might be something important in the message she was receiving from her body, even though it did not seem particularly relevant to her in that moment to rest in her sense of being tired. I did not know where it would go, but decided to ask Melanie to pause, turn aside from her expressed agenda, and indeed to notice the sensations and energy level of her body before we continued.

We both closed our eyes and Melanie took some time to scan her body and connect with her breath and to notice what her body was feeling and "saying," and to see what she might simply notice, without passing judgment or jumping to conclusions about what she experienced. She simply paused to "take off her shoes" and feel the ground of being in that moment.

After a few minutes of this body-focused meditation, Melanie opened her eyes. She said, in a soft, slower voice than usual, that she noticed how deeply tired she felt in her bones. Her eyes felt softer, she noticed, and there was an achy feeling in her lower back. She had felt this before in sharp moments of pain, but she usually chose to override this intrusion of pain into her day, as she was busily focused on the task in front of her.

At a certain point, as Melanie continued to connect with her breath and the sensations in her body, she began to sigh heavily. Her shoulders seemed to drop away from her ears. She was quiet for a while longer. We began to explore where God might be found in the sensations she was noticing in her body. The "felt sense" that Melanie perceived was that she was indeed deeply tired, and that she wanted to stop "doing" so much. The aching and pain in her lower back bespoke to her a sense of needing more support, more help to hold her up in her life. As she slowed down long enough to feel what her body was actually experiencing, even though it was not comfortable, Melanie had a realization about her sense of God in that moment.

Perhaps, Melanie said, her God did not expect her to carry the world on her back. Perhaps, just maybe, God wanted Melanie to slow down, to allow God to carry more of the burden with her. Perhaps she might allow herself to be held in the arms of a gentle, nurturing God who would be there for her, to help hold her as she was holding so many others in her life. She saw in that encounter that she had been overriding the messages her body, and her God, had been sending in attempts to get her attention, via subtle and not-so-subtle signals. Melanie needed to turn aside from her habitual path, take off her "shoes" of habitual doing and protective thinking, and settle in to notice the sacred messages that turned her toward a fresh and relational sense of God's presence in her life.

Melanie continued to work with the issues of willfulness and softening surrender that she uncovered in this session. This important turning point in her Jewish spiritual direction practice was engendered by the wise truth of her physical self trying, like a burning bush, to get her attention, to get her to slow down, listen, and hear the nonverbal and sacred language of her body. In the direction sessions that followed, Melanie continued to practice the art of listening to the felt senses of her body. She knew on a deep level that somehow God's mysterious manifestation in her life was happening through the vessel of her body. Had Melanie not chosen to listen to that signal of fatigue and an aching lower back, but instead continued to pursue what she thought was going to be her agenda for the spiritual direction work, she might never have come to notice the still, small voice of God speaking through the authentic experience of her body.

Hachnasat Orchim: Grounding Body Awareness Exercise

"As we enter the body with great awareness, supported by another's loving presence, focused on our breath and willing to let go, we [can] enter another domain of being—the domain of spirit."[10] The following is an exercise that a spiritual director can facilitate to help a directee not just think about his body, but drop into it and experience what is happening in the moment. This practice is one way of "taking off one's shoes" and turning to notice the holy ground of being on which the self stands.

Invite the directee to sit comfortably and to close her eyes. Explain that there is no need to fix or change, or understand, what she notices. She needs only to notice what is happening where she brings her attention. Then, the director might offer the following grounding practice:

Bring your awareness to your feet. Breathe into the soles of your feet. Notice where the weight is distributed on your feet right now; the front, the back, the inside, the outside of your feet. No need to change anything, just notice.

Now, bring attention to your ankles. Which parts are working to keep you upright? Do your ankles feel strong, wobbly? Just notice what is happening. With the next breath in, draw your awareness to your shins. Your calves. Notice what is happening there. Exhale, and with your next in-breath, direct your inner gaze to the knees. Notice if your knees are working to hold your body upright, or if they seem relaxed. As you breathe in next, breathe awareness into your thighs: inside, outside, front, and back. What do you notice about your thighs? Let this go with your next out-breath.

Now bring your attention to your pelvis, groin, and but-tocks. Notice if the breath can enter easily into these areas of your body, or if there is constriction or any tightening. Again, no need to do or be anything other than notice what is happening in this moment. Now, your abdominal region. Do you notice areas of hardness, of softness, of fullness or emptiness, any areas of more sensation, or less?

As you inhale next, breathe awareness into your chest, rib cage, and solar plexus. Notice where the breath goes easily and where it might not, and what happens in the rib cage. Next, your shoulders. Notice where your shoulders feel themselves to be in this moment in relation to your chest and trunk. Just notice. Bring awareness now to your arms, in relation to the rest of your body. Do the arms and hands rest easily? Do you feel tension?

Now, bring awareness to your lower back. Midback. Upper back. Notice areas of tightness or those that are working to keep you upright. Notice areas that feel relaxed, soft. No need to change a thing. Just bring breath and awareness to your back.

Inhale next to your neck, the back of your neck, and your

throat. Notice which parts seem to be working to keep your head upright. Notice areas of tension, of ease. And now, the base of your skull; your scalp; your face; the entirety of your head. Feel the density of your head, holding itself upright on your body.

Now, with your next in-breath, scan your entire body, front, back, and left and right sides. Notice which parts of your body seem at ease, which seem to be working hard. Notice the parts of your body that are harmonious, if any are in conflict with each other. Bring breath to the whole body, and let it go.

Again, breathe in a deep breath of air, letting it fill your entire body, and then release. This time, as you breathe in, see if you notice God's presence in your body, right now. There is no need to force or change anything. Just notice what is there. Where is God in this breath? In this body? In this moment? Continue to breathe in connection with your body for as long as you like. When you feel complete with this process, let your eyes open.

At the conclusion of this exercise, the directee might share her experience with the director.

Nishmat Hayyim *(The Breath of Life)*: *Awareness of Breath, Flow of Spirit*

Jim and I sat together in a direction session and were reflecting on a painful situation, and how the loss he had been experiencing was impacting his sense of God in his life. Where was God, and what was God, if God was not coming to help Jim in his time of need? Who was this God that would allow the suffering Jim was enduring? As Jim was spewing these words out, his usually full, deep breathing became noticeably more shallow. He paused, unable to speak.

I asked him to follow what was happening in his body, to turn from tracking his feelings to just noticing his breath and the physical sensations. He was turning his deep listening skills toward the "speaking" that his body, through this changed breathing pattern, was offering. Jim closed his eyes. His brow furrowed and his chin tucked toward his throat as he allowed his body to follow the tension held in his breath. After some moments, Jim's breath returned to a longer flow. He sighed a deep and long exhalation; his eyes opened and he rolled his face toward the ceiling, stretching his throat open. He sighed again, and his shoulders relaxed a little. Next, his eyes and mine met, and, without words, we "spoke" our witnessing of his breath to guide him through this experience of emotional and spiritual pain. It was Jim's breath that got his attention.

Jim continued in this session to reflect on his experience of God at this difficult time in his life. We did not put into language what happened to Jim as his breath constricted so utterly as he deepened into the experience of psychospiritual pain he allowed to surface. Yet, our mutual honoring and tending to Jim's flow and halt of breath was an important dimension of Jim's "speaking," and listening, to the flow of his spiritual life and discernment process during this spiritual direction session. In Jewish spiritual direction, breath is an essential, not tangential, dialect of the vernacular of this discourse.

In Genesis 2:7, God breathes the breath of life—*nishmat hayyim*—into Adam, that first, archetypal human being, and Adam becomes a living being. Breath sustains us moment by moment and is our most constant reminder of the spirit moving in us every second, sustaining us.[11] The fact that in the Hebrew, *neshimah,* breath, is spelled exactly as *neshamah,* one of the words for *soul,* but just vocalized differently, is noteworthy. The breath and the soul are so overlapping as to be in some sense, one. Our ability to breathe deeply, to take in breath, is thus connected to our ability to receive, or embrace, "soulfullness" in our lived experience.

In Jewish spiritual direction, then, another central aspect of embodiment involves awareness of the breath and how breath moves through our bodies. If a director can hold in her awareness the movement of breath in a directee, she might pick up on subtle or not-so-subtle cues as to the movement of spirit within that person. Such awareness might help guide the flow of reflection and perhaps open up areas of discussion or prayer.

When breath flows easily and deeply, there tends to be freedom to experience and express emotions, perceptions, desires, and many other forms of life energy—*nishmat hayyim*—as it courses through the body. Such awareness can be noted overtly, or needn't be, but is nonetheless a valuable sensitivity for the director to hold.

As a director sits with a directee, he might look to notice if the directee's breath seems shallow, and short, or if it flows into the entire body, long, and if there are sighs, pauses to allow a breath to enter and release fully.

In *The Particulars of Rapture: Reflections on Exodus*,[12] Aviva Gottlieb Zornberg describes vividly a state of spiritual dis-ease that is reflected physically by the inability to take in deep breaths. When, in Exodus, the Israelites were enslaved, they were not able to listen to Moses and his promise of freedom, "out of shortness of breath *(kotzer ruach)* and hard work" (Exodus 6:9). The Hebrew phrase *kotzer ruach* not only means "shortness of breath," but also, "shortness of spirit." When a person or a people is so densely oppressed, constricted, or depressed that they are enslaved, they cannot hear words of consolation, they cannot breathe deeply into their situation, nor can they deeply receive spiritual nourishment. The double bind of being in such a constricted state physically or psychically, Zornberg points out, is that when one is unable to breathe deeply, this state prevents the very thing from happening that could help release one from this enslavement: a deep, receptive breath that reaches into one's body and soul, penetrating every cell with fresh *nishmat hayyim,* vitality and awareness. As more breath is allowed into the body, as more breath is deeply released, movement and renewal become increasingly possible. Sometimes, however, "a prisoner cannot free himself from prison";[13] with the help of a loving presence devoted to that person's well-being, however, one can become free.

As a spiritual director you can bring your discerning gaze to your directee's flow of breath. If you notice that his breath is shallow, or if the flow of talking is so rapid that pauses for breath seem few and far between, you might suggest that you both pause and invite the directee to breathe deeply and slowly. You might further suggest in that moment that the directee focus on his breath, and return to felt body sense before attempting to bring the reflections to language. As discussed earlier, it is the felt sense experienced in the body, not the mind's thoughts *about* the body, that are the basis for grounded discernment and integrated experience. As a Hasidic teaching from the *Sefat Emet* instructs, in order to hear deeply God's presence, it is important to clear oneself from distractions and obstructions. One can then better hear the voice of the Divine stirring within.[14]

In Jewish spiritual direction, as a director tends to the flow of breath in the room, there can be a tending to the flow of God's unfolding mystery in the life of the directee. Just as important, there can be discernment as to whether there might be a restriction in that flow, which can be explored.

Also, the spiritual director can note the flow of her own breath in a session, as a tool to discern her own state of being in a moment. If you notice your breath becoming shallow, you might ask yourself if your freedom of discernment has narrowed. If so, why might that be? You might pause, take in a deep, slow breath, and exhale, as you give space for your spirit to return, your breath and presence together again more fully available to your directee and to God's presence within you and in the relationship.

Kol Haneshamah Tehallel Yah (Let Each Breath Praise God): Breathing Practice in Jewish Spiritual Direction

You can use the following exercise as a tool in a spiritual direction session to help focus on breath moving through the body. You can guide the directee through this meditation, reading the words slowly so that the directee has time to experience and notice what you are cueing. You can also adapt this practice for your own use before, after, or during a session.

> Sit comfortably with your spine upright. Let your shoulders roll up toward the ears, and then down your back. Settle onto your buttocks. Your feet should rest comfortably on the floor, and your hands can rest easily on your lap. Let your eyes close.
>
> Bring awareness to the breath as it moves in and out through your nostrils. Just become aware of the flow of this breath. [*Pause for several seconds.*] Notice where the breath moves easily, where it is constricted. On the next in-breath, direct your gaze and the breath to your throat. Let it fill with breath, then release.
>
> Now, breathe into your heart. Feel the lungs expand with oxygen. Notice what happens in the upper back. As you release the breath, watch it leave the body. On the next inhale, direct your mind's eye to your belly. Notice what happens. Does the breath travel easily into the abdominal area? Is it difficult to bring breath

there? Do not try to fix or change the breath, just notice how this breath moves in and out of your body.

Next, breathe into your lower back. Notice if the lower back broadens and fills with breath, or where the breath is or isn't. Exhale. Now breathe into your entire body, aware of the breath filling you up from the crown of your head down to the toes. Exhale fully; empty the body of this breath. Notice the pause in between exhale and the next inhale.

Continue to breathe in and out, in and out, at your own pace. You might focus on God's presence filling each breath as it enters and leaves your body. [*Pause for several moments.*] When you feel complete with this meditation, you can let your eyes open.

You can spend some time in reflection about this exercise, exploring any openings, challenges, or awareness of the directee's inner life or relationship with God that may have emerged. Remember that there is no "right" way for this meditation to happen, no results you are intending other than helping to assist in the connection between breath, body, awareness, and the spiritual life of the directee, however she understands this process.

A sampling of questions for reflection might include:

- Where does God's presence in your life feel constricted?
- Where does it flow freely?
- What does it mean to take God in with each breath? To "breathe deeply" or "shallowly," and in relation to your relationship with God?
- What happens to your sense of God in the moments of exhalation?
- How do you experience the moments in between breaths when the body is empty?
- What happens if your body is unable to take in breath? Consolation?

Movements of the Soul: Gesture and Movement as an Embodied Walk with God

Body language is a phrase that evokes, literally, the language our bodies speak in order to communicate. A phrase my own spiritual director uses often when asking me to articulate a feeling or awareness about something in my life or about God, is to "put language to that." Putting language to the inchoate urges, sensibilities, awareness, yearnings, pain, or insights of our spirit sometimes means listening to the grammar of somatic communication. We speak through our bodies, sometimes in ways more direct than verbal words because there are levels of awareness and experience that are preverbal, nonverbal, and immediate. As directors, we honor our directees if we can learn their body language as well as the verbal ways of expression they share.

At times this can manifest by following cues from the directee's breathing or body posture, as discussed earlier. In other instances, gesture or movement may be the most authentic and immediate means through which we share what we are experiencing. A director can sensitize herself to moments when spiritual expression takes form through embodied expression. Through our own body language as well as with our words, we can provide safe haven for such expression, and can help directees honor the sacred dimensions of their own embodied spirits. Do we sit comfortably alert, with an open heart and chest, with relaxed shoulders? Is our facial expression one of invitation and warmth? How might you, as a director, allow your body to communicate a message of receptivity and support for the one in whose service you are sitting?

In addition to being aware of the language your body is speaking as you are present in a spiritual direction session, you might also bring awareness to the gestures and movements that a directee is sharing, and understand that he might actually be "speaking" coherently and potently, if only his grammar were understood.

For example, Kara often spoke in Jewish spiritual direction sessions about her longing for connection with God, and about her pain at feeling a distance from God and not knowing quite how to sustain that contact. After several months, we began to notice that most times as Kara deepened in her reflections about this dynamic of her spiritual life, her right hand would move up to her heart area, pause, and then rise up toward her throat. She touched her heart and her throat lightly each time. I grew curious about this gesture, and began to wonder if perhaps there might be something that Kara's body was telling us about her spiritual yearning. As it turns out, Kara had not been "conscious" that her body was moving in this patterned way that "spoke" when she was in a contemplative, prayerful time of spiritual reflection. It was a moment of integration of body and spirit brought through to the light of conscious awareness that helped Kara made this connection, and through it she began to forge a deeper intimacy with her body and her movements toward her God.

How many times do our bodies move and gesture, while our minds are elsewhere, not paying attention to the physical activity of the present moment? Perhaps these moments are many. An opportunity in spiritual direction is to "sit" with what flows through us, to notice the postures, gestures, and sacred expressions that may be surfacing before our very eyes even as we are devoting our attention to "other" areas. In Kara's situation, as we explored what this gesture of lifting the hand to heart and then to throat might mean, Kara discerned that a deep prayer was being uttered through this nonverbal gesture. The raising of the hand to the heart and then to the throat bespoke, for Kara, her longing to allow the stirrings of desire for God to be expressed. In fact, the hand gestures were themselves the expression of that prayerful longing. Sharing this moment of awareness together was a kind of "Amen" to that prayer.

There may be gestures or movements, or various expressions of body language, that a director will sense are significant for the directee. The director might gently point out this gesture to the directee and invite the directee's own reflection on the significance or possible meaning behind the movement. Just as a director would want to invite the directee to name her own experience, rather than doing so for her, in any other realm of the spiritual direction discourse, so too with bodily movements, postures, or stances, the meaning or authenticity of which lies in their relevance for the directee. Associations and valences that the directee brings with the gesture are theirs to discern. Thus, it can be useful to invite the directee to reflect on the gesture, perhaps to repeat it with awareness, and bring it to prayer and reflection. It is usually less helpful for a director to impose a meaning or association on a movement, even when it might seem quite obvious to a director that a gesture clearly means something. For example, prostrating on the floor might recall for a director the bowing that is done in many Jewish services on Yom Kippur. Yet, for a directee, there might be quite a different sense of what that gesture means or expresses for him were he to embody that posture in a spiritual direction session.

As a Jewish spiritual director, each of us can consciously create an environment of safety and respect for the body's languages of expression in the growth of the spirit, and respect for the sanctity and uniqueness of each person's journey. There may be times when a directee is searching for words to clarify or express her relationship to God or her spiritual life. Yet, words are not found. It may be that tears, sighs, crying, shaking, or allowing the body to move in the moment will be the language that is sought. Just as the cries of Hannah were understood to be holy and sacred expressions of the soul (even as they were misunderstood and devalued by some), so too might one embody prayers or states of the soul through gestured movement or soundings that find a different grammar than the spoken word. As a spiritual director, each of us can honor the unfolding presence of God in the lives of our directees by learning to listen for, respect, and converse with, the fullness of bodily expression as it manifests with each breath and through each gesture. We can practice the art of holy listening, not only by listening to the words that are spoken, but to the sighs, the silences, the uplifted eyes, or the outstretched arms, remembering that in those places, too, might God's presence be found.

Notes

1. Job 19:26.
2. A central tenet of Hasidic spirituality is that God's presence fills the entire creation, that nothing is devoid of the revealed and physical dimension of the Divine.
3. The nexus between what we perceive, feel, and "know" through our bodies, and how we experience and "know" God's presence in our lives, is vast and nuanced. Some of the realms of embodied experience not touched upon in this chapter include sexual identity and sexuality; pregnancy and giving birth; infertility; menopause; illness, dying, and death; and action-oriented embodiments of spirituality, such as social justice and athletics.
4. See Norvene West, ed., *Tending the Holy: Spiritual Direction Across Traditions* (Harrisburg, PA: Morehouse Publishing, 2003), for an examination of how human responses to the Divine are refracted through various religious and cultural traditions and help shape the contours of spiritual direction within a given faith tradition.
5. Diane Bloomfield, *Torah Yoga: Experiencing Jewish Wisdom through Classic Postures* (San Francisco: Jossey-Bass, 2004), 95.
6. A belief central to Hasidic spirituality is that God sustains and fills creation each and every moment, breath by breath. If this were not the case, existence as we know it would simply, suddenly, cease to be.

7. See Zalman Schachter-Shalomi, *First Steps to a New Jewish Spirit: Reb Zalman's Guide to Recapturing Intimacy and Ecstasy in Your Relationship with God* (Woodstock, VT: Jewish Lights Publishing, 2003), 41ff.

8. Exodus 3:1–5ff.

9. See Aharon Yaakov Greenberg, *Itturei Torah*, English translation *(Torah Gems)*, vol. II, trans. Samuel Himelstein (Tel Aviv: Yavneh Publishing House Ltd., 1998), 26–27.

10. Michael Lee, *Phoenix Rising Yoga Therapy: A Bridge from Body to Soul* (Deerfield Beach, FL: Health Communications, Inc., 1997), 42–46.

11. See Jonathan Slater, *Mindful Jewish Living: Compassionate Practice* (New York: Aviv Press, 2004), 183–187, for a detailed reflection on how the process of respiration in the body reflects deep awareness of the movement of God in one's life, as based in both Hasidic teaching and mindfulness practice.

12. Aviva Gottlieb Zorenberg, *The Particulars of Rapture: Reflections on Exodus* (New York: Doubleday, 2001), 110–111ff.

13. Brachot 5b.

14. Zorenberg, 111ff.

Suggested Reading

Gilman, Sander. *The Jew's Body.* New York: Routledge, 1991.

Rabbi Myriam Klotz is a cofounder and codirector of the Yoga and Jewish Spirituality Teacher Certification Program at Elat Chayyim Jewish Retreat Center. She is director of Yoga and Movement Practices at the Institute of Jewish Spirituality, serves as a spiritual guide at the Reconstructionist Rabbinical College, and a mentor for Morei Derekh training program for Jewish spiritual direction.

New Horizons: Poetry and Spiritual Direction

Jennifer (Jinks) Hoffman

L et me tell you my story of being a spiritual companion and about the way I use poetry in spiritual direction sessions. Being a spiritual director is a gift and a privilege beyond description. To sit with another, as he seeks to discern the movement of God in his life, is profound. The following are *composites* of two of the people with whom I work, so as to preserve their privacy and the sacredness of our time together.

Arthur is a man who struggles with his prayer life. He is comfortable with the liturgy in shul, he enjoys the Shabbat services and those of the *chaggim* (holidays), but he yearns, with such a deep longing, to have a more personal relationship with God. I talk quietly with him about the difference between *keva* (liturgical prayer) and *kavannah* (intentional, personal prayer.) I talk about a contemplative approach to God, and remind him of Psalm 46:10: "*Be still and* know that I am God." I invite him into silence, and he expresses a little fear, saying that he has never sought God in this way. With my encouragement, however, he sits quietly, as do I. Our eyes are closed for several minutes, as we attempt to be receptive to God's presence. "Nothing," he says flatly after fifteen minutes. I suggest that before our next session he sit quietly with his eyes closed every day for fifteen minutes or so, simply trying to be present, to bring himself intentionally before God's presence. I show him a *shiviti* and explain he may want to use this sacred painting or illustration as an aid to prayer and contemplation of God's presence. Based on the verse from Psalm 16:8, "I set YHVH before me always," the *shiviti* has traditionally been used to aid devotion. I invite him to try an elegantly simple way of sitting in silent contemplation with the desire to open his mind, heart, and soul to God, the Ultimate Mystery, beyond words or even thoughts. I ask, as we sit in prayer once more, for a name to come to Arthur that he can use gently as a way to go inside and to center on God, when his mind wanders. Arthur does receive a name, very clearly, and I ask him not to tell me, but to keep it totally private between him and God. I say we will reflect in our next session about his experiences.

When Arthur returns, one month later, he tells me that he has been very faithful. He has sat in silence for twenty minutes each day, using the name that came to him in our previous session, not as a mantra, but to return to his attention to God's presence. "I say the name gently, silently," he tells me, "just as you suggested, as gently as you kiss the head of a child after saying the bedtime *Shema*."

Yet he says he was unable to still his mind, and he feels very disconsolate. "I just cannot reach God," he says grimly. "I understand," I say and I reach for this poem.

Kavannah

In dawn's darkness
I lie in prayer
seeking You.
I yearn for the stillness,
the quiet, the nothingness
that affirms Your presence.
I ache for the inner silence
that is infused with divinity.
Instead
my "monkey mind" chatters,
thought upon thought
wish upon wish
longing upon longing.
But a single thought
has an urgent insistence
and gains my attention.
"Your *kavannah*" You whisper
"your *kavannah*."
You love my intention.
You welcome my deep desire
to be present to Your Presence.
I "show up," You tell me
over and over.
And that is Your desire.

Your desire is that I seek You,
in silence,
in noise,
in every single aspect
of my life.
Moment upon moment.
Your desire
is my *kavannah*,
my conscious intention
to connect with You.
"Do not chastise yourself"
You say
as You kiss me,
Your *ruach* upon my face.
"Your *kavannah*,
your intention
is gold."

Arthur looks at me quietly. "Thank you," he says.

I have been a psychotherapist since 1978. That was my second profession. I was a speech therapist until then. I have served as a spiritual director since 2003. There is, however, a certain graceful logic and order to this movement in my life. I trained to become a spiritual director with Lev Shomea (which means "listening heart"), the first ever training program in Jewish spiritual direction, and very soon into my training felt that I was home. I spent most of all four residential weeks in tears, tears that I have come to call my "God-tears," my own visceral confirmation of God's presence. My whole life, particularly my relationship with God, has been transformed through this process. Indeed, I suspect God's main reason for "hauling" me into the training program was so I would become more aware of the reality that God is at the center of my life, at the center of everything.

Very early in my work as a psychotherapist, I began writing poetry. Most of my poems are about God, about my own spiritual joys and wrestlings, and those of my clients, family, and friends. Fairly soon, I came to realize that God is the cocreator of my poems. When something is stirring my consciousness, either because I am joyous or "in trouble," I sit quietly and ask, "A poem please, Beloved." When I do not understand something, or need God to guide me, I ask for guidance, and nine times out of ten, a poem arrives in short order, often taking just a few minutes to create. I have been blessed to discover that poetry expands my consciousness and helps me tap into depths of truth that are not otherwise available to me. Writing poetry is numinous for me. It is prayer, an act of love. Poetry is the language of my soul. And when the poem is completed, I often read it to discover what God and I have cocreated ... and cry more "God-tears."

I have come to believe that I receive holy guidance through my poetry and also through dreams. I have experienced many significant dreams that seem to issue from a place of expanded consciousness, which I identify with God. I once had a dream that said, You have five keys. I knew these to be the five ways that God guides me, keys to my relationship with God: dreams; reflection on my relationships and *gemilut chasidim* (acts of loving-kindness); my poetry writing; my daily walks, during which I pray and meditate; and study of Torah and other spiritual matters. Five keys. Five ways I experience divine love and guidance.

I had a dream that said, Study the Torah for poetry and meaning, (gorgeous, huh?) and, Some dreams and some poems are meant to be shared. Since I utterly believe that God cocreates both dreams and poems, how appropriate that I am to share them, with directees, clients, family, and friends. It seems odd, then perhaps not, that often a poem I have written that very morning seems to have relevance for something a directee later brings for reflection. And sometimes, as I sit with someone, I discern that a poem, maybe even one written some time ago, may be a possible offering. I imagine that God is whispering these suggestions into my heart, and of course I never really know if it is God's voice or my own. But I have learned to trust such impulses, and quite often they seem helpful.

I believe deeply that there is a profound need within the soul for creativity. We need to create and I believe that God desires human creation and addresses us through its imagery. Is not God the greatest artist of all? Creativity within the context of spiritual direction need not be restricted to sharing the director's own compositions. It can involve placing a few flowers in a vase or arranging scarves or candles with consciousness to beautify the direction setting. It can include, when appropriate, inviting directees to capture the immediacy of their own experiences in prose or verse. It also may include the director lovingly sharing poems composed by others, artistically offered at just the right moment, when continued discourse, lessons from tradition, or even the richness of silence won't do. God does not have human hands with which to write or select poems, but we do. As it says in Psalm 90:17:

> Let the work of our hands prosper
> O prosper the work of our hands.

Sarah has recently begun to work with me. She is thinking of becoming a spiritual director herself, and is looking for guidance as to whether this is right at this time in her life. Her son Jake is eight and although her husband is very supportive, she feels that she is facing a big decision that requires a big commitment. "How do I know that God really wants me to become a spiritual director, that it is not just my own selfish desire? I worry about leaving Jake for the four residential weeks of training. And I will be much busier when I am at home." I offer this poem to her.

God's Guidance

"How do you *know*," I am often asked,
I ask myself,
"how do you *know*
that you are hearing the voice of God
that you are discerning God's guidance?"
And my answer is simple.
You don't *know.*
You can only follow
what you understand to be the guidance,
and then, like Moses,
hidden in the cleft of a rock,
you can watch God's back as God retreats.
You can only be a little wiser, after the fact.
"I believe I understood correctly that
God was saying thus-and-so.
I followed the guidance
and the outcome was good."
It is frightening not to *know* ...
Yet as the Book of Job teaches us

Fear of the Lord is the beginning of wisdom (Job:
    28:28)
Most of us, though,
receive indications that we are on the right track:
a feeling of well-being,
heat in the belly,
an intuition,
a deep sense of knowing,
words that compel,
a dream.
For myself, I am blessed.
My "God-tears" are my gift.
When someone is talking with me,
and my "God-tears" arrive,
I discern that they are speaking a "soul-truth."
And when I write or pray
for my own guidance
and grateful tears inform me,
I have a keener sense
of God's desire for me.
My "God-tears" now,
as I write these words
affirm this understanding.

Sarah also cries when something seems numinous and deeply right; she weeps quiet tears as I read the poem. I tell her that her discernment process will need to continue for a long while. She indicates that she will pray many times until we meet again, asking God if she should become a spiritual director. I suggest that she journal and pay attention to her dreams. She has recently read *Jewish Spiritual Guidance* by Carol Ochs and Kerry Olitzky, and wonders whether God also speaks to her through the books she reads and the conversations she overhears. I comment that she is broadening her perspective on God's presence in her life and suggest that she hold her question about becoming a spiritual director close to her heart. We sit in silence as she asks God's guidance in the present moment. I keep private my own sense that she is likely to be a gifted guide: This is between her and God. She sits for a long while, crying quietly through her time of contemplation.

Then opens her eyes. "I believe God is saying *yes*, but like Moses seeing God from behind, I will only know in retrospect, over time."

When Sarah leaves, I sit in the quiet of my sacred room, reflecting on the gift and privilege of working with her and my other directees. I think of my own director who tells me regularly, that direction is "working," when both directee and director are transformed. In my quiet and beautiful room, I ponder the reality that we really do "tend the Holy."

Remove Your Shoes

Remove your shoes,
for the place on which you stand
is Holy ground.
In truth,
we should all walk barefooted,
at all times,
for there is no place, no *makom*,
empty of God,
no place empty of holiness.
Yet it is very clear
that certain places
or certain times
create *kedushah*, create holiness.
In the room
where I meet with others,
where we gather, shoeless,
for spiritual direction,
specifically to seek God,
there are times
when the very air shimmers,
when I cannot cease weeping,
God-tears.
Then I know the truth
of the biblical statement:
for whenever two or more
are gathered in My name,
there I am in the midst of them.
I do not know
why certain people

or certain times
are simply more numinous.
All I know is the undeniable truth
that sometimes
I am on Holy ground.
And with reverence
and with awe
I am grateful
that I have removed my shoes.
For I stand naked before God.

Sarah returns a month later feeling a quiet and clear sense that she is meant to pursue the training. She states that she will only know in the future if this is God's desire for her. In this situation, as in most, she cannot see how she could make a "mistake." In a certain way, there are no "mistakes." With a tearful smile, I offer her this poem:

Who Can Possibly Know?

I prepare to spend some time with You
at my deepest level,
in the cocreation of a poem.
And suddenly a steady raucous noise outside,
a harsh *thrum, thrum, thrum* …
I think I cannot descend.
But then You tug at me with Your "come."
There is frequently noise in life,
outside and within,
You suggest,
and You are always present within,
waiting …
Grateful for the encouragement
I descend to the cool, warm *Makom*,
the place of Rock solid, angel gentle Eternity.
"What?" I ask, "what?"
Even the question, the very question,
brings my God-tears.
You whisper that You spoke to me
when I read Torah this morning.
You told me in Ecclesiastes,

Who can possibly know
what is best to do,
for a woman, in life? (6:12)
You say that even *You* do not know,
because although You are *Ehyeh*
I shall be,
You and I cocreate my life
all the time.
So we are both individuating
You and I.
You have a huge role in my present and my future,
and I do in Yours too.
You whisper to me
that it is not only I
who does not know
what is best for me to do, in life.
We discover together,
as we cocreate my life.

Arthur returns for a direction session some time later that same week. He mentions how helpful it was to hear the poem "Kavannah." His sense of failure at his difficulty in connecting with God through silence has diminished. He feels sure that God welcomes his "showing up daily for his appointment." Although he seldom "hears" anything during his prayer, he feels his life is slowly changing in positive ways. "That's what *they* say will happen," I smile.

As *mashpi'im* we are vessels through whom God's holy spirit, God's *shefa*, can flow. The better our own relationships with God, the cleaner the vessel, the more we are able to remove ourselves and allow God to be the guide. My primary way of "cleaning the vessel" is through poetry, a gift through which God guides me. To my humble joy, I have discovered it can guide others too.

Avodah Yomi (My Daily Work)

At night I yearn for You with all my being (Isaiah
    26:9),
I seek You with all the spirit in me.
At night I seek You in my dreams,

by day, I seek You
in all of my waking life,
but most importantly Beloved,
I seek You
in my painstaking writing.
I have never understood so well
the deep significance
of my morning worship.
For when I say my blessings
upon awakening
when I study Torah,
but most importantly, Holy One of Being
when I *write* in cocreation with You
I enter the alchemical vessel.
Or do I actually *become*
the alchemical vessel?
My daily reflective writing,
my poems, my dreams,
my thoughts, my musings, my feelings
bring me closer, a little, each day
to You.
I pray.
I study Torah.
I write.
Each day I am being cleansed.
I am the *mashpia*, the vessel
being cleansed
of my thoughts, my feelings, my musings,
of past and present hurts and wounds,
I am being cleansed,
so that Your *shefa*, Your flow
is freer to move within, and through me.
I seek You with all the spirit in me.
Or
Is my spirit
Yours
seeking me?

Suggested Readings: Sacred Poetry

Bly, Robert, ed. *Soul Is Here for Its Own Joy: Sacred Poems from Many Cultures*. Ecco Press, 1995.

Hanh, Thich Nhat. *Call Me by My True Names: The Collected Poems of Thich Nhat Hanh*. Berkeley, CA: Parallax Press, 1993.

Ladinsky, Daniel. *Love Poems from God: Twelve Sacred Voices from the East and West*. New York: Penguin Compass, 2002.

Mitchell, Stephen. *The Enlightened Heart: An Anthology of Sacred Poetry*. New York: Harper & Row, 1989.

Stephens, William. *Souls on Fire*. Cullowhee, NC: Oceanic Press, 1998.

Jennifer (Jinks) Hoffmann is a psychotherapist and a spiritual director in private practice in Toronto. She serves as poetry editor for *Presence: An International Journal of Spiritual Direction*. Her poems and prose appear regularly in professional journals and synagogue publications.

God Danced the Day You Were Born: Jewish Spiritual Direction and the Sacred Body

Julie Leavitt Kutzen

The Holy Receiver

"The full activation of the entire body in holy actions is thus a therapy of total joy" (Rebbe Nachman of Breslov).[1]

Centuries ago, the great Hasidic teacher Nachman of Bratzlav taught that you cannot have a spiritual experience without telling your body. His insight lies at the heart of this essay.

Truly, we are our bodies. Genesis 1 states that we, flesh and blood human beings, are created in God's image. Enlarging on this teaching, kabbalistic lore posits a correspondence between *Adam Kadmon* (Primordial Adam), a humanlike configuration of the *sefirot* (divine attributes), and the integral structure of our bodies. If this is so, might it be possible for us to access this correspondence through direct experience, to sense the presence or absence of God on a physical level?

As my Aunt Harice would say, "Good question, Julie!" She would say this with her whole body, raising her fists in the air and shaking them as if she had found the golden key to the next secret room. Perhaps our bodies are those secret rooms. Kinesthetic attention, the body's listening sense, can access a profound spiritual wisdom and healing, and act as a doorway to the sanctum where God's presence always is.

How do we begin to listen to the body as a holy receiver?

Breathe. Feel your breath as it leaves your body and returns. Take a moment, pause, close your eyes. Uncross your legs and open more fully to the sensation of your breath. Where do you feel the breath in your body? No special technique needed. Just take time to sense this breathful movement.

While you are here, sense your feet on the ground, your back against the chair or couch. Feel your weight however the furniture holds you. More than a head taking in ideas, you are a body engaged. Breathe, sense, center, ground.

Hineni—Here I am.

Hinenu—Here we are.

Recently a student gave me a phrase I want to offer here: Essential Words. In Hebrew, "breath," *neshimah,* is such an essential word, as honored as the word "snow" is in Eskimo. It shares its root with the word for "soul," *neshamah*; *ruach* (wind) and *nefesh* (literally, the trachea), words used to indicate spirit and soul, also relate to breathing. During creation God breathed into the human body and through that "inspiration," we became living beings. According to the Zohar, God breathes us into being every day. When God "exhales," the breath extends from God's innermost being into the human soul. The breath is never severed from God. Through the breath, the human soul is always connected to the Holy One.[2]

Prior to learning the practice of spiritual direction, I was a student and practitioner of a discipline known as Authentic Movement. Janet Adler, mystic, writer, and foremost teacher of Authentic Movement, calls us away from abstract conceptualization as a way of knowing and into embodied experiential knowledge. "How do you know this in your body?" she asks. "Be specific as you track this." When I breathe with attention to my body, I feel the brilliance and mystery of connection to a place in me called *soul*. I sense my spine from sacrum to a warm, tingly place just atop the back of my head. I sense this same warm, vibrating sensation from my heart to the top of my belly. I sense it right above my skin as well. I feel a slight pulse in the vibration. In that lifting through my spine and the pulsing life in and around my body, in its simultaneous buoyancy and weight, I experience soul.

For me, Authentic Movement and spiritual direction are twin practices. Integrating the two disciplines, I have been able to deepen and expand the wisdom of both.

Let Us Enter with Dance

"Draw forth the spirit until you see and know for certain that it is bound to you perpetually, inseparably, engraved within you.

Sanctify your limbs and adorn them with good deeds, making yourself into a throne for the divine presence, your body an ark for Shekhinah."[3]

Our hearts beat, we breathe, and our organs sustain us, usually without our conscious attention. Such is God's movement in our lives. Neglecting these sensations imprisons much of our wisdom and vitality. Attention to the body's voice, however, deepens our capacity to viscerally experience our bodies as Holy Arks for the *Shechinah*. The lungs, in a sense, become Two Tablets of the Covenant; the spine, Trees of Life, *Etzei Chayyim*, supporting our inner Torah (Psalm 40). Longing and attunement to the sacred gift of our body may well provide us entrée to the Holy of Holies within.

I have found one such portal through movement and dance. This kinesthetic entry can be accomplished in solitude, in *chevruta* (paired study), or in a group setting. Rebbe Nachman teaches that dance and movement are paths to knowing God's Presence, that in the world to come the righteous will find God at the head of each *mahol*, each dance troupe.[4] Dance is an expression of the body's life force, the body's birthright. Therefore, the able-bodied do not have an exclusive deed to this channel; it is for each of us to permit the voice of our soul to come through as our own listening bodies uniquely permit.

In the practice of Authentic Movement, movement as meditation grows from and returns to silence. Through this form, I have discovered that the body is a self-healing organism on the spiritual and emotional, as well as the physical, plane. It is amazing that a gash in the skin heals without much intervention. The body's wisdom does the same for our souls and psyches when we can unleash its extraordinary, ordinary healing power. When I let my body move according to its own will, I am taken exactly where I need to go. This organic design is created by the divinely brilliant choreographer, *HaKadosh Baruch Hu*, the Holy One of Blessing.[5]

Integrating Spiritual Direction and Authentic Movement in Groups

As spiritual directors, we invite our directees into silence and listen for God's "voice" as it moves through the stillness within. In Authentic Movement, we ask that our bodies become instruments for the Mystery and pay attention as we are moved by a power greater than ourselves.

When I lead groups integrating Authentic Movement and spiritual direction, I begin by inviting people to wait in the silence for their body's offering. Our *kavannah,* sacred intention, is to honor the emptiness and mystery of beginnings and ask for Creation to work through us as holy vessels through the vehicle of our bodies. I offer a teaching about will and surrender, and how they exist on a continuum of choice. The movement that emerges in the group is not rehearsed or decided on beforehand. We practice a willingness to let go into what arrives as impulse through our muscles and senses.

Though we practice willingness and spontaneous movement as prayer, I remind participants that we can choose what we allow to come through our moving bodies, so that safety and respect for each person's limits is affirmed. I offer guidelines for safety so we can form a container for what will unfold in the next few minutes. The leap of faith to not only sit in the emptiness, but also literally to be moved by it, requires the creation of a safe and holy space in which to enter the embodiment of each moment.

> My body
> this beggar's bowl of bone
> cracks open
> pours out
> lets the light in.[6]

What emerges in the group may be anything on the continuum between stillness and ecstatic dance. Sound may be a part of this movement, for the voice is a part of the body. Neither movement nor sound come from conscious decision, but from surrender to the prompting of the kinesthetic sense. Our eyes closed, we move to increase inner focus and decrease visual distraction, including the temptation to socialize. Open eyes can engage the brain in a way that may limit sensory experience. This sensory experience is our doorway to the embodied feeling of God as choreographer, of God's ongoing creation with us as dancers, instruments of each moment's unfolding.

Embodied Discernment

"The movements of dance thus express a desire for divinity....
Dance is a deeply transformational grammar."[7]

Like spiritual direction, a sacred companionship exists within Authentic Movement. As a spiritual guide companions a seeker, in Authentic Movement, a witness companions a mover. This dyadic relationship supports the mover as she enters into the mystery of the moment. Except for any sound born of inner necessity, there is continual silence. Each gesture of flow and feeling can mirror the mover's experience of God's presence or absence. Simultaneously, by attending to the mover completely, the witness grows in his ability to discern the Presence within the mover and himself.

Witnessing is analogous to holy listening. As a spiritual companion, I listen with all my senses to the seeker's words and the spaces between them. As a witness, I perceive kinesthetically the mover before me. Like Moses at the Burning Bush, perception becomes witnessing when my sustained attention brings me more completely into the reality and wonder of what and who is moving before me. It represents an opportunity for embodied discernment, to sense the *Shechinah* and affirm "… as for me, God knows, and is my witness!"[8]

After transitioning from the Authentic Movement time, mover and witness join within a still circle comprising other movers and witnesses. The mover always speaks first, trying to articulate those essential words that will bring her movement to a level of greater awareness. The witness then speaks, if it is the mover's wish to hear what she has to say. Committed to a clear discernment that transcends projection, interpretation, analysis, and judgment, the witness might track the actual movements she saw and speak of her own inner response. Like a spiritual director, the witness responds spontaneously and intuitively.

The mover's experience initially unfolds in the solitude of her own focused attention. Now hearing the words of her witness, she may feel seen in a way that raises her experience to greater awareness. It may emphasize or remind her of moments she had forgotten. Her own veils of self-judgment and interpretation may lift to reveal God's presence beneath.

Moving with Your Power

"Let those whom you move with your power
Speak it out loud
For your kindness pierces time" (Psalm 118:4,
  adapted).

Let me recount one morning of offering Authentic Movement as spiritual direction at Elat Chayyim: The Jewish Retreat Center.

It is early morning. We sing *Modeh Ani,* thanking God for the gift of this day. As we chant, our eyes close to enhance our *kavannah* and deep listening. Our voices reach inward and outward until we arrive at that communally sensed moment of quiet that follows voiced prayer. It is delicious; we savor the silence.

This morning, I will serve as the only witness in order to offer these movers the full experience of embodied prayerfulness. Movers now close their eyes, knowing that the end of our chant signals the beginning of "moving time."

One woman lies on her back, very still. Her arms rise above her head. Suddenly, she goes to the chair where she has left her belongings. She takes out her tallit and again closes her eyes. She moves with the tallit as her partner.

Another mover sits with still attention. A few tears stream from her eyes. I feel peaceful, grateful, and sad. My own body wants to push out at the sides, wanting to make space for myself. I don't know if this has anything to do with her experience; it may be my own kinesthetic projection placed over the purity of her movement. I clear my attention and continue to witness.

The "tallit dancer" has covered her head with the prayer shawl and is rocking. It looks like a kind of primordial *shuckling,* a visceral crying out and crying in to God. Her arms open to the sides and her tallit extends across her back and down her arms like wings. I feel lifted as I watch her. I am filled with love. She dips and sways, stepping rhythmically, her feet in place.

I see her tallit as wings, *chuppah,* cloud. However, this act of interpretation begins to take me away from her experience. She is still now. Her shawl wraps around her. I feel quiet and connected to the Sacred in her presence.

My eyes return to the other mover. She is standing and swaying. Her arms form an open circle before her. I sense that she is not alone, that she is waltzing with the Divine.

Softly, I begin to chant a *niggun,* a wordless melody. I have told them ahead of time that I will call them back with this song. They return slowly.

Soon, we sit together again in our circle. They gradually join me in the *niggun,* some with eyes closed, others rubbing theirs as if coming to from a waking dream.

We now journal and rest in silent transition time.

Returning to the circle, we speak from our experiences. The "waltzing mover" speaks first. She has become aware of "contracting," of sacrificing her own authentic involvement in life to make room for others. Often she gives her prerogatives away to others and then becomes angry and frustrated. When she first moved, she sat up from the floor stretching her arms out in front of her. She felt her anger become strength; using the muscles in her arms filled her with a sense of power. She took all the space she sensed she needed and wanted on the movement floor. Feeling loved and valued, she discerned that God wants her to take her rightful space, to experience her own sense of *adamat kodesh,* holy ground. She said:

> … really moving into my own, into spaciousness toward God … in silence led by the heart. I was claiming space, my body. My body doing the prayer, my heart led me to my prayer dance. I needed an inner sense of openness to come to God in that way.
>
> What came to me was a response of thanksgiving through movement and song.
>
> My whole being crouched to scoop as much energy from the earth as needed. My heart and voice sang, "*Barchu,* dear one." I reached up, swaying back and forth, arms reaching to touch the edges of our connection to God. I sang, "In the light of Your light, I come home."

It is my turn to share as her witness. I tell her of the opening that unfolded in me and of my sense of witnessing a divinely partnered duet. She nods and beams. The experience of being witnessed in a way that has internal congruence increases a mover's feelings of affirmation and trust in her own experience.

As the "tallit dancer" journaled, morning blessings flowed, like fresh fish at sunrise, jumping into her net.

Under Your tallit
My breathing heart
as the wind of Your breath
    Seven times I turn around myself
with Your great prayer shawl
    Sheva Berachot of Your Spirit
    I fall to the ground
in supplication to You, *Yah*
On Holy Ground
        Modah ani l'fanecha
Your ground ...
It is all holy
    You paint the skies
in the morning
and bring dusk and darkness
in the evening
        L'havdil
You separate—You join—and separate
You love
    Morning into night
man to woman
mother to child
unborn to born
and then back again
    Oh *Yah,* how great You are
    Under this prayer shawl
breathing wings
of *Shechinah*
    Adonai Adonai sefatai tiftach
ufi yagid t'hilatecha
    Ufros aleynu succat shlomecha
        Life, *Yah,* Master of this great cosmos
It is all a dance of prayer
for You, oh God
    Pray for the children
Pray for the parents
Pray for the elders

Pray for the earth and the sky
for the wind and the rain
for the sun and the moon
for the light and the darkness
Pray for the light—Choose Life
It is *commanded*
It is necessary!
   Each and every one of us
is needed and
must be counted
not by the hundreds and thousands
but by the ones
Each and Every One
   Eli Eli shelo yegamer l'olam
Hachol v'hayam
Rishrush shel hamayim
V'rach hashamayim
Tefilat ha-adam.

When she invites my witnessing, I say, "Amen." She smiles, knowing that in this one word, I have received her morning blessing.[9]

I speak to each as her witness, sharing some of what I've written here and more. I say that without the others knowing, they each danced with God. Ending, we stand together in speaking blessings to and for each other, leaving others unspoken in the open space of the circle between us, there for silent reflection or to be realized when we gather again.

As witness, I find that I see more than I consciously know. Who is it in me that sees? Who is it in me that knows? To quote e.e. cummings," … now the eyes of my eyes are open, now the ears of my ears can see …"[10]

"Blessels"

My soul is for your blessing (Psalm 103:1, adapted).

When I teach Movement and Healing at Lesley University in Cambridge, Massachusetts, we practice listening to our bodies for the beginning, middle, and end of any movement.

For me, this essay has been a many-worded dance. As this "movement" concludes, my shoulders relax, my heart and sacrum feel warm, my breath becomes quiet and easy. I release other gestures I might have made or different directions we may have taken. It is time for this dance to end.

I sit on a wooden bench at the end of a long field of very green, newly mown grass. The breeze is warm and soft. At my feet are smooth horse chestnuts. The thorny husks they cracked out from are beside them like small, prehistoric orange peels. Dried leaves are everywhere. A large orange and black butterfly sails by. The wind shakes more leaves from a nearby apple tree. Scratchy sounds are dotted by the plunk here and there of a newly released horse chestnut. My light breath precedes a slight breeze.

It is the second day of Rosh Hashanah, the Jewish New Year, 5766. Sitting amid the transitions of autumn, I witness the truth articulated by our High Holy Day prayers. We do not know ahead of time what the length of our days, the duration of the gesture of our lives will be. However, my daughter Tali taught me something when she was five years old that I would like to share with you. As my daughters and I were driving home one day, listening to Hanna Tiferet Siegel's beautiful version of *Mah Tovu,* we sang at the top of our joyful lungs:

> Blessings flow into the world
> from the source of Life,
> Be a vessel for the love song of God.[11]

From the back seat Tali asked me, "Mommy, what is a blessel?"

"A what?"

"You know, a *blessel* for the love song of God."

At that moment, a new word was born.

In that spirit:

May we allow our bodies to be the blessels they were created to be, blessels for wholeness, prayer, and God's sacred work.

May our thorny husks open at the right time to the beauty of what is inside: our breath, a heartbeat, and an ever-present, visceral connection to *Shechinah,* the living Presence of God.

May we come to experience the whole world as a blessel for the love song of God.

And may we dance before God as we imagine God danced on the day we were born.

Notes

1. Michael Fishbane, *The Exegetical Imagination: On Jewish Thought and Theology* (Cambridge, MA: Harvard University Press, 1998), 181.
2. Aryeh Kaplan, *Inner Space* (Jerusalem: Moznaim Publishing Co., 1990), 17.
3. Daniel Matt, *The Essential Kabbalah: The Heart of Jewish Mysticism* (HarperSanFrancisco, 1996), 123.
4. *Likkutei Maharan* II, 24.
5. On God as eschatological choreographer, see *Ta'anit* 31a.
6. Jeanne Castle, "Weaving Words: Voices from Green Gulch" in *A Moving Journal, Ongoing Expressions of Authentic Movement*, vol. 11, no. 2 (Summer 2004): 10.
7. Fishbane, *Exegetical Imagination,* 175–176.
8. Janet Adler, "Who Is the Witness?" *Contact Quarterly*, Winter 1987: 20–29.
9. Many thanks to the movers who have shared their experiences with me here and in between the lines on these pages. Special thanks to Ellen Stromberg and Vivian Aviva Feintech (tallit prayer) for their gracious permission to use their writings in the body of this chapter.
10. e.e. cummings, *Poems 1923–1954* (New York: Harcourt, Brace, 1954), 464.
11. Hanna Tiferet Siegal, *Awaken, Arise*, CD (recorded at Studio Fast Forward, Montreal, 2002; available at www.hannatiferet.com).

Suggested Readings

Adler, Janet. *Offering from the Conscious Body: The Discipline of Authentic Movement*. Rochester, VT: Inner Traditions, 2002.

Frankel, Estelle. *Sacred Therapy: Jewish Spiritual Teachings on Emotional Healing and Inner Wholeness*. Boston: Shambala, 2003.

Frankiel, Tamar, and Judy Greenfield. *Minding the Temple of the Soul: Balancing Body, Mind and Spirit through Traditional Jewish Prayer, Movement and Meditation*. Woodstock, VT: Jewish Lights Publishing, 1997.

Sachs, Curt. *World History of the Dance*. Translated by Bessie Schoenberg. New York: Norton, 1965.

Julie Leavitt Kutzen is a body-centered psychotherapist and spiritual guide residing in the Boston area with her daughters, Amielle and Talia. A twenty-year practitioner of authentic movement, she serves as artist in residence on the Lev Shomea faculty and teaches dance therapy at Lesley University.

Opening Doors, Windows, and Vistas: Integrating Spiritual Direction and Visual Creativity

Laine Barbanell Schipper

My Journey

Art and spirituality have been intimate and inseparable partners during the last fifteen years of my life. The dance between these elements called me forward from my upbringing, steeped in science with little room for the notion of God. By the time I became a dentist, I had lost track of my love of handcraft and my deep connection to nature, both of which initially led me toward the natural sciences and dentistry. Somewhere along my accelerated path to success, I lost my sense of connection and meaning. But lingering somewhere in my consciousness, mostly unnoticed, was my intuitive, artful, and poetic shadow waiting for the opportunity to emerge and heal.

At a critical crossroads in my life, I left dentistry and found great solace and the opportunity for deep self-discovery through the quiet and meditative process of weaving. Weaving provided me with the opportunity for reflection and repatterning of my understandings and relationship to the Spiritual. At that time I also began my exploration of Judaism. These two paths merged as I began to weave tallitot. Long days of weaving offered me focused meditative time. During these eight quiet years of weaving and exploring visual art, I began to find a way back to my authentic self. My intuitive nature, which I had grown to mistrust during my academic years, once again became my teacher.

As I entered spiritual direction, I found a sacred space in which to explore and name much of what I was discovering in the spaciousness of my weaving studio. I began to acknowledge my insights, and weave them into a coherent fabric of understanding that drew from my intuitive, artistic, and creative nature as well as from my tradition. I began the deep process of return to God, exploring the issues that had obscured my connection on many levels.

I began the work of softening the harsh edges of my linearly trained mind. I looked at the ways in which my upbringing had taught me to view God and religion with suspicion, as a crutch, and as an indication of weakness. I never struggled with the childhood images of God, having been raised in an essentially atheist household. Yet I discovered that the messages that emerged from my intuitive source and spiritual center were often altered and judged by the internalized, authoritarian voice of my father. Much of my spiritual direction work began to soften the many voices of my upbringing, my early training, and my perfectionism so that I could become more and more available to the still, small, and clear voice within.

Throughout my training and my practice as a spiritual director, I have explored ways in which visual creativity can be integrated into the spiritual direction process. Several understandings and ideas have emerged and continue to evolve. I have learned the power of communication through visual imagery. I have explored the use of simple opportunities for visual art expression during group spiritual direction. Also, I have created a spiritual practice of written and visual journaling during the *Omer*. For the last three years, I have creatively explored my inner spiritual journey from the constriction of Egypt to the Revelation at Sinai, one day at a time for forty-nine days. Based on the learning and growth that I have experienced from my practice, I have begun to share this *Omer*-based experience with others.

Images and Words

Visual imagery offers a very useful approach to exploring the Spiritual. Throughout my practice of spiritual direction, I have noticed that the imagery that enters my consciousness as I listen to the reflections of others is helpful in reaching directees on an intuitive level. I have worked with directees who lean more heavily toward the "left side" and others who lean more heavily toward the "right side" of their brains. In both cases my ability to respond to them using imagery has been helpful at times, as together we listen for God within their lives.

Carol Eckerman's description of emergent words and images in the spiritual direction session offers further illumination of the use of visual imagery. She regards images as "important gifts, tools, or aids in the spiritual journey ... that may embody key aspects of our journey before words can."[1] She describes the power of words that either emerge out of a person's inner experience or, when offered by another, fit a person's inner experiences and images.

> ... [these] emergent words stand in sharp contrast to words used to grasp at and manage experiences. They function powerfully as labels for images, serving to reinstate images in their fullness and communicate clearly and quickly with others who share these images. Words like these have aided in fleshing out the fuller meaning of the experience, in drawing attention to aspects of images previously overlooked, and in realizing important connections given similar labels where these experiences had not previously been reflected upon together.[2]

My spiritual direction sessions with Rebeccah offer an example of the use of emergent words and imagery as we communicated about the spiritual stirrings in her life. Our first session centered on imagery of Rebeccah's vulnerability (visualized as a sprouting plant), a critical voice (visualized as a pointing hand), and faith (visualized as sunshine in which to grow and flourish). We looked at the meaning of each element in this image and how they related to one another. We also explored how Rebeccah could relax the hand from a stance of a punitive pointing finger to one of nurturing openness. Using imagery, we were able to move through concepts that would have required many, many more words. This very immediate visual language was filled with the light of God, which infused the images we shared. As we have worked together over the last three years, we have repeatedly referred to this imagery as Rebeccah goes ever more deeply into the process of spiritual direction and the healing involved in relaxing the hand and accepting the nurturance of God.

Brother Don Bisson, a pioneer in Jungian psychology and spiritual direction, quotes William Blake as saying "Imagination is the source to the Divine." Brother Bisson goes on to explain, "If you don't have an imagination, you can't recognize how God works."[3] He continues by pointing out that human beings often need imagery to take us where our rational/linear minds cannot go. It is through our imagination that we can move to realms ungraspable by our rational/linear thinking. The realm of imagination plays a central role in my spiritual direction relationship with Rebeccah.

During the following spiritual direction session, the issue of love and failed relationships emerged. Rebeccah wondered how to remain open to love after many disappointing and painful experiences. She even questioned whether love was a fairy tale or a reality. I suggested that we take one of her questions: "Where does love come from?" into silence. After the silence, Rebeccah responded that "Love is gathered in containers but it comes from a bigger Source. Containers can be broken, overwhelmed; containers can be damaged by old hurts." Later in our conversation I suggested that perhaps she could find an image that was both container and connection: elastic and supple. She mused about webbing and interconnection, imagining the porosity and elasticity of a spiritual container as opposed to the brittle container of love she had first imagined. At our next session Rebeccah commented she had reflected on spiritual containers and their elastic qualities during her meditation. As she focused on her breathing, she realized that lungs, which change dimension to accommodate our breath, are our internal spiritual containers.

Rebeccah's meditation practice of focused breathing allowed her to move to a deeper and more open place of consciousness. The very practice of breathing put her in touch with the archetypal imagery of *ruach,* understood in Hebrew as "spirit" and "wind" and related to emotions and constant movement throughout the body.[4] In the quiet of her centered self, she reached through her constricted consciousness to a broader, deeper, and more resilient experience of love. Rebeccah's first images of separate, brittle, damaged, inanimate, and therefore irreparable containers gave way to a living and breathing image deeply rooted in Jewish tradition and connected to the Source of Love. Rebeccah's image of lungs as internal spiritual containers reflected an opening to the soul level, the *neshamah* whose Hebrew root is the same as "breath."

This shared image broadened my understanding of a very personally evocative visual metaphor of spiritual direction, the container. As I sit with another I am often aware of the container, which I create in safety and opening to the presence of God. My sense of the container is always changing. Sometimes I envision the container as cocoon, a space of warmth and holding, a space for growth in the darkness. At other times I am perched at the rim of the container and holding it open so that the directee can venture past resistance and the places of constriction that we often deal with. And at other times I sense myself together with the directee in an opened and spacious container of shared movement. Rebeccah's insights helped me to understand container as an organic and living system that itself breathes and changes in response to the need of the directee in the present moment.

The Group

Group spiritual direction is another format in which I have explored the use of visual imagery. As I planned my second year of group spiritual direction for the Kehilla Community Synagogue Group Spiritual Direction Program, *Chevrah L'Ruach,* in Berkeley, California, I began to introduce the use of art and visual expression to deepen and enrich our time together. Because people can sometimes be threatened or fearful when invited to create and share artwork, I made it clear that my primary purpose was for the group to be a safe container in which group members could sense and explore experiences and understandings of the Divine. I explained that the art opportunity was optional and simple and intended only as a vehicle for sharing spiritual experiences in a new way.

Because our groups began shortly after the High Holy Days, I started my group with a short poem I had written on some spiritual themes of Sukkot:

> My sanctuary is a Sukkah
> Open to the stars
> Fragile before the heavens
> Vulnerable to the elements
>
> It is the simple framework
> Holding my heart open
> It is the temporary dwelling
> I am constantly building
>
> Building in surrender
> Opening to Mystery

I explained to the group that together we would be creating *s'chach*, the protective canopy of the sukkah, which stands open to the stars and moon. We would create our *sukkat shalom*, shelter of peace, the framework of opening that we would build together. I cut strips of varicolored handmade paper and provided oil pastels and Sharpie markers. I explained that whatever each of them were called to draw or write on their strip of paper would be an illuminated offering of their heart. Each prayer, each offering of the heart would form an essential element of our temporary dwelling, our *sukkat shalom*, which we would build as a group.

Over the course of four meetings we drew, wrote, and shared. After each meeting I wove the art strips together with much thinner strips of paper. The woven *s'chach* from each meeting formed the basis of the contemplative centerpiece for our next gathering. By the end of the group, I had created a centerpiece that incorporated all our weavings. The group agreed to allow the finished piece to be displayed at our synagogue, where it is currently hanging.

Example of woven *s'chach*.

Sukkat Shalom piece created from the four *s'chach* weavings.

Weaving is a very apt and beautiful metaphor for the group spiritual direction process. The identity and artwork of each person is preserved in its individuality, while simultaneously bound into the weave of the group as well as the Great Weaver, whose sacred presence was felt during the sessions. The use of artwork enriched the spiritual direction process in many ways, as described by one member's reflections on the group, offered after the end of our last session:

> The creative expression portion of our sessions was helpful in a number of ways. To me, much of spiritual experience is nonverbal and intangible. To be able to draw and write after a period of

guided meditation gave us all an opportunity to express our connection to whatever we had experienced during the meditation. Because we only had a limited time to draw and write, the images were strong and direct, because we didn't have time to think about it or do a lot of revision. Afterwards, we had the opportunity to share what we had drawn or written, and this enabled us to talk about things that are usually difficult to articulate.

The creative expression portion was beneficial in other ways. The room setup required us all to get down on the floor and work at the same round table (we met in the nursery). This brought us closer together in a literal physical way, and that physical closeness while drawing stayed with us for the rest of the session. The fact that we had to share supplies had a similar effect. The simple request of "Could you please pass the silver marker?" formed a connection, a way of feeling less separate, since we were all drawing together.

Finally, the creative expression portion led to us being more open and vulnerable with each other. Few of us had artistic experience, so the mere act of drawing something and sharing the drawing with the group was taking an incredible risk. Because of the limited time, even members with artistic experience could only produce some kind of quick sketch, so it was a risk for them, too. The process brought up all kinds of doubts about our artistic abilities, but in the end it was a great confidence builder, because everyone discovered that in a few minutes they could draw and/or write something that had meaning, that they could express themselves creatively, even if they didn't consider themselves a creative person. The group was always respectful of the members' drawings and writings, and this reinforced the feeling of a safe place.

As the facilitator, I found that the timing of creating and sharing the artwork affected the quality and depth of the sharing. My format included three periods of silence. One period of silence allowed group members to "get centered" before our "spiritual check-in" with each other. A short focusing reading preceded a longer period of silence and sharing, and then a final period of silence readied group members to share any final stirrings that came up during our time together. We created our artwork after the second, longer period of silence and verbal sharing. I noticed that some members were unable to visually express the depths of their silence. As a result, their sharing did not probe as deeply as when the opportunity for drawing followed immediately after the longer silence. By first sharing verbally after the longer silence and then drawing, group members were able to utilize multiple modalities to express themselves. Their drawings incorporated their silent experience as well as their verbal sharing. After we created art for ten minutes, we briefly shared any additional insights that may have occurred as we drew. One disadvantage of this approach was that it required additional time, but the group unanimously agreed to add fifteen minutes to our two-hour session so the artwork could continue.

My group attracted a diverse mix of individuals. While people were aware that my group would involve some creative aspects, one member joined because it was the only time that she could attend. She told me that she was completely art-phobic and wasn't sure this group would be right for her. I assured her that the art aspect was optional and would only take ten minutes of the group time. As the group experience unfolded, she fully participated in the creative portion at each opportunity, as did everyone else in the group.

Perhaps most telling are the words of another group member who came with a very intellectual approach and found in the creative expression experience an opportunity to "shift" his consciousness.

> In drawing on the strips in successive sessions, I reached deeper into myself to a place where the layers of intellectual self-protection were gently stripped away (with some convulsion on my part). I was able to express myself, in the moment. This was freed expression and that was different. It was different each time. It was play in an open and free manner. Yet it was deeply serious, strenuous, and stringent. In other words, my experience was one of getting in touch with a joyful core and a wounded core—but no longer bleeding, thanks to this weaving over of the wounds.

Art Journaling

Another means by which the creative process can merge with spiritual direction is art journaling. Marianne Hieb describes art journaling "as a prayer form and a tool that can be used in the direction relationship in a way that can support and enhance our gazing and our contemplative presence to those places of revelation."[5] She also describes art journaling as "the use of simple art materials to help focus, express, or respond to prayer."[6]

Marianne Hieb's article, "The Prayer of Art-Journaling and Spiritual Direction," combined with Julia Cameron's book, *The Artist's Way: A Spiritual Path to Higher Creativity,* inspired me to design my own format of creative/spiritual journaling. My journal consists of at least one page of centering writing and one contemplative drawing for each of the forty-nine days that mark the counting of the *Omer* between Pesach and Shavuot. I have learned year after year to more fully express myself visually, to sit in front of a blank page, sense the invitation to experiment, and let the creative process sweep me along. Sometimes I have a general idea of what I want to draw and sometimes I don't. In either case, finding myself in the midst of creation, I am focused and present, and the image evolves in the moment. The result has been a number of quite varied images that I could never have planned. It has been an enriching, ongoing contemplation. Over the last three years, I have filled several journals, one day at a time. This had been a lesson in valuing each day and each moment in the context of a period of time. I have also watched a body of work emerge out of the moment, teaching me to respond more fully to each moment as it emerges.

The Visual and the Spiritual

In her book, *Spirit Taking Form,* Nancy Azara explains the essential value of visual expression as one contemplates the spiritual:

> [By creating and] viewing work that has a visual presence, we enter a more spacious dimension than words can offer. This visual dimension offers the possibility of wisdom as well as an expression of experience. Because it is a different kind of dimension from what we usually know through words, time spent with the visual can be a healing experience, a communication with spirit, and a way to make a connection to the divine.[7]

The realm of visual creativity offers an important venue in which a spiritual director can be present for a directee. The opportunity to express

 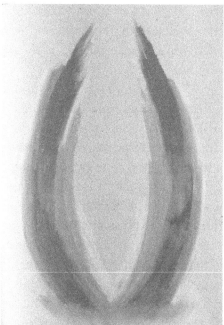

Omer journal oil pastel reflections.

spiritual experiences through imagery provides a powerful intuitive approach to exploring one's relationship to God. While more traditional modes of Jewish prayer use language as the primary medium of Divine-human encounter, imagery and visual art offer additional modes through which human beings can both receive and express experiences of the Mystery we call God. For me, the practice of art has opened doors, windows, and vistas of spiritual understanding and deepened my compassion as I listen to those who entrust me with the gift of their spiritual experiences.

Notes

1. Carol Eckerman, "Images, Words, and Spiritual Direction," *Presence: An International Journal of Spiritual Direction* 9, no. 2 (June 2003): 11.
2. Ibid., 11.
3. Brother Donald Bisson, FMS, "Dreams: Redeeming the Darkness" an audiotaped lecture (October 5, 2002; available for purchase at www.donbisson.com).
4. Rabbi David A. Cooper, *God Is a Verb: Kabbalah and the Practice of Mystical Judaism* (New York: Riverhead Books, 1997), 97.

5. Marianne Hieb, RSM, "The Prayer of Art-Journaling and Spiritual Direction," *Presence: An International Journal of Spiritual Direction* 2, no. 1 (January 1996): 5.
6. Ibid., 5.
7. Nancy Azara, *Spirit Taking Form: Making a Spiritual Practice of Making Art* (Boston: Red Wheel, 2002), 1.

Suggested Reading

Cameron, Julia. *The Artist's Way: A Spiritual Path to Higher Creativity.* New York: J. P. Tarcher/Putnam, 2002.

Laine Barbanell Schipper is a spiritual director in San Francisco who integrates visual creativity into spiritual direction with individuals and groups. She weaves together her insights from her intuitive, artistic, and creatively based understandings as well as from Judaism.

Glossary

Adam Kadmon: In Kabbalah, the humanlike configuration of the ten traits of God's personality configured as Primordial Adam, based on the idea that humans are shaped in the divine image.

adamat kodesh: "Holy ground."

Adonai Echad: "YHVH is One"; the last phrase of the *Shema*; in Hasidic thought it connotes the Divine Unity that underlies and pervades all of reality.

Agus, Jacob: Twentieth-century American rabbi, scholar, and advocate of interfaith dialogue.

ahavah: "Love."

anavah: "Humility."

annanei hakavod: The cloud of glory that guided the Israelites in the wilderness.

aravi'im zeh ba-zeh: (All of Israel) "is responsible one for another"; implies Jewish or, by extension, human interconnectedness.

Arba Olamot: The Four Worlds, or dimensions of reality, interposed between *Ayn Sof,* the infinite, unknowable Divine, and our world; the divine light of each successive descending world becomes ever more obscured as its coarseness and physicality increase; on the psychological level, the worlds have been correlated to the spiritual, intellectual, emotional, and instinctually active capacities of human beings.

Aseret HaDibrot: The Ten Commandments.

Asiyah: "Doing and action"; see also *Olam Ha-asiyah.*

Atzey Hayyim: "Trees of Life"; the two wooden rollers affixed to the parchment of a Torah scroll.

Atzilut: "Divine emanation"; see also *Olam Ha-atzilut.*

Avinu Malkenu: "Our Father, Our King"; major petitionary prayer recited as part of the High Holy Day liturgy.

avodah: "Service"; the sacrificial rites performed in the First and Second Holy Temples in ancient Jerusalem and the section of the Yom Kippur liturgy that describes them; also used to connote "prayer."

Ayn Sof: God the Mystery, boundless, seamless and unknowable.

Azikri, Eliezer: Sixteenth-century Gallilean mystic; composer of love poem to God, *Yedid Nefesh.*

B'not Esh: "Daughters of Fire"; American Jewish feminist spirituality collective.

b'tzelem Elohim: "In the image of God."

ba'alei teshuvah: "Masters of return"; previously non-Orthodox Jews who embrace Orthodox observance and lifestyle.

Baal Shem Tov, Israel: Eighteenth-century Eastern European rabbi and mystic; founder of Hasidism.

bakashot: "Requests"; petitionary prayers.

Barry, William A.: Jesuit priest, author, and noted authority on the spiritual practices of Saint Ignatius of Loyola.

Beit HaMidrash: House of Study.

Beit HaMikdash: The Holy Temple in ancient Jerusalem.

benoni: "Average"; neither saintly nor wicked.

berachot: Blessings.

berur: Clarification of the sacred from the mundane and profane; used in spiritual direction to denote the discernment process.

berurim: Discernment practices.

binah: "Understanding"; a *sefirah* on the Tree of Life, also called *Ima,* Supernal Mother; being differentiates and unfolds within *binah* the way the zygote develops into the various organs and limbs of the fetus in the womb.

Bisson, Don: Marist brother and pioneer in advancing the dialogue between Christianity and Jungian psychology.

bitachon: "Trust."

Boorstein, Sylvia: Author and a leading western teacher of mindfulness meditation.

Briyah: "Creation"; see also *Olam Ha-Briyah.*

bubbe: Yiddish term of endearment for "grandmother."

Chabad: Sect of Hasidism founded in White Russia by Shneur Zalman of Liadi during the late eighteenth century; currently headquartered in Brooklyn, New York, it stresses outreach to Jews throughout the world; its name is an acronym for three divine attributes: *chochmah* (wisdom), *binah* (understanding), and *da'at* (knowledge).

chavurat ruach: "Fellowship of spirit"; group spiritual direction.

chesed: "Loving-kindness, devotion"; in Kabbalah the third manifestation of the divine personality on the Tree of Life.

chochmah: "Wisdom," also known as Supernal Father, *Abba;* a *sefirah* on the Tree of Life, encapsulated within it are the encoded archetypes of all being.

chutzpah: Yiddish term for gumption or arrogance.

dam: "Blood"; represents our human life force and the embodied aspect of **Adam,** the first human.

Dayan HaEmet: "The True (or Ultimate) Judge"; term for God most commonly used in relation to human finitude and death.

devekut: "Cleaving" to God; heightened spiritual state leading to continual awareness of the Divine in all aspects of reality; seen as the ultimate goal of life in Hasidism.

din: "Judgment" or *gevurah,* "power"; a *sefirah* on the Tree of Life; the aspect of God that sets limits and boundaries; *din* is to *chesed* as form is to content.

Dougherty, Rose Mary: Roman Catholic School sister of Notre Dame and former director of the group spiritual direction program at the Shalem Institute for Spiritual Formation in the Christian Contemplative tradition.

Edwards, Tilden: Episcopal priest and founding director of the Shalem Institute.

einfuhlung: "To feel into another person's experience"; German term used in self-psychology.

El Emunah: God, the Faithful; connotes divine reliability in the face of human uncertainty.

eli machmad libi: "My God is the desire of my heart"; from the third stanza of the sixteenth-century love poem to God, *"Yedid Nefesh"*; expresses longing to feel God's presence as opposed to merely petitioning God to grant our requests as indicated by an alternative version of the text *"Eleh chamdah libi*—These are the desires of my heart."

emunah: "Faith."

erev Shabbat: "Sabbath eve"; Friday night, which ushers in the Sabbath at dusk.

Etz Chayyim: The kabbalistic configuration of the ten aspects of God's personality as the Tree of Life.

Eyn HaChayyim: The "Wellspring of Life"; given the prevalence of well imagery associated with Miriam the prophetess and the matriarchs Rebecca and Rachel, this term for God has special resonance in Jewish feminist circles.

Ezra, Abraham ibn: Twelfth-century Spanish Jewish poet, scientist, Hebrew grammarian, and scriptural commentator.

Feuerbach, Ludwig: Nineteenth-century German philosopher; demonstrated the connection between philosophical idealism and religion.

Four Worlds: The kabbalistic tenet that our physical world descended from God through four worlds of increasing physical coarseness: *Olam Ha-Atzilut,* the World of Emanation; *Olam Ha-Briyah,* the World of Creating; *Olam Ha-Yetzirah,* the World of Formation; and *Olam Ha-asiyah,* the archetype of our World of Physical Action.

Friedman, Debbie: Composer and performer of popular contemporary Jewish folk music.

gadlut: State of spiritual and mental expansiveness; also referred to as *mochin de gadlut,* expanded mind and consciousness.

galut: "Exile"; connotes geographic exile or existential alienation.

gematria: System of numerology based on the notion that every Hebrew letter has a numerical equivalent, which can reveal hidden connections between seemingly unrelated or even conflicting verses, expressions, and individuals.

Green, Arthur: American rabbi, mystic, theologian, and leading authority on Hasidic thought.

guru: Hindu spiritual teacher.

ha'arachah: "Evaluative judgment."

hachnasat orchim: Hospitality; welcoming guests.

Haggadah: The "Telling" prayer book used at the Passover seder; also can connote rabbinic folklore.

HaKadosh Baruch Hu: Term emphasizing God's sanctity; alternately translated as "The Blessed Holy One," "The Holy One of Blessing," or "The Holy One, Blessed be He."

halachah: Jewish law.

HaLevi, Yehuda: Twelfth-century Spanish rabbi and philosopher; greatest of the medieval Jewish poets.

halichah b'drachav: "Walking in His [God's] ways"; spiritual imperative of Imitatio Dei, based on Deuteronomy 10.

HaMakom: "The Place"; term for God denoting divine omnipresence; in Hasidic theology it connotes a pantheistic view of God Who simultaneously envelopes and pervades all that is.

hana'ah: Benefit in the form of pleasure or financial gain; viewed in Hasidic thought as a sign of self-centeredness and an impediment to godliness.

HaRachaman: God the Compassionate.

HaShem: "The Name"; divine appellation used so as not to risk taking God's name in vain.

hashgachah pratit: Individual or personal divine providence.

hashpa'ah: "Spiritual guidance."

hasidut: "Saintliness"; used specifically to denote Hasidism, a pietist movement begun in eighteenth-century Eastern Europe by Rabbi Israel Baal Shem Tov.

havchanah: "Distinction"; term used to connote discernment by carefully distinguishing among different aspects of a situation.

havdalah: "Separation"; most frequently used to describe the Saturday night service separating the Sabbath from the upcoming week; sometimes used to denote the discernment process.

hazarah: "Return, repeat"; in spiritual direction connotes the continuing process of discernment over time.

hen: "Favor" or "grace"; God's love given as an unearned gift.

Heschel, Abraham Joshua: Leading twentieth-century rabbi, theologian, and social activist; born in Poland to a prominent Hasidic family, he emigrated to the United States during World War II.

Hillel: First-century CE rabbi and talmudic sage.

Hineni: "Here I am"; Abraham's response when initially called by God in the Binding of Isaac tale in Genesis; connotes being fully present before God; also the name of a special petitionary prayer recited by the cantor on the High Holy Days.

hister panim: "Hiding of God's face"; abandonment by God, also *hastarat* or *hester panim*.

hitbodedut: "Self-seclusion"; contemplative practice of isolating oneself and speaking aloud to God.

hitbonen, hitbonenut: "Making oneself understand"; generic Hebrew term for "contemplation."

hitlahavut: "Burning enthusiasm"; religious fervor or zeal.

hod: Divine splendor that refracts and conveys the defining energy of *din* to the lower world, keeping the forces of chaos and entropy at bay; a *sefirah* on the Tree of Life.

hodesh: Month; drawn from the word *hadash*, meaning "new," denoting that the months begin when the newly visible crescent appears following the full effacement of the moon.

imam: Muslim religious leader.

iyun: "Analysis"; according to Luzzatto, the step in the discernment process during which the behavioral effects of a considered option are examined.

Jacobson, Burt: Contemporary American rabbi and pioneer in the field of Jewish spiritual direction.

James, William: Nineteenth-century American pragmatist philosopher and phenomenonologist of religion; author of *Varieties of the Religious Experience.*

kabbalat ol malchut shamayim: "Accepting the yoke of divine rule"; submission to God.

kabbalat ol mitzvot: "Accepting the yoke of the commandments"; accepting the authority of Jewish law by observing its commandments.

Kaddish: A prayer in Aramaic that stresses the sanctity of God; most frequently used to denote a specific version of this prayer recited by mourners following the death of an immediate relative.

kallah: Conclave; can also mean a bride.

Kaplan, Aryeh: Twentieth-century American rabbi, scientist and mystic; helped introduce Jewish meditation practices to contemporary Jewry.

Kaplan, Mordecai: Twentieth-century rabbi, theologian, and founder of Reconstructionist Judaism.

katnut: A state of spiritual and mental constriction; also referred to as *mochin de katnut,* the contracted mind.

kavannah: Intentionality; often used to connote spiritual fervor during prayer.

kavod: "Honor, glory"; can also refer to the Divine Presence, as in *Kavod HaShem.*

kedushah: "Sanctity"; specifically used to denote those communal prayers during the *Amidah,* the standing prayer of silent devotion, which invoke the imagery of the angels in Isaiah's vision chanting, "Holy, holy, holy is YHVH of Hosts...."

kelipot: Shells or husks of physical desire and materiality that envelope and obscure the *netzotzot* (divine sparks); Kabbalah asserts that the performance of mitzvot with the proper *kavannah* can free the *netzotzot* and elevate them back to their source in the Tree of Life as acts of *tikkun olam,* cosmic repair and redemption.

keter: "Supernal Crown"; a *sefirah* on the Tree of Life, it's the point of transition from potential to actuality.

kippot: Skullcaps worn for devotional purposes or as a sign of Jewish identity; also known in Yiddish as yarmulkes.

kol d'mamma dakka: "Still small voice" or "thin voice of silence"; God's voice as heard by Elijah at the mouth of the cave in I Kings.

kol haneshama tehallel yah: "Let each breath praise God"; concluding verse of Psalm 150, indicating that human breath is the most sublime instrument with which to praise God.

Kook, Abraham Isaac: Twentieth-century mystic and author; chief rabbi of the Jewish community in Israel prior to the establishment of the state.

kotzer ruach: "Shortness of breath"; impatient or diminished spirit.

Kotzker Rebbe (Menachem Mendel Morganstern): Nineteenth-century Polish Hasidic rebbe who became literally obsessed with his search for truth.

Kübler-Ross, Elisabeth: Twentieth-century psychiatrist and author of the groundbreaking book, *On Death and Dying.*

lechem: "Bread."

lev shomea: "Hearing heart"; found in Solomon's request to God in I Kings 5.

Lubavitch: An alternative name for Chabad Hasidism; based on the name of the town in White Russia where the movement was headquartered from the time of its second rebbe, Dov Ber of Lubavitch.

Lurianic: Pertaining to the ideas of the sixteenth-century kabbalistic master, Rabbi Isaac Luria of Safed, also known as the Holy Lion, Ari Hakadosh.

Luzzatto, Moshe Chayyim: Eighteenth-century Italian rabbi and mystic; author of *Mesilat Yesharim, The Path of the Upright;* often referred to by the acronym of his name, RaMCHaL.

ma'asim tovim: "Good deeds."

machshavot zarot: "Strange or alienating thoughts"; illicit sexual, idolatrous, prideful, or even murderous desires.

Maimonides, Moses: Twelfth-century rabbi, physician and scholar; greatest of the medieval Jewish philosophers; often called by the acronym of his name, RaMbaM.

mashgiach (pl. *mashgichim*): "Supervisor, overseer"; denotes a spiritual director in an Orthodox yeshiva; more commonly used to refer to a kashrut supervisor who oversees food preparation according to the dictates of Jewish law.

Mashiach: "Messiah."

mashpia (pl. *mashpi'im*): "Prompter"; denotes a spiritual guide who assists the rebbe in Hasidic communities; Hebrew title adopted by many contemporary spiritual guides.

May, Gerald: Twentieth-century American scholar and author; known for his pioneering work in the field of contemplative psychology.

Mekor HaChayyim: God as the Source of Life.

Melech: "King"; God the Sovereign; can be understood as an acronym representing the divine image embodied in humanity: *moach* (brain), *lev* (heart), *k'layot* (kidneys).

merchav-Yah: "Spacious freedom divine" from Psalm 118.

middah (pl. *middot*): Soul traits.

midrash: Rabbinic homily; also refers to anthologies of such texts compiled between the first and tenth centuries CE.

milchama: "War."

mishkal hahasidut: "Deliberation leading to saintliness"; term for a three-step discernment process found in Luzzatto's *Path of the Upright.*

Mishna: Initial section of the Talmud compiled by Rabbi Judah the Prince in 200 CE.

mishpacha: "Family."

mishpat: "Justice"; legal rulings reflecting the letter of the law; often contrasted with *rachamim,* mercy, and *chesed,* loving-kindness.

misserat nefesh: "Self-sacrifice."

mitzvah (pl. mitzvot): "Divine commandments."

mochin de gadlut: See *gadlut.*

mochin de katnut: See *katnut.*

Modah ani l'fanecha: "I give thanks before You ..."; first prayer a Jew recites upon awakening in the morning, thanking God for the restoration of the soul.

Morei Derekh: "A guide along the way."

motzi: Blessing praising God "Who brings forth bread from the ground"; often called HaMotzi.

Mughal: Islamic-ruled kingdom in Northwest India during the sixteenth and seventeenth centuries.

Musaf: Additional prayer of standing silent devotion recited on Shabbat and Holy Days to commemorate the special sacrificial offerings brought to the ancient Holy Temple on those occasions.

Mussar: Literature and practices leading to ethical and spiritual self-improvement; specifically refers to the Moralist movement begun in nineteenth-century Europe by Rabbi Israel Lipkin Salanter.

mutual irradiation: Term originated in the twentieth century by Douglas Steere to describe a dynamic that impels participants to reexamine and gain new understanding of their own traditions in light of their encounters with those of other faiths.

Nachman of Breslov: Eighteenth-century Hasidic rebbe and great-grandson of the Baal Shem Tov; known for his highly original existential theology.

Nachmanides, Moses: Leading thirteenth-century Spanish rabbi, kabbalist, and legalist, often referred to by his acronym, RaMBaN.

nefesh: "Soul"; in kabbalistic psychology it describes the instinctual function of the psyche that humans share with all other creatures.

neshamah: "Spirit"; in kabbalistic psychology it connotes the intellectual, reflective, and meditative functions of the psyche.

neshimah, nishmat hayyim: "Breath, breath of life."

netzach: A *sefirah* on the Tree of Life, it's the eternal, enduring nature of God.

netzotzot: Sparks of divine light scattered throughout the world when the seven lower *sefirot* could no longer contain the fullness of the divine radiant energy and shattered during Creation; also known as *netzotzot kedushah,* sparks of holiness, or *netzotzot elohut,* sparks of godliness.

niggun: A wordless melody originally chanted as a contemplative or ecstatic practice in Hasidic communities.

Nisan: Month during which Passover occurs; also known in the Bible as Aviv, the month of spring.

nishmat kol chai: "The breath of all that lives ..."; prayer in the morning service for Sabbath and Holy Days; the words can be alternately translated as "Every living breath praises you God," indicating that contemplative, wordless breathing also constitutes prayer.

Ochs, Carol: Scholar, writer and philosopher; pioneer in introducing the practice of spiritual direction to the liberal Jewish community; coauthor of *Jewish Spiritual Guidance.*

Olam Ha'Asiyah: Fourth of the four worlds; concerns the importance of attention to physicality, logistics, and action.

Olam Ha'Atzilut: First of the four worlds; the transcendent dimension of the four aspects of spiritual practice found within Hasidic and kabbalistic traditions; where you connect beyond the known or conceivable and experience pure, unified being.

Olam Ha-Briyah: Second of the four worlds; concerns ideas, thoughts, and innovations.

Olam Ha-Yetzirah: Third of the four worlds; deals with the formation and addressing of feelings.

Omer: Forty-nine-day period between the second day of Passover and Shavuot.

oneg: "Delight"; often used to refer to the array of desserts following Friday evening services known as the *Oneg Shabbat.*

p'sak halachah: A binding legal ruling.

parasha: "Portion"; weekly Sabbath Torah reading; also called a *sedra.*

parnassah: "Livelihood."

penimiyut: Inwardness; usually contrasted with *hitzoniyut,* externality.

Pesach: "Passover."

pilpul: Intricate talmudic argument, often over details that have no real-life applicability, to demonstrate scholarly acuity.

prishut: "Isolation"; connotes solitude or separating oneself from defilement.

Purim: The Feast of Lots, commemorating the victory of Esther and Mordechai over Haman in ancient Persia.

rachamim: "Compassion; mercy."

Rachmana liba Ba-ei: "The compassionate God desires the heart"; talmudic aphorism indicating that beyond religious observance, God asks for human openness, fervor, and love.

rasha: "Wicked," "evil," or "unredeemed."

Rashi (Solomon ben Isaac): Eleventh-century French rabbi and scholar; author of the normative Hebrew commentaries on the Bible and the Talmud.

rebbe: Rabbinic leader of a Hasidic sect; seen by his followers as an intermediary between humanity and God.

Ribbono shel Olam: Master or Sovereign of the Universe.

Rosh Hashanah: Jewish New Year.

roshi: "Elder"; Taoist or Zen Buddhist sage.

Ruach: "Wind" or "Soul"; in kabbalistic psychology it connotes the social and emotional functions of the psyche.

Ruach HaKodesh: The "Holy Spirit"; thought to convey clairvoyance and prophesy.

Schachter-Shalomi, Zalman: Rabbi, mystic, and guiding spiritual leader of the Jewish Renewal movement.

schmoozim: Lectures on Jewish observance and the inner life offered by the mashgiach at the yeshiva, often in advance of Holy Days.

seder: Ritual meal celebrated on the initial nights of Passover.

Sefat Emet: "Language of Truth"; appellation for late nineteenth-century Polish mystic and Hasidic leader Rabbi Yehudah Leib Alter of Ger, based on the name of his famous commentary on the Torah and Jewish Festivals.

sefirah, sefirot: The ten manifestations of the divine personality most frequently configured as the kabbalistic *Etz Chayyim,* the Tree of Life.

Shavuot: "Feast of Weeks," which commemorates the Revelation at Sinai; in the Torah it is known as the Feast of the First Fruits.

Shefa: The divine radiant energy of *Ayn Sof,* which flows along the twenty-two paths of the Tree of Life to the *sefirot;* the *sefirot,* in turn, mediate the blessings of the *shefa* to our world below.

Shechinah: God's Indwelling Presence, Divine Immanence; in Kabbalah it is identified with the tenth *sefirah* on the Tree of Life, *Malchut,* and is seen as a feminine aspect of the Divine

sheikh: Sufi spiritual master.

shelemut halev: "Wholeheartedness."

Shema: "Hear O Israel, YHVH our God, YHVH is One" (Deuteronomy 6:4); prayer affirming God's unity and uniqueness; calls us to listen for the divine unity that underlies the diverse narratives of our lives.

Sheva Berachot: Traditional Seven Blessings recited during a Jewish wedding ceremony.

shevach: "Praise."

shevirat hakelim: "The Breaking of the Vessels"; in Kabbalah, during creation, the seven lower *sefirot* shattered, causing the *netzotzot* to scatter; helps account for the initial misalignment of the *Etz Chayyim.*

shiviti: A contemplative plaque or picture, usually placed on the eastern wall of a sanctuary near the Ark, containing the Divine Name, often amid a design of biblical verses or kabbalistic phrases; based on Psalms 16:8: "*Shiviti YHVH l'negdi tamid*—I place the Eternal One before me always."

Shneur Zalman of Liadi: Eighteenth-century mystic and founder of Chabad Hasidism; seminal figure in the spread of Hasidism to White Russia.

shofar: Ram's horn sounded on Rosh Hashanah.

shul: "School"; Yiddish term for a synagogue, stressing its role as a house of study.

Steere, Douglas: Twentieth-century Quaker scholar, author, and religious leader; cofounder of the Ecumenical Institute on Spirituality.

sukkah: Hut, tabernacle; temporary dwelling erected for use on Sukkot to commemorate the wandering of the Israelites in the Sinai wilderness.

Sukkot: "Feast of Tabernacles."

tallit: Prayer shawl; also known as *tallis.*

Talmud: Primary compendium of rabbinic law and lore containing sources dated from 200 BCE to approximately 750 CE.

teshuvah: "Repentance"; "return."

tiferet: A *sefirah* on the Tree of Life; beauty that comes when *chesed* and *din* are in balance.

tikkun olam: "Repairing the world"; used to denote social action and awareness; in Kabbalah it connotes redemptive acts aimed at spiritually repairing the fissures in our broken world and in God, Godself; see *kelipot.*

timimut lev: "Purity of heart"; initial step of the discernment process during which one purges oneself of self-serving attitudes and focuses on pleasing God; also called *timimut hamachshavah,* "purifying one's thoughts."

Tisha B'av: "Ninth of Av"; full-day fast commemorating the destruction of the First and Second Temples in Jerusalem; traditionally, the saddest day of the Jewish calendar year.

Tomchei-Temimim: "Upholders of the Pure"; educational system of Chabad Hasidism.

Tu b'Av: Fifteenth day of Av; a day of courting and merriment in ancient Israel.

Tvi Elimelech Shapira of Dinov: Early eighteenth-century Galician scholar, kabbalist, and Hasidic rebbe; often referred to by the name of his most famous text, the *B'nai Yissaschar.*

tzaddikim: Righteous, pious or saintly ones; sometimes used to connote Hasidic rebbes.

tzedakah: "Righteousness"; charity and community service.

tzitzit: Fringes on the four corners of a prayer shawl; based on Numbers 15.

yeridah: Descent; can connote descent into despair or desolation as a prelude to further spiritual growth, as in *yeridah l'tzorech aliyah*—descent for the sake of ascent.

yeshiva: Talmudic academy.

yesod: "Foundation"; a *sefirah* on the Tree of Life alternately called *tzaddik* (righteous) for the "righteous are the foundation of the world" (Proverbs 10:25); when the ten *sefirot* are depicted in human form, *yesod* corresponds to the male generative organ, since it focuses the *shefa's* potency from the upper *sefirot* and emits it downward.

yetzer: "Inclination"; according to rabbinic psychology each individual has two inclinations; the *yetzer hatov* is our good inclination, our altruistic drive; the *yetzer hara* is our harmful, evil inclination, our susceptibility to temptation, and our drive for self-aggrandizement.

YHVH: The Ineffable four-letter name of God; often translated as "The Lord" or "The Eternal."

Yirah: "Fear, awe"; reverence for God.

yotzei: Fulfillment of one's religious/legal obligations; can have connotations of perfunctory, uninspired observance.

zman simchateynu: "Season of our Rejoicing"; Sukkot; similarly, Passover is called *zman charuteynu,* "Season of our Liberation," and Shavuot is called *zman matan torateynu,* "Season of the Giving of the Torah."

Where Do I Go from Here?
Resources in Jewish Spiritual Guidance

If you wish to learn more about the evolving field of Jewish spiritual direction please feel free to contact us. Howard Avruhm Addison can be reached at rabbia@juno.com and Barbara Eve Breitman can be reached at bahirachava@aol.com.

For information about our two-year, retreat-based spiritual direction training program, Lev Shomea, please consult Elat Chayyim at www.jewishretreatcenter.org (click Training Institutes) or go to www.LevShomea.org.

The Yedidya Center for Jewish Spiritual Direction offers resources to support the advancement of spiritual direction in the Jewish community, including its Morei Derekh training program. For further information, see www.yedidyacenter.org.

A number of regional centers offer programs in contemplative Judaism and spiritual guidance. While this list is not exhaustive they include:

Ruach: A New Center for Spirituality (Cleveland): www.ruachprograms.org

Makom: The Center for Mindfulness (New York): www.jccnyc.org

Chochmat HaLev: A Center for Jewish Spirituality (San Francisco): www.chochmat.org

Gesher Center (Virginia): www.geshercenter.org

Lev Tahor: A Center for Jewish Soulwork (Washington, D.C.): www.levtahor.org

We are most interested in learning about the existence and development of other Jewish spiritual guidance centers and invite you to contact us so that the list might become ever more complete

There are currently two listservs available. These help Jewish spiritual directors network, share information, and publicize events of common interest, including advanced training seminars and the Jewish spiritual directors meeting that follows the annual Spiritual Directors

International (SDI) Convention. If you have questions or wish to enroll, please contact: Amy Brenner at abrenner@rrc.edu or Sandy Jardine at sandyjardine@cox.net.

SDI is a worldwide umbrella organization offering support and fellowship to spiritual directors of all faiths and traditions. Among its activities are its yearly convention and the publication of *Presence: An International Journal of Spiritual Direction.* SDI can be reached at www.sdiworld.org.

Index of Terms and Concepts

Index of Classical Sources
Cited (Biblical and Rabbinic)

Children's Books

What You Will See Inside a Synagogue

By Rabbi Lawrence A. Hoffman and Dr. Ron Wolfson; Full-color photos by Bill Aron

A colorful, fun-to-read introduction that explains the ways and whys of Jewish worship and religious life. Full-page photos; concise but informative descriptions of the objects used, the clergy and laypeople who have specific roles, and much more. For ages 6 & up.

8½ x 10½, 32 pp, Full-color photos, Hardcover, ISBN 1-59473-012-1 **$17.99** *(A SkyLight Paths book)*

Because Nothing Looks Like God

By Lawrence and Karen Kushner

What is God like? Introduces children to the possibilities of spiritual life. Real-life examples of happiness and sadness invite us to explore, together with our children, the questions we all have about God.

11 x 8½, 32 pp, Full-color illus., Hardcover, ISBN 1-58023-092-X **$16.95** *For ages 4 & up*

Also Available: **Because Nothing Looks Like God Teacher's Guide**

8½ x 11, 22 pp, PB, ISBN 1-58023-140-3 **$6.95** *For ages 5–8*

Board Book Companions to *Because Nothing Looks Like God*

5 x 5, 24 pp, Full-color illus., SkyLight Paths Board Books *For ages 0–4*

What Does God Look Like? ISBN 1-893361-23-3 **$7.95**

How Does God Make Things Happen? ISBN 1-893361-24-1 **$7.95**

Where Is God? ISBN 1-893361-17-9 **$7.99**

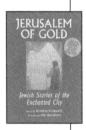

The 11th Commandment: Wisdom from Our Children

By The Children of America

"If there were an Eleventh Commandment, what would it be?" Children of many religious denominations across America answer in their own drawings and words.

8 x 10, 48 pp, Full-color illus., Hardcover, ISBN 1-879045-46-X **$16.95** *For all ages*

Jerusalem of Gold: Jewish Stories of the Enchanted City

Retold by Howard Schwartz. Full-color illus. by Neil Waldman.

A beautiful and engaging collection of historical and legendary stories for children. Based on Talmud, midrash, Jewish folklore, and mystical and Hasidic sources.

8 x 10, 64 pp, Full-color illus., Hardcover, ISBN 1-58023-149-7 **$18.95** *For ages 7 & up*

The Book of Miracles: A Young Person's Guide to Jewish Spiritual Awareness

By Lawrence Kushner. All-new illustrations by the author.

6 x 9, 96 pp, 2-color illus., Hardcover, ISBN 1-879045-78-8 **$16.95** *For ages 9–13*

In Our Image: God's First Creatures

By Nancy Sohn Swartz

9 x 12, 32 pp, Full-color illus., Hardcover, ISBN 1-879045-99-0 **$16.95** *For ages 4 & up*

Also Available as a Board Book: **How Did the Animals Help God?**

5 x 5, 24 pp, Board, Full-color illus., ISBN 1-59473-044-X **$7.99** *For ages 0–4 (A SkyLight Paths book)*

From SKYLIGHT PATHS PUBLISHING

Becoming Me: A Story of Creation

By Martin Boroson. Full-color illus. by Christopher Gilvan-Cartwright.

Told in the personal "voice" of the Creator, a story about creation and relationship that is about each one of us.

8 x 10, 32 pp, Full-color illus., Hardcover, ISBN 1-893361-11-X **$16.95** *For ages 4 & up*

Ten Amazing People: And How They Changed the World

By Maura D. Shaw. Foreword by Dr. Robert Coles. Full-color illus. by Stephen Marchesi.

Black Elk • Dorothy Day • Malcolm X • Mahatma Gandhi • Martin Luther King, Jr. • Mother Teresa • Janusz Korczak • Desmond Tutu • Thich Nhat Hanh • Albert Schweitzer.

8½ x 11, 48 pp, Full-color illus., Hardcover, ISBN 1-893361-47-0 **$17.95** *For ages 7 & up*

Where Does God Live? *By August Gold and Matthew J. Perlman*

Helps young readers develop a personal understanding of God.

10 x 8½, 32 pp, Full-color photo illus., Quality PB, ISBN 1-893361-39-X **$8.99** *For ages 3–6*

Current Events/History

The Story of the Jews: A 4,000-Year Adventure—A Graphic History Book
Written & illustrated by Stan Mack
Witty, illustrated narrative of all the major happenings from biblical times to the twenty-first century. 6 x 9, 288 pp., illus., Quality PB, ISBN 1-58023-155-1 **$16.95**

Hannah Senesh: Her Life and Diary, the First Complete Edition
By Hannah Senesh; Foreword by Marge Piercy; Preface by Eitan Senesh
6 x 9, 352 pp, Hardcover, ISBN 1-58023-212-4 **$24.99**

The Jewish Prophet: Visionary Words from Moses and Miriam to Henrietta Szold and A. J. Heschel *By Rabbi Michael J. Shire*
6½ x 8½, 128 pp, 123 full-color illus., Hardcover, ISBN 1-58023-168-3 **Special gift price $14.95**

Shared Dreams: Martin Luther King, Jr. & the Jewish Community
By Rabbi Marc Schneier. Preface by Martin Luther King III.
6 x 9, 240 pp, Hardcover, ISBN 1-58023-062-8 **$24.95**

"Who Is a Jew?": Conversations, Not Conclusions *By Meryl Hyman*
6 x 9, 272 pp, Quality PB, ISBN 1-58023-052-0 **$16.95**

Ecology

Ecology & the Jewish Spirit: Where Nature & the Sacred Meet
Edited by Ellen Bernstein 6 x 9, 288 pp, Quality PB, ISBN 1-58023-082-2 **$16.95**

Torah of the Earth: Exploring 4,000 Years of Ecology in Jewish Thought
Vol. 1: Biblical Israel: One Land, One People; Rabbinic Judaism: One People, Many Lands
Vol. 2: Zionism: One Land, Two Peoples; Eco-Judaism: One Earth, Many Peoples
Edited by Rabbi Arthur Waskow
Vol. 1: 6 x 9, 272 pp, Quality PB, ISBN 1-58023-086-5 **$19.95**
Vol. 2: 6 x 9, 336 pp, Quality PB, ISBN 1-58023-087-3 **$19.95**

The Way Into Judaism and the Environment
By Jeremy Benstein, PhD
6 x 9, 225 pp (est.), Hardcover, ISBN 1-58023-268-X **$24.99**

Grief/Healing

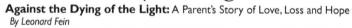

Against the Dying of the Light: A Parent's Story of Love, Loss and Hope
By Leonard Fein
5½ x 8½, 176 pp, Quality PB, ISBN 1-58023-197-7 **$15.99;** Hardcover, ISBN 1-58023-110-1 **$19.95**

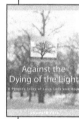

Grief in Our Seasons: A Mourner's Kaddish Companion *By Rabbi Kerry M. Olitzky*
4½ x 6½, 448 pp, Quality PB, ISBN 1-879045-55-9 **$15.95**

Healing of Soul, Healing of Body: Spiritual Leaders Unfold the Strength & Solace in Psalms *Edited by Rabbi Simkha Y. Weintraub, C.S.W.*
6 x 9, 128 pp, 2-color illus. text, Quality PB, ISBN 1-879045-31-1 **$14.99**

Jewish Paths toward Healing and Wholeness: A Personal Guide to Dealing with Suffering *By Rabbi Kerry M. Olitzky. Foreword by Debbie Friedman.*
6 x 9, 192 pp, Quality PB, ISBN 1-58023-068-7 **$15.95**

Mourning & Mitzvah, 2nd Edition: A Guided Journal for Walking the Mourner's Path through Grief to Healing *By Anne Brener, L.C.S.W.*
7½ x 9, 304 pp, Quality PB, ISBN 1-58023-113-6 **$19.95**

The Perfect Stranger's Guide to Funerals and Grieving Practices
A Guide to Etiquette in Other People's Religious Ceremonies *Edited by Stuart M. Matlins*
6 x 9, 240 pp, Quality PB, ISBN 1-893361-20-9 **$16.95** *(A SkyLight Paths book)*

Tears of Sorrow, Seeds of Hope: A Jewish Spiritual Companion for Infertility and Pregnancy Loss *By Rabbi Nina Beth Cardin*
6 x 9, 192 pp, Hardcover, ISBN 1-58023-017-2 **$19.95**

A Time to Mourn, A Time to Comfort, 2nd Edition: A Guide to Jewish Bereavement and Comfort *By Dr. Ron Wolfson*
7 x 9, 336 pp, Quality PB, ISBN 1-58023-253-1 **$19.99**

When a Grandparent Dies: A Kid's Own Remembering Workbook for Dealing with Shiva and the Year Beyond *By Nechama Liss-Levinson, Ph.D.*
8 x 10, 48 pp, 2-color text, Hardcover, ISBN 1-879045-44-3 **$15.95** *For ages 7–13*

Holidays/Holy Days

Yom Kippur Readings: Inspiration, Information and Contemplation
Edited by Rabbi Dov Peretz Elkins with section introductions from Arthur Green's These Are the Words
An extraordinary collection of readings, prayers and insights that enable the modern worshiper to enter into the spirit of the Day of Atonement in a personal and powerful way, permitting the meaning of Yom Kippur to enter the heart.
6 x 9, 348 pp, Hardcover, ISBN 1-58023-271-X **$24.99**

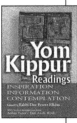

Leading the Passover Journey
The Seder's Meaning Revealed, the Haggadah's Story Retold
By Rabbi Nathan Laufer
Uncovers the hidden meaning of the Seder's rituals and customs.
6 x 9, 208 pp, Hardcover, ISBN 1-58023-211-6 **$24.99**

Reclaiming Judaism as a Spiritual Practice: Holy Days and Shabbat
By Rabbi Goldie Milgram
Provides a framework for understanding the powerful and often unexplained intellectual, emotional, and spiritual tools that are essential for a lively, relevant, and fulfilling Jewish spiritual practice. 7 x 9, 272 pp, Quality PB, ISBN 1-58023-205-1 **$19.99**

7th Heaven: Celebrating Shabbat with Rebbe Nachman of Breslov
By Moshe Mykoff with the Breslov Research Institute
Explores the art of consciously observing Shabbat and understanding in-depth many of the day's spiritual practices. 5⅛ x 8¼, 224 pp, Deluxe PB w/flaps, ISBN 1-58023-175-6 **$18.95**

The Women's Passover Companion
Women's Reflections on the Festival of Freedom
Edited by Rabbi Sharon Cohen Anisfeld, Tara Mohr, and Catherine Spector
Groundbreaking. A provocative conversation about women's relationships to Passover as well as the roots and meanings of women's seders.
6 x 9, 352 pp, Quality PB, ISBN 1-58023-231-0 **$19.99**; Hardcover, ISBN 1-58023-128-4 **$24.95**

The Women's Seder Sourcebook
Rituals & Readings for Use at the Passover Seder
Edited by Rabbi Sharon Cohen Anisfeld, Tara Mohr, and Catherine Spector
Gathers the voices of more than one hundred women in readings, personal and creative reflections, commentaries, blessings, and ritual suggestions that can be incorporated into your Passover celebration.
6 x 9, 384 pp, Quality PB, ISBN 1-58023-232-9 **$19.99**; Hardcover, ISBN 1-58023-136-5 **$24.95**

Creating Lively Passover Seders: A Sourcebook of Engaging Tales, Texts & Activities
By David Arnow, Ph.D. 7 x 9, 416 pp, Quality PB, ISBN 1-58023-184-5 **$24.99**

Hanukkah, 2nd Edition: The Family Guide to Spiritual Celebration
By Dr. Ron Wolfson. Edited by Joel Lurie Grishaver.
7 x 9, 240 pp, illus., Quality PB, ISBN 1-58023-122-5 **$18.95**

The Jewish Family Fun Book: Holiday Projects, Everyday Activities, and Travel Ideas with Jewish Themes *By Danielle Dardashti and Roni Sarig. Illus. by Avi Katz.*
6 x 9, 288 pp, 70+ b/w illus. & diagrams, Quality PB, ISBN 1-58023-171-3 **$18.95**

The Jewish Gardening Cookbook: Growing Plants & Cooking for
Holidays & Festivals *By Michael Brown* 6 x 9, 224 pp, 30+ illus., Quality PB, ISBN 1-58023-116-0 **$16.95**

The Jewish Lights Book of Fun Classroom Activities: Simple and Seasonal
Projects for Teachers and Students *By Danielle Dardashti and Roni Sarig*
6 x 9, 240 pp, Quality PB, ISBN 1–58023–206–X **$19.99**

Passover, 2nd Edition: The Family Guide to Spiritual Celebration
By Dr. Ron Wolfson with Joel Lurie Grishaver 7 x 9, 352 pp, Quality PB, ISBN 1-58023-174-8 **$19.95**

Shabbat, 2nd Edition: The Family Guide to Preparing for and Celebrating the Sabbath
By Dr. Ron Wolfson 7 x 9, 320 pp, illus., Quality PB, ISBN 1-58023-164-0 **$19.95**

Sharing Blessings: Children's Stories for Exploring the Spirit of the Jewish Holidays
By Rahel Musleah and Michael Klayman
8½ x 11, 64 pp, Full-color illus., Hardcover, ISBN 1-879045-71-0 **$18.95** *For ages 6 & up*

Inspiration

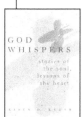

God in All Moments
Mystical & Practical Spiritual Wisdom from Hasidic Masters
Edited and translated by Or N. Rose with Ebn D. Leader
Hasidic teachings on how to be mindful in religious practice and cultivating every-day ethical behavior—*hanhagot*. 5½ x 8½, 192 pp, Quality PB, ISBN 1-58023-186-1 **$16.95**

Our Dance with God: Finding Prayer, Perspective and Meaning in the Stories of Our Lives *By Karyn D. Kedar*
Inspiring spiritual insight to guide you on your life journeys and teach you to live and thrive in two conflicting worlds: the rational/material and the spiritual.
6 x 9, 176 pp, Quality PB, ISBN 1-58023-202-7 **$16.99**

Also Available: **The Dance of the Dolphin** (Hardcover edition of *Our Dance with God*)
6 x 9, 176 pp, Hardcover, ISBN 1-58023-154-3 **$19.95**

The Empty Chair: Finding Hope and Joy—Timeless Wisdom from a Hasidic Master, Rebbe Nachman of Breslov *Adapted by Moshe Mykoff and the Breslov Research Institute*
4 x 6, 128 pp, 2-color text, Deluxe PB w/flaps, ISBN 1-879045-67-2 **$9.95**

The Gentle Weapon: Prayers for Everyday and Not-So-Everyday Moments—
Timeless Wisdom from the Teachings of the Hasidic Master, Rebbe Nachman of Breslov *Adapted by Moshe Mykoff and S. C. Mizrahi, together with the Breslov Research Institute*
4 x 6, 144 pp, 2-color text, Deluxe PB w/flaps, ISBN 1-58023-022-9 **$9.99**

God Whispers: Stories of the Soul, Lessons of the Heart *By Karyn D. Kedar*
6 x 9, 176 pp, Quality PB, ISBN 1-58023-088-1 **$15.95**

An Orphan in History: One Man's Triumphant Search for His Jewish Roots
By Paul Cowan. Afterword by Rachel Cowan. 6 x 9, 288 pp, Quality PB, ISBN 1-58023-135-7 **$16.95**

Restful Reflections: Nighttime Inspiration to Calm the Soul, Based on Jewish Wisdom
By Rabbi Kerry M. Olitzky & Rabbi Lori Forman 4½ x 6½, 448 pp, Quality PB, ISBN 1-58023-091-1 **$15.95**

Sacred Intentions: Daily Inspiration to Strengthen the Spirit, Based on Jewish Wisdom
By Rabbi Kerry M. Olitzky and Rabbi Lori Forman 4½ x 6½, 448 pp, Quality PB, ISBN 1-58023-061-X **$15.95**

Kabbalah/Mysticism/Enneagram

Awakening to Kabbalah: The Guiding Light of Spiritual Fulfillment
By Rav Michael Laitman, PhD
A distinctive, personal and awe-filled introduction to this ancient wisdom tradition.
6 x 9, 192 pp, Hardcover, ISBN 1-58023-264-7 **$21.99**

Seek My Face: A Jewish Mystical Theology
By Dr. Arthur Green
This classic work of contemporary Jewish theology, revised and updated, is a pro-found, deeply personal statement of the lasting truths of Jewish mysticism and the basic faith claims of Judaism. 6 x 9, 304 pp, Quality PB, ISBN 1-58023-130-6 **$19.95**

Zohar: Annotated & Explained
Translation and annotation by Dr. Daniel C. Matt. Foreword by Andrew Harvey
Offers insightful yet unobtrusive commentary to the masterpiece of Jewish mys-ticism. 5½ x 8½, 160 pp, Quality PB, ISBN 1-893361-51-9 **$15.99** (*A SkyLight Paths book*)

Cast in God's Image: Discover Your Personality Type Using the Enneagram and Kabbalah
By Rabbi Howard A. Addison
7 x 9, 176 pp, Quality PB, Layflat binding, 20+ journaling exercises, ISBN 1-58023-124-1 **$16.95**

Ehyeh: A Kabbalah for Tomorrow *By Dr. Arthur Green*
6 x 9, 224 pp, Quality PB, ISBN 1-58023-213-2 **$16.99**; Hardcover, ISBN 1-58023-125-X **$21.95**

The Enneagram and Kabbalah, 2nd Edition: Reading Your Soul
By Rabbi Howard A. Addison 6 x 9, 192 pp, Quality PB, ISBN 1-58023-229-9 **$16.99**

Finding Joy: A Practical Spiritual Guide to Happiness *By Dannel I. Schwartz with Mark Hass*
6 x 9, 192 pp, Quality PB, ISBN 1-58023-009-1 **$14.95**

The Gift of Kabbalah: Discovering the Secrets of Heaven, Renewing Your Life on Earth
By Tamar Frankiel, Ph.D.
6 x 9, 256 pp, Quality PB, ISBN 1-58023-141-1 **$16.95**; Hardcover, ISBN 1-58023-108-X **$21.95**

The Way Into Jewish Mystical Tradition *By Lawrence Kushner*
6 x 9, 224 pp, Quality PB, ISBN 1-58023-200-0 **$18.99**; Hardcover, ISBN 1-58023-029-6 **$21.95**

Life Cycle
Marriage / Parenting / Family / Aging

Jewish Fathers: A Legacy of Love
Photographs by Lloyd Wolf. Essays by Paula Wolfson. Foreword by Harold S. Kushner.
Honors the role of contemporary Jewish fathers in America. Each father tells in his own words what it means to be a parent and Jewish, and what he learned from his own father. Insightful photos. 9½ x 9⅞, 144 pp with 100+ duotone photos, Hardcover, ISBN 1-58023-204-3 **$30.00**

The New Jewish Baby Album: Creating and Celebrating the Beginning of a Spiritual Life—A Jewish Lights Companion
By the Editors at Jewish Lights. Foreword by Anita Diamant. Preface by Sandy Eisenberg Sasso.
A spiritual keepsake that will be treasured for generations. More than just a memory book, *shows you how—and why it's important*—to create a Jewish home and a Jewish life. 8 x 10, 64 pp, Deluxe Padded Hardcover, Full-color illus., ISBN 1-58023-138-1 **$19.95**

The Jewish Pregnancy Book: A Resource for the Soul, Body & Mind during Pregnancy, Birth & the First Three Months
By Sandy Falk, M.D., and Rabbi Daniel Judson, with Steven A. Rapp
Includes medical information, prayers and rituals for each stage of pregnancy, from a liberal Jewish perspective. 7 x 10, 208 pp, Quality PB, b/w illus., ISBN 1-58023-178-0 **$16.95**

Celebrating Your New Jewish Daughter: Creating Jewish Ways to Welcome Baby Girls into the Covenant—New and Traditional Ceremonies
By Debra Nussbaum Cohen 6 x 9, 272 pp, Quality PB, ISBN 1-58023-090-3 **$18.95**

The New Jewish Baby Book, 2nd Edition: Names, Ceremonies & Customs—A Guide for Today's Families *By Anita Diamant* 6 x 9, 336 pp, Quality PB, ISBN 1-58023-251-5 **$19.99**

Parenting As a Spiritual Journey: Deepening Ordinary and Extraordinary Events into Sacred Occasions *By Rabbi Nancy Fuchs-Kreimer* 6 x 9, 224 pp, Quality PB, ISBN 1-58023-016-4 **$16.95**

Judaism for Two: A Spiritual Guide for Strengthening and Celebrating Your Loving Relationship *By Rabbi Nancy Fuchs-Kreimer and Rabbi Nancy H. Wiener*
Addresses the ways Jewish teachings can enhance and strengthen committed relationships. 6 x 9, 208 pp, Quality PB, ISBN 1-58023-254-X **$16.99**

Embracing the Covenant: Converts to Judaism Talk About Why & How
By Rabbi Allan Berkowitz and Patti Moskowitz 6 x 9, 192 pp, Quality PB, ISBN 1-879045-50-8 **$16.95**

The Guide to Jewish Interfaith Family Life: An InterfaithFamily.com Handbook
Edited by Ronnie Friedland and Edmund Case 6 x 9, 384 pp, Quality PB, ISBN 1-58023-153-5 **$18.95**

Introducing My Faith and My Community
The Jewish Outreach Institute Guide for the Christian in a Jewish Interfaith Relationship
By Rabbi Kerry M. Olitzky 6 x 9, 176 pp, Quality PB, ISBN 1-58023-192-6 **$16.99**

Making a Successful Jewish Interfaith Marriage: The Jewish Outreach Institute Guide to Opportunities, Challenges and Resources
By Rabbi Kerry M. Olitzky with Joan Peterson Littman 6 x 9, 176 pp, Quality PB, ISBN 1-58023-170-5 **$16.95**

The Creative Jewish Wedding Book: A Hands-On Guide to New & Old Traditions, Ceremonies & Celebrations *By Gabrielle Kaplan-Mayer*
Provides the tools to create the most meaningful Jewish traditional or alternative wedding by using ritual elements to express your unique style and spirituality. 9 x 9, 288 pp, b/w photos, Quality PB, ISBN 1-58023-194-2 **$19.99**

Divorce Is a Mitzvah: A Practical Guide to Finding Wholeness and Holiness When Your Marriage Dies *By Rabbi Perry Netter. Afterword by Rabbi Laura Geller.*
6 x 9, 224 pp, Quality PB, ISBN 1-58023-172-1 **$16.95**

A Heart of Wisdom: Making the Jewish Journey from Midlife through the Elder Years
Edited by Susan Berrin. Foreword by Harold Kushner. 6 x 9, 384 pp, Quality PB, ISBN 1-58023-051-2 **$18.95**

So That Your Values Live On: Ethical Wills and How to Prepare Them
Edited by Jack Riemer and Nathaniel Stampfer 6 x 9, 272 pp, Quality PB, ISBN 1-879045-34-6 **$18.99**

Meditation

The Handbook of Jewish Meditation Practices
A Guide for Enriching the Sabbath and Other Days of Your Life
By Rabbi David A. Cooper
Easy-to-learn meditation techniques. 6 x 9, 208 pp, Quality PB, ISBN 1-58023-102-0 **$16.95**

Discovering Jewish Meditation: Instruction & Guidance for Learning an Ancient
Spiritual Practice *By Nan Fink Gefen, Ph.D.* 6 x 9, 208 pp, Quality PB, ISBN 1-58023-067-9 **$16.95**

A Heart of Stillness: A Complete Guide to Learning the Art of Meditation
By Rabbi David A. Cooper 5½ x 8½, 272 pp, Quality PB, ISBN 1-893361-03-9 **$16.95**
(A SkyLight Paths book)

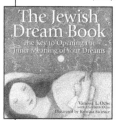

Meditation from the Heart of Judaism: Today's Teachers Share Their
Practices, Techniques, and Faith *Edited by Avram Davis*
6 x 9, 256 pp, Quality PB, ISBN 1-58023-049-0 **$16.95**

Silence, Simplicity & Solitude: A Complete Guide to Spiritual Retreat at Home
By Rabbi David A. Cooper 5½ x 8½, 336 pp, Quality PB, ISBN 1-893361-04-7 **$16.95**
(A SkyLight Paths book)

The Way of Flame: A Guide to the Forgotten Mystical Tradition of Jewish
Meditation *By Avram Davis* 4½ x 8, 176 pp, Quality PB, ISBN 1-58023-060-1 **$15.95**

Ritual/Sacred Practice/Journaling

The Jewish Dream Book: The Key to Opening the Inner Meaning of
Your Dreams *By Vanessa L. Ochs with Elizabeth Ochs; Full-color illus. by Kristina Swarner*
Instructions for how modern people can perform ancient Jewish dream practices
and dream interpretations drawn from the Jewish wisdom tradition. For anyone
who wants to understand their dreams—and themselves.
8 x 8, 120 pp, Full-color illus., Deluxe PB w/flaps, ISBN 1-58023-132-2 **$16.95**

The Jewish Journaling Book: How to Use Jewish Tradition to Write
Your Life & Explore Your Soul *By Janet Ruth Falon*
Details the history of Jewish journaling throughout biblical and modern times,
and teaches specific journaling techniques to help you create and maintain a vital
journal, from a Jewish perspective. 8 x 8, 304 pp, Deluxe PB w/flaps, ISBN 1-58023-203-5 **$18.99**

The Book of Jewish Sacred Practices: CLAL's Guide to Everyday & Holiday
Rituals & Blessings *Edited by Rabbi Irwin Kula and Vanessa L. Ochs, Ph.D.*
6 x 9, 368 pp, Quality PB, ISBN 1-58023-152-7 **$18.95**

Jewish Ritual: A Brief Introduction for Christians
By Rabbi Kerry M. Olitzky and Rabbi Daniel Judson
5½ x 8½, 144 pp, Quality PB, ISBN 1-58023-210-8 **$14.99**

The Rituals & Practices of a Jewish Life: A Handbook for Personal Spiritual
Renewal *Edited by Rabbi Kerry M. Olitzky and Rabbi Daniel Judson*
6 x 9, 272 pp, illus., Quality PB, ISBN 1-58023-169-1 **$18.95**

Science Fiction/ Mystery & Detective Fiction

Mystery Midrash: An Anthology of Jewish Mystery & Detective Fiction
Edited by Lawrence W. Raphael. Preface by Joel Siegel.
6 x 9, 304 pp, Quality PB, ISBN 1-58023-055-5 **$16.95**

Criminal Kabbalah: An Intriguing Anthology of Jewish Mystery & Detective Fiction
Edited by Lawrence W. Raphael. Foreword by Laurie R. King.
6 x 9, 256 pp, Quality PB, ISBN 1-58023-109-8 **$16.95**

Wandering Stars: An Anthology of Jewish Fantasy & Science Fiction
Edited by Jack Dann. Introduction by Isaac Asimov.
6 x 9, 272 pp, Quality PB, ISBN 1-58023-005-9 **$16.95**

More Wandering Stars: An Anthology of Outstanding Stories of Jewish Fantasy and
Science Fiction *Edited by Jack Dann. Introduction by Isaac Asimov.*
6 x 9, 192 pp, Quality PB, ISBN 1-58023-063-6 **$16.95**

Spirituality

Does the Soul Survive? A Jewish Journey to Belief in Afterlife, Past Lives & Living with Purpose   *By Rabbi Elie Kaplan Spitz. Foreword by Brian L. Weiss, M.D.*
Spitz relates his own experiences and those shared with him by people he has worked with as a rabbi, and shows us that belief in afterlife and past lives, so often approached with reluctance, is in fact true to Jewish tradition.
6 x 9, 288 pp, Quality PB, ISBN 1-58023-165-9 **$16.99**; Hardcover, ISBN 1-58023-094-6 **$21.95**

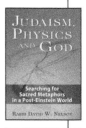

First Steps to a New Jewish Spirit: Reb Zalman's Guide to Recapturing the Intimacy & Ecstasy in Your Relationship with God
By Rabbi Zalman M. Schachter-Shalomi with Donald Gropman
An extraordinary spiritual handbook that restores psychic and physical vigor by introducing us to new models and alternative ways of practicing Judaism. Offers meditation and contemplation exercises for enriching the most important aspects of everyday life.   6 x 9, 144 pp, Quality PB, ISBN 1-58023-182-9 **$16.95**

God in Our Relationships: Spirituality between People from the Teachings of Martin Buber   *By Rabbi Dennis S. Ross*
On the eightieth anniversary of Buber's classic work, we can discover new answers to critical issues in our lives. Inspiring examples from Ross's own life— as congregational rabbi, father, hospital chaplain, social worker, and husband— illustrate Buber's difficult-to-understand ideas about how we encounter God and each other. 5½ x 8½, 160 pp, Quality PB, ISBN 1-58023-147-0 **$16.95**

Judaism, Physics and God: Searching for Sacred Metaphors in a Post-Einstein World   *By Rabbi David W. Nelson*
In clear, non-technical terms, this provocative fusion of religion and science examines the great theories of modern physics to find new ways for contemporary people to express their spiritual beliefs and thoughts.
6 x 9, 352 pp, Hardcover, ISBN 1-58023-252-3 **$24.99**

The Jewish Lights Spirituality Handbook: A Guide to Understanding, Exploring & Living a Spiritual Life   *Edited by Stuart M. Matlins*
What exactly is "Jewish" about spirituality? How do I make it a part of my life? Fifty of today's foremost spiritual leaders share their ideas and experience with us.
6 x 9, 456 pp, Quality PB, ISBN 1-58023-093-8 **$19.95**; Hardcover, ISBN 1-58023-100-4 **$24.95**

Bringing the Psalms to Life: How to Understand and Use the Book of Psalms
By Dr. Daniel F. Polish
6 x 9, 208 pp, Quality PB, ISBN 1-58023-157-8 **$16.95**; Hardcover, ISBN 1-58023-077-6 **$21.95**

God & the Big Bang: Discovering Harmony between Science & Spirituality
By Dr. Daniel C. Matt 6 x 9, 216 pp, Quality PB, ISBN 1-879045-89-3 **$16.95**

Godwrestling—Round 2: Ancient Wisdom, Future Paths
By Rabbi Arthur Waskow 6 x 9, 352 pp, Quality PB, ISBN 1-879045-72-9 **$18.95**

One God Clapping: The Spiritual Path of a Zen Rabbi   *By Rabbi Alan Lew with Sherril Jaffe*
5½ x 8½, 336 pp, Quality PB, ISBN 1-58023-115-2 **$16.95**

The Path of Blessing: Experiencing the Energy and Abundance of the Divine
By Rabbi Marcia Prager 5½ x 8½, 240 pp., Quality PB, ISBN 1-58023-148-9 **$16.95**

Six Jewish Spiritual Paths: A Rationalist Looks at Spirituality   *By Rabbi Rifat Sonsino*
6 x 9, 208 pp, Quality PB, ISBN 1-58023-167-5 **$16.95**; Hardcover, ISBN 1-58023-095-4 **$21.95**

Soul Judaism: Dancing with God into a New Era
By Rabbi Wayne Dosick 5½ x 8½, 304 pp, Quality PB, ISBN 1-58023-053-9 **$16.95**

Stepping Stones to Jewish Spiritual Living: Walking the Path Morning, Noon, and Night   *By Rabbi James L. Mirel and Karen Bonnell Werth*
6 x 9, 240 pp, Quality PB, ISBN 1-58023-074-1 **$16.95**; Hardcover, ISBN 1-58023-003-2 **$21.95**

There Is No Messiah ... and You're It: The Stunning Transformation of Judaism's Most Provocative Idea   *By Rabbi Robert N. Levine, D.D.*
6 x 9, 192 pp, Quality PB, ISBN 1-58023-255-8 **$16.99**; Hardcover, ISBN 1-58023-173-X **$21.95**

These Are the Words: A Vocabulary of Jewish Spiritual Life   *By Dr. Arthur Green*
6 x 9, 304 pp, Quality PB, ISBN 1-58023-107-1 **$18.95**

Spirituality/The Way Into... Series

The Way Into... Series offers an accessible and highly usable "guided tour" of the Jewish faith, people, history and beliefs—in total, an introduction to Judaism that will enable you to understand and interact with the sacred texts of the Jewish tradition. Each volume is written by a leading contemporary scholar and teacher, and explores one key aspect of Judaism. *The Way Into...* enables all readers to achieve a real sense of Jewish cultural literacy through guided study.

The Way Into Encountering God in Judaism *By Neil Gillman*
6 x 9, 240 pp, Quality PB, ISBN 1-58023-199-3 **$18.99**; Hardcover, ISBN 1-58023-025-3 **$21.95**

Also Available: **The Jewish Approach to God: A Brief Introduction for Christians**
By Neil Gillman 5½ x 8½, 192 pp, Quality PB, ISBN 1-58023-190-X **$16.95**

The Way Into Jewish Mystical Tradition *By Lawrence Kushner*
6 x 9, 224 pp, Quality PB, ISBN 1-58023-200-0 **$18.99**; Hardcover, ISBN 1-58023-029-6 **$21.95**

The Way Into Jewish Prayer *By Lawrence A. Hoffman*
6 x 9, 224 pp, Quality PB, ISBN 1-58023-201-9 **$18.99**; Hardcover, ISBN 1-58023-027-X **$21.95**
6 x 9, 225 pp (est.), Hardcover, ISBN 1-58023-267-1 **$24.99**

The Way Into Judaism and the Environment *By Jeremy Benstein, PhD*
6 x 9, 225 pp (est.), Hardcover, ISBN 1-58023-268-X **$24.99**

The Way Into *Tikkun Olam* (Repairing the World) *By Elliot N. Dorff*
6 x 9, 320 pp, Hardcover, ISBN 1-58023-269-8 **$24.99**

The Way Into Torah *By Norman J. Cohen*
6 x 9, 176 pp, Quality PB, ISBN 1-58023-198-5 **$16.99**; Hardcover, ISBN 1-58023-028-8 **$21.95**

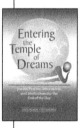

Spirituality and Wellness

Aleph-Bet Yoga
Embodying the Hebrew Letters for Physical and Spiritual Well-Being
By Steven A. Rapp. Foreword by Tamar Frankiel, Ph.D., and Judy Greenfeld. Preface by Hart Lazer
7 x 10, 128 pp, b/w photos, Quality PB, Layflat binding, ISBN 1-58023-162-4 **$16.95**

Entering the Temple of Dreams
Jewish Prayers, Movements, and Meditations for the End of the Day
By Tamar Frankiel, Ph.D., and Judy Greenfeld
7 x 10, 192 pp, illus., Quality PB, ISBN 1-58023-079-2 **$16.95**

Jewish Paths toward Healing and Wholeness: A Personal Guide to Dealing with Suffering *By Rabbi Kerry M. Olitzky. Foreword by Debbie Friedman.*
6 x 9, 192 pp, Quality PB, ISBN 1-58023-068-7 **$15.95**

Minding the Temple of the Soul
Balancing Body, Mind, and Spirit through Traditional Jewish Prayer, Movement, and Meditation *By Tamar Frankiel, Ph.D., and Judy Greenfeld*
7 x 10, 184 pp, illus., Quality PB, ISBN 1-879045-64-8 **$16.95**
Audiotape of the Blessings and Meditations: 60 min. **$9.95**
Videotape of the Movements and Meditations: 46 min. **$20.00**

Spirituality/Lawrence Kushner

Filling Words with Light: Hasidic and Mystical Reflections on Jewish Prayer
By Lawrence Kushner and Nehemia Polen
Reflects on the joy, gratitude, mystery and awe embedded in traditional prayers and blessings, and shows how you can imbue these familiar sacred words with your own sense of holiness. 5½ x 8¼, 176 pp, Hardcover, ISBN 1-58023-216-7 **$21.99**

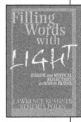

The Book of Letters: A Mystical Hebrew Alphabet
Popular Hardcover Edition, 6 x 9, 80 pp, 2-color text, ISBN 1-879045-00-1 **$24.95**
Collector's Limited Edition, 9 x 12, 80 pp, gold foil embossed pages, w/limited edition silkscreened print, ISBN 1-879045-04-4 **$349.00**

The Book of Miracles: A Young Person's Guide to Jewish Spiritual Awareness
6 x 9, 96 pp, 2-color illus., Hardcover, ISBN 1-879045-78-5 **$16.95** *For ages 9–13*

The Book of Words: Talking Spiritual Life, Living Spiritual Talk
6 x 9, 160 pp, Quality PB, ISBN 1-58023-020-2 **$16.95**

Eyes Remade for Wonder: A Lawrence Kushner Reader *Introduction by Thomas Moore*
6 x 9, 240 pp, Quality PB, ISBN 1-58023-042-3 **$18.95;** Hardcover, ISBN 1-58023-014-8 **$23.95**

God Was in This Place & I, i Did Not Know
Finding Self, Spirituality and Ultimate Meaning 6 x 9, 192 pp, Quality PB, ISBN 1-879045-33-8 **$16.95**

Honey from the Rock: An Introduction to Jewish Mysticism
6 x 9, 176 pp, Quality PB, ISBN 1-58023-073-3 **$16.95**

Invisible Lines of Connection: Sacred Stories of the Ordinary
5½ x 8¼, 160 pp, Quality PB, ISBN 1-879045-98-2 **$15.95**

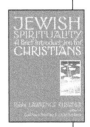

Jewish Spirituality—A Brief Introduction for Christians
5½ x 8¼, 112 pp, Quality PB Original, ISBN 1-58023-150-0 **$12.95**

The River of Light: Jewish Mystical Awareness 6 x 9, 192 pp, Quality PB, ISBN 1-58023-096-2 **$16.95**

The Way Into Jewish Mystical Tradition
6 x 9, 224 pp, Quality PB, ISBN 1-58023-200-0 **$18.99;** Hardcover, ISBN 1-58023-029-6 **$21.95**

Spirituality/Prayer

Pray Tell: A Hadassah Guide to Jewish Prayer
By Rabbi Jules Harlow, with contributions from Tamara Cohen, Rochelle Furstenberg, Rabbi Daniel Gordis, Leora Tanenbaum, and many others
Enriched with insight and wisdom from a broad variety of viewpoints.
8½ x 11, 400 pp, Quality PB, ISBN 1-58023-163-2 **$29.95**

My People's Prayer Book Series

Traditional Prayers, Modern Commentaries *Edited by Rabbi Lawrence A. Hoffman*
Provides diverse and exciting commentary to the traditional liturgy, helping modern men and women find new wisdom in Jewish prayer, and bring liturgy into their lives. Each book includes Hebrew text, modern translation, and commentaries from all perspectives of the Jewish world.

Vol. 1—The *Sh'ma* and Its Blessings
7 x 10, 168 pp, Hardcover, ISBN 1-879045-79-6 **$24.99**

Vol. 2—The *Amidah*
7 x 10, 240 pp, Hardcover, ISBN 1-879045-80-X **$24.95**

Vol. 3—*P'sukei D'zimrah* (Morning Psalms)
7 x 10, 240 pp, Hardcover, ISBN 1-879045-81-8 **$24.95**

Vol. 4—*Seder K'riat Hatorah* (The Torah Service)
7 x 10, 264 pp, Hardcover, ISBN 1-879045-82-6 **$23.95**

Vol. 5—*Birkhot Hashachar* (Morning Blessings)
7 x 10, 240 pp, Hardcover, ISBN 1-879045-83-4 **$24.95**

Vol. 6—*Tachanun* and Concluding Prayers
7 x 10, 240 pp, Hardcover, ISBN 1-879045-84-2 **$24.95**

Vol. 7—Shabbat at Home
7 x 10, 240 pp, Hardcover, ISBN 1-879045-85-0 **$24.95**

Vol. 8—*Kabbalat Shabbat* (Welcoming Shabbat in the Synagogue)
7 x 10, 240 pp, Hardcover, ISBN 1-58023-121-7 **$24.99**

Vol. 9—Welcoming the Night: *Minchah* and *Ma'ariv* (Afternoon and Evening Prayer) 7 x 10, 272 pp, Hardcover, ISBN 1-58023-262-0 **$24.99**

Spirituality/Women's Interest

The Quotable Jewish Woman: Wisdom, Inspiration & Humor from the Mind & Heart *Edited and compiled by Elaine Bernstein Partnow*
The definitive collection of ideas, reflections, humor, and wit of over 300 Jewish women.
6 x 9, 496 pp, Hardcover, ISBN 1-58023-193-4 **$29.99**

Lifecycles, Vol. 1: Jewish Women on Life Passages & Personal Milestones
Edited and with introductions by Rabbi Debra Orenstein 6 x 9, 480 pp, Quality PB, ISBN 1-58023-018-0 **$19.95**

Lifecycles, Vol. 2: Jewish Women on Biblical Themes in Contemporary Life
Edited and with introductions by Rabbi Debra Orenstein and Rabbi Jane Rachel Litman
6 x 9, 464 pp, Quality PB, ISBN 1-58023-019-9 **$19.95**

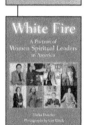

Moonbeams: A Hadassah Rosh Hodesh Guide *Edited by Carol Diament, Ph.D.*
8½ x 11, 240 pp, Quality PB, ISBN 1-58023-099-7 **$20.00**

ReVisions: Seeing Torah through a Feminist Lens *By Rabbi Elyse Goldstein*
5½ x 8½, 224 pp, Quality PB, ISBN 1-58023-117-9 **$16.95**

White Fire: A Portrait of Women Spiritual Leaders in America
By Rabbi Malka Drucker. Photographs by Gay Block.
7 x 10, 320 pp, 30+ b/w photos, Hardcover, ISBN 1-893361-64-0 **$24.95** *(A SkyLight Paths book)*

Women of the Wall: Claiming Sacred Ground at Judaism's Holy Site
Edited by Phyllis Chesler and Rivka Haut 6 x 9, 496 pp, b/w photos, Hardcover, ISBN 1-58023-161-6 **$34.95**

The Women's Haftarah Commentary: New Insights from Women Rabbis on the 54 Weekly Haftarah Portions, the 5 Megillot & Special Shabbatot
Edited by Rabbi Elyse Goldstein 6 x 9, 560 pp, Hardcover, ISBN 1-58023-133-0 **$39.99**

The Women's Torah Commentary: New Insights from Women Rabbis on the 54 Weekly Torah Portions *Edited by Rabbi Elyse Goldstein*
6 x 9, 496 pp, Hardcover, ISBN 1-58023-076-8 **$34.95**

The Year Mom Got Religion: One Woman's Midlife Journey into Judaism
By Lee Meyerhoff Hendler 6 x 9, 208 pp, Quality PB, ISBN 1-58023-070-9 **$15.95**

See Holidays for *The Women's Passover Companion: Women's Reflections on the Festival of Freedom* and *The Women's Seder Sourcebook: Rituals & Readings for Use at the Passover Seder.* Also see Bar/Bat Mitzvah for *The JGirl's Guide: The Young Jewish Woman's Handbook for Coming of Age.*

Travel

Israel—A Spiritual Travel Guide, 2nd Edition
A Companion for the Modern Jewish Pilgrim
By Rabbi Lawrence A. Hoffman 4¾ x 10, 256 pp, Quality PB, illus., ISBN 1-58023-261-2 **$18.99**

Also Available: **The Israel Mission Leader's Guide** ISBN 1-58023-085-7 **$4.95**

12 Steps

100 Blessings Every Day Daily Twelve Step Recovery Affirmations, Exercises for Personal Growth & Renewal Reflecting Seasons of the Jewish Year
By Rabbi Kerry M. Olitzky. Foreword by Rabbi Neil Gillman.
One-day-at-a-time monthly format. Reflects on the rhythm of the Jewish calendar to bring insight to recovery from addictions.
4½ x 6½, 432 pp, Quality PB, ISBN 1-879045-30-3 **$15.99**

Recovery from Codependence: A Jewish Twelve Steps Guide to Healing Your Soul
By Rabbi Kerry M. Olitzky 6 x 9, 160 pp, Quality PB, ISBN 1-879045-32-X **$13.95**

Renewed Each Day: Daily Twelve Step Recovery Meditations Based on the Bible
By Rabbi Kerry M. Olitzky and Aaron Z.
Vol. 1—Genesis & Exodus: 6 x 9, 224 pp, Quality PB, ISBN 1-879045-12-5 **$14.95**
Vol. 2—Leviticus, Numbers & Deuteronomy: 6 x 9, 280 pp, Quality PB, ISBN 1-879045-13-3 **$18.99**

Twelve Jewish Steps to Recovery: A Personal Guide to Turning from Alcoholism & Other Addictions—Drugs, Food, Gambling, Sex...
By Rabbi Kerry M. Olitzky and Stuart A. Copans, M.D. Preface by Abraham J. Twerski, M.D.
6 x 9, 144 pp, Quality PB, ISBN 1-879045-09-5 **$14.95**

Theology/Philosophy

Aspects of Rabbinic Theology
By Solomon Schechter. New Introduction by Dr. Neil Gillman.
6 x 9, 448 pp, Quality PB, ISBN 1-879045-24-9 **$19.95**

Broken Tablets: Restoring the Ten Commandments and Ourselves
Edited by Rachel S. Mikva. Introduction by Lawrence Kushner. Afterword by Arnold Jacob Wolf.
6 x 9, 192 pp, Quality PB, ISBN 1-58023-158-6 **$16.95**; Hardcover, ISBN 1-58023-066-0 **$21.95**

Creating an Ethical Jewish Life
A Practical Introduction to Classic Teachings on How to Be a Jew
By Dr. Byron L. Sherwin and Seymour J. Cohen
6 x 9, 336 pp, Quality PB, ISBN 1-58023-114-4 **$19.95**

The Death of Death: Resurrection and Immortality in Jewish Thought
By Dr. Neil Gillman 6 x 9, 336 pp, Quality PB, ISBN 1-58023-081-4 **$18.95**

Evolving Halakhah: A Progressive Approach to Traditional Jewish Law
By Rabbi Dr. Moshe Zemer
6 x 9, 480 pp, Quality PB, ISBN 1-58023-127-6 **$29.95**; Hardcover, ISBN 1-58023-002-4 **$40.00**

Hasidic Tales: Annotated & Explained
By Rabbi Rami Shapiro. Foreword by Andrew Harvey, SkyLight Illuminations series editor.
5½ x 8½, 240 pp, Quality PB, ISBN 1-893361-86-1 **$16.95** *(A SkyLight Paths Book)*

A Heart of Many Rooms: Celebrating the Many Voices within Judaism
By Dr. David Hartman 6 x 9, 352 pp, Quality PB, ISBN 1-58023-156-X **$19.95**

The Hebrew Prophets: Selections Annotated & Explained
Translation & Annotation by Rabbi Rami Shapiro. Foreword by Zalman M. Schachter-Shalomi
5½ x 8½, 224 pp, Quality PB, ISBN 1-59473-037-7 **$16.99** *(A SkyLight Paths book)*

Keeping Faith with the Psalms: Deepen Your Relationship with God Using the
Book of Psalms *By Daniel F. Polish* 6 x 9, 320 pp, Quality PB, ISBN 1-58023-300-7 **$18.99**;
Hardcover, ISBN 1-58023-179-9 **$24.95**

The Last Trial
On the Legends and Lore of the Command to Abraham to Offer Isaac as a Sacrifice
By Shalom Spiegel. New Introduction by Judah Goldin.
6 x 9, 208 pp, Quality PB, ISBN 1-879045-29-X **$18.95**

A Living Covenant: The Innovative Spirit in Traditional Judaism
By Dr. David Hartman 6 x 9, 368 pp, Quality PB, ISBN 1-58023-011-3 **$20.00**

Love and Terror in the God Encounter
The Theological Legacy of Rabbi Joseph B. Soloveitchik
By Dr. David Hartman
6 x 9, 240 pp, Quality PB, ISBN 1-58023-176-4 **$19.95**; Hardcover, ISBN 1-58023-112-8 **$25.00**

The Personhood of God: Biblical Theology, Human Faith and the Divine Image
By Dr. Yochanan Muffs; Foreword by Dr. David Hartman
6 x 9, 240 pp, Hardcover, ISBN 1-58023-265-5 **$24.99**

The Spirit of Renewal: Finding Faith after the Holocaust
By Rabbi Edward Feld 6 x 9, 224 pp, Quality PB, ISBN 1-879045-40-0 **$16.95**

Tormented Master: *The Life and Spiritual Quest of Rabbi Nahman of Bratslav*
By Dr. Arthur Green 6 x 9, 416 pp, Quality PB, ISBN 1-879045-11-7 **$19.99**

Your Word Is Fire: The Hasidic Masters on Contemplative Prayer
Edited and translated by Dr. Arthur Green and Barry W. Holtz
6 x 9, 160 pp, Quality PB, ISBN 1-879045-25-7 **$15.95**

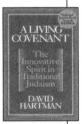

I Am Jewish
Personal Reflections Inspired by the Last Words of Daniel Pearl
Almost 150 Jews—both famous and not—from all walks of life, from all around
the world, write about Identity, Heritage, Covenant / Chosenness and Faith,
Humanity and Ethnicity, and *Tikkun Olam* and Justice.
Edited by Judea and Ruth Pearl
6 x 9, 304 pp, Deluxe PB w/flaps, ISBN 1-58023-259-0 **$18.99**; Hardcover, ISBN 1-58023-183-7 **$24.99**
Download a free copy of the *I Am Jewish Teacher's Guide* at our website:
www.jewishlights.com

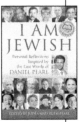

About Jewish Lights

People of all faiths and backgrounds yearn for books that attract, engage, educate, and spiritually inspire.

Our principal goal is to stimulate thought and help all people learn about who the Jewish People are, where they come from, and what the future can be made to hold. While people of our diverse Jewish heritage are the primary audience, our books speak to people in the Christian world as well and will broaden their understanding of Judaism and the roots of their own faith.

We bring to you authors who are at the forefront of spiritual thought and experience. While each has something different to say, they all say it in a voice that you can hear.

Our books are designed to welcome you and then to engage, stimulate, and inspire. We judge our success not only by whether or not our books are beautiful and commercially successful, but by whether or not they make a difference in your life.

For your information and convenience, at the back of this book we have provided a list of other Jewish Lights books you might find interesting and useful. They cover all the categories of your life:

Bar/Bat Mitzvah	Life Cycle
Bible Study / Midrash	Meditation
Children's Books	Parenting
Congregation Resources	Prayer
Current Events / History	Ritual / Sacred Practice
Ecology	Spirituality
Fiction: Mystery, Science Fiction	Theology / Philosophy
Grief / Healing	Travel
Holidays / Holy Days	Twelve Steps
Inspiration	Women's Interest
Kabbalah / Mysticism / Enneagram	

Stuart M. Matlins, Publisher

Or phone, mail or e-mail to: **JEWISH LIGHTS Publishing**
An imprint of Turner Publishing Company
4507 Charlotte Avenue • Suite 100 • Nashville, Tennessee 37209
Tel: (615) 255-2665 • www.jewishlights.com
Prices subject to change.

Printed in the USA
CPSIA information can be obtained
at www.ICGtesting.com
JSHW022205140824
68134JS00018B/881